The Voyages and Adventures of Captain Hatteras

Jules Verne

Alpha Editions

This edition published in 2024

ISBN : 9789364739610

Design and Setting By
Alpha Editions
www.alphaedis.com
Email - info@alphaedis.com

As per information held with us this book is in Public Domain.
This book is a reproduction of an important historical work. Alpha Editions uses the best technology to reproduce historical work in the same manner it was first published to preserve its original nature. Any marks or number seen are left intentionally to preserve its true form.

Contents

PART I. THE ENGLISH AT THE NORTH POLE. .... - 1 -
CHAPTER I. ....- 3 -
CHAPTER II. ....- 13 -
CHAPTER III. ....- 16 -
CHAPTER IV. ....- 27 -
CHAPTER V. ....- 38 -
CHAPTER VI. ....- 51 -
CHAPTER VII. ....- 58 -
CHAPTER VIII. ....- 68 -
CHAPTER IX. ....- 78 -
CHAPTER X. ....- 86 -
CHAPTER XI. ....- 95 -
CHAPTER XII. ....- 105 -
CHAPTER XIII. ....- 114 -
CHAPTER XIV. ....- 121 -
CHAPTER XV. ....- 129 -
CHAPTER XVI. ....- 136 -
CHAPTER XVII. ....- 145 -
CHAPTER XVIII. ....- 151 -
CHAPTER XIX. ....- 156 -
CHAPTER XX. ....- 163 -
CHAPTER XXI. ....- 172 -
CHAPTER XXII. ....- 181 -
CHAPTER XXIII. ....- 188 -
CHAPTER XXIV. ....- 197 -
CHAPTER XXV. ....- 203 -

CHAPTER XXVI.	- 213 -
CHAPTER XXVII.	- 219 -
CHAPTER XXVIII.	- 226 -
CHAPTER XXIX.	- 230 -
CHAPTER XXX.	- 242 -
CHAPTER XXXI.	- 249 -
CHAPTER XXXII.	- 258 -
PART II. THE DESERT OF ICE.	- 267 -
CHAPTER I.	- 269 -
CHAPTER II.	- 279 -
CHAPTER III.	- 288 -
CHAPTER IV.	- 296 -
CHAPTER V.	- 306 -
CHAPTER VI.	- 315 -
CHAPTER VII.	- 325 -
CHAPTER VIII.	- 334 -
CHAPTER IX.	- 344 -
CHAPTER X.	- 352 -
CHAPTER XI.	- 361 -
CHAPTER XII.	- 371 -
CHAPTER XIII.	- 381 -
CHAPTER XIV.	- 393 -
CHAPTER XV.	- 400 -
CHAPTER XVI.	- 411 -
CHAPTER XVII.	- 421 -
CHAPTER XVIII.	- 428 -
CHAPTER XIX.	- 434 -
CHAPTER XX.	- 447 -

CHAPTER XXI.	- 458 -
CHAPTER XXII.	- 466 -
CHAPTER XXIII.	- 477 -
CHAPTER XXIV.	- 484 -
CHAPTER XXV.	- 492 -
CHAPTER XXVI.	- 502 -
CHAPTER XXVII.	- 511 -

PART I.
THE ENGLISH AT THE NORTH POLE.

CHAPTER I.

THE FORWARD.

"To-morrow, at the turn of the tide, the brig *Forward*, K. Z., captain, Richard Shandon, mate, will clear from New Prince's Docks; destination unknown."

This announcement appeared in the *Liverpool Herald* of April 5, 1860.

The sailing of a brig is not a matter of great importance for the chief commercial city of England. Who would take notice of it in so great a throng of ships of all sizes and of every country, that dry-docks covering two leagues scarcely contain them?

Nevertheless, from early morning on the 6th of April, a large crowd collected on the quays of the New Prince's Docks; all the sailors of the place seemed to have assembled there. The workingmen of the neighboring wharves had abandoned their tasks, tradesmen had left their gloomy shops, and the merchants their empty warehouses. The many-colored omnibuses which pass outside of the docks were discharging, every minute, their load of sight-seers; the whole city seemed to care for nothing except watching the departure of the *Forward*.

The *Forward* was a vessel of one hundred and seventy tons, rigged as a brig, and carrying a screw and a steam-engine of one hundred and twenty horse-power. One would have very easily confounded it with the other brigs in the harbor. But if it presented no especial difference to the eye of the public, yet those who were familiar with ships noticed certain peculiarities which could not escape a sailor's keen glance.

Thus, on the *Nautilus*, which was lying at anchor near her, a group of sailors were trying to make out the probable destination of the *Forward*.

"What do you say to her masts?" said one; "steamers don't usually carry so much sail."

"It must be," answered a red-faced quartermaster, "that she relies more on her sails than on her engine; and if her topsails are of that size, it's probably because the lower sails are to be laid back. So I'm sure the *Forward* is going either to the Arctic or Antarctic Ocean, where the icebergs stop the wind more than suits a solid ship."

"You must be right, Mr. Cornhill," said a third sailor. "Do you notice how straight her stem is?"

"Besides," said Mr. Cornhill, "she carries a steel ram forward, as sharp as a razor; if the *Forward*, going at full speed, should run into a three-decker, she would cut her in two."

"That's true," answered a Mersey pilot, "for that brig can easily run fourteen knots under steam. She was a sight to see on her trial trip. On my word, she's a swift boat."

"And she goes well, too, under sail," continued the quartermaster; "close to the wind, and she's easily steered. Now that ship is going to the polar seas, or my name is not Cornhill. And then, see there! Do you notice that large helm-port over the head of her rudder?"

"That's so," said some of the sailors; "but what does that prove?"

"That proves, my men," replied the quartermaster with a scornful smile, "that you can neither see nor think; it proves that they wanted to leave the head of the rudder free, so that it might be unshipped and shipped again easily. Don't you know that's what they have to do very often in the ice?"

"You are right," answered the sailors of the *Nautilus*.

"And besides," said one, "the lading of the brig goes to prove what Mr. Cornhill has said. I heard it from Clifton, who has shipped on her. The *Forward* carries provisions for five or six years, and coal in proportion. Coal and provisions are all she carries, and a quantity of woollen and sealskin clothing."

"Well," said Mr. Cornhill, "there's no doubt about it. But, my friend, since you know Clifton, hasn't he told you where she's bound?"

"He couldn't tell me, for he didn't know; the whole crew was shipped in that way. Where is he going? He won't know till he gets there."

"Nor yet if they are going to Davy Jones's locker," said one scoffer, "as it seems to me they are."

"But then, their pay," continued the friend of Clifton enthusiastically,—"their pay! it's five times what a sailor usually gets. If it had not been for that, Richard Shandon would not have got a man. A strangely shaped boat, going no one knows where, and as if it never intended coming back! As for me, I should not have cared to ship in her."

"Whether you would or not," answered Mr. Cornhill, "you could never have shipped in the *Forward*."

"Why not?"

"Because you would not have answered the conditions. I heard that married men were not taken. Now you belong to that class. So you need not say what you would or would not do, since it's all breath thrown away."

The sailor who was thus snubbed burst out laughing, as did his companions, showing in this way that Mr. Cornhill's remarks were true.

"There's nothing but boldness about the ship," continued Cornhill, well pleased with himself. "The *Forward*,—forward to what? Without saying that nobody knows who her captain is."

"O, yes, they do!" said a young sailor, evidently a green-hand.

"What! They do know?"

"Of course."

"My young friend," said Cornhill, "do you think Shandon is the captain of the *Forward?*"

"Why—" answered the boy.

"Shandon is only the mate, nothing else; he's a good and brave sailor, an old whaler, a good fellow, able to take command, but he's not the captain; he's no more captain than you or I. And who, under God, is going to have charge of the ship, he does not know in the least. At the proper time the captain will come aboard, I don't know how, and I don't know where; for Richard Shandon didn't tell me, nor has he leave to tell me in what direction he was first to sail."

"Still, Mr. Cornhill," said the young sailor, "I can tell you that there's some one on board, some one who was spoken of in the letter in which Mr. Shandon was offered the place of mate."

"What!" answered Cornhill, "do you mean to tell me that the *Forward* has a captain on board?"

"Yes, Mr. Cornhill."

"You tell me that?"

"Certainly, for I heard it from Johnson, the boatswain."

"Boatswain Johnson?"

"Yes, he told me himself."

"Johnson told you?"

"Not only did he tell me, but he showed him to me."

"He showed him to you!" answered Cornhill in amazement.

"He showed him to me."

"And you saw him?"

"I saw him with my own eyes."

"And who is it?"

"It's a dog."

"A dog?"

"A four-footed dog?"

"Yes."

The surprise of the sailors of the *Nautilus* was great. Under any other circumstances they would have burst out laughing. A dog captain of a one hundred and seventy ton brig! It was certainly amusing enough. But the *Forward* was such an extraordinary ship, that one thought twice before laughing, and before contradicting it. Besides, Quartermaster Cornhill showed no signs of laughing.

"And Johnson showed you that new sort of captain, a dog?" he said to the young sailor. "And you saw him?"

"As plainly as I see you, with all respect."

"Well, what do you think of that?" asked the sailors, turning to Cornhill.

"I don't think anything," he answered curtly, "except that the *Forward* is a ship of the Devil, or of fools fit for Bedlam."

Without saying more, the sailors continued to gaze at the *Forward*, which was now almost ready to depart; and there was no one of them who presumed to say that Johnson, the boatswain, had been making fun of the young sailor.

This story of the dog had already spread through the city, and in the crowd of sight-seers there were many looking for the captain-dog, who were inclined to believe that he was some supernatural animal.

Besides, for many months the *Forward* had been attracting the public attention; the singularity of its build, the mystery which enshrouded it, the incognito maintained by the captain, the manner in which Richard Shandon received the proposition of superintending its outfit, the careful selection of the crew, its unknown destination, scarcely conjectured by any,—all combined to give this brig a reputation of something more than strangeness.

For a thoughtful, dreamy mind, for a philosopher, there is hardly anything more touching than the departure of a ship; the imagination is ready to follow her in her struggles with the waves, her contests with the winds, in her perilous course, which does not always end in port; and if only there is something unusual about her, the ship appears like something fantastic, even to the least imaginative minds.

So it was with the *Forward*. And if most of the spectators were unable to make the ingenious remarks of Quartermaster Cornhill, the rumors which had been prevailing for three months were enough to keep all the tongues of Liverpool busy.

The brig had been built at Birkenhead, a suburb of the city on the left bank of the Mersey, and connected with it by numerous ferry-boats.

The builders, Scott & Co., as skilful as any in England, had received from Richard Shandon careful plans and drawings, in which the tonnage, dimensions, and model of the brig were given with the utmost exactness. They bore proof of the work of an experienced sailor. Since Shandon had ample means at his command, the work began, and, in accordance with the orders of the unknown owner, proceeded rapidly.

Every care was taken to have the brig made exceedingly strong; it was evidently intended to withstand enormous pressure, for its ribs of teak, an East Indian wood remarkable for its solidity, were further strengthened by thick iron braces. The sailors used to ask why the hull of a ship, which was intended to be so strong, was not made of iron like other steamers. But they were told that the mysterious designer had his own reasons for having it built in that way.

Gradually the shape of the brig on the stocks could be clearly made out, and the strength and beauty of her model were clear to the eye of all competent judges. As the sailors of the *Nautilus* had said, her stem formed a right angle with the keel, and she carried, not a ram, but a steel cutter from the foundry of R. Hawthorn, of Newcastle. This metallic prow, glistening in the sun, gave a singular appearance to the brig, although there was nothing warlike about it. However, a sixteen-pound gun was placed on her forecastle; its carriage was so arranged that it could be pointed in any direction. The same thing can be said of the cannon as of her bows, neither were positively warlike.

On the 5th of February, 1860, this strange vessel was successfully launched in the sight of an immense number of spectators.

But if the brig was not a man-of-war, nor a merchant-vessel, nor a pleasure-yacht, for no one takes a pleasure trip with provisions for six years in the hold, what could she be?

A ship intended for the search of the *Erebus* and the *Terror*, and of Sir John Franklin? No; for in 1859, the previous year, Captain MacClintock had returned from the Arctic Ocean, with convincing proof of the loss of that ill-fated expedition.

Did the *Forward* want to try again the famous Northwest Passage? What for? Captain MacClure had discovered it in 1853, and his lieutenant, Cresswell, had the honor of first skirting the American continent from Behring Strait to Davis Strait.

It was nevertheless absolutely certain to all competent observers that the *Forward* was preparing for a voyage to icy regions. Was it going to push towards the South Pole, farther than the whaler Wedell, farther than Captain James Ross? But what was the use, and with what intention?

It is easy to see that, although the field for conjecture was very limited, the imagination could easily lose itself.

The day after the launching of the brig her machinery arrived from the foundry of R. Hawthorn at Newcastle.

The engine, of one hundred and twenty horse-power, with oscillating cylinders, took up but little space; its force was large for a vessel of one hundred and seventy tons, which carried a great deal of sail, and was, besides, remarkably swift. Of her speed the trial trips left no doubt, and even the boatswain, Johnson, had seen fit to express his opinion to the friend of Clifton in these terms,—

"When the *Forward* is under both steam and sail, she gets the most speed from her sails."

Clifton's friend had not understood this proposition, but he considered anything possible in a ship commanded by a dog.

After the engines had been placed on board, the stowage of provisions began; and that was no light task, for she carried enough for six years. They consisted of salted and dried meats, smoked fish, biscuit, and flour; mountains of coffee and tea were deposited in the store-room. Richard Shandon superintended the arrangement of this precious cargo with the air of a man who perfectly understood his business; everything was put in its place, labelled, and numbered with perfect precision; at the same time there was stowed away a large quantity of pemmican, an Indian preparation, which contains a great deal of nutriment in a small compass.

This sort of supply left no doubt as to the length of the cruise; but an experienced observer would have known at once that the *Forward* was to sail in polar waters, from the barrels of lime-juice, of lime lozenges, of bundles of mustard, sorrel, and of cochlearia,—in a word, from the abundance of powerful antiscorbutics, which are so necessary in journeys in the regions of the far north and south. Shandon had doubtless received word to take particular care about this part of the cargo, for he gave to it especial attention, as well as to the ship's medicine-chest.

If the armament of the vessel was small enough to calm the timid souls, on the other hand, the magazine was filled with enough powder to inspire some uneasiness. The single gun on the forecastle could not pretend to require so large a supply. This excited curiosity. There were, besides, enormous saws and strong machinery, such as levers, masses of lead, hand-saws, huge axes, etc., without counting a respectable number of blasting-cylinders, which might have blown up the Liverpool custom-house. All this was strange, if not alarming, not to mention the rockets, signals, lights, and lanterns of every sort.

Then, too, the numerous spectators on the quays of the New Prince's Docks gazed with admiration at a long mahogany whale-boat, a tin canoe covered with gutta-percha, and a number of halkett-boats, which are a sort of india-rubber cloaks, which can be inflated and thereby turned into canoes. Every one felt more and more puzzled, and even excited, for with the turn of the tide the *Forward* was to set sail for its unknown destination.

CHAPTER II.

AN UNEXPECTED LETTER.

This is a copy of the letter received by Richard Shandon eight months previously:—

ABERDEEN, August 2, 1859.

MR. RICHARD SHANDON, *Liverpool.*

SIR,—This letter is to advise you of a remittance of £16,000, deposited with Messrs. Marcuart & Co., bankers, at Liverpool. Enclosed you will find a series of drafts, signed by me, which will enable you to draw upon Messrs. Marcuart & Co. to the amount mentioned above.

You do not know me. No matter; I know you, and that is enough. I offer you the position of mate on board of the brig *Forward*, for a voyage which may be long and perilous.

If you decline, well and good. If you accept, five hundred pounds will be assigned you as salary, and at the end of each year of the voyage your pay will be increased one tenth.

The brig *Forward* does not exist. You will be obliged to have it built so that it will be possible to set to sea in the beginning of April, 1860, at the latest.

Enclosed is a drawing with estimates. You will follow them exactly. The ship will be built in the stocks of Scott & Co., who will arrange everything with you.

I beg of you to be specially cautious in selecting the crew of the *Forward;* it will consist of a captain (myself), a mate (you), a second mate, a boatswain, two engineers, an ice-master, eight sailors, two stokers, in all eighteen men, including Dr. Clawbonny of this city, who will join you at the proper time.

Those who are shipped on board of the *Forward* must be Englishmen, independent, with no family ties, single and temperate; for the use of spirits, and even of beer, will be strictly forbidden on shipboard: the men must be ready to undertake and endure everything.

In your selection you will prefer those of a sanguine temperament, and so inclined to maintain a higher degree of animal heat.

You will offer the crew five times their usual pay, to be increased one tenth at the end of each year. At the end of the voyage each one shall receive five hundred pounds, and you yourself two thousand. The requisite sum shall be deposited with the above-named Messrs. Marcuart & Co.

The voyage will be long and difficult, but one sure to bring renown. You need not hesitate, then, Mr. Shandon.

Send your answer to the initials K. Z., at Gottenburg, Sweden, *poste restante.*

P. S. On the 15th of February next you will receive a large Danish dog, with hanging lips, of a dark tawny color, with black stripes running crosswise.

You will find place for him on board, and you will feed him on barley bread mixed with a broth of lard. You will acknowledge the receipt of this dog by a letter to the same initials at Leghorn, Italy.

The captain of the *Forward* will appear and make himself known at the proper time. As you are about setting sail you will receive new instructions.

K. Z.,
Captain of the Forward.

CHAPTER III.

DR. CLAWBONNY.

Richard Shandon was a good sailor; for a long time he had commanded whalers in the Arctic seas, with a well-deserved reputation throughout all Lancaster. Such a letter was well calculated to astonish him; he was astonished, it is true, but with the calmness of a man who is accustomed to surprises.

He suited all the required conditions; no wife, child, nor relatives. He was as independent as man could be. There being no one whose opinion he needed to consult, he betook himself to Messrs. Marcuart & Co.

"If the money is there," he said to himself, "the rest is all right."

At the banking-house he was received with the respect due to a man who has sixteen thousand pounds deposited to his credit; having made that point sure, Shandon asked for a sheet of white paper, and in his large sailor's handwriting he sent his acceptance of the plan to the address given above.

That very day he made the necessary arrangements with the builders at Birkenhead, and within twenty-four hours the keel of the *Forward* was laid on the stocks.

Richard Shandon was a man about forty years old, strong, energetic, and fearless, three qualities most necessary for a sailor, for they give him confidence, vigor, and coolness. He was known to be severe and very hard to please; hence he was more feared than loved by his men. But this reputation was not calculated to interfere with his selection of a crew, for he was known to be skilful in avoiding trouble.

Shandon feared that the mysterious nature of the expedition might stand in his way.

"In that case," he said, "it's best not to say anything about it; there will always be plenty of men who will want to know the why and the wherefore of the whole matter, and, since I don't know anything about it myself, I should find it hard to answer them. This K. Z. is certainly an odd stick; but, after all, he knows me, he depends on me, and that is enough. As for his ship, it will be a good one, and if it's not going to the Arctic Ocean, my name is not Richard Shandon. But I shall keep that fact for myself and my officers."

Thereupon Shandon began to choose his crew, bearing in mind the captain's wishes about the independence and health of the men.

He knew a very capital fellow, and a good sailor, James Wall by name. Wall might have been about thirty years old, and had already made some voyages in the northern seas. Shandon offered him the place of second mate, and Wall accepted it at once; all he cared for was to be at sea. Shandon confided all the details of the affair to him and to a certain Johnson, whom he took as boatswain.

"All right," answered James Wall, "that's as good as anything. Even if it's to seek the Northwest Passage, some have come back from that."

"Not all," said Johnson, "but that's no reason that we should not try it."

"Besides, if our guesses are right," said Shandon, "it must be said that we start with a fair chance of success. The *Forward* will be a stanch ship and she will carry good engines. She can go a great distance. We want a crew of only eighteen men."

"Eighteen men," answered Johnson; "that's the number the American, Kane, took with him on his famous voyage towards the North Pole."

"It's strange," said Wall, "that a private person should try to make his way from Davis Strait to Behring Strait. The expeditions in search of Sir John Franklin have already cost England more than seven hundred and sixty thousand pounds, without producing any practical good. Who in the world wants to throw away his money for such a purpose?"

"In the first place, James," answered Shandon, "we are in the dark about it all. I don't know whether we are going to the northern or the southern seas. Perhaps there's some new discovery to be tried. At any rate, some day or other a Dr. Clawbonny is to come aboard who will probably know more about it and will be able to tell us. We shall see."

"Let us wait, then," said Johnson; "as for me, I'm going to look after some good men, and I'll answer now for their animal heat, as the captain calls it. You can depend on me."

Johnson was an invaluable man; he was familiar with high latitudes. He had been quartermaster aboard of the *Phoenix*, which belonged to one of the expeditions sent out in 1853 in search of Franklin; he had been an eye-witness of the death of the French lieutenant Bellot, whom he had accompanied in his expedition across the ice. Johnson knew all the sailors in Liverpool, and immediately set about engaging a crew.

"Johnson knew all the sailors in Liverpool, and immediately set about engaging a crew."

Shandon, Wall, and he succeeded in filling the number by the middle of December, but they met with considerable difficulty; many who were attracted by the high pay were alarmed by the danger, and more than one who had boldly enlisted came later to say that he had changed his mind on account of the dissuasion of his friends. They all tried to pierce the mystery, and pursued Shandon with their questions. He used to refer them to Johnson.

"What can I say, my man?" the boatswain used to answer; "I don't know any more about it than you do. At any rate you will be in good company, with men who won't shirk their work; that's something! So don't be thinking about it all day: take it or leave it!" And the greater number took it.

"You understand," added Johnson, sometimes, "my only trouble is in making my choice. High pay, such as no sailor ever had before, with the certainty of finding a round sum when we get back. That's very tempting."

"The fact is," answered the sailors, "that it is hard to refuse. It will support a man all the rest of his life."

"I won't hide from you," continued Johnson, "that the voyage will be long, difficult, and dangerous; that's all stated in our instructions; it's well to know beforehand what one undertakes to do; probably it's to try all that men can possibly do, and perhaps even more. So, if you haven't got a bold heart and a strong body, if you can't say you have more than twenty chances to one of staying there, if, in short, you are particular about leaving your body in one place more than another, here rather than there, get away from here and let some bolder man have your place!"

"But, at least," said the confused sailor,—"at least, you know the captain?"

"The captain is Richard Shandon, my friend, until we receive another."

Now it must be said that was what the commander thought; he allowed himself to think that at the last moment he would receive definite instructions as to the object of the voyage, and that he would remain in command of the *Forward*. He was fond of spreading this opinion about, either in conversation with his officers or in superintending the building of the brig, of which the timbers were now rising in the Birkenhead ship-yard like the sides of a huge whale.

Shandon and Johnson conformed strictly with the recommendation about the health of the crew; they all looked hardy and possessed enough animal heat to run the engines of the *Forward;* their elastic limbs, their clear and ruddy skin, showed that they were fit to encounter intense cold. They were bold, determined men, energetic and stoutly built; they were not all equally vigorous. Shandon had even hesitated about accepting some of them; for instance, the sailors Gripper and Garry, and the harpooner Simpson, who seemed to him too thin; but, on the other hand, they were well built, they were earnest about it, and they were shipped.

All the crew were members of the same church; in their long voyage their prayers and the reading of the Bible would call them together and console them in the hours of depression; so that it was advisable that there should be no diversity on this score. Shandon knew from experience the usefulness of this practice and its good influence on the men, so valuable that it is never neglected on board of ships which winter in the polar seas.

When all the crew had been engaged, Shandon and his two officers busied themselves with the provisions; they followed closely the captain's instructions, which were definite, precise, and detailed, in which the quality and quantity of the smallest articles were clearly set down. Thanks to the drafts placed at the commander's order, every article was paid for, cash down, with a discount of eight per cent, which Richard carefully placed to the credit of K. Z.

Crew, provisions, and outfit were all ready in January, 1860; the *Forward* was approaching completion. Shandon never let a day pass without visiting Birkenhead.

On the morning of the 23d of January he was, as usual, on one of the double-ended ferry-boats which ply between the two shores of the Mersey; everything was enveloped in one of the ordinary fogs of that region, which compel the pilot to steer by compass, although the trip is one of but ten minutes.

"Everything was enveloped in one of the ordinary fogs of that region."

However, the thickness of the fog could not prevent Shandon from noticing a short, rather stout man, with a refined, agreeable face and pleasant expression, who came towards him, seized both his hands, and pressed them with a warmth and familiarity which a Frenchman would have said was "very southern."

But if this stranger was not from the South, he had escaped it narrowly; he spoke and gesticulated freely; his thoughts seemed determined to find expression, even if they had to burst out. His eyes, small like the eyes of witty men, his large and mobile mouth, were safety-valves which enabled him to rid himself of too strong a pressure on his feelings; he talked; and he talked so much and joyously, that, it must be said, Shandon could not make out what he was saying.

Still the mate of the *Forward* was not slow in recognizing this short man whom he had never seen; it flashed into his mind, and the moment that the other stopped to take breath, Shandon uttered these words,—

"Dr. Clawbonny?"

"The same, in person, Commander! For nearly a quarter of an hour I have been looking after you, asking for you of every one and everywhere. Imagine my impatience. Five minutes more and I should have lost my head! So this is you, officer Shandon? You really exist? You are not a myth? Your hand, your hand! Let me press it again in mine! Yes, that is indeed the hand of Richard Shandon. Now, if there is a commander Richard, there is a brig *Forward* which he commands; and if he commands it, it will sail; and if it sails, it will take Dr. Clawbonny on board."

"Well, yes, Doctor, I am Richard Shandon, there is a brig *Forward*, and it will sail."

"There's logic," answered the doctor, taking a long breath,—"there's logic. So I am delighted, enchanted! For a long time I've been waiting for something of this sort to turn up, and I've been wanting to try a voyage of this sort. Now, with you—"

"Excuse me—" said Shandon.

"With you," continued Clawbonny, paying him no attention, "we are sure of going far without turning round."

"But—" began Shandon.

"For you have shown what stuff you are made of, and I know all you've done. Ah, you are a good sailor!"

"If you please—"

"No, I sha'n't let your courage and skill be doubted for a moment, even by yourself. The captain who chose you for mate is a man who knew what he was about; I can tell you that."

"But that is not the question," said Shandon, impatiently.

"What is it, then? Don't keep me anxious any longer."

"But you won't let me say a word. Tell me, Doctor, if you please, how you came to join this expedition of the *Forward?*"

"By a letter, a capital letter; here it is,—the letter of a brave captain, very short, but very full."

With these words he handed Shandon a letter running as follows:—

INVERNESS, January 22, 1860.

To DR. CLAWBONNY, *Liverpool.*

If Dr. Clawbonny wishes to sail on the *Forward* for a long voyage, he can present himself to the mate, Richard Shandon, who has been advised concerning him.

> K. Z.,
> *Captain of the Forward.*

"The letter reached me this morning, and I'm now ready to go on board of the *Forward*."

"But," continued Shandon, "I suppose you know whither we are bound."

"Not the least idea in the world; but what difference does it make, provided I go somewhere? They say I'm a learned man; they are wrong; I don't know anything, and if I have published some books which have had a good sale, I was wrong; it was very kind of the public to buy them! I don't know anything, I tell you, except that I am very ignorant. Now I have a chance offered me to complete, or, rather, to make over my knowledge of medicine, surgery, history, geography, botany, mineralogy, conchology, geodesy, chemistry, physics, mechanics, hydrography; well, I accept it, and I assure you, I didn't have to be asked twice."

"Then," said Shandon in a tone of disappointment, "you don't know where the *Forward* is going."

"O, but I do, commander; it's going where there is something to be learned, discovered; where one can instruct himself, make comparisons, see other customs, other countries, study the ways of other people; in a word, it's going where I have never been."

"But more precisely?" cried Shandon.

"More precisely," answered the doctor, "I have understood that it was bound for the Northern Ocean. Well, good for the North!"

"At any rate," said Shandon, "you know the captain?"

"Not at all! But he's a good fellow, you may depend on it."

The mate and the doctor stepped ashore at Birkenhead; Shandon gave his companion all the information he had, and the mystery which lay about it all excited highly the doctor's imagination. The sight of the *Forward* enchanted him. From that time he was always with Shandon, and he came every morning to inspect the hull of the *Forward*.

In addition he was specially intrusted with the providing of the ship's medicine-chest.

For Clawbonny was a physician, and a good one, although he had never practised much. At twenty-five he was an ordinary young doctor, at forty he was a learned man; being known throughout the whole city, he became a leading member of the Literary and Philosophical Society of Liverpool. His moderate fortune allowed him to give some advice which was no less valuable for being without charge; loved as a thoroughly kind-hearted man must be, he did no harm to any one else nor to himself; quick and garrulous, if you please, but with his heart in his hand, and his hand in that of all the world.

When the news of his intended journey on board the *Forward* became known in the city, all his friends endeavored to dissuade him, but they only made him cling more obstinately to his intention; and when the doctor had absolutely determined on anything, he was a skilful man who could make him change.

From that day the rumors, conjectures, and apprehensions steadily increased; but that did not interfere with the launching of the *Forward* on the 5th of February, 1860. Two months later she was ready for sea.

On the 15th of March, as the captain's letter had said, a Danish dog was sent by rail from Edinburgh to Liverpool, to the address of Richard Shandon. He seemed morose, timid, and almost wicked; his expression was very strange. The name of the *Forward* was engraved on his collar.

The commander gave him quarters on board, and sent a letter, with the news of his arrival, to Leghorn.

Hence, with the exception of the captain, the crew of the *Forward* was complete. It was composed as follows:—

1. K. Z., captain; 2. Richard Shandon, first mate, in command; 3. James Wall, second mate; 4. Dr. Clawbonny; 5. Johnson, boatswain; 6. Simpson, harpooner; 7. Bell, carpenter; 8. Brunton, first engineer; 9. Plover, second engineer; 10. Strong (negro), cook; 11. Foker, ice-master; 12. Wolston, gunner; 13. Bolton, sailor; 14. Garry, sailor; 15. Clifton, sailor; 16. Gripper, sailor; 17. Pen, sailor; 18. Warren, stoker.

CHAPTER IV.

THE DOG-CAPTAIN.

The 5th of April, the day of departure, came. The fact that the doctor had joined the expedition gave some comfort to those on board. Wherever he could go they could follow. Still, most of the sailors were very uneasy, and Shandon, fearing that their number might be diminished by desertion, was very anxious to get to sea. The land once out of sight, the men would soon be resigned.

Dr. Clawbonny's cabin was situated on the poop, occupying the extreme after-part of the ship. The cabins of the captain and mate opened on the deck. That of the captain was kept tightly closed, after it had been provided with various instruments, furniture, clothing, books, and utensils, all of which had been set down in detail in a letter. As he had asked, the key was sent to the captain at Lübeck; so he alone had admission into the cabin.

This fact annoyed Shandon, and diminished his chances of having chief command. As for his own cabin, he had arranged it suitably for the presumed voyage, for he knew very well what was necessary for a polar expedition.

The second mate's cabin was on the lower deck, where the sailors were domiciled; the crew had very comfortable quarters; they would hardly have had such accommodations in any other ship. They were treated as if they were a valuable cargo; a huge stove stood in the middle of their sleeping-room.

Dr. Clawbonny was very enthusiastic about it; he took possession of his cabin on the 6th of February, the day after the ship was launched.

"The happiest animal in the world," he used to say, "would be a snail who could make himself just such a shell as he wanted; I shall try to be an intelligent snail."

And, in fact, for a shell which he was not going to leave for some time, his cabin presented a very comfortable appearance; the doctor took a scientific or childlike pleasure in arranging his scientific paraphernalia. His books, his specimens, his cases, his instruments, his physical apparatus, his thermometers, barometers, field-glasses, compasses, sextants, charts, drawings, phials, powder, and medicine-bottles, all were classified in a way which would have done honor to the British Museum. This space of six feet square contained incalculable wealth; the doctor needed only to stretch out his hand without rising, to become at once a physician, a mathematician, an astronomer, a geographer, a botanist, or a conchologist.

"This space of six feet square contained incalculable wealth."

To tell the truth, he was proud of his arrangements, and very contented in his floating sanctum, which three of his thinnest friends would have completely filled. They used to crowd there in great numbers, so that even so good-natured a man as the doctor was occasionally put out; and, like Socrates, he came at last to say,—

"My house is small, but may Heaven grant that it never be filled with friends!"

To complete our account of the *Forward*, it is only necessary to add that a kennel for the huge Danish dog was built just beneath the window of the closed cabin; but he preferred to keep himself between decks and in the hold; it seemed impossible to tame him; no one ever conquered his shyness; he could be heard, at night especially, howling dismally in the ship's hold.

Was it because he missed his master? Had he an instinctive dread of the dangers of the voyage? Had he a presentiment of the coming perils? The sailors were sure that he had, and more than one said the same in jest, who in his heart regarded the dog as a sort of diabolic animal.

PEN.

Pen, a very brutal man, one day, while trying to kick him, slipped, and fell on the corner of the capstan in such a way that he cut his head badly. It is easy to see how the sailors put all the blame upon the dog.

CLIFTON.

Clifton, who was the most superstitious man in the crew, made, one day, the strange observation that the dog, when on the poop, would always walk on the windward side; and afterwards, when the brig was at sea and under sail, this singular animal would shift his position to the other side after every tack, so as to be windward, as the captain of the *Forward* would have done.

Dr. Clawbonny, who by his gentleness and caresses would have almost tamed the heart of a tiger, tried in vain to make friends with the dog; he met with no success.

The dog, too, did not answer to any of the usual names of his kind. So the men used to call him "Captain," for he seemed perfectly familiar with all the ways on shipboard. He had evidently been to sea before.

It is hence easy to understand the boatswain's answer to Clifton's friend, and how this idea found but few sceptics; more than one would repeat it jestingly, who was fully prepared to see the dog, some fine day, take human shape, and with a loud voice assume command.

If Richard Shandon did not share such apprehensions, he was far from being undisturbed, and on the eve of departing, on the night of April 5th, he was talking on this subject with the doctor, Wall, and Johnson, in the mess-room.

These four persons were sipping their tenth grog, which was probably their last, too; for, in accordance with the letter from Aberdeen, all the crew, from the captain to the stoker, were teetotalers, never touching beer, wine, nor spirits, except in case of sickness, and by the advice of the doctor.

For an hour past they had been talking about their departure. If the captain's instructions were to be completely carried out, Shandon would the next day receive a letter containing his last orders.

"If that letter," said the mate, "doesn't tell me the captain's name, it must at least tell us whither we are bound. If not, in what direction shall we sail?"

"Upon my word," answered the impatient doctor, "if I were in your place, Shandon, I should set sail even without getting a letter; one will come after us, you may be sure."

"You have a great deal of faith, Doctor. But, if you please, to what part of the world would you sail?"

"Towards the North Pole, of course; there can be no doubt about that."

"No doubt indeed!" said Wall. "Why not towards the South Pole?"

"The South Pole! Never!" cried the doctor. "Would the captain ever have thought of sending a brig across the whole Atlantic Ocean? Just think for a moment, my dear Wall."

"The doctor has an answer for everything," was his only reply.

"Granted it's northward," resumed Shandon. "But tell me, Doctor, is it to Spitzbergen, Greenland, or Labrador that we have to sail, or to Hudson's Bay? If all these routes come to the same end at last,—the impassable ice,—there is still a great number of them, and I should find it very hard to choose between them. Have any definite answer to that, Doctor?"

"No," answered the doctor, annoyed that he had nothing to say; "but if you get no letter, what shall you do?"

"I shall do nothing; I shall wait."

"You won't set sail!" cried Clawbonny, twirling his glass in his despair.

"No, certainly not."

"That's the best course," said Johnson, mildly; while the doctor walked around the table, being unable to sit quiet any longer. "Yes, that's the best course; and still, too long a delay might have very disastrous consequences. In the first place, the season is a good one, and if it's north we are going, we ought to take advantage of the mild weather to get through Davis Straits; besides, the crew will get more and more impatient; the friends and companions of the men are urging them to leave the *Forward*, and they might succeed in playing us a very bad turn."

"And then, too," said James Wall, "if any panic should arise among the men, every one would desert us; and I don't know, Commander, how you could get together another crew."

"But what is to be done?" cried Shandon.

"What you said," answered the doctor: "wait; but wait till to-morrow before you despair. The captain's promises have all been fulfilled so far with such regularity that we may have the best hopes for the future; there's no reason to think that we shall not be told of our destination at the proper time. As for me, I don't doubt in the least that to-morrow we shall be sailing in the Irish Sea. So, my friends, I propose one last drink to a happy voyage; it begins in a mysterious way, but, with such sailors as you, there are a thousand chances of its ending well."

And they all touched their glasses for the last time.

"Now, Commander," resumed Johnson, "I have one piece of advice to give you, and that is, to make everything ready for sailing. Let the crew think you are certain of what you are about. To-morrow, whether a letter comes or not, set sail; don't start your fires; the wind promises to hold; nothing will be easier than to get off; take a pilot on board; at the ebb of the tide leave the docks; then anchor beyond Birkenhead Point; the crew will have no more communication with the land; and if this devilish letter does come at last, it can find us there as well as anywhere."

"Well said, Johnson!" exclaimed the doctor, reaching out his hand to the old sailor.

"That's what we shall do," answered Shandon.

Each one then withdrew to his cabin, and took what sleep he could get till morning.

The next day the first distribution of letters took place in the city, but there was none for Commander Richard Shandon.

Nevertheless he made his preparations for departure; the news spread immediately throughout the city, and, as we have seen, a great concourse of spectators thronged the piers of the New Prince's Docks.

"The news spread immediately throughout the city, and a great concourse of spectators thronged the piers."

A great many people came on board the brig,—some to bid a friend good by, or to urge him to leave the ship, or to gaze at this strange vessel; others to ascertain the object of the voyage; and there were many murmurs at the unusual silence of the commander.

For that he had his reasons.

Ten o'clock struck. Eleven. The tide was to turn at half past twelve. Shandon, from the upper deck, gazed with anxious eyes at the crowd, trying in vain to read on some one's face the secret of his fate. But in vain. The sailors of the

Forward obeyed his orders in silence, keeping their eyes fixed upon him, ever awaiting some information which he did not give.

Johnson was finishing the preparations for setting sail. The day was overcast, and the sea, outside of the docks, rather high; a stiff southwest breeze was blowing, but they could easily leave the Mersey.

At twelve o'clock still nothing. Dr. Clawbonny walked up and down uneasily, looking about, gesticulating, and "impatient for the sea," as he said. In spite of all he could do, he felt excited. Shandon bit his lips till the blood came.

At this moment Johnson came up to him and said,—

"Commander, if we are going to take this tide, we must lose no time; it will be a good hour before we can get off from the docks."

Shandon cast one last glance about him, and looked at his watch. It was after the time of the midday distribution of letters.

"Cast off!" he said to his boatswain.

"All ashore who are going!" cried the latter, ordering the spectators to leave the deck of the *Forward*.

Thereupon the crowd, began to move toward the gangway and make its way on to the quay, while the crew began to cast off the last moorings.

At once the inevitable confusion of the crowd, which was pushed about without much ceremony by the sailors, was increased by the barking of the dog. He suddenly sprang from the forecastle right through the mass of visitors, barking sullenly.

All made way for him. He sprang on the poop-deck, and, incredible as it may seem, yet, as a thousand witnesses can testify, this dog-captain carried a letter in his mouth.

"A letter!" cried Shandon; "but is *he* on board?"

"*He* was, without doubt, but he's not now," answered Johnson, showing the deck cleared of the crowd.

"Here, Captain! Captain!" shouted the doctor, trying to take the letter from the dog, who kept springing away from him. He seemed to want to give the letter to Shandon himself.

"Here, Captain!" he said.

The dog went up to him; Shandon took the letter without difficulty, and then Captain barked sharply three times, amid the profound silence which prevailed on board the ship and along the quay.

Shandon held the letter in his hand, without opening it.

"Read it, read it!" cried the doctor. Shandon looked at it. The address, without date or place, ran simply,—"Commander Richard Shandon, on board the brig *Forward*."

Shandon opened the letter and read:—

You will sail towards Cape Farewell. You will reach it April 20. If the captain does not appear on board, you will pass through Davis Strait and go up Baffin's Bay as far as Melville Sound.

K. Z.,
Captain of the Forward.

Shandon folded carefully this brief letter, put it in his pocket, and gave the order to cast off. His voice, which arose alone above the roaring of the wind, sounded very solemn.

Soon the *Forward* had left the docks, and under the care of a pilot, whose boat followed at a distance, put out into the stream. The crowd hastened to the outer quay by the Victoria Docks to get a last look at the strange vessel. The two topsails, the foresail, and staysail were soon set, and under this canvas the *Forward*, which well deserved its name, after rounding Birkenhead Point, sailed away into the Irish Sea.

CHAPTER V.

AT SEA.

The wind, which was uncertain, although in general favorable, was blowing in genuine April squalls. The *Forward* sailed rapidly, and its screw, as yet unused, did not delay its progress. Towards three o'clock they met the steamer which plies between Liverpool and the Isle of Man, and which carries the three legs of Sicily on its paddle-boxes. Her captain hailed them, and this was the last good-by to the crew of the *Forward*.

At five o'clock the pilot resigned the charge of the ship to Richard Shandon, and sailed away in his boat, which soon disappeared from sight in the southwest.

Towards evening the brig doubled the Calf of Man, at the southern extremity of the island of that name. During the night the sea was very high; the *Forward* rode the waves very well, however, and leaving the Point of Ayr on the northwest, she ran towards the North Channel.

"Towards evening the brig doubled the Calf of Man."

Johnson was right; once at sea the sailors readily adapted themselves instinctively to the situation. They saw the excellence of their vessel and forgot the strangeness of their situation. The ship's routine was soon regularly established.

The doctor inhaled with pleasure the sea-air; he paced up and down the deck in spite of the fresh wind, and showed that for a student he had very good sea-legs.

"The sea is a fine thing," he said to Johnson, as he went upon the bridge after breakfast; "I am a little late in making its acquaintance, but I shall make up for my delay."

"You are right, Dr. Clawbonny; I would give all the land in the world for a bit of ocean. People say that sailors soon get tired of their business; but I've been sailing for forty years, and I like it as well as I did the first day."

"What a pleasure it is to feel a stanch ship under one's feet! and, if I'm not mistaken, the *Forward* is a capital sea-boat."

"You are right, Doctor," answered Shandon, who had joined the two speakers; "she's a good ship, and I must say that there was never a ship so well equipped for a voyage in the polar regions. That reminds me that, thirty years ago, Captain James Ross, going to seek the Northwest Passage—"

"Commanded the *Victory*," said the doctor, quickly, "a brig of about the tonnage of this one, and also carrying machinery."

"What! did you know that?"

"Say for yourself," retorted the doctor. "Steamers were then new inventions, and the machinery of the *Victory* was continually delaying him. Captain Ross, after in vain trying to patch up every piece, at last took it all out and left it at the first place he wintered at."

"The deuce!" said Shandon. "You know all about it, I see."

"More or less," answered the doctor. "In my reading I have come across the works of Parry, Ross, Franklin; the reports of MacClure, Kennedy, Kane, MacClintock; and some of it has stuck in my memory. I might add that MacClintock, on board of the *Fox*, a propeller like ours, succeeded in making his way more easily and more directly than all his successors."

"That's perfectly true," answered Shandon; "that MacClintock is a good sailor; I have seen him at sea. You might also say that we shall be, like him, in Davis Strait in the month of April; and if we can get through the ice our voyage will be very much advanced."

"Unless," said the doctor, "we should be as unlucky as the *Fox* in 1857, and should be caught the first year by the ice in the north of Baffin's Bay, and we should have to winter among the icebergs."

"We must hope to be luckier, Mr. Shandon," said Johnson; "and if, with a ship like the *Forward*, we can't go where we please, the attempt must be given up forever."

"Besides," continued the doctor, "if the captain is on board he will know better than we what is to be done, and so much the better because we are perfectly ignorant; for his singularly brief letter gives us no clew to the probable aim of the voyage."

"It's a great deal," answered Shandon, with some warmth, "to know what route we have to take; and now for a good month, I fancy, we shall be able to get along without his supernatural intervention and orders. Besides, you know what I think about him."

"Ha, ha!" laughed the doctor; "I used to think as you did, that he was going to leave the command of the ship in your hands, and that he would never come on board; but—"

"But what?" asked Shandon, with some ill-humor.

"But since the arrival of the second letter, I have altered my views somewhat."

"And why so, doctor?"

"Because, although this letter does tell you in which direction to go, it still does not inform you of the final aim of the voyage; and we have yet to know whither we are to go. I ask you how can a third letter reach us now that we are on the open sea. The postal service on the shore of Greenland is very defective. You see, Shandon, I fancy that he is waiting for us at some Danish settlement up there,—at Holsteinborg or Upernavik. We shall find that he has been completing the supply of seal-skins, buying sledges and dogs,—in a word, providing all the equipment for a journey in the arctic seas. So I shall not be in the least surprised to see him coming out of his cabin some fine morning and taking command in the least supernatural way in the world."

"Possibly," answered Shandon, dryly; "but meanwhile the wind's freshening, and there's no use risking our topsails in such weather."

Shandon left the doctor, and ordered the topsails furled.

"He still clings to that idea," said the doctor to the boatswain.

"Yes," was the answer, "and it's a pity; for you may very well be right, Dr. Clawbonny."

Towards the evening of Saturday the *Forward* rounded the Mull of Galloway, on which the light could be seen in the northeast. During the night they left the Mull of Cantire to the north, and on the east Fair Head, on the Irish coast. Towards three o'clock in the morning, the brig, passing Rathlin Island on its starboard quarter, came out from the North Channel into the ocean.

That was Sunday, April 8. The English, and especially sailors, are very observant of that day; hence the reading of the Bible, of which the doctor gladly took charge, occupied a good part of the morning.

The wind rose to a gale, and threatened to drive the ship back upon the Irish coast. The waves ran very high; the vessel rolled a great deal. If the doctor was not sea-sick, it was because he was determined not to be, for nothing would have been easier. At midday Malin Head disappeared from their view in the south; it was the last sight these bold sailors were to have of Europe, and more than one gazed at it for a long time who was doubtless fated never to set eyes on it again.

By observation the latitude then was 55° 57', and the longitude, according to the chronometer, 7° 40'.*

* Meridian of Greenwich.

The gale abated towards nine o'clock of the evening; the *Forward*, a good sailer, kept on its route to the northwest. That day gave them all a good opportunity to judge of her sea-going qualities; as good judges had already said at Liverpool, she was well adapted for carrying sail.

During the following days, the *Forward* made very good progress; the wind veered to the south, and the sea ran high. The brig set every sail. A few petrels and puffins flew about the poop-deck; the doctor succeeded in shooting one of the latter, which fortunately fell on board.

Simpson, the harpooner, seized it and carried it to the doctor.

"It's an ugly bird, Dr. Clawbonny," he said.

"But then it will make a good meal, my friend."

"What, are you going to eat it?"

"And you shall have a taste of it," said the doctor, laughing.

"Never!" answered Simpson; "it's strong and oily, like all sea-birds."

"True," said the doctor; "but I have a way of dressing such game, and if you recognize it to be a sea-bird, I'll promise never to kill another in all my life."

"So you are a cook, too, Dr. Clawbonny?" asked Johnson.

"A learned man ought to know a little of everything."

"Then take care, Simpson," said the boatswain; "the doctor is a clever man, and he'll make us take this puffin for a delicious grouse."

In fact, the doctor was in the right about this bird; he removed skilfully the fat which lies beneath the whole surface of the skin, principally on its thighs, and with it disappeared all the rancid, fishy odor with which this bird can be justly charged. Thus prepared, the bird was called delicious, even by Simpson.

During the recent storm, Richard Shandon had made up his mind about the qualities of his crew; he had tested his men one by one, as every officer should do who wishes to be prepared for future dangers; he knew on whom he could rely.

James Wall, who was warmly attached to Richard, was intelligent and efficient, but he had very little originality; as second officer he was exactly in his place.

Johnson, who was accustomed to the dangers of the sea, and an old sailor in arctic regions, lacked neither coolness nor courage.

Simpson, the harpooner, and Bell, the carpenter, were steady men, obedient and well disciplined. The ice-master, Foker, an experienced sailor, who had sailed in northern waters, promised to be of the greatest service.

Of the other men, Garry and Bolton seemed to be the best; Bolton was a jolly fellow, always laughing and joking; Garry, a man about thirty-five years old, had an energetic, but rather pale and sad face.

The three sailors, Clifton, Gripper, and Pen, seemed to be the least enthusiastic and determined; they were inclined to grumbling. Gripper had even wished to break his engagement when the time came for sailing, and only a feeling of shame prevented him. If things went well, if they encountered no excessive dangers, and their toil was not too severe, these three men could be counted on; but they were hard to please with their food, for they were inclined to gluttony. In spite of their having been forewarned, they were by no means pleased with being teetotalers, and at their meals they used to miss their brandy or gin; but they made up for it with the tea and coffee which were distributed with a lavish hand.

As for the two engineers, Brunton and Plover, and the stoker, Warren, they had been so far well satisfied with having nothing to do.

Shandon knew therefore what to expect from each man.

On the 14th of April, the *Forward* crossed the Gulf Stream, which, after following the eastern coast of America as far as Newfoundland, turns to the northeast and moves towards the shore of Norway. They were then in latitude 51° 37', and longitude 22° 37', two hundred miles from the end of Greenland. The weather grew colder; the thermometer fell to 32°, the freezing-point.

The doctor, without yet putting on his arctic winter dress, was wearing a suit of sea-clothes, like all the officers and sailors; he was an amusing sight in his high boots, in which he could not bend his legs, his huge tarpaulin hat, his trousers and coat of the same material; in heavy rain, or when the brig was shipping seas, the doctor used to look like a sort of sea-monster, a comparison which always flattered him.

For two days the sea was very rough; the wind veered to the northwest, and delayed the *Forward*. From the 14th to the 16th of April there was still a high sea running; but on Monday there fell a heavy shower which almost immediately had the effect of calming the sea. Shandon called the doctor's attention to it.

"Well," said the doctor, "that confirms the curious observations of the whaler Scoresby, who was a member of the Royal Society of Edinburgh, of which I have the honor to be a corresponding member. You see that while the rain is falling the waves are hardly to be noticed, even when the wind is strong. On the other hand, in dry weather the sea would be rougher even with a gentler wind."

"But what is the explanation of it, Doctor?"

"It's very simple; there is no explanation."

At that moment the ice-master, who was on watch in the topmast crosstrees, cried out that there was a floating mass on the starboard quarter, about fifteen miles to windward.

"An iceberg in these latitudes!" cried the doctor.

Shandon turned his glass in that direction, and corroborated the lookout's words.

"That's strange," said the doctor.

"Are you surprised?" asked the commander, laughing. "What! are we lucky enough to find anything that will surprise you?"

"I am surprised without being surprised," answered the doctor, smiling, "since the brig *Ann Poole*, of Greenspond, was caught in the ice in the year 1813, in the forty-fourth degree of north latitude, and Dayement, her captain, saw hundreds of icebergs."

"Good," said Shandon; "you can still teach us a great deal about them."

"O, not so very much!" answered Clawbonny, modestly, "except that ice has been seen in very much lower latitudes."

"That I know, my dear Doctor, for when I was a cabin-boy on the sloop-of-war, *Fly*—"

"In 1818," continued the doctor, "at the end of March, or it might have been the beginning of April, you passed between two large fields of floating ice, in latitude forty-two."

"That is too much!" exclaimed Shandon.

"But it's true; so I have no need to be surprised, now that we are two degrees farther north, at our sighting an iceberg."

"You are bottled full of information, Doctor," answered the commander; "one needs only draw the cork."

"Very well, I shall be exhausted sooner than you think; and now, Shandon, if we can get a nearer view of this phenomenon, I should be the gladdest of doctors."

"Exactly, Johnson," said Shandon, summoning the boatswain; "I think the wind is freshening."

"Yes, Commander," answered Johnson, "we are making very little headway, and soon we shall feel the currents from Davis Strait."

"You are right, Johnson, and if we mean to make Cape Farewell by the 20th of April, we must go under steam, or we shall be cast on the coast of Labrador.—Mr. Wall, give the order to light the fires."

The mate's orders were obeyed; an hour later the engines were in motion; the sails were furled; and the screw, turning through the waves, was driving the *Forward* rapidly in the teeth of the northwest wind.

CHAPTER VI.

THE GREAT POLAR CURRENT.

Soon more numerous flocks of birds, petrels, puffins, and others which inhabit those barren shores, gave token of their approach to Greenland. The *Forward* was moving rapidly northward, leaving behind her a long line of dark smoke.

Tuesday, the 17th of April, the ice-master caught the first sight of the *blink** of the ice. It was visible at least twenty miles off to the north-northwest. In spite of some tolerably thick clouds it lighted up brilliantly all the air near the horizon. No one of those on board who had ever seen this phenomenon before could fail to recognize it, and they felt assured from its whiteness that this blink was due to a vast field of ice lying about thirty miles farther than they could see, and that it came from the reflection of its luminous rays.

> * A peculiar and brilliant color of the air above a large expanse of ice.

Towards evening the wind shifted to the south, and became favorable; Shandon was able to carry sail, and as a measure of economy they extinguished the furnace fires. The *Forward* under her topsails, jib, and foresail, sailed on towards Cape Farewell.

At three o'clock on the 18th they made out an ice-stream, which, like a narrow but brilliant band, divided the lines of the water and sky. It was evidently descending rather from the coast of Greenland than from Davis Strait, for the ice tended to keep on the western side of Baffin's Bay. An hour later, and the *Forward* was passing through the detached fragments of the ice-stream, and in the thickest part the pieces of ice, although closely welded together, were rising and falling with the waves.

At daybreak the next morning the watch saw a sail; it was the *Valkyria*, a Danish corvette, sailing towards the *Forward*, bound to Newfoundland. The current from the strait became perceptible, and Shandon had to set more sail to overcome it.

At that moment the commander, the doctor, James Wall, and Johnson were all together on the poop-deck, observing the force and direction of the current. The doctor asked if it were proved that this current was felt throughout Baffin's Bay.

"There's no doubt of it," answered Shandon; "and sailing-vessels have hard work in making headway against it."

"And it's so much the harder," added James Wall, "because it's met on the eastern coast of America, as well as on the western coast of Greenland."

"Well," said the doctor, "that serves to confirm those who seek a Northwest Passage. The current moves at the rate of about five miles an hour, and it is hard to imagine that it rises at the bottom of a gulf."

"That is very likely, Doctor," answered Shandon, "because, while this current flows from north to south, there is a contrary current in Behring Strait, which flows from south to north, and which must be the cause of this one."

"Hence," said the doctor, "you must admit that America is completely separated from the polar regions, and that the water from the Pacific skirts its whole northern coast, until it reaches the Atlantic. Besides, the greater elevation of the water of the Pacific is another reason for its flowing towards the European seas."

"But," said Shandon, "there must be some facts which support this theory; and if there are," he added with gentle irony, "our learned friend must be familiar with them."

"Well," answered the latter, complacently, "if it interests you at all I can tell you that whales, wounded in Davis Strait, have been found afterwards on the coast of Tartary, still carrying a European harpoon in their side."

"And unless they doubled Cape Horn, or the Cape of Good Hope," answered Shandon, "they must have gone around the northern coast of America. There can be no doubt of that, Doctor."

"And if you were not convinced, my dear Shandon," said the doctor, smiling, "I could produce still other evidence, such as the floating wood with which Davis Strait is filled, larch, aspen, and other southern kinds. Now we know that the Gulf Stream could not carry them into the strait; and if they come out from it they must have got in through Behring Strait."

"I am perfectly convinced, Doctor, and I must say it would be hard to maintain the other side against you."

"See there," said Johnson, "there's something that will throw light on this discussion. It's a large piece of wood floating on the water; if the commander will give us leave, we can put a rope about it, hoist it on board, and ask it the name of its country."

"That's the way!" said the doctor; "after the rule we have the example."

Shandon gave the necessary orders; the brig was turned towards the piece of wood, and soon the crew were hoisting it aboard, although not without considerable trouble.

It was the trunk of a mahogany-tree, eaten to its centre by worms, which fact alone made it light enough to float.

"This is a real triumph," exclaimed the doctor, enthusiastically, "for, since the Atlantic currents could not have brought it into Davis Strait, since it could not have reached the polar waters from the rivers of North America, as the tree grows under the equator, it is evident that it must have come direct from Behring Strait. And besides, see those sea-worms which have eaten it; they belong to warm latitudes."

"It certainly gives the lie to those who deny the existence of a Northwest Passage."

"It fairly kills them," answered the doctor. "See here, I'll give you the route of this mahogany-tree: it was carried to the Pacific Ocean by some river of the Isthmus of Panama or of Guatemala; thence the current carried it along the coast of America as far as Behring Strait, and so it was forced into the polar waters; it is neither so old nor so completely water-logged that we cannot set its departure at some recent date; it escaped all the obstacles of the many straits coming into Baffin's Bay, and being quickly seized by the arctic current it came through Davis Strait to be hoisted on board the *Forward* for the great joy of Dr. Clawbonny, who asks the commander's permission to keep a piece as a memorial."

"Of course," answered Shandon; "but let me tell you in my turn that you will not be the only possessor of such a waif. The Danish governor of the island of Disco—"

"On the coast of Greenland," continued the doctor, "has a mahogany table, made from a tree found in the same way; I know it, my dear Shandon. Very well; I don't grudge him his table, for if there were room enough on board, I could easily make a sleeping-room out of this."

On the night of Wednesday the wind blew with extreme violence; drift-wood was frequently seen; the approach to the coast became more dangerous at a time when icebergs are numerous; hence the commander ordered sail to be shortened, and the *Forward* went on under merely her foresail and forestay-sail.

The thermometer fell below the freezing-point. Shandon distributed among the crew suitable clothing, woollen trousers and jackets, flannel shirts, and thick woollen stockings, such as are worn by Norwegian peasants. Every man received in addition a pair of water-proof boots.

As for Captain, he seemed contented with his fur; he appeared indifferent to the changes of temperature, as if he were thoroughly accustomed to such a life; and besides, a Danish dog was unlikely to be very tender. The men seldom laid eyes on him, for he generally kept himself concealed in the darkest parts of the vessel.

Towards evening, through a rift in the fog, the coast of Greenland could be seen in longitude 37° 2' 7". Through his glass the doctor was able to distinguish mountains separated by huge glaciers; but the fog soon cut out this view, like the curtain of a theatre falling at the most interesting part of a play.

On the morning of the 20th of April, the *Forward* found itself in sight of an iceberg one hundred and fifty feet high, aground in this place from time immemorial; the thaws have had no effect upon it, and leave its strange shape unaltered. Snow saw it; in 1829 James Ross took an exact drawing of it; and in 1851 the French lieutenant, Bellot, on board of the *Prince Albert*, observed it. Naturally the doctor wanted to preserve a memorial of the famous mountain, and he made a very successful sketch of it.

It is not strange that such masses should run aground, and in consequence become immovably fixed to the spot; as for every foot above the surface of the water they have nearly two beneath, which would give to this one a total height of about four hundred feet.

At last with a temperature at noon as low as 12°, under a snowy, misty sky, they sighted Cape Farewell. The *Forward* arrived at the appointed day; the unknown captain, if he cared to assume his place in such gloomy weather, would have no need to complain.

"Then," said the doctor to himself, "there is this famous cape, with its appropriate name! Many have passed it, as we do, who were destined never to see it again! Is it an eternal farewell to one's friends in Europe? You have all passed it, Frobisher, Knight, Barlow, Vaughan, Scroggs, Barentz, Hudson, Blosseville, Franklin, Crozier, Bellot, destined never to return home; and for you this cape was well named Cape Farewell!"

It was towards the year 970 that voyagers, setting out from Iceland, discovered Greenland. Sebastian Cabot, in 1498, went as high as latitude 56°; Gaspard and Michel Cotréal, from 1500 to 1502, reached latitude 60°; and in 1576 Martin Frobisher reached the inlet which bears his name.

To John Davis belongs the honor of having discovered the strait, in 1585; and two years later in a third voyage this hardy sailor, this great whaler, reached the sixty-third parallel, twenty-seven degrees from the Pole.

Barentz in 1596, Weymouth in 1602, James Hall in 1605 and 1607, Hudson, whose name was given to the large bay which runs so far back into the continent of America, James Poole in 1611, went more or less far into the straits, seeking the Northwest Passage, the discovery of which would have greatly shortened the route between the two worlds.

Baffin, in 1616, found in the bay of that name Lancaster Sound; he was followed in 1619 by James Monk, and in 1719 by Knight, Barlow, Vaughan, and Scroggs, who were never heard of again.

In 1776, Lieutenant Pickersgill, sent to meet Captain Cook, who tried to make his way through Behring Strait, reached latitude 68°; the next year, Young, on the same errand, went as far as Woman's Island.

Then came James Ross, who in 1818 sailed all around the shores of Baffin's Bay, and corrected the errors on the charts of his predecessors.

Finally, in 1819 and 1820, the famous Parry made his way into Lancaster Sound. In spite of numberless difficulties he reached Melville Island, and won the prize of five thousand pounds offered by act of Parliament to the English sailors who should cross the meridian at a latitude higher than the seventy-seventh parallel.

In 1826, Beechey touched at Chamisso Island; James Ross wintered, from 1829 to 1833, in Prince Regent's Inlet, and, among other important services, discovered the magnetic pole.

During this time Franklin, by a land-journey, defined the northern coast of America, from Mackenzie River to Turnagain Point; Captain Back followed the same route from 1823 to 1835; and these explorations were completed in 1839 by Dease, Simpson, and Dr. Rae.

At last, Sir John Franklin, anxious to discover the Northwest Passage, left England in 1845, with the *Erebus* and the *Terror;* he entered Baffin's Bay, and since his leaving Disco Island there has been no news of his expedition.

His disappearance started numerous search-expeditions, which have effected the discovery of the passage, and given the world definite information about the rugged coasts of the polar lands. The boldest sailors of England, France, and the United States hastened to these terrible latitudes; and, thanks to their exertions, the tortuous, complicated map of these regions has at last been placed in the archives of the Royal Geographical Society of London.

The strange history of these lands crowded on the imagination of the doctor, as he stood leaning on the rail, and gazing on the long track of the brig. The names of those bold sailors thronged into his memory, and it seemed to him that beneath the frozen arches of the ice he could see the pale ghosts of those who never returned.

CHAPTER VII.

THE ENTRANCE OF DAVIS STRAIT.

During that day the *Forward* made easy progress through the loose ice; the breeze was in a good quarter, but the temperature was very low; the wind coming across the ice-fields was thoroughly chilled.

At night the strictest care was necessary; the icebergs crowded together in this narrow passage; often they could be counted by the hundred on the horizon; they had been loosened from the lofty coasts by the incessant beating of the waves and the warmth of the spring month, and they were floating down to melt away in the depths of the ocean. Often, too, they came across large masses of floating wood, which they were obliged to avoid, so that the crow's-nest was placed in position on the top of the foremast; it consisted of a sort of tub, in which the ice-master, partly sheltered from the wind, scanned the sea, giving notice of the ice in sight, and even, if necessary, directing the ship's course.

The nights were short; since the 31st of January the sun had reappeared in refraction, and was every day rising higher and higher above the horizon. But it was hid by the snow, which, if it did not produce utter darkness, rendered navigation difficult.

April 21st, Cape Desolation appeared through the mist; hard work was wearying the crew; since the brig had entered the ice, the sailors had had no rest; it was now necessary to have recourse to steam to force a way through the accumulated masses.

The doctor and Johnson were talking together on the after-deck, while Shandon was snatching a few hours of sleep in his cabin. Clawbonny was very fond of talking with the old sailor, whose numerous voyages had given him a valuable education. The two had made great friends of one another.

"You see, Dr. Clawbonny," said Johnson, "this country is not like any other; its name is Greenland, but there are very few weeks of the year in which it deserves this name."

"But, Johnson," answered the doctor, "who can say whether in the tenth century this name did not suit it? More than one change of this sort has taken place on the globe, and I should astonish you much more by saying that, according to Icelandic chroniclers, two hundred villages flourished on this continent eight or nine hundred years ago."

"You astonish me so much, Dr. Clawbonny, that I can't believe you; for it's a sterile country."

"Well, sterile as it is, it supports a good many inhabitants, and among them are some civilized Europeans."

"Without doubt; at Disco and at Upernavik we shall find men who are willing to live in such a climate; but I always supposed they stayed there from necessity, and not because they liked it."

"I think you are right; still, men get accustomed to everything, and these Greenlanders appear to me better off than the workingmen of our large cities; they may be unfortunate, but they are not miserable. I say unfortunate, but that is not exactly what I mean; in fact, if they are not quite as comfortable as those who live in temperate regions, they, nevertheless, are accustomed to the severity of the climate, and find in it an enjoyment which we should never imagine."

"We have to think so, Dr. Clawbonny, because Heaven is just; but I have often visited these coasts, and I am always saddened at the sight of its gloomy loneliness; the capes, promontories, and bays ought to have more attractive names, for Cape Farewell and Cape Desolation are not of a sort to cheer sailors."

"I have often made the same remark," answered the doctor; "but these names have a geographical value which is not to be forgotten; they describe the adventures of those who gave them; along with the names of Davis, Baffin, Hudson, Ross, Parry, Franklin, Bellot, if I find Cape Desolation, I also find soon Mercy Bay; Cape Providence makes up for Port Anxiety, Repulse Bay brings me to Cape Eden, and after leaving Point Turnagain I rest in Refuge Bay; in that way I have under my eyes the whole succession of dangers, checks, obstacles, successes, despairs, and victories connected with the great names of my country; and, like a series of antique medals, this nomenclature gives me the whole history of these seas."

"Well reasoned, Doctor; and may we find more bays of Success in our journey than capes of Despair!"

"I hope so, Johnson; but, tell me, have the crew got over their fears?"

"Somewhat, sir; and yet, to tell the truth, since we entered these straits, they have begun to be very uneasy about the unknown captain; more than one expected to see him appear at the end of Greenland; and so far no news of him. Between ourselves, Doctor, don't you think that is a little strange!"

"Yes, Johnson, I do."

"Do you believe the captain exists?"

"Without any doubt."

"But what reason can he have had for acting in this way?"

"To speak frankly, Johnson, I imagine that he wants to get the crew so far away that it will be impossible for them to turn back. Now, if he had appeared on board when we set sail, and every one had known where we were going, he might have been embarrassed."

"How so?"

"Why, if he wants to try any superhuman enterprise, if he wants to go where so many have failed, do you think he would have succeeded in shipping a crew? But, once on the way, it is easy to go so far that to go farther becomes an absolute necessity."

"Possibly, Doctor; I have known more than one bold explorer, whose name alone would have frightened every one, and who would have found no one to accompany him on his perilous expeditions—"

"Except me," said the doctor.

"And me," continued Johnson. "I tell you our captain is probably one of those men. At any rate, we shall know sooner or later; I suppose that at Upernavik or Melville Bay he will come quietly on board, and let us know whither he intends to take the ship."

"Very likely, Johnson; but the difficulty will be to get to Melville Bay; see how thick the ice is about us! The *Forward* can hardly make her way through it. See there, that huge expanse!"

"We whalers call that an ice-field, that is to say, an unbroken surface of ice, the limits of which cannot be seen."

"And what do you call this broken field of long pieces more or less closely connected?"

"That is a pack; if it's round we call it a patch, and a stream if it is long."

"And that floating ice?"

"That is drift-ice; if a little higher it would be icebergs; they are very dangerous to ships, and they have to be carefully avoided. See, down there on the ice-field, that protuberance caused by the pressure of the ice; we call that a hummock; if the base were under water, we should call it a cake; we have to give names to them all to distinguish them."

"Ah, it is a strange sight," exclaimed the doctor, as he gazed at the wonders of the northern seas; "one's imagination is touched by all these different shapes!"

"True," answered Johnson, "the ice takes sometimes such curious shapes; and we men never fail to explain them in our own way."

"See there, Johnson; see that singular collection of blocks of ice! Would one not say it was a foreign city, an Eastern city, with minarets and mosques in the moonlight? Farther off is a long row of Gothic arches, which remind us of the chapel of Henry VII., or the Houses of Parliament."

"Would one not say it was a foreign city, an Eastern city, with minarets and mosques in the moonlight?"

"Everything can be found there; but those cities or churches are very dangerous, and we must not go too near them. Some of those minarets are tottering, and the smallest of them would crush a ship like the *Forward*."

"And yet men have dared to come into these seas under sail alone! How could a ship be trusted in such perils without the aid of steam?"

"Still it has been done; when the wind is unfavorable, and I have known that happen more than once, it is usual to anchor to one of these blocks of ice; we should float more or less around with them, but we would wait for a fair wind; it is true that, travelling in that way, months would be sometimes wasted where we shall need only a few days."

"It seems to me," said the doctor, "that the temperature is falling."

"That would be a pity," answered Johnson, "for there will have to be a thaw before these masses separate, and float away into the Atlantic; besides, they are more numerous in Davis Strait, because the two stretches of land approach one another between Cape Walsingham and Holsteinborg; but above latitude 67° we shall find in May and June more navigable seas."

"Yes; but we must get through this first."

"We must get through, Doctor; in June and July we should have found the passage free, as do the whalers; but our orders were strict; we had to be here in April. If I'm not very much mistaken, our captain is a sound fellow with an idea firm in his head; his only reason for leaving so early was to go far. Whoever survives will see."

The doctor was right about the falling of the temperature; at noon the thermometer stood at 6°, and a breeze was blowing from the northwest, which, while it cleared the sky, aided the current in accumulating the floating ice in the path of the *Forward*. It did not all follow the same course; often some pieces, and very high ones, too, floated in the opposite direction under the influence of a submarine current.

The difficulties of this navigation may be readily understood; the engineers had no repose; the engines were controlled from the bridge by means of levers, which started, stopped, and reversed them instantly, at the orders of the officer in command. Sometimes it was necessary to hasten forward to enter an opening in the ice, again to race with a mass of ice which threatened to block up their only egress, or some piece, suddenly upsetting, obliged the brig to back quickly, in order to escape destruction. This mass of ice, carried and accumulated by the great polar current, was hurried through the strait, and if the frost should unite it, it would present an impassable barrier to the *Forward*.

In these latitudes numberless birds were to be found; petrels and contremaitres were flying here and there, with deafening cries; there were also many gulls, with their large heads, short necks, and small beaks, which were extending their long wings and braving the snow which the storm was whirling about. This profusion of winged beings enlivened the scene.

Numerous pieces of wood were drifting along, clashing continually into one another; a few whales with large heads approached the ship; but they could not think of chasing them, although Simpson, the harpooner, earnestly desired it. Towards evening several seals were seen, which, with their noses just above the water, were swimming among the great pieces of ice.

On the 22d the temperature was still falling; the *Forward* carried a great deal of steam to reach an easier sailing-place; the wind blew steadily from the northwest; the sails were furled.

During Sunday the sailors had little to do. After divine service, which was read by Shandon, the crew betook themselves to chasing wild birds, of which they caught a great many. These birds, prepared according to Dr. Clawbonny's method, were an agreeable addition to the messes of the officers and crew.

At three o'clock in the afternoon, the *Forward* sighted the Kin of Sael, which lay east one quarter northeast, and the Mount Sukkertop, southeast one quarter east half-east; the sea was very high; from time to time a dense fog descended suddenly from the gray sky. Notwithstanding, at noon they were able to take an observation. The ship was found to be in latitude 65° 20' and longitude 54° 22'. They would have to go two degrees farther north before they would find clearer sailing.

During the three following days, the 24th, 25th, and 26th of April, they had uninterruptedly to fight with the ice; the management of the engines became very tedious; every minute steam was shut off or reversed, and escaped from the safety-valve.

In the dense mist their approach to the icebergs could be known only by the dull roar of the avalanches; then the vessel would shift its course at once; then there was the danger of running into the masses of frozen fresh water, which were as clear as crystal and as hard as stone. Richard Shandon used to take aboard a quantity of this ice every day to supply the ship with fresh water.

The doctor could not accustom himself to the optical illusions produced by refraction; indeed, an iceberg ten or twelve miles distant used to seem to him to be a small piece of ice close by; he tried to get used to this strange phenomenon, in order to be able by and by to overcome the mistakes of his eyesight.

At last, both by towing the brig along the fields of ice and by pushing off threatening blocks with poles, the crew was thoroughly exhausted; and yet, on the 27th of April, the *Forward* was still detained on the impassable Polar Circle.

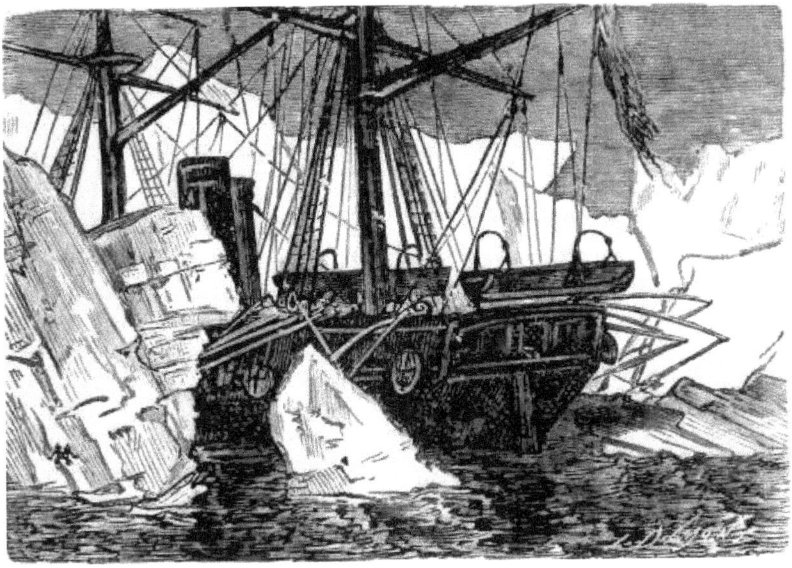

CHAPTER VIII.

THE TALK OF THE CREW.

Nevertheless, by taking advantages of such openings as there were, the *Forward* succeeded in getting a few minutes farther north; but, instead of escaping the enemy, it would soon be necessary to attack it; ice-fields of many miles in extent were drawing together, and as these moving masses often represent a pressure of ten millions of tons, they were obliged to take every precaution against being crushed by them. Ice-saws were placed outside the vessel, where they could be used without delay.

Some of the crew endured their hard toil without a murmur, but others complained or even refused to obey orders. While they were putting the saws in place, Garry, Bolton, Pen, and Gripper exchanged their diverse opinions as follows.

"Deuce take it," said Bolton, cheerfully; "I don't know why it just occurs to me that in Water Street there's a comfortable tavern, where one might be very well off between a glass of gin and a bottle of porter. Can you see it from here, Gripper?"

"To tell the truth," answered the sailor who had been addressed, and who generally pretended to be very sullen, "I must say I can't see it from here."

"That's merely your way of talking, Gripper; it is evident that, in those snow towns which Dr. Clawbonny is always admiring, there's no tavern where a poor sailor can moisten his throat with a drink or two of brandy."

"You may be sure of that, Bolton; and you might add that on board of this ship there's no way of getting properly refreshed. A strange idea, sending people into the northern seas, and giving them nothing to drink!"

"Well," answered Garry, "have you forgotten, Gripper, what the doctor said? One must go without spirits if he expects to escape the scurvy, remain in good health, and sail far."

"I don't care to sail far, Garry; and I think it's enough to have come as far as this, and to try to get through here where the Devil doesn't mean to let us through."

"Well, we sha'n't get through," retorted Pen. "O, when I think I have already forgotten how gin tastes!"

"But," said Bolton, "remember what the doctor said."

"O," answered Pen, with his rough voice, "that's all very well to say! I fancy that they are economizing it under the pretext of saving our health."

"Perhaps that devil Pen is right," said Gripper.

"Come, come!" replied Bolton, "his nose is too red for that; and if a little abstinence should make it a trifle paler, Pen won't need to be pitied."

"Don't trouble yourself about my nose," was the answer, for Pen was rather vexed. "My nose doesn't need your advice; it doesn't ask for it; you'd better mind your own business."

"Come, don't be angry, Pen; I didn't think your nose was so tender. I should be as glad as any one else to have a glass of whiskey, especially on such a cold day; but if in the long run it does more harm than good, why, I'm very willing to get along without it."

"You may get along without it," said Warren, the stoker, who had joined them, "but it's not everybody on board who gets along without it."

"What do you mean, Warren?" asked Garry, looking at him intently.

"I mean that for one purpose or another there is liquor aboard, and I fancy that aft they don't get on without it."

"What do you know about it?" asked Garry.

Warren could not answer; he spoke for the sake of speaking.

"You see, Garry," continued Bolton, "that Warren knows nothing about it."

"Well," said Pen, "we'll ask the commander for a ration of gin; we deserve it, and we'll see what he'll say."

"I advise you not to," said Garry.

"Why not?" cried Pen and Gripper.

"Because the commander will refuse it. You knew what the conditions were when you shipped; you ought to think of that now."

"Besides," said Bolton, who was not averse to taking Garry's side, for he liked him, "Richard Shandon is not master; he's under orders like the rest of us."

"Whose orders?" asked Pen.

"The captain's."

"Ah, that ridiculous captain's!" cried Pen. "Don't you know there's no more captain than there is tavern on the ice? That's a mean way of refusing politely what we ask for."

"But there is a captain," persisted Bolton; "and I'll wager two months' pay that we shall see him before long."

"All right!" said Pen; "I should like to give him a piece of my mind."

"Who's talking about the captain?" said a new speaker.

It was Clifton, who was inclined to be superstitious and envious at the same time.

"Is there any news about the captain?" he asked.

"No," a single voice answered.

"Well, I expect to find him settled in his cabin some fine morning, and without any one's knowing how or whence he came aboard."

"Nonsense!" answered Bolton; "you imagine, Clifton, that he's an imp, a hobgoblin such as are seen in the Scotch Highlands."

"Laugh if you want to, Bolton; that won't alter my opinion. Every day as I pass the cabin I peep in through the keyhole, and one of these days I'll tell you what he looks like, and how he's made."

"O, the devil!" said Pen; "he'll look like everybody else. And if he wants to lead us where we don't want to go, we'll let him know what we think about it."

"All right," said Bolton; "Pen doesn't know him, and wants to quarrel with him already."

"Who doesn't know all about him?" asked Clifton, with the air of a man who has the whole story at his tongue's end; "I should like to know who doesn't."

"What do you mean?" asked Gripper.

"I know very well what I mean."

"But we don't."

"Well, Pen has already had trouble with him."

"With the captain?"

"Yes, the dog-captain; for it's the same thing precisely."

The sailors gazed at one another, incapable of replying.

"Dog or man," muttered Pen, between his teeth, "I'll bet he'll get his account settled one of these days."

"Why, Clifton," asked Bolton, seriously, "do you imagine, as Johnson said in joke, that that dog is the real captain?"

"Certainly, I do," answered Clifton, with some warmth; "and if you had watched him as carefully as I have, you'd have noticed his strange ways."

"What ways? Tell us."

"Haven't you noticed the way he walks up and down the poop-deck as if he commanded the ship, keeping his eye on the sails as if he were on watch?"

"That's so," said Gripper; "and one evening I found him with his paws on the wheel."

"Impossible!" said Bolton.

"And then," continued Clifton, "doesn't he run out at night on the ice-fields without caring for the bears or the cold?"

"That's true," said Bolton.

"Did you ever see him making up to the men like an honest dog, or hanging around the kitchen, and following the cook when he's carrying a savory dish to the officers? Haven't you all heard him at night, when he's run two or three miles away from the vessel, howling so that he makes your blood run cold, and that's not easy in weather like this? Did you ever seen him eat anything? He never takes a morsel from any one; he never touches the food that's given him, and, unless some one on board feeds him secretly, I can say he lives without eating. Now, if that's not strange, I'm no better than a beast myself."

"Upon my word," answered Bell, the carpenter, who had heard all of Clifton's speech, "it may be so."

But all the other sailors were silent.

"Well, as for me," continued Clifton, "I can say that if you don't believe, there are wiser people on board who don't seem so sure."

"Do you mean the mate?" asked Bolton.

"Yes, the mate and the doctor."

"Do you think they fancy the same thing?"

"I have heard them talking about it, and they could make no more out of it than we can; they imagined a thousand things which did not satisfy them in the least."

"Did they say the same things about the dog that you did, Clifton?" asked the carpenter.

"If they were not talking about the dog," answered Clifton, who was fairly cornered, "they were talking about the captain; it's exactly the same thing, and they confessed it was all very strange."

"Well, my friends," said Bell, "do you want to hear my opinion?"

"What is it!" they all cried.

"It is that there is not, and there will not be, any other captain than Richard Shandon."

"And the letter?" said Clifton.

"The letter was genuine," answered Bell; "it is perfectly true that some unknown person has equipped the *Forward* for an expedition in the ice; but the ship once off, no one will come on board."

"Well," asked Bolton, "where is the ship going to?"

"I don't know; at the right time, Richard Shandon will get the rest of the instructions."

"But from whom?"

"From whom?"

"Yes, in what way?" asked Bolton, who was becoming persistent.

"Come, Bell, an answer," said the other sailors.

"From whom? in what way? O, I'm sure I don't know!"

"Well, from the dog!" cried Clifton. "He has already written once, and he can again. O, if I only knew half as much as he does, I might be First Lord of the Admiralty!"

"So," added Bolton, in conclusion, "you persist in saying that dog is the captain?"

"Yes, I do."

"Well," said Pen, gruffly, "if that beast doesn't want to die in a dog's skin, he'd better hurry and turn into a man; for, on my word, I'll finish him."

"Why so?" asked Garry.

"Because I want to," answered Pen, brutally; "and I don't care what any one says."

"You have been talking long enough, men," shouted the boatswain, advancing at the moment when the conversation threatened to become dangerous; "to work, and have the saws put in quicker! We must get through the ice."

"Good! on Friday too," answered Clifton, shrugging his shoulders. "You won't find it so easy to cross the Polar Circle."

Whatever the reason may have been, the exertions of the crew on that day were nearly fruitless. The *Forward*, plunging, under a full head of steam, against the floes, could not separate them; they were obliged to lie at anchor that night.

On Saturday, the temperature fell still lower under the influence of an east-wind; the sky cleared up, and they all had a wide view over the white expanse, which shone brilliantly beneath the bright rays of the sun. At seven o'clock in the morning, the thermometer stood at 8° above zero.

The doctor was tempted to remain quietly in his cabin, or read over the accounts of arctic journeys; but he asked himself, following his usual habit, what would be the most disagreeable thing he could do at that moment. He thought that to go on deck on such a cold day and help the men would not be attractive. So, faithful to his line of conduct, he left his well-warmed cabin, and went out to help tow the ship. He looked strange with his green glasses, which he wore to protect his eyes against the brilliancy of the sun, and after that he always took good care to wear snow-spectacles as a security against the inflammation of the eyes, which is so common in these latitudes.

By evening the *Forward* had got several miles farther north, thanks to the energy of the men and the intelligence of Shandon, who was quick at utilizing every favorable circumstance; at midnight they crossed the sixty-sixth parallel, and the lead announcing a depth of twenty-three fathoms, Shandon knew that he was in the neighborhood of the shoal on which her Majesty's ship *Victory* grounded. Land lay thirty miles to the east.

But then the mass of ice, which had hitherto been stationary, separated, and began to move; icebergs seemed to rise in all points of the horizon; the brig was caught in a number of whirlpools of irresistible force; controlling her became so hard, that Garry, the best steersman, took the helm; the masses began to close behind the brig, hence it was necessary to cut through the ice; both prudence and duty commanded them to go forward. The difficulties were enhanced by the impossibility of Shandon's fixing the direction of the brig among all the changing points, which were continually shifting and presenting no definite point to be aimed at.

The crew were divided into two forces, and one stationed on the starboard, the other on the larboard side; every man was given a long iron-headed pole, with which to ward off threatening pieces of ice. Soon the *Forward* entered such a narrow passage between two lofty pieces, that the ends of the yards touched its solid walls; gradually it penetrated farther into a winding valley filled with a whirlwind of snow, while the floating ice was crashing ominously all about.

But soon it was evident that there was no outlet to this gorge; a huge block, caught in the channel, was floating swiftly down to the *Forward;* it seemed impossible to escape it, and equally impossible to return through an already closed path.

Shandon and Johnson, standing on the forward deck, were viewing their position. Shandon with his right hand signalled to the man at the wheel what direction he was to take, and with his left hand he indicated to James Wall the orders for the engines.

"What will be the end of this?" asked the doctor of Johnson.

"What pleases God," answered the boatswain.

The block of ice, eight hundred feet high, was hardly more than a cable's length from the *Forward*, and threatened to crush it.

Pen broke out with a fearful oath.

"Silence!" cried a voice which it was impossible to recognize in the roar of the hurricane.

The mass appeared to be falling upon the brig, and there was an indefinable moment of terror; the men, dropping their poles, ran aft in spite of Shandon's orders.

Suddenly, a terrible noise was heard; a real water-spout fell on the deck of the brig, which was lifted in the air by a huge wave. The crew uttered a cry of terror, while Garry, still firm at the wheel, kept the course of the *Forward* steady, in spite of the fearful lurch.

And when they looked for the mountain of ice, it had disappeared; the passage was free, and beyond, a long channel, lit up by the sun, allowed the brig to continue her advance.

"Well, Dr. Clawbonny," said Johnson, "can you explain that?"

"It's very simple, my friend," answered the doctor. "It happens very often; when these floating masses get detached in a thaw, they float away in perfect equilibrium; but as they get towards the south, where the water is relatively warmer, their base, eaten away by running into other pieces, begins to melt, and be undermined; then comes a moment when the centre of gravity is displaced, and they turn upside down. Only, if this had happened two minutes later, it would have fallen on the brig and crushed us beneath it."

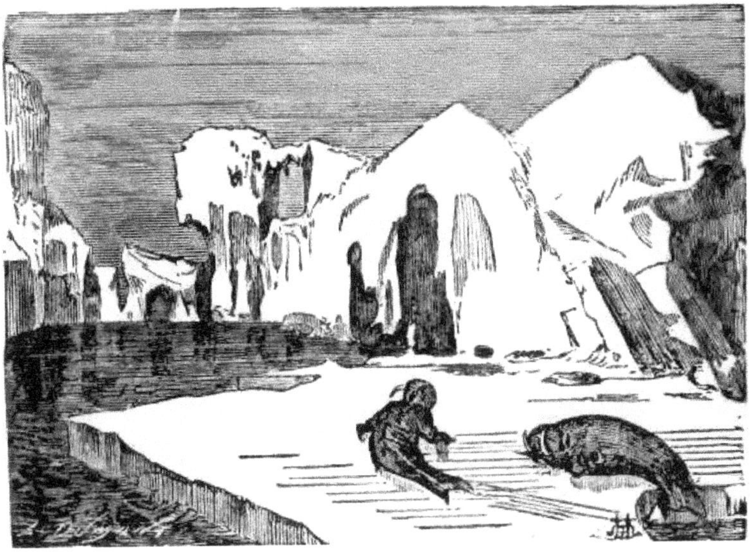

CHAPTER IX.

ANOTHER LETTER.

The Polar Circle was crossed at last; on the 30th of April, at midday, the *Forward* passed by Holsteinborg; picturesque mountains arose in the east. The sea appeared almost free of ice, or, more exactly, the ice could be avoided. The wind was from the southeast, and the brig, under foresail, staysail, and topsails, sailed up Baffin's Bay.

That day was exceptionally calm and the crew was able to get some rest; numerous birds were swimming and flying about the ship; among others, the doctor noticed some wild birds which were very like teal, with black neck, wings, and back, and a white breast; they were continually diving, and often remained more than forty seconds under water.

This day would not have been marked by any new incident, if the following extraordinary fact had not taken place.

At six o'clock in the morning, on returning to his cabin after his watch was over, Richard Shandon found on his table a letter, addressed as follows:—

To COMMANDER RICHARD SHANDON,
    On board the *Forward*,
        BAFFIN'S BAY.

Shandon could not believe his eyes; but before reading it, he summoned the doctor, James Wall, and the boatswain, and showed them the letter.

"It's getting interesting," said Johnson.

"It's delightful," thought the doctor.

"Well," cried Shandon, "at last we shall know his secret."

He tore open the envelope rapidly, and read the following:—

COMMANDER: The captain of the *Forward* is satisfied with the coolness, skill, and courage which the crew, officers, and you, yourself, have shown of late; he begs of you to express his thanks to the crew.

Be good enough to sail due north towards Melville Bay, and thence try to penetrate into Smith's Sound.

K. Z.,
Captain of the Forward.

Monday, April 30, OFF CAPE WALSINGHAM.

"And is that all?" cried the doctor.

"That's all," answered Shandon.

The letter fell from his hands.

"Well," said Wall, "this imaginary captain says nothing about coming on board. I don't believe he ever will."

"But how did this letter get here?" asked Johnson.

Shandon was silent.

"Mr. Wall is right," answered the doctor, who had picked up the letter, and who was turning it over with hands as well as in his mind. "The captain won't come on board, and for an excellent reason."

"What is it?" asked Shandon, quickly.

"Because he's on board now," answered the doctor, simply.

"Now!" exclaimed Shandon, "what do you mean?"

"How else can you explain the arrival of this letter?"

Johnson nodded approvingly.

"Impossible!" said Shandon, warmly. "I know all the men in the crew; can he have smuggled himself into their number since we left? It's impossible, I tell you. For more than two years I've seen every one of them more than a hundred times in Liverpool; so your conjecture, Doctor, is untenable."

"Well, what do you admit, Shandon?"

"Everything, except that. I admit that the captain or some tool of his, for all I know, may have taken advantage of the darkness, the mist, or whatever you please, to slip on board; we are not far from shore; there are the kayaks of the Esquimaux which could get through the ice without our seeing them; so some one may have come on board the ship, left the letter,—the fog was thick enough to make this possible."

"And to prevent them from seeing the brig," answered the doctor; "if we didn't see the intruder slip aboard the *Forward*, how could he see the *Forward* in the fog?"

"That's true," said Johnson.

"So I return to my explanation," said the doctor; "what do you think of it, Shandon?"

"Whatever you please," answered Shandon, hotly, "except that the man is on board."

"Perhaps," added Wall, "there is some man in the crew who is acting under his instructions."

"Perhaps," said the doctor.

"But who can it be?" asked Shandon. "I've known all my men for a long time."

"At any rate," resumed Johnson, "if this captain presents himself, whether as man or devil, we shall receive him; but there's something else to be drawn from this letter."

"What is that?" asked Shandon.

"It is that we must go not only into Melville Bay, but also into Smith's Sound."

"You are right," said the doctor.

"Smith's Sound," repeated Shandon, mechanically.

"So it's very plain," continued Johnson, "that the *Forward* is not intended to seek the Northwest Passage, since we leave to the left, the only way towards it, that is to say, Lancaster Sound. This would seem to promise a difficult journey in unknown seas."

"Yes, Smith's Sound," replied Shandon; "that's the route Kane, the American, took in 1853, and it was full of dangers. For a long time he was given up for lost. Well, if we must go, we'll go. But how far? To the Pole?"

"And why not?" cried the doctor.

The mention of such a foolhardy attempt made the boatswain shrug his shoulders.

"Well," said James Wall, "to come back to the captain, if he exists. I don't see that there are any places on the coast of Greenland except Disco and Upernavik, where he can be waiting for us; in a few days that question will be settled."

"But," asked the doctor of Shandon, "are you not going to tell the crew about this letter?"

"With the commander's permission," answered Johnson, "I should not do so."

"And why not?" asked Shandon.

"Because everything mysterious and extraordinary tends to discourage the men; they are already very much troubled, as it is, about the nature of the journey. Now, if any supernatural circumstances should become known, it might be harmful, and perhaps at a critical moment we should not be able to count on them. What do you think, Commander?"

"And what do you think, Doctor?" asked Shandon.

"Boatswain Johnson seems to me to reason well," answered the doctor.

"And you, James?"

"Having no better opinion, I agree with these gentlemen."

Shandon reflected for a few minutes; he reread the letter attentively.

"Gentlemen," said he, "your opinion is certainly worthy of respect, but I cannot adopt it."

"Why not, Shandon?" asked the doctor.

"Because the instructions in this letter are formal; it tells me to give the captain's thanks to the crew; now, hitherto I have strictly obeyed his orders, in whatever way they have been given to me, and I cannot—"

"Still—" interposed Johnson, who had a warrantable dread of the effect of such communications on the men's spirits.

"My dear Johnson," said Shandon, "I understand your objection; your reasons are very good, but read that:—

"He begs of you to express his thanks to the crew."

"Do as he bids," replied Johnson, who was always a strict disciplinarian. "Shall I assemble the crew on deck?"

"Yes," answered Shandon.

The news of a message from the captain was immediately whispered throughout the ship. The sailors took their station without delay, and the commander read aloud the mysterious letter.

It was received with dead silence; the crew separated under the influence of a thousand suppositions; Clifton had plenty of material for any superstitious vagaries; a great deal was ascribed by him to the dog-captain, and he never failed to salute him every time he met him.

"Didn't I tell you," he used to say to the sailors, "that he knew how to write?"

No one made any answer, and even Bell, the carpenter, would have found it hard to reply.

Nevertheless, it was plain to every one, that if the captain was not on board, his shade or spirit was watching them; henceforth, the wisest kept their opinions to themselves.

At midday of May 1st, their observation showed them that they were in latitude 68° and longitude 56° 32'. The temperature had risen, the thermometer standing at 25° above zero.

The doctor amused himself with watching the gambols of a she-bear and two cubs on some pack-ice near the shore. Accompanied by Wall and Simpson, he tried to chase them in a canoe; but she was in a very peaceful mood, and ran away with her young, so that the doctor had to give up his attempt.

During the night a favorable breeze carried them well to the north, and soon the lofty mountains of Disco were peering above the horizon; Godharn Bay, where the governor of the Danish settlements lived, was left on the right. Shandon did not consider it necessary to land, and he soon passed by the canoes of the Esquimaux, who had put out to meet him.

The island of Disco is also called Whale Island; it is from here that, on the 12th of July, 1845, Sir John Franklin wrote to the Admiralty for the last time, and it was also here that Captain MacClintock stopped on his way back, bringing too sure proofs of the loss of that expedition.

This coincidence was not unknown to the doctor; the place was one of sad memories, but soon the heights of Disco were lost to view.

There were many icebergs on its shores, which no thaws ever melt away; this gives the island a singular appearance from the sea.

The next day, at about three o'clock, Sanderson's Hope appeared in the northeast; land lay about fifteen miles to starboard; the mountains appeared of a dusky red hue. During the evening many fin-backs were seen playing in the ice, and occasionally blowing.

It was in the night of May 3d, that the doctor for the first time saw the sun touch the horizon without setting; since January 31st its orbit had been getting longer every day, and now there was unbroken daylight.

For those who were unaccustomed to it, this continuance of the day is a cause of perpetual surprise, and even of weariness; it is difficult to believe how necessary the darkness of the night is for the eyes; the doctor actually suffered from the continual brilliancy, which was increased by the reflection from the ice.

May 5th the *Forward* passed the sixty-second parallel. Two months later they would have met numerous whalers in these latitudes; but the straits were not yet free enough to allow easy ingress into Baffin's Bay.

The next day, the brig, after passing Woman's Island, came in sight of Upernavik, the northernmost station of Denmark in these lands.

CHAPTER X.

DANGEROUS SAILING.

Shandon, Dr. Clawbonny, Johnson, Foker, and Strong, the cook, got into one of the boats and made their way to shore.

The Governor, his wife and five children, all Esquimaux, received their visitors kindly. The doctor, who was the philologist of the party, knew enough Danish to establish friendly relations; moreover, Foker, the interpreter of the party as well as ice-master, knew a dozen or two words of the language of the Greenlanders, and with that number of words one can express a great deal, if he is not too ambitious.

The Governor was born on the island of Disco, and he has never left the place; he did the honors of his capital, which consisted of three wooden houses, for himself and the Lutheran minister, of a school, and shops which were supplied by what was cast upon the shore from wrecked ships. The rest of the town consisted of snow huts, into which the Esquimaux crawl through a single opening.

A great part of the population came out to meet the *Forward*, and more than one of them went as far as the middle of the bay in his kayak, fifteen feet long and two broad at the widest part.

The doctor knew that the word Esquimaux meant "eater of raw fish"; but he knew too that this name is considered an insult in this country, so he forbore giving it to the inhabitants of Greenland.

And yet, from the oily sealskin clothes and boots, from their squat, fat figures, which make it hard to distinguish the men from the women, it was easy to declare the nature of their food; besides, like all fish-eating people, they were somewhat troubled by leprosy, but their general health was not impaired by it.

The Lutheran minister and his wife, with whom the doctor had promised himself an interesting talk, happened to be away on the shore of Proven, south of Upernavik; hence he was compelled to seek the company of the Governor. The chief magistrate did not appear to be very well informed: a little less, he would have been a fool; a little more, and he would have known how to read.

In spite of that, the doctor questioned him about the commerce, habits, and manners of the Esquimaux; and he learned, by means of gestures, that the seals were worth about forty pounds when delivered at Copenhagen; a bear-skin brought forty Danish dollars, the skin of a blue fox four, and of a white fox two or three dollars.

In order to make his knowledge complete, the doctor wanted to visit an Esquimaux hut; a man who seeks information is capable of enduring anything; fortunately the opening of these huts was too small, and the enthusiastic doctor could not get through. It was fortunate for him, for there is nothing more repulsive than the sight of that crowd of living and dead objects, of seal's bodies and Esquimaux-flesh, decayed fish and unclean clothing, which fill a Greenland hut; there is no window to renew that suffocating air; there is only a hole at the top of the cabin which lets the smoke out, but gives no relief to the stench.

"Fortunately the opening of these huts was too small, and the enthusiastic doctor could not get through."

Foker gave all these details to the doctor, but he none the less bewailed his portliness. He wanted to judge for himself these emanations *sui generis*.

"I am sure," said he, "that one could get used to it in time." *In time* shows clearly the doctor's character.

During these ethnographic studies on his part, Shandon was busying himself, according to his instructions, with procuring means of travel on the ice; he was obliged to pay four pounds for a sledge and six dogs, and the natives were reluctant to sell even at this price.

Shandon would have liked to engage Hans Christian, the skilful driver of the dogs, who accompanied Captain MacClintock, but Hans was then in Southern Greenland.

Then came up the great question of the day; was there at Upernavik a European awaiting the arrival of the *Forward?* Did the Governor know of any stranger, probably an Englishman, who had come into these latitudes? How recently had they seen any whalers or other ships?

To these questions the Governor answered that no stranger had landed on that part of the coast for more than ten months.

Shandon asked the names of the whalers which had last arrived; he recognized none. He was in despair.

"You must confess, Doctor, that it passes all comprehension," he said to his companion. "Nothing at Cape Farewell! nothing at Disco! nothing at Upernavik!"

"Tell me in a few days from now, nothing at Melville Bay, my dear Shandon, and I will salute you as sole captain of the *Forward.*"

The boat returned to the brig towards evening, bringing back the visitors to the shore; Strong had bought several dozen eider-duck's eggs, which were twice as large as hen's eggs, and of a greenish color. It was not much, but it was very refreshing for a crew accustomed to little but salt meat.

The next day the wind was fair, but yet Shandon did not set sail; he wanted to wait another day, and, to satisfy his conscience, to give time for any member of the human race to rejoin the *Forward;* he even fired off, every hour, the ship's gun, which re-echoed among the icebergs; but he only succeeded in frightening the flocks of molly-mokes* and rotches.* During the night many rockets were set off; but in vain. He had to give the order to set sail.

 * Sea-birds common in these latitudes.

The 8th of May, at six o'clock in the morning, the *Forward*, under her topsails, foresail, and main-top-gallant-sail, soon lost sight of the station of Upernavik, and hideous long poles on which were hanging along the shore the seals' entrails and deers' stomachs.

The wind was southeast, the thermometer stood at 32°. The sun pierced through the fog and the ice melted a little.

The reflection, however, injured the sight of many of the crew. Wolston, the armorer, Gripper, Clifton, and Bell were attacked by snow-blindness, which is very common in the spring, and which totally blinds many of the Esquimaux. The doctor advised all, the unharmed as well as the suffering, to cover their faces with a green veil, and he was the first to follow his own recommendation.

The dogs bought by Shandon at Upernavik were rather wild; but they soon got used to their new quarters, and Captain showed no dislike of his new companions; he seemed to know their ways. Clifton was not the last to remark that Captain seemed to be familiar with the dogs of Greenland. And they, always half starved on shore, only thought of making up for it when at sea.

The 9th of May the *Forward* passed within a few cable-lengths of the westernmost of the Baffin Islands. The doctor noticed many rocks between the islands and the mainland which were what are called crimson cliffs; they were covered with snow as red as carmine, which Dr. Kane says is of purely vegetable origin; Clawbonny wanted to examine this singular phenomenon, but the ice forbade their approaching them; although the temperature was rising, it was easy to see that the icebergs and ice-streams were accumulating toward the north of Baffin's Bay.

After leaving Upernavik the land presented a different appearance, and huge glaciers were sharply defined against the gray horizon. On the 10th the *Forward* left on its right Kingston Bay, near the seventy-fourth degree of latitude; Lancaster Sound opened into the sea many hundred miles to the west.

But then this vast expanse of water was hidden beneath enormous fields of ice, in which arose the hummocks, uniform as a homogeneous crystallization. Shandon had the furnace-fires lighted, and until the 11th of

May the *Forward* advanced by a tortuous course, tracing with her smoke against the sky the path she was following through the water.

But new obstacles soon presented themselves; the passages were closing in consequence of the incessant crowding of the floating masses; every moment threatened to close up the clear water before the *Forward*, and if she were nipped, it would be hard to get her out. Every one knew it and was thinking about it.

Hence, on board of this ship without any definite aim, any known destination, which was blindly pushing on northward, some symptoms of hesitation began to appear; among these men accustomed to dangers, many, forgetting the advantages which were promised them, regretted having ventured so far. A certain demoralization became common, which was further increased by the fears of Clifton and the talk of two or three ringleaders, such as Pen, Gripper, Warren, and Wolston.

Exhausting fatigue was added to the moral disquiet of the crew, for, on the 12th of May, the brig was caught fast; the steam was of no avail. A path had to be cut through the ice. It was no easy task to manage the saws in the floes which were six or seven feet thick; when two parallel grooves had divided the ice for a hundred feet, it was necessary to break the part that lay between with axes and bars; next they had to fasten anchors in a hole made by a huge auger; then the crew would turn the capstan and haul the ship along by the force of their arms; the greatest difficulty consisted in driving the detached pieces beneath the floes, so as to give space for the vessel, and they had to be pushed under by means of long iron-headed poles.

Moreover, this continued toil with saws, capstan, and poles, all of which was persistent, compulsory, and dangerous, amid the dense fog or snow, while the air was so cold, and their eyes so exposed, their doubt so great, did much to weaken the crew of the *Forward* and to act on their imagination.

When sailors have to deal with a man who is energetic, bold, and determined, who knows what he wants, whither he is going, what aim he has in view, confidence animates them all in spite of themselves; they are firmly united to their leader, strong with his force and calm with his calmness. But on board of the brig they were aware of the commander's uncertainty, they knew that he hesitated before the unknown aim and destination. In spite of the energy of his character, his uncertainty was clearly to be seen by his uncertain orders, incomplete manoeuvres, his sudden outbursts, and a thousand petty details which could not escape the sharp eyes of the crew.

And then, Shandon was not the captain of the ship, the master under God, which was enough to encourage the discussion of his orders; and from discussion to disobedience is but a short step.

The malcontents soon brought over to their number the first engineer, who, hitherto, had been a slave to his duty.

The 16th of May, six days after the *Forward* had reached the ice, Shandon had not made two miles to northward. They were threatened with being detained in the ice until the next season. Matters had a serious look.

Towards eight o'clock of the evening, Shandon and the doctor, accompanied by Garry, went out to reconnoitre the vast plains; they took care not to go too far from the ship, for it was hard to find any fixed points in this white solitude, which was ever changing in appearance. Refraction kept producing strange effects, much to the doctor's astonishment; at one place, where he thought he had but an easy jump before him, he had to leap some five or six feet; or else the contrary happened, and in either case the result was a tumble, which if not dangerous was at any rate painful, for the ice was as hard and slippery as glass.

Shandon and his two companions went out to seek a possible passage; three miles from the ship, they succeeded with some difficulty in ascending an iceberg about three hundred feet high. From that point nothing met their eyes but a confused mass, like the ruins of a vast city, with shattered monuments, overthrown towers, and prostrate palaces,—a real chaos. The sun was just peering above the jagged horizon, and sent forth long, oblique rays of light, but not of heat, as if something impassable for heat lay between it and this wild country.

The sea appeared perfectly covered as far as eye could reach.

"How shall we get through?" asked the doctor.

"I don't know," answered Shandon; "but we shall get through, if we have to blow our way through with powder. I certainly sha'n't stay in the ice till next spring."

"But that happened to the *Fox*, and not far from here. Bah!" said the doctor; "we shall get through with a little philosophy. You will see that is worth all the machinery in the world."

"I must say," answered Shandon, "this year does not begin very well."

"True, Shandon, and I notice also that Baffin's Bay seems to be returning to the state it was in before 1817."

"Don't you think, Doctor, it has always been as it is now?"

"No, my dear Shandon, from time to time there have been great breakings of the ice which no one can explain; so, up to 1817 this sea was continually full, when an enormous sort of inundation took place, which cast the icebergs into the ocean, most of which reached the banks of Newfoundland. From that day Baffin's Bay was nearly free, and was visited by whalers."

"So," asked Shandon, "from that time voyages to the North became easier?"

"Incomparably; but for some years it has been noticed that the bay seems to be resuming its old ways and threatens to become closed, possibly for a long time, to sailors. An additional reason, by the way, for pushing on as far as possible. And yet it must be said, we look like people who are pushing on in unknown ways, with the doors forever closing behind us."

"Would you advise me to go back?" asked Shandon, trying to read into the depths of the doctor's eyes.

"I! I have never retreated yet, and, even if we should never get back, I say go on. Still, I want to make it clear that if we act imprudently, we do it with our eyes open."

"And you, Garry, what do you think about it?" asked Shandon of the sailor.

"I, Commander, should go straight on; I agree with Dr. Clawbonny; but do as you please; command, we shall obey."

"They don't all talk as you do, Garry," resumed Shandon; "they are not all ready to obey. And if they refuse to obey my orders?"

"I have given you my opinion, Commander," answered Garry, coldly, "because you asked for it; but you are not obliged to follow it."

Shandon did not answer; he scanned the horizon closely, and then descended with his companions to the ice-fields.

CHAPTER XI.

THE DEVIL'S THUMB.

During the commander's absence the men had been variously busied in attempts to relieve the ship from the pressure of the ice. Pen, Clifton, Bolton, Gripper, and Simpson had this in charge; the fireman and the two engineers came to the aid of their comrades, for, as soon as the engines did not require their attention, they became sailors, and as such could be employed in all that was going on aboard the ship.

But there was a great deal of discontent among them.

"I declare I've had enough," said Pen; "and if we are not free in three days, I swear I sha'n't stir a finger to get the ship out."

"Not stir a finger!" answered Plover; "you'd better use them in getting back. Do you think we want to stay here till next year?"

"It certainly would be a hard winter," said Pen, "for we are exposed on all sides."

"And who knows," said Brunton, "whether next spring the sea will be any freer than it is now?"

"Never mind about next spring," answered Pen; "to-day is Thursday; if the way is not clear Sunday morning, we shall turn back to the south."

"Good!" cried Clifton.

"Don't you agree with me?" asked Pen.

"We do," cried his companions.

"That's so," said Warren; "for if we have to work in this way and haul the ship along with our own arms, I think it would be as well to haul her backwards."

"We shall do that on Sunday," said Wolston.

"Only give me the order," resumed Brunton, "and my fires shall be lighted."

"Well," remarked Clifton, "we shall light them ourselves."

"If any officer," said Pen, "is anxious to spend the winter here, he can; we can leave him here contentedly; he'll find it easy to build a hut like the Esquimaux."

"Not at all, Pen," retorted Brunton, quickly; "we sha'n't abandon any one here; do you understand that, all of you? I think it won't be hard to persuade the commander; he seems to me to be very much discouraged, and if we propose it to him gently—"

"But," interrupted Plover, "Richard Shandon is often very obstinate; we shall have to sound him cautiously."

"When I think," said Bolton, with a sigh of longing, "that in a month we might be back in Liverpool! We can easily pass the line of ice at the south! Davis Strait will be open by the beginning of June, and then we shall have nothing but the free Atlantic before us."

"Besides," said the cautious Clifton, "if we take the commander back with us, and act under his commands, we shall have earned our pay; but if we go back without him, it's not so sure."

"True," said Plover; "Clifton talks sense. Let's try not to get into any trouble with the Admiralty, that's safer, and don't let us leave any one behind."

"But if they refuse to come with us?" continued Pen, who wished to compel his companions to stand by him.

They found it hard to answer the question thus squarely put them.

"We shall see about that when the time comes," replied Bolton; "it will be enough to bring Richard Shandon over to our side, and I fancy that won't be hard."

"There's one I shall leave here," exclaimed Pen with fierce oaths, "even if he should bite my arm off."

"O, the dog!" said Plover.

"Yes, that dog! I shall soon settle accounts with him."

"So much the better," retorted Clifton, returning to his favorite theory; "he is the cause of all our troubles."

"He has thrown an evil spell upon us," said Plover.

"He led us into the ice," remarked Gripper.

"He brought more ice in our way," said Wolston, "than was ever seen at this season."

"He made my eyes sore," said Brunton.

"He shut off the gin and brandy," cried Pen.

"He's the cause of everything," they all exclaimed excitedly.

"And then," added Clifton, "he's the captain."

"Well, you unlucky Captain," cried Pen, whose unreasonable fury grew with the sound of his own words, "you wanted to come here, and here you shall stay!"

"But how shall we get hold of him?" said Plover.

"Well, now is a good time," answered Clifton. "The commander is away; the second mate is asleep in his cabin; the fog is so thick that Johnson can't see us—"

"But the dog?" said Pen.

"He's asleep in the coal," answered Clifton, "and if any one wants—"

"I'll see to it," replied Pen, angrily.

"Take care, Pen; his teeth would go through a bar of iron."

"If he stirs, I'll rip him open," answered Pen, drawing his knife.

And he ran down between decks, followed by Warren, who was anxious to help him.

Soon they both returned, carrying the dog in their arms; his mouth and paws were securely tied; they had caught him asleep, and the poor dog could not escape them.

"Hurrah for Pen!" cried Plover.

"And what are you going to do with him now?" asked Clifton.

"Drown him, and if he ever comes back—" answered Pen with a smile of satisfaction.

Two hundred feet from the vessel there was a hole in the ice, a sort of circular crevasse, made by the seals with their teeth, and always dug out from the inside to the outside; it was there that the seals used to come to breathe on the surface of the ice; but they were compelled to take care to prevent the aperture from closing, for the shape of their jaws did not permit them to make the hole from the outside, and in any danger they would not be able to escape from their enemies.

Pen and Warren hastened to this crevasse, and then, in spite of his obstinate struggles, the dog was pitilessly cast into the sea; a huge cake of ice they then rolled over the aperture, closing all means of escape for the poor dog, thus locked in a watery prison.

"A pleasant journey, Captain!" cried the brutal sailor.

Soon they returned on board; Johnson had seen nothing of it all; the fog was growing thick about the ship, and the snow was beginning to fall with violence.

An hour later, Richard Shandon, the doctor, and Garry regained the *Forward*.

Shandon had observed in the northeast a passage, which he determined to try. He gave his orders to that effect; the crew obeyed with a certain activity; they wanted to convince Shandon of the impossibility of a farther advance, and besides, they had before them three days of obedience.

During a part of the following night and day the sawing and towing went on busily; the *Forward* made about two miles of progress. On the 18th they were in sight of land, five or six cable-lengths from a strange peak, to which its singular shape had given the name of the Devil's Thumb.

At this very place the *Prince Albert*, in 1851, the *Advance*, with Kane, in 1853, had been caught in the ice for many weeks.

The odd shape of the Devil's Thumb, the barren and desolate surroundings, which consisted of huge icebergs often more than three hundred feet high, the cracking of the ice, repeated indefinitely by the echo, made the position of the *Forward* a very gloomy one. Shandon saw that it was necessary to get away from there; within twenty-four hours, he calculated he would be able to get two miles from the spot. But that was not enough. Shandon felt himself embarrassed by fear, and the false position in which he was placed benumbed his energy; to obey his instructions in order to advance, he had brought his ship into a dangerous position; the towing wore out his men; more than three hours were necessary to cut a canal twenty feet in length through ice which was generally four or five feet thick; the health of the crew gave signs of failing. Shandon was astonished at the silence of the men, and their unaccustomed obedience; but he feared it was only the calm that foreboded a storm.

We can, then, easily judge of the painful surprise, disappointment, and even despair which seized upon him, when he noticed that by means of an imperceptible movement in the ice, the *Forward* lost in the night of the 18th all that had been gained by such toilsome efforts; on Saturday morning he was opposite the Devil's Thumb, in a still more critical position; the icebergs increased in number and passed by in the mist like phantoms.

Shandon was thoroughly demoralized; it must be said that fear seized both this bold man and all his crew. Shandon had heard of the disappearance of the dog; but he did not dare to punish the guilty persons; he feared exciting a mutiny.

The weather during that day was horrible; the snow, caught up in dense whirls, covered the brig with an impenetrable veil; at times, under the influence of the hurricane, the fog would rise, and their terror-stricken eyes beheld the Devil's Thumb rising on the shore like a spectre.

The *Forward* was anchored to a large piece of ice; there was nothing to be done, nothing to be tried; darkness was spreading about them, and the man at the helm could not see James Wall, who was on watch forward.

Shandon withdrew to his cabin, a prey to perpetual disquiet; the doctor was arranging his notes of the expedition; some of the crew were on the deck, others in the common room.

At a moment when the violence of the storm was redoubling, the Devil's Thumb seemed to rise immoderately from the mist.

"Great God!" exclaimed Simpson, recoiling with terror.

"What's the matter?" asked Foker.

Soon shouts were heard on all sides.

"It's going to crush us!"

"We are lost!"

"Mr. Wall, Mr. Wall!"

"It's all over!"

"Commander, Commander!"

All these cries were uttered by the men on watch.

Wall hastened to the after-deck; Shandon, followed by the doctor, flew to the deck and looked out.

Through a rift in the mist, the Devil's Thumb appeared to have suddenly come near the brig; it seemed to have grown enormously in size; on its summit was balanced a second cone, upside down, and revolving on its point; it threatened to crush the ship with its enormous mass; it wavered, ready to fall down. It was an alarming sight. Every one drew back instinctively, and many of the men, jumping upon the ice, abandoned the ship.

"Let no one move!" cried the commander with a loud voice; "every one to his place!"

"My friends, don't be frightened," said the doctor, "there is no danger! See, Commander, see, Mr. Wall, that's the mirage and nothing else."

"You are right, Dr. Clawbonny," replied Johnson; "they've all been frightened by a shadow."

When they had heard what the doctor said, most of the sailors drew near him, and from terror they turned to admiration of this wonderful phenomenon, which soon passed from their view.

"They call that a mirage," said Clifton; "the Devil's at the bottom of it, I'm sure."

"That's true," growled Gripper.

But the break in the fog had given the commander a glimpse of a broad passage which he had not expected to find; it promised to lead him away from the shore; he resolved to make use of it at once; men were sent out on each side of the canal; hawsers were given them, and they began to tow the ship northward.

During long hours this work was prosecuted busily but silently; Shandon had the furnace-fires lighted to help him through this passage so providentially discovered.

"That's great luck," he said to Johnson, "and if we can only get on a few miles, we may be free. Make a hot fire, Mr. Brunton, and let me know as soon as you get steam on. Meanwhile, men, the farther on we get, the more gained! You want to get away from the Devil's Thumb; well, now is your chance!"

Suddenly the brig stopped. "What's the matter?" shouted Shandon. "Wall, have the tow-ropes broken?"

"No," answered Wall, leaning over the railing. "See, there are the men running back; they are climbing on board; they seem very much frightened."

"What's happened?" cried Shandon, running forward.

"On board, on board!" cried the sailors, evidently exceedingly terrified.

Shandon looked towards the north, and shuddered in spite of himself.

A strange animal, with alarming motions, whose steaming tongue hung from huge jaws, was bounding along within a cable's length from the ship; it seemed more than twenty feet high; its hair stood on end; it was chasing the sailors as if about to seize them, while its tail, which was at least ten feet long, lashed the snow and tossed it about in dense gusts. The sight of the monster froze the blood in the veins of the boldest.

"A strange animal was bounding along within a cable's length from the ship."

"It's an enormous bear," said one.

"It's the beast of Gévaudan!"

"It's the lion of the Apocalypse!"

Shandon ran to his cabin to get a gun which he kept always loaded; the doctor seized his arms, and made ready to fire at the beast, which by its size, recalled antediluvian monsters.

It drew near with long leaps; Shandon and the doctor fired at the same time, and suddenly the report of the pieces agitated the air and produced an unlooked-for effect.

The doctor gazed attentively, and could not help bursting out laughing. "It's refraction!" said he.

"Refraction!" cried Shandon.

But a terrible cry from the crew interrupted them.

"The dog!" shouted Clifton.

"The dog-captain!" repeated his companions.

"It's he!" cried Pen.

In fact, it was the dog who had burst his bonds and had made his way to the surface of the ice through another hole. At that moment the refraction, by a phenomenon common in these latitudes, exaggerated his size, and this had only been broken by the report of the guns; but, notwithstanding, a disastrous impression had been produced upon the minds of the sailors, who were not very much inclined to admit any explanation of the fact from physical causes. The adventure of the Devil's Thumb, the reappearance of the dog under such peculiar circumstances, completely upset them, and murmurs arose on all sides.

CHAPTER XII.

CAPTAIN HATTERAS.

The *Forward* was advancing rapidly under steam between the ice-fields and the mountains of ice. Johnson was at the helm. Shandon was examining the horizon with his snow-spectacles; but his joy was brief, for he soon saw that the passage was blocked up by a circle of mountains.

Nevertheless, he preferred to take his chances with pushing on, to returning.

The dog followed the brig on the ice, but he kept at a respectful distance. Only, if he lagged too far, there was to be heard a singular whistle which at once brought him on.

The first time that this whistle was heard, the sailors looked around; they were alone on the deck, talking together; there was no unknown person there; and yet this whistle was often repeated.

Clifton was the first to take alarm.

"Do you hear that?" he said; "and do you see how the dog starts as soon as he hears it?"

"It's past belief," said Gripper.

"Very well!" cried Pen; "I'm not going any farther."

"Pen is right," said Brunton; "it's tempting Providence."

"Tempting the Devil," answered Clifton. "I should rather give up all my share of the pay than go on."

"We shall never get back," said Bolton, dejectedly.

The crew was exceedingly demoralized.

"Not a foot farther!" cried Wolston; "is that your opinion?"

"Yes, yes!" answered the sailors.

"Well," said Bolton, "let's go find the commander; I'll undertake to tell him."

The sailors in a dense group made their way to the quarter-deck.

The *Forward* was then advancing into a large arena, which had a diameter of about eight hundred feet; it was completely closed, with the exception of one place through which the ship entered.

Shandon saw that he was locking himself in. But what was to be done? How could he retreat? He felt all the responsibility, and his hand nervously grasped his glass.

The doctor looked on in silence, with folded arms; he gazed at the walls of ice, the average height of which was about three hundred feet. A cloud of fog lay like a dome above the gulf.

Then it was that Bolton spoke to the commander.

"Commander," said he in a broken voice, "we can't go any farther."

"What's that you are saying?" said Shandon, who felt enraged at the slight given to his authority.

"We have come to say, Commander," resumed Bolton, "that we have done enough for this invisible captain, and that we have made up our minds not to go on any farther."

"Made up your minds?" cried Shandon. "Is that the way you talk to me, Bolton? Take care."

"You need not threaten," retorted Pen, brutally, "we are not going any farther."

Shandon stepped towards the mutinous sailors, when the boatswain said to him in a low voice,—

"Commander, if we want to get out of this place, we have not a moment to lose. There's an iceberg crowding towards the entrance; it may prevent our getting out and imprison us here."

Shandon returned to look at the state of affairs.

"You will account for this afterwards," he said to the mutineers. "Now, go about!"

The sailors hastened to their places. The *Forward* went about rapidly; coal was heaped on the fires; it was necessary to beat the iceberg. There was a race between them; the brig stood towards the south, the berg was drifting northward, threatening to bar the way.

"Put on all the steam, Brunton, do you hear?" said Shandon.

The *Forward* glided like a bird through the broken ice, which her prow cut through easily; the ship shook with the motion of the screw, and the gauge indicated a full pressure of steam, the deafening roar of which resounded above everything.

"Load the safety-valve!" cried Shandon.

The engineer obeyed at the risk of bursting the boilers.

But these desperate efforts were vain; the iceberg, driven by a submarine current, moved rapidly towards the exit; the brig was still three cable-lengths distant, when the mountain, entering the vacant space like a wedge, joined itself to its companions, and closed the means of escape.

"We are lost!" cried Shandon, who was unable to restrain that unwise speech.

"Lost!" repeated the crew.

"Lower the boats!" cried many.

"To the steward's pantry!" cried Pen and some of his set; "if we must drown, let us drown in gin!"

The wildest confusion raged among these half-wild men. Shandon felt unable to assert his authority; he wanted to give some orders; he hesitated, he stammered; his thoughts could find no words. The doctor walked up and down nervously. Johnson folded his arms stoically, and said not a word.

Suddenly a strong, energetic, commanding voice was heard above the din, uttering these words:—

"Every man to his place! Prepare to go about!"

Johnson shuddered, and, without knowing what he did, turned the wheel rapidly.

It was time; the brig, going under full steam, was about crashing against the walls of its prison.

But while Johnson instinctively obeyed, Shandon, Clawbonny, the crew, all, even down to Warren the fireman, who had abandoned his fires, and Strong the cook, who had fled from his galley, were collected on the deck, and all saw issuing from the cabin, the key of which he alone possessed, a man.

This man was the sailor Garry.

"Sir!" cried Shandon, turning pale, "Garry—by what right do you give orders here?"

"Duke!" said Garry, repeating the whistle which had so surprised the crew.

The dog, on hearing his real name, sprang on the quarter-deck, and lay down quietly at his master's feet.

The crew did not utter a word. The key which the captain alone should possess, the dog which he had sent and which had identified him, so to speak, the tone of command which it was impossible to mistake,—all this had a strong influence on the minds of the sailors, and was enough to establish firmly Garry's authority.

Besides, Garry was hardly to be recognized; he had removed the thick whiskers which had surrounded his face, thereby giving it a more impassible, energetic, and commanding expression; he stood before them clothed in a captain's uniform, which he had had placed in his cabin.

So the crew of the *Forward*, animated in spite of themselves, shouted,—

"Hurrah, hurrah, hurrah for the captain!"

"Shandon," he said to his first officer, "have the crew put in line; I want to inspect them."

Shandon obeyed, and gave the requisite orders with an agitated voice.

The captain walked in front of the officers and men, saying a word to each, and treating him according to his past conduct.

When he had finished his inspection, he went back to the quarter-deck, and calmly uttered these words:—

"Officers and sailors, I am an Englishman like you all, and my motto is that of Lord Nelson,—'England expects every man to do his duty.'

"As Englishmen, I am unwilling, we are unwilling, that others should go where we have not been. As Englishmen, I shall not endure, we shall not endure, that others should have the glory of going farther north than we. If human foot is ever to reach the Pole, it must be the foot of an Englishman! Here is the flag of our country. I have equipped this ship, I have devoted my fortune to this undertaking, I shall devote to it my life and yours, but this flag shall float over the North Pole. Fear not. You shall receive a thousand pounds sterling for every degree that we get farther north after this day. Now we are at the seventy-second, and there are ninety in all. Figure it out. My name will be proof enough. It means energy and patriotism. I am Captain Hatteras."

"Captain Hatteras!" cried Shandon. And this name, familiar to them all, soon spread among all the crew.

"Now," resumed Hatteras, "let us anchor the brig to the ice; let the fires be put out, and every one return to his usual occupation. Shandon, I want to speak with you about the ship. You will join me in my cabin with the doctor, Wall, and the boatswain. Johnson, dismiss the men."

Hatteras, calm and cold, quietly left the poop-deck, while Shandon had the brig made fast to the ice.

Who was this Hatteras, and why did his name make so deep an impression upon the crew?

John Hatteras, the only son of a London brewer, who died in 1852, worth six million pounds, took to the sea at an early age, unmindful of the large fortune which was to come to him. Not that he had any commercial designs, but a longing for geographical discovery possessed him; he was continually dreaming of setting foot on some spot untrodden of man.

When twenty years old, he had the vigorous constitution of thin, sanguine men; an energetic face, with well-marked lines, a high forehead, rising straight from the eyes, which were handsome but cold, thin lips, indicating a mouth chary of words, medium height, well-knit muscular limbs, indicated a man ready for any experience. Any one who saw him would have called him bold, and any one who heard him would have called him coldly passionate; he was a man who would never retreat, and who would risk the lives of others as coldly as his own. One would hence think twice before following him in his expeditions.

John Hatteras had a great deal of English pride, and it was he who once made this haughty reply to a Frenchman.

The Frenchman said with what he considered politeness, and even kindness,—

"If I were not a Frenchman, I should like to be an Englishman."

"If I were not an Englishman, I should like to be an Englishman!"

That retort points the nature of the man.

He would have liked to reserve for his fellow-countrymen the monopoly of geographical discovery; but much to his chagrin, during previous centuries, they had done but little in the way of discovery.

America was discovered by the Genoese, Christopher Columbus; the East Indies by the Portuguese, Vasco de Gama; China by the Portuguese, Fernao d'Andrada; Terra del Fuego by the Portuguese, Magellan; Canada by the Frenchman, Jacques Cartier; the islands of Sumatra, Java, etc., Labrador, Brazil, the Cape of Good Hope, the Azores, Madeira, Newfoundland, Guinea, Congo, Mexico, White Cape, Greenland, Iceland, the South Pacific Ocean, California, Japan, Cambodia, Peru, Kamschatka, the Philippine Islands, Spitzbergen, Cape Horn, Behring Strait, New Zealand, Van Diemen's Land, New Britain, New Holland, the Louisiana, Island of Jan-Mayen, by Icelanders, Scandinavians, Frenchmen, Russians, Portuguese, Danes, Spaniards, Genoese, and Dutchmen; but no Englishmen figured among them, and it was a constant source of grief to Hatteras to see his fellow-countrymen excluded from the glorious band of sailors who made the great discoveries of the fifteenth and sixteenth centuries.

Hatteras consoled himself somewhat when he considered modern times: the English took their revenge with Stuart, McDougall Stuart, Burke, Wells, King, Gray, in Australia; with Palliser in America; with Havnoan in Syria;

with Cyril Graham, Waddington, Cunningham, in India; and with Barth, Burton, Speke, Grant, and Livingstone in Africa.

But this was not enough; for Hatteras these men were rather finishers than discoverers; something better was to be done, so he invented a country in order to have the honor of discovering it.

Now he had noticed that if the English were in a minority with regard to the early discoveries, that if it was necessary to go back to Cook to make sure of New Caledonia in 1774, and of the Sandwich Islands where he was killed in 1778, there was nevertheless one corner of the globe on which they had centred all their efforts.

This was the northern seas and lands of North America.

In fact, the list of polar discoveries runs as follows:—

Nova Zembla, discovered by Willoughby in 1553.
Island of Wiegehts, discovered by Barrow in 1556.
West Coast of Greenland, discovered by Davis in 1585.
Davis Strait, discovered by Davis in 1587.
Spitzbergen, discovered by Willoughby in 1596.
Hudson's Bay, discovered by Hudson in 1610.
Baffin's Bay, discovered by Baffin in 1616.

During recent years Hearne, Mackenzie, John Ross, Parry, Franklin, Richardson, Beechey, James Ross, Back, Dease, Simpson, Rae, Inglefield, Belcher, Austin, Kellet, Moore, MacClure, Kennedy, MacClintock, were incessantly exploring these unknown regions.

The northern coast of America had been accurately made out, the Northwest Passage nearly discovered, but that was not enough; there was something greater to be done, and this John Hatteras had twice tried, fitting out ships at his own expense; he wanted to reach the Pole itself, and thus to crown the list of English discoveries by a glorious success.

To reach the Pole itself was the aim of his life.

After many successful voyages in the southern seas, Hatteras tried for the first time in 1846 to reach the North through Baffin's Bay, but he could get no farther than latitude 74°; he sailed in the sloop *Halifax*; his crew suffered terribly, and John Hatteras carried his temerity so far that henceforth sailors were averse to undertaking a similar expedition under such a leader.

Notwithstanding, in 1850, Hatteras succeeded in obtaining for the schooner *Farewell* about twenty determined men, but who were persuaded especially by the high pay offered their boldness. It was then that Dr. Clawbonny began to correspond with John Hatteras, whom he did not know, about accompanying him; but the post of surgeon was filled, fortunately for the doctor.

The *Farewell*, following the route taken by the *Neptune* of Aberdeen in 1817, went to the north of Spitzbergen, as far as latitude 76°. There they were obliged to winter; but their sufferings were such, and the cold so intense, that of all on board, Hatteras alone returned to England. He was picked up by a Danish whaler after he had walked more than two hundred miles across the ice.

The excitement produced by the return of this man alone was intense; who, after this, would accompany Hatteras in his bold attempts? Still he did not abandon the hope of trying again. His father, the brewer, died, and he came into possession of an enormous fortune.

Meanwhile something had happened which cut John Hatteras to the heart.

A brig, the *Advance*, carrying seventeen men, equipped by Mr. Grinnell, a merchant, commanded by Dr. Kane, and sent out in search of Franklin, went as far north, through Baffin's Bay and Smith's Sound, as latitude 82°, nearer to the Pole than any of his predecessors had gone.

Now this was an American ship. Grinnell was an American, Kane was an American!

It is easy to understand how the customary disdain of the Englishman for the Yankee turned to hatred in the heart of Hatteras; he made up his mind, at any price, to beat his bold rival, and to reach the Pole itself.

For two years he lived at Liverpool incognito. He was taken for a sailor. He saw in Richard Shandon the man he wanted; he presented his plans by an anonymous letter to him and to Dr. Clawbonny. The *Forward* was built and equipped. Hatteras kept his name a secret; otherwise no one would have gone with him. He resolved only to take command of the brig at some critical juncture, and when his crew had gone too far to be able to retreat; he kept in reserve, as we have seen, the power of making generous offers to the men, so that they would follow him to the end of the world.

In fact, it was to the end of the world that he wanted to go.

Now matters looked very serious, and John Hatteras made himself known.

His dog, the faithful Duke, the companion of his expeditions, was the first to recognize him, and fortunately for the bold, and unfortunately for the timid, it was firmly established that the captain of the *Forward* was John Hatteras.

"John Hatteras."

CHAPTER XIII.

THE CAPTAIN'S PLANS.

The appearance of this famous person was variously received by the different members of the crew: some allied themselves strongly with him, moved both by boldness and by avarice; others took renewed interest in the expedition, but they reserved to themselves the right of protesting later; besides, at that time, it was hard to make any resistance to such a man. Hence every man went back to his place. The 20th of May was Sunday, and consequently a day of rest for the crew.

The officers took counsel together in the doctor's cabin; there were present Hatteras, Shandon, Wall, Johnson, and the doctor.

"Gentlemen," said the captain, with his peculiarly gentle but impressive voice, "you know my project of going to the Pole; I want to get your opinion of the undertaking. What do you think about it, Shandon?"

"I have not to think, Captain," answered Shandon, coldly; "I have only to obey."

Hatteras was not surprised at this answer.

"Richard Shandon," he resumed with equal coldness, "I ask your opinion about our probable chance of success."

"Well, Captain," answered Shandon, "facts must answer for me; all attempts hitherto have failed; I hope we may be more fortunate."

"We shall be. And, gentlemen, what do you think?"

"As for me," replied the doctor, "I consider your design practicable, Captain; and since there is no doubt but that at some time or other explorers will reach the Pole, I don't see why we should not do it."

"There are very good reasons why we should," answered Hatteras, "for we have taken measures to make it possible, and we shall profit by the experience of others. And, Shandon, you must accept my thanks for the care you have given to the equipment of the brig; there are some ill-disposed men in the crew, whom I shall soon bring to reason; but on the whole, I can give nothing but praise."

Shandon bowed coldly. His position on the *Forward*, of which he had thought himself commander, was a false one. Hatteras understood this, and said nothing more about it.

"As for you, gentlemen," he resumed, addressing Wall and Johnson, "I could not myself have chosen officers more skilled and intrepid."

"On my word, Captain, I am your man," answered Johnson; "and although I think your plan a very bold one, you can count on me to the end."

"And on me too," said Wall.

"As for you, Doctor, I know your worth—"

"Well, you know then a great deal more than I do," answered the doctor, quickly.

"Now, gentlemen," said Hatteras, "it is well that you should know on what good grounds I have made up my mind about the accessibility of the Pole. In 1817 the *Neptune*, of Aberdeen, went to the north of Spitzbergen, as far as latitude 82°. In 1826 the celebrated Parry, after his third voyage in polar seas, started also from the extremity of Spitzbergen, and on sledges went one hundred and fifty miles farther north. In 1852, Captain Inglefield reached, through Smith's Sound, latitude 78° 35'. All these were English ships, and were commanded by Englishmen, our fellow-countrymen."

Here Hatteras paused.

"I ought to add," he resumed with some formality, and as if he could hardly bring himself to utter the words,—"I ought to add that in 1854 the

American, Captain Kane, in the brig *Advance*, went still farther north, and that his lieutenant, Morton, journeying over the ice, hoisted the United States flag beyond the eighty-second degree. Having once said this, I shall not return to it. Now the main point is that the captains of the *Neptune*, the *Enterprise*, the *Isabella*, and the *Advance* agree in the statement that beyond these high latitudes there is an open polar sea, entirely free from ice."

"Free from ice!" cried Shandon, interrupting the captain, "it's impossible!"

"You will notice, Shandon," observed Hatteras, quietly, while his eye lighted up for an instant, "that I quote both facts and authorities. I must add that in 1851, when Penny was stationed by the side of Wellington Channel, his lieutenant, Stewart, found himself in the presence of an open sea, and that his report was confirmed when, in 1853, Sir Edward Belcher wintered in Northumberland Bay, in latitude 76° 52', and longitude 99° 20'; these reports are indisputable, and one must be very incredulous not to admit them."

"Still, Captain," persisted Shandon, "facts are as contradictory—"

"You're wrong, Shandon, you're wrong!" cried Dr. Clawbonny; "facts never contradict a scientific statement; the captain will, I trust, excuse me."

"Go on, Doctor!" said Hatteras.

"Well, listen to this, Shandon; it results very clearly from geographical facts, and from the study of isothermal lines, that the coldest spot on the globe is not on the Pole itself; like the magnetic pole, it lies a few degrees distant. So the calculations of Brewster, Berghaus, and other physicists prove that in our hemisphere there are two poles of extreme cold: one in Asia in latitude 79° 30' N., and longitude 120° E.; the other is in America, in latitude 78° N., and longitude 97° W. This last alone concerns us, and you see, Shandon, that it is more than twelve degrees below the Pole. Well, I ask you why, then, the sea should not be as free from ice as it often is in summer in latitude 66°, that is to say, at the southern end of Baffin's Bay?"

"Well put," answered Johnson; "Dr. Clawbonny talks of those things like a man who understands them."

"It seems possible," said James Wall.

"Mere conjectures! nothing but hypotheses!" answered Shandon, obstinately.

"Well, Shandon," said Hatteras, "let us consider the two cases; either the sea is free from ice, or it is not, and in neither case will it be impossible to reach the Pole. If it is free, the *Forward* will take us there without difficulty; if it is frozen, we must try to reach it over the ice by our sledges. You will confess that it is not impracticable; having once come with our brig to latitude 83°, we shall have only about six hundred miles between us and the Pole."

"And what are six hundred miles," said the doctor, briskly, "when it is proved that a Cossack, Alexis Markoff, went along the frozen sea, north of Russia, on sledges drawn by dogs, for a distance of eight hundred miles, in twenty-four days?"

"You hear him, Shandon," answered Hatteras, "and will you say that an Englishman cannot do as much as a Cossack?"

"Never!" cried the enthusiastic doctor.

"Never!" repeated the boatswain.

"Well, Shandon?" asked the captain.

"Captain," answered Shandon, coldly, "I can only repeat what I have said,— I shall obey you."

"Well. Now," continued Hatteras, "let us consider our present situation; we are caught in the ice, and it seems to me impossible for us to reach Smith's Sound this year. This is what we must do."

Hatteras unfolded on the table one of the excellent charts published in 1859 by the order of the Admiralty.

"Be good enough to look here. If Smith's Sound is closed, Lancaster Sound is not, to the west of Baffin's Bay; in my opinion, we ought to go up this sound as far as Barrow Strait, and thence to Beechey Island. This has been done a hundred times by sailing-vessels; we shall have no difficulty, going under steam. Once at Beechey Island, we shall follow Wellington Sound as far northward as possible, to where it meets the channel, connecting it with Queen's Sound, at the place where the open sea was seen. It is now only the 20th of May; if nothing happens, we shall be there in a month, and from there we shall start for the Pole. What do you say to that, gentlemen?"

"Evidently," said Johnson, "it's the only way open to us."

"Well, we shall take it, and to-morrow. Let Sunday be a day of rest; you will see, Shandon, that the Bible is read as usual; the religious exercises do the men good, and a sailor more than any one ought to put his trust in God."

"Very well, Captain," answered Shandon, who went away with the second officer and the boatswain.

"Doctor," said Hatteras, pointing at Shandon, "there's an offended man, whose pride has ruined him; I can no longer depend upon him."

Early the next day the captain had the launch lowered; he went to reconnoitre the icebergs about the basin, of which the diameter was hardly more than two hundred yards. He noticed that by the gradual pressure of the ice, this space threatened to grow smaller; hence it became necessary to make a breach somewhere, to save the ship from being crushed; by the means he employed, it was easy to see that John Hatteras was an energetic man.

In the first place he had steps cut, by which he climbed to the top of an iceberg; from that point he saw it would be easy to open a path to the southwest; by his orders an opening was made in the middle of an iceberg, a task which was completed by Monday evening.

Hatteras could not depend on his blasting-cylinders of eight or ten pounds of powder, whose action would have been insignificant against such large masses; they were only of use to break the field-ice; hence he placed in the opening a thousand pounds of powder, carefully laying it where it should be of the utmost service. This chamber, to which ran a long fuse, surrounded by gutta-percha, opened on the outside. The gallery, leading thereto, was filled with snow and lumps of ice, to which the cold of the next night gave the consistency of granite. In fact, the temperature, under the influence of the east-wind, fell to 12°.

The next day at seven o'clock the *Forward* was under steam, ready to seize any chance of escape. Johnson was charged with lighting the mine; the fuse was calculated to burn half an hour before exploding the powder. Hence Johnson had plenty of time to get back to the ship; indeed, within ten minutes he was at his post.

The crew were all on deck; the day was dry and tolerably clear; the snow was no longer falling; Hatteras, standing on the deck with Shandon and the doctor, counted the minutes on his watch.

At thirty-five minutes after eight a dull explosion was heard, much less deafening than had been anticipated. The outline of the mountains was suddenly changed, as by an earthquake; a dense white smoke rose high in the air, and long cracks appeared in the side of the iceberg, of which the upper part was hurled to a great distance, and fell in fragments about the *Forward*.

But the way was by no means free yet; huge lumps of ice were suspended upon the neighboring icebergs, and their fall threatened to close the exit.

Hatteras saw their situation in a flash of the eye.

"Wolston!" he shouted.

The gunner hastened to him.

"Captain!" he said.

"Put a triple charge in the forward gun, and ram it in as hard as possible!"

"Are we going to batter the iceberg down with cannon-balls?" asked the doctor.

"No," answered Hatteras. "That would do no good. No balls, Wolston, but a triple charge of powder. Be quick!"

In a few moments the gun was loaded.

"What is he going to do without a ball?" muttered Shandon between his teeth.

"We'll soon see," answered the doctor.

"We are all ready, Captain," cried Wolston.

"Well," answered Hatteras. "Brunton!" he shouted to the engineer, "make ready! Forward a little!"

Brunton opened the valves, and the screw began to move; the *Forward* drew near the blown-up iceberg.

"Aim carefully at the passage!" cried the captain to the gunner.

He obeyed; when the brig was only half a cable-length distant, Hatteras gave the order,—

"Fire!"

A loud report followed, and the fragments of ice, detached by the commotion of the air, fell suddenly into the sea. The simple concussion had been enough.

"Put on full steam, Brunton!" shouted Hatteras. "Straight for the passage, Johnson!"

Johnson was at the helm; the brig, driven by the screw, which tossed the water freely, entered easily the open passage. It was time. The *Forward* had hardly passed through the opening, before it closed behind it.

It was an exciting moment, and the only calm and collected man on board was the captain. So the crew, amazed at the success of this device, could not help shouting,—

"Hurrah for John Hatteras!"

CHAPTER XIV.

THE EXPEDITIONS IN SEARCH OF FRANKLIN.

Wednesday, the 21st of May, the *Forward* resumed her perilous voyage, making her way dexterously through the packs and icebergs, thanks to steam, which is seldom used by explorers in polar seas; she seemed to sport among the moving masses; one would have said she felt the hand of a skilled master, and that, like a horse under a skilful rider, she obeyed the thought of her captain.

The weather grew warmer. At six o'clock in the morning the thermometer stood at 26°, at six in the evening at 29°, and at midnight at 25°; the wind was light from the southeast.

Thursday, at about three o'clock in the morning, the *Forward* arrived in sight of Possession Bay, on the American shore, at the entrance of Lancaster Sound; soon Cape Burney came into sight. A few Esquimaux came out to the ship; but Hatteras could not stop to speak with them.

The peaks of Byam Martin, which rise above Cape Liverpool, were passed on the left, and they soon disappeared in the evening mist; this hid from them Cape Hay, which has a very slight elevation, and so is frequently confounded with ice about the shore, a circumstance which very often renders the determination of the coast-line in polar regions very difficult.

Puffins, ducks, and white gulls appeared in great numbers. By observation the latitude was 74° 1', and the longitude, according to the chronometer, 77° 15'.

The two mountains, Catherine and Elizabeth, raised their snowy heads above the clouds.

At ten o'clock on Friday Cape Warrender was passed on the right side of the sound, and on the left Admiralty Inlet, a bay which has never been fully explored by navigators, who are always hastening westward. The sea ran rather high, and the waves often broke over the bows, covering the deck with small fragments of ice. The land on the north coast presented a strange appearance with its high, flat table-lands sparkling beneath the sun's rays.

Hatteras would have liked to skirt these northern lands, in order to reach the sooner Beechey Island and the entrance of Wellington Channel; but, much to his chagrin, the bank-ice obliged him to take only the passes to the south.

Hence, on the 26th of May, in the midst of a fog and a snow-storm, the *Forward* found herself off Cape York; a lofty, steep mountain was soon recognized; the weather got a little clearer, and at midday the sun appeared long enough to permit an observation to be taken: latitude 74° 4', and longitude 84° 23'. The *Forward* was at the end of Lancaster Sound.

Hatteras showed the doctor on the chart the route he had taken and that which he was to follow. At that time the position of the brig was interesting.

"I should have liked to be farther north," he said, "but it was impossible; see, here is our exact position."

The captain pointed to a spot near Cape York.

"We are in the middle of this open space, exposed to every wind; into it open Lancaster Sound, Barrow Strait, Wellington Channel, and Regent's Inlet; here, of necessity, come all northern explorers."

"Well," answered the doctor, "so much the worse for them; it is indeed an open space, where four roads meet, and I don't see any sign-post to point out the right way! What did Parry, Ross, and Franklin do?"

"They didn't do anything in particular; they let themselves be governed by circumstances; they had no choice, I can assure you; at one time Barrow Strait would be closed against one, and the next year it would be open for another; again the ship would be irresistibly driven towards Regent's Inlet. In this way we have at last been able to learn the geography of these confused seas."

"What a strange region!" said the doctor, gazing at the chart. "How everything is divided and cut up, without order or reason! It seems as if all the land near the Pole were divided in this way in order to make the approach harder, while in the other hemisphere it ends in smooth, regular points, like Cape Horn or the Cape of Good Hope, and the Indian peninsula! Is it the greater rapidity at the equator which has thus modified things, while the land lying at the extremity, which was fluid at the beginning of the world, could not condense and unite as elsewhere, on account of slower rotation?"

"That may be, for there is a reason for everything, and nothing happens without a cause, which God sometimes lets students find out; so, Doctor, find it out if you can."

"I shall not waste too much time over it, Captain. But what is this fierce wind?" added the doctor, wrapping himself up well.

"The north-wind is the common one, and delays our progress."

"Still it ought to blow the ice toward the south, and leave our way free."

"It ought to, Doctor, but the wind doesn't always do what it ought to. See, that ice looks impenetrable. We shall try to reach Griffith Island, then to get around Cornwallis Island to reach Queen's Channel, without going through Wellington Channel. And yet I am anxious to touch at Beechey Island to get some more coal."

"How will you do that?" asked the astonished doctor.

"Easily; by order of the Admiralty, a great amount has been placed on this island, to supply future expeditions, and although Captain MacClintock took some in 1859, I can assure you there is still some left for us."

"In fact, these regions have been explored for fifteen years, and until certain proof of Franklin's death was received, the Admiralty always kept five or six ships cruising in these waters. If I'm not mistaken, Griffith Island, which I see in the middle of the open space, has become a general rendezvous for explorers."

"'True, Doctor, and Franklin's ill-fated expedition has been the means of our learning so much about these parts."

"Exactly; for there have been a great many expeditions since 1845. It was not till 1848 that there was any alarm about the continued non-appearance of the *Erebus* and the *Terror*, Franklin's two ships. Then the admiral's old friend, Dr. Richardson, seventy years of age, went through Canada, and descended Coppermine River to the Polar Sea; on the other side, James Ross, in command of the *Enterprise* and the *Investigator*, sailed from Upernavik in 1848, and reached Cape York, where we are now. Every day he threw overboard a cask containing papers telling where he was; during fogs he fired cannon; at night he burned signal-fires and sent off rockets, carrying always but little sail; finally, he wintered at Leopold's Harbor in 1848-49; there he caught a large number of white foxes; he had put on their necks copper collars on which was engraved a statement of the position of the ship and where supplies had been left, and he drove them away in every direction; then, in the spring, he explored the coast of North Somerset on sledges, amid dangers and privations which disabled nearly all his men. He built cairns, enclosing copper cylinders with instructions to the absent expedition; during his absence, Lieutenant MacClure explored fruitlessly the northern coast of Barrow Strait. It is noteworthy, Captain, that James Ross had among his officers two men who afterwards became celebrated,—MacClure, who found the Northwest Passage, and MacClintock, who found the last remains of the Franklin expedition."

"He caught a large number of white foxes; he had put on their necks copper collars."

"Two good and brave captains, two brave Englishmen; go on, Doctor, with this account which you know so well; there is always something to be learned from the account of bold adventurers."

"Well, to conclude with James Ross, I have only to add that he tried to go farther west from Melville Island; but he nearly lost his ships, and being caught in the ice he was carried, against his will, to Baffin's Bay."

"Carried," said Hatteras, frowning,—"carried against his will!"

"He had discovered nothing," resumed the doctor; "it was only after 1850 that English ships were always exploring there, when a reward of twenty thousand pounds was offered to any one who should discover the crews of the *Erebus* and *Terror*. Already, in 1848, Captains Kellet and Moore, in command of the *Herald* and the *Plover*, tried to make their way through by Behring Strait. I ought to say that the winter of 1850-51, Captain Austin passed at Cornwallis Island; Captain Penny, with the *Assistance* and *Resolute*, explored Wellington Channel; old John Ross, who discovered the magnetic pole, started in his yacht, the *Felix*, in search of his friend; the brig *Prince Albert* made her first voyage at the expense of Lady Franklin; and, finally, two American ships, sent out by Grinnell, under Captain Haven, carried beyond Wellington Channel, were cast into Lancaster Sound. It was during this year that MacClintock, Austin's lieutenant, pushed on to Melville Island and to Cape Dundas, the extreme points reached by Parry in 1819, and on Beechey Island were found traces of Franklin's wintering there in 1845."

"Yes," answered Hatteras, "three of his sailors were buried there, three fortunate men!"

"From 1851 to 1852," continued the doctor, with a gesture of agreement, "we find the *Prince Albert* making a second attempt with the French lieutenant, Bellot; he winters at Batty Bay in Prince Regent's Sound, explores the southwest of Somerset, and reconnoitres the coast as far as Cape Walker. Meanwhile, the *Enterprise* and *Investigator*, having returned to England, came under the command of Collinson and MacClure, and they rejoined Kellet and Moore at Behring Strait; while Collinson returned to winter at Hong-Kong, MacClure went on, and after three winters, 1850-51, 1851-52, and 1852-53, he discovered the Northwest Passage without finding any traces of Franklin. From 1852 to 1853, a new expedition, consisting of three sailing-vessels, the *Assistance*, the *Resolute*, the *North Star*, and two steam-vessels, the *Pioneer* and the *Intrepid*, started out under the orders of Sir Edward Belcher, with Captain Kellet second in command; Sir Edward visited Wellington Channel, wintered in Northumberland Bay, and explored the coast, while Kellet, pushing on as far as Brideport on Melville Island, explored that region without success. But then it was rumored in England that two ships, abandoned in the ice, had been seen not far from New Caledonia. At once Lady Franklin fitted out the little screw-steamer *Isabella*, and Captain Inglefield, after ascending Baffin's Bay to Victoria Point, at the eightieth parallel, returned to Beechey Island with equal unsuccess. At the beginning of 1855 the American Grinnell defrays the expense of a new expedition, and Dr. Kane, trying to reach the Pole—"

"But he did not succeed," cried Hatteras with violence, "and thank God he did not! What he did not do, we shall!"

"I know it, Captain," answered the doctor, "and I only speak of it on account of its connection with the search for Franklin. Besides, it accomplished nothing. I nearly forgot to say that the Admiralty, regarding Beechey Island as a general rendezvous, ordered the steamer *Phoenix*, Captain Inglefield, in 1853, to carry provisions there; he sailed with Lieutenant Bellot, who for the second, and last, time offered his services to England; we can get full details about the catastrophe, for Johnson, our boatswain, was eye-witness of this sad affair."

"Lieutenant Bellot was a brave Frenchman," said Hatteras, "and his memory is honored in England."

"Then," resumed the doctor, "the ships of Belcher's squadron began to return one by one; not all, for Sir Edward had to abandon the *Assistance* in 1854, as McClure had the *Investigator* in 1853. Meanwhile Dr. Rae, in a letter dated July 29, 1854, written from Repulse Bay, gave information that the Esquimaux of King William's Land had in their possession different objects belonging to the *Erebus* and *Terror;* then there was no doubt possible about the fate of the expedition; the *Phoenix*, the *North Star*, and the ship of Collinson returned to England; there was then no English ship in these waters. But if the government seemed to have lost all hope, Lady Franklin did not despair, and with what was left of her fortune she fitted out the *Fox*, commanded by MacClintock; he set sail in 1857, wintered about where you made yourself known to us, Captain; he came to Beechey Island, August 11, 1858; the next winter he passed at Bellot Sound; in February, 1859, he began his explorations anew; on the 6th of May he found the document which left no further doubt as to the fate of the *Erebus* and *Terror*, and returned to England at the end of the same year. That is a complete account of all that has been done in these regions during the last fifteen years; and since the return of the *Fox*, no ship has ventured among these dangerous waters!"

"Well, we shall try it!" said Hatteras.

CHAPTER XV.

THE FORWARD DRIVEN SOUTHWARD.

Towards evening the weather cleared up, and land was clearly to be seen between Cape Sepping and Cape Clarence, which juts out to the east, then to the south, and is connected to the mainland on the west by a low tongue of land. There was no ice at the entrance of Regent's Sound; but it was densely massed beyond Leopold Harbor, as if to form an impassable barrier to the northward progress of the *Forward*.

Hatteras, who, although he carefully concealed his feelings, was exceedingly annoyed, had to blow out a way with powder in order to enter Leopold Harbor; he reached it at midday, on Sunday, May 27th; the brig was securely anchored to the large icebergs, which were as firm, solid, and hard as rock.

At once the captain, followed by the doctor, Johnson, and his dog Duke, leaped out upon the ice and soon reached the land. Duke leaped about with joy; besides, since the captain had made himself known, he had become very sociable and very gentle, preserving his ill-temper for some of the crew, whom his master disliked as much as he did.

The harbor was free from the ice which is generally forced there by the east-wind; the sharp peaks, covered with snow, looked like a number of white waves. The house and lantern, built by James Ross, were still in a tolerable state of preservation; but the provisions appeared to have been eaten by foxes, and even by bears, of which fresh traces were to be seen; part of the devastation was probably due to the hand of man, for some ruins of Esquimaux huts were to be seen on the shores of the bay.

The six tombs, enclosing six sailors of the *Enterprise* and the *Investigator*, were recognizable by little mounds of earth; they had been respected by all, by both men and beasts.

On first setting his foot on this northern earth, the doctor was really agitated; it would not be easy to describe the emotions one feels at the sight of these ruined houses, tents, huts, supplies, which nature preserves so perfectly in cold countries.

"There," said he to his companions,—"there is the spot which James Ross himself named Camp Refuge! If Franklin's expedition had reached this spot, it would have been saved. Here is the engine which was taken out and left here, and the furnace which warmed the crew of the *Prince Albert* in 1851; everything remains as it was left, and one might fancy that Kennedy, her captain, had sailed away from here yesterday. This is the launch that sheltered them for some days, for Kennedy was separated from his ship, and only saved by Lieutenant Bellot, who braved the cold of October to join him."

"A brave and excellent officer he was," said Johnson. "I knew him."

While the doctor eagerly sought for traces of previous winterings there, Hatteras busied himself with collecting the scanty fragments of fuel and provisions which lay there. The next day was devoted to carrying them on board ship. The doctor explored the whole neighborhood, never going too far from the brig, and sketched the most remarkable views. The weather gradually grew milder; the snow-drifts began to melt. The doctor made a tolerably large collection of northern birds, such as gulls, divers, mollynochtes, and eider-ducks, which resemble ordinary ducks, with a white back and breast, a blue belly, the top of the head blue, the rest of the plumage white, shaded with different tints of green; many of them had already plucked from their bellies the eider-down, which both the male and the female devote to lining their nests. The doctor also saw great seals breathing at the surface of the water, but he was unable to draw one.

In his wanderings he discovered the stone on which is engraved the following inscription:—

[E I]
1849,

which marks the passage of the *Enterprise* and *Investigator;* he pushed on to Cape Clarence, to the spot where, in 1833, John and James Ross waited so impatiently for the ice to thaw. The earth was covered with the skulls and bones of animals, and traces of the dwellings of Esquimaux were to be seen.

The doctor thought of erecting a cairn at Leopold Harbor, and of leaving a letter there to indicate the passage of the *Forward* and the aim of the expedition. But Hatteras formally objected; he did not wish to leave behind him any traces which might be of use to a rival. In spite of all he could say, the doctor was obliged to yield to the captain's will. Shandon was ready enough to blame this obstinacy, for, in case of accident, no ship could have put out to the aid of the *Forward*.

Hatteras refused to comply. Having completed his preparations on Monday, he tried once more to go to the north through the ice, but, after dangerous efforts, he was obliged to descend again Regent's Channel; he was utterly averse to remaining at Leopold's Harbor, which is open one day and closed the next by the unheralded motion of the ice,—a frequent phenomenon in these seas, and one against which navigators have to be ever on their guard.

If Hatteras kept his anxiety from the others, he was at heart very anxious; he wanted to go northward, and he was obliged to retreat to the south! Where would that bring him? Was he going as far back as Victoria Harbor in the Gulf of Boothia, where Sir John Ross wintered in 1833? Should he find Bellot Sound free at this time, and, by going around North Somerset, could he ascend through Peel Sound? Or should he, like his predecessors, be caught for many winters, and be obliged to consume all his supplies and provisions?

These fears tormented him; but he had to decide; he put about and started for the south.

Prince Regent's Channel is of nearly uniform width from Leopold's Harbor to Adelaide Bay. The *Forward* went rapidly through the ice, with better fortune than many other ships, most of which required a month to descend the channel, even in a better season; it is true that none of these ships, except the *Fox*, had steam at their command, and were obliged to do their best against frequent unfavorable winds.

The crew seemed overjoyed at leaving the northern regions; they had but a slight desire to reach the Pole; they were alarmed at Hatteras's plans, for his reputation as a fearless man inspired them with but little confidence. Hatteras tried to make use of every opportunity to go forward, whatever the consequences might be. And yet in these parts, to advance is all very well, but one must also maintain his position and not run the risk of losing it.

The *Forward* went on under full steam; the black smoke whirled in spirals about the sparkling summits of the icebergs; the weather was changeable, turning from a dry cold to a snowstorm with inconceivable rapidity. Since the brig drew but little water, Hatteras hugged the west shore; he did not want to miss the entrance of Bellot Sound, for the Gulf of Boothia has no other entrance towards the south than the slightly known sound of the *Fury* and the *Hecla;* hence the gulf would be impassable, if Bellot Sound were missed or found impracticable.

By evening the *Forward* was in sight of Elwin Bay, which was recognized by its high, steep cliffs; Tuesday morning Batty Bay was seen, where, on the 10th of September, 1851, the *Prince Albert* anchored for the winter. The doctor examined the coast with interest through his glass. From this point started the expeditions which determined the shape of North Somerset. The weather was clear enough for them to see the deep ravines surrounding the bay.

The doctor and Johnson were probably the only ones who took any interest in these deserted countries. Hatteras, always studying his charts, talked little; his silence increased as the ship drew southward; he often went upon the quarter-deck, and there he would remain for hours, with folded arms, gazing absently at the horizon. His orders, when he gave any, were short and quick. Shandon maintained a cold silence, and drawing more and more into himself, he had nothing more to do with Hatteras than was officially required; James Wall remained devoted to Shandon, and modelled his conduct after that of his friend. The rest of the crew waited for whatever might turn up, ready to make the best use of it for their own profit. On board there was none of the unanimity which is so necessary for the accomplishment of great things. Hatteras knew this well.

During the day two whalers[2] were seen making toward the south; a white bear, too, was saluted with a few rifle-shots, but apparently without success.

The captain knew the worth of an hour at that time, and refused permission to chase the animal.

Wednesday morning the end of Regent Channel was passed; the angle of the west coast was followed by a deep curve in the land. On examining his chart, the doctor recognized Somerset-House Point, or Point Fury.

"There," he said to his usual companion,—"there is where the first English ship was lost that was sent to these seas in 1815, in Parry's third voyage; the *Fury* was so much injured by the ice in her second winter, that the crew were obliged to abandon her and to return to England in her companion, the *Hecla*."

"A good reason for having another ship," answered Johnson; "that is a precaution which polar explorers should not neglect; but Captain Hatteras was not the man to burden himself with a companion!"

"Do you consider him rash, Johnson?" asked the doctor.

"I? O, I don't say anything of the sort, Dr. Clawbonny! But see those piles there, with fragments of a tent hanging to them."

"Yes, Johnson, it is there Parry unloaded all his ship's supplies, and, if my memory serves me right, the roof of the hut he built was made out of a mainsail covered by the running-rigging of the *Fury*."

"That must have changed a good deal since 1825."

"Not so very much. In 1829, John Ross kept his crew safe and sound in this light building. In 1851, when Prince Albert sent out an expedition, this hut was still standing; Captain Kennedy repaired it nine years ago. It would be interesting to visit it, but Hatteras is unwilling to stop."

"And he is probably right, Dr. Clawbonny; if in England time is money, here it is safety, and for the delay of a day, of an hour even, the whole voyage might be rendered useless. We must let him do as he pleases."

On Thursday, June 1st, the *Forward* sailed diagonally across Creswell Bay; from Point Fury the coast rises in steep rocks three hundred feet high; towards the south, it is lower; a few snowy summits are to be seen, of a regular shape, while others, more fantastic, were hidden in the clouds.

During that day the weather grew milder, but cloudier; they lost sight of land; the thermometer rose to 32°; a few water-quail were to be seen, and flocks of wild geese flew toward the north; the crew laid aside some of their thick clothes; they began to be aware of the approach of summer in the arctic regions.

Toward evening the *Forward* doubled Cape Garry, a quarter of a mile from the shore. The lead marked ten to twelve fathoms, and they bore along the shore to Brentford Bay. In this latitude they were to find Bellot Sound, a sound which entirely escaped the notice of Sir John Ross in his expedition of 1828; his charts indicated an unbroken coast-line, with the least irregularities indicated with the utmost care; hence it is to be supposed that when he passed by the entrance of the sound, it was completely closed with ice and so could not be distinguished from the land.

This sound was really discovered by Captain Kennedy in an excursion made in April, 1852; he named it after Lieutenant Bellot, as "a just tribute," as he said, "to the important services rendered to our expedition by the French officer."

CHAPTER XVI.

THE MAGNETIC POLE.

As Hatteras drew near this sound he felt his anxiety redoubling; in fact, the success of his expedition was at stake; so far he had done nothing more than his predecessors, the most successful of whom, MacClintock, had consumed fifteen months in reaching this spot; but that was little, indeed nothing, if he could not make Bellot Sound; being unable to return, he would be kept a prisoner until the next year.

Hence he took upon himself the care of examining the coast; he went up to the lookout, and on Saturday passed many hours there.

The crew were all acquainted with the situation of the ship; an unbroken silence reigned on board; the engine was slackened; the *Forward* ran as near shore as possible; the coast was lined with ice which the warmest summers could not melt; a practised eye was needed to make out an entrance through them.

Hatteras was comparing his charts with the coast-line. The sun having appeared for a moment at noon, Shandon and Wall took an observation, the result of which was at once told him.

There was half a day of anxiety for all. But suddenly, at about two o'clock, these words were shouted from aloft,—

"Head to the west, and put on all steam."

The brig obeyed at once, turning to the point directed; the screw churned the water, and the *Forward* plunged under a full head of steam between two swiftly running ice-streams.

The path was found; Hatteras came down to the quarter-deck, and the ice-master went aloft.

"Well, Captain," said the doctor, "we have entered this famous sound at last!"

"Yes," answered Hatteras; "but entering is not all, we have got to get out of it too."

And with these words he went to his cabin.

"He is right," thought the doctor; "we are in a sort of trap, without much space to turn about in, and if we had to winter here!—well, we shouldn't be the first to do it, and where others lived through it, there is no reason why we should not!"

The doctor was right. It was at this very place, in a little sheltered harbor called Port Kennedy by MacClintock himself, that the *Fox* wintered in 1858. At that moment it was easy to recognize the lofty granite chains, and the steep beaches on each side.

Bellot Sound, a mile broad and seventeen long, with a current running six or seven knots, is enclosed by mountains of an estimated height of sixteen hundred feet; it separates North Somerset from Boothia; it is easy to see that there is not too much sailing room there. The *Forward* advanced carefully, but still she advanced; tempests are frequent in this narrow pass, and the brig did not escape their usual violence; by Hatteras's orders, all the topsail-yards were lowered, and the topmasts also; in spite of everything the ship labored fearfully; the heavy seas kept the deck continually deluged with water; the smoke flew eastward with inconceivable rapidity; they went on almost at haphazard through the floating ice; the barometer fell to $29°$; it was hard to stay on deck, so most of the men were kept below to spare them unnecessary exposure.

Hatteras, Johnson, and Shandon remained on the quarter-deck, in spite of the whirlwinds of snow and rain; and the doctor, who had just asked himself what was the most disagreeable thing to be done at that time, soon joined them there; they could not hear, and hardly could they see, one another; so he kept his thoughts to himself.

Hatteras tried to pierce the dense cloud of mist, for, according to his calculation, they should be through the strait at six o'clock of the evening. At that time exit seemed closed, and Hatteras was obliged to stop and anchor to an iceberg; but steam was kept up all night.

The weather was terrible. Every moment the *Forward* threatened to snap her cables; there was danger, too, lest the mountain should be driven by the wind and crush the brig. The officers kept on the alert, owing to their extreme anxiety; besides the snow, large lumps of frozen spray were blown about by the hurricane like sharp arrows.

The temperature arose strangely in that terrible night; the thermometer marked 57°; and the doctor, to his great surprise, thought he noticed some flashes of lightning followed by distant thunder. This seemed to corroborate the testimony of Scoresby, who noticed the same phenomenon above latitude 65°. Captain Parry also observed it in 1821.

Towards five o'clock in the morning the weather changed with singular rapidity; the temperature fell to the freezing-point; the wind shifted to the north and grew quiet. The western opening of the strait could be seen, but it was entirely closed. Hatteras gazed anxiously at the coast, asking himself if there really were any exit.

Nevertheless, the brig put out slowly into the ice-streams, while the ice crushed noisily against her bows; the packs at this time were six or seven feet thick; it was necessary carefully to avoid them, for if the ship should try to withstand them, it ran the risk of being lifted half out of the water and cast on her beam-ends.

At noon, for the first time, a magnificent solar phenomenon could be observed, a halo with two parhelions; the doctor observed it, and took its exact dimensions; the exterior arc was only visible for about thirty degrees each side of the horizontal diameter; the two images of the sun were remarkably clear; the colors within the luminous area were, going toward the outside, red, yellow, green, faint blue, and last of all white, gently fading away, without any sharp line of termination.

The doctor remembered Thomas Young's ingenious theory about these meteors; he supposed that certain clouds composed of prisms of ice are hanging in the air; the sun's rays falling on these prisms are refracted at angles of sixty and ninety degrees. The halos can only be formed in a clear sky. The doctor thought this an ingenious explanation.

Sailors, who are familiar with northern seas, consider this phenomenon a forerunner of heavy snow. If this should be the case, the position of the *Forward* was very critical. Hence Hatteras resolved to push on; during the rest of that day and the next night he took no rest, but examined the horizon through his glass, entering every inlet, and losing no opportunity to get out of the strait.

But in the morning he was compelled to stop before the impenetrable ice. The doctor joined him on the quarter-deck. Hatteras led him clear aft where they could talk without fear of being overheard.

"We are caught," said Hatteras. "It's impossible to go on."

"Impossible?" said the doctor.

"Impossible! All the powder on board the *Forward* would not open a quarter of a mile to us."

"What are we to do?" asked the doctor.

"I don't know. Curse this unlucky year!"

"Well, Captain, if we must go into winter-quarters, we'll do it. As well here as anywhere else!"

"Of course," said Hatteras in a low voice, "but we ought not to be going into winter-quarters, especially in the month of June. It is demoralizing, and bad for the health. The spirits of the crew are soon cast down during this long rest among real sufferings. So I had made up my mind to winter at a latitude nearer the Pole."

"Yes, but, unluckily, Baffin's Bay was closed."

"Any one else would have found it open," cried Hatteras; "that American, that—"

"Come, Hatteras," said the doctor, purposely interrupting him, "it's now only the 5th of June; we should not despair; a path may open before us suddenly; you know the ice often breaks into separate pieces, even when the weather is calm, as if it were driven apart by some force of repulsion; at any moment we may find the sea free."

"Well, if that happens, we shall take advantage of it. It is not impossible that beyond Bellot Strait we might get northward through Peel Sound or MacClintock Channel, and then—"

"Captain," said James Wall, approaching, "the ice threatens to tear away the rudder."

"Well," answered Hatteras, "never mind; I sha'n't unship it; I want to be ready at any hour, day or night. Take every precaution, Mr. Wall, and keep the ice off; but don't unship it, you understand."

"But—" began Wall.

"I don't care to hear any remarks, sir," said Hatteras, severely. "Go!"

Wall returned to his post.

"Ah!" said Hatteras, angrily, "I would give five years of my life to be farther north! I don't know any more dangerous place; and besides, we are so near the magnetic pole that the compass is of no use; the needle is inactive, or always shifting its direction."

"I confess," said the doctor, "that it is not plain sailing; but still, those who undertook it were prepared for such dangers, and there is no need to be surprised."

"Ah, Doctor! the crew has changed very much, and you have seen that the officers have begun to make remarks. The high pay offered the sailors induced them to ship; but they have their bad side, for as soon as they are off they are anxious to get back. Doctor, I have no encouragement in my undertaking, and if I fail, it won't be the fault of such or such a sailor, but of the ill-will of certain officers. Ah, they'll pay dearly for it!"

"You are exaggerating, Hatteras."

"Not at all! Do you fancy the crew are sorry for the obstacles we are meeting? On the contrary, they hope I shall be compelled to abandon my plans. So they do not murmur, and when the *Forward* is headed for the south, it will be the same thing. Fools! They imagine they are returning to England! But when I'm turned towards the north, you will see a difference! I swear solemnly that no living being shall make me swerve from my course! Give me a passage, an opening through which my brig can go, and I shall take it, if I have to leave half her sheathing behind!"

The desires of the captain were destined to be satisfied in a measure. As the doctor had foretold, there was a sudden change in the evening; under some influence of the wind, the ice-fields separated; the *Forward* pushed on boldly, breaking the ice with her steel prow; all the night they advanced, and towards six o'clock they were clear of Bellot Strait.

But great was Hatteras's anger at finding the way to the north closed! He was able to hide his despair; and as if the only open path were the one of his choice, he turned the *Forward* towards Franklin Sound. Being unable to go up Peel Sound, he determined to go around Prince of Wales Land, to reach MacClintock Channel. But he knew that Shandon and Wall could not be deceived, and were conscious of the failure of his hopes.

Nothing especial happened on the 6th of June; snow fell, and the prophecy of the halo came true.

For thirty-six hours the *Forward* followed the sinuosities of the coast of Boothia, without reaching Prince of Wales Land. Hatteras put on all steam, burning his coal extravagantly; he still intended to get further supplies on Beechey Island; on Thursday he arrived at Franklin Sound, and he still found the way northward impassable.

His position was a desperate one; he could not return; the ice pushed him onward, and he saw his path forever closing behind him, as if there were no open sea where he had passed but an hour before.

Hence, not only was the *Forward* unable to go toward the north, but she could not stop for a moment lest she should be imprisoned, and she fled before the ice like a ship before a storm.

Friday, June 7th, she arrived near the coast of Boothia, at the entrance of James Ross Sound, which had to be avoided because its only exit is to the west, close to the shore of America.

The observations taken at noon showed them to be in latitude 70° 5' 17", and longitude 96° 46' 45"; when the doctor heard this he examined his chart, and found that they were at the magnetic pole, at the very point where James Ross, the nephew of Sir John, came to determine its situation.

The land was low near the coast, and it rose only about sixty feet at the distance of a mile from the sea.

The boiler of the *Forward* needed cleaning; the captain anchored his ship to a field of ice, and gave the doctor leave to go ashore with the boatswain. For himself, being indifferent to everything outside of his own plans, he shut himself up in his cabin, and studied the chart of the Pole.

The doctor and his companion easily reached land; the first-named carried a compass for his experiments; he wanted to test the work of James Ross; he easily made out the mound of stones erected by him; he ran towards it; an opening in the cairn let him see a tin box in which James Ross had placed an account of his discovery. No living being had visited this lonely spot for thirty years.

At this place a needle suspended as delicately as possible assumed a nearly vertical position under the magnetic influence; hence the centre of attraction was near, if not immediately beneath, the needle.

The doctor made the experiment with all care. But if James Ross, owing to the imperfection of his instruments, found a declination of only 89° 50', the real magnetic point is found within a minute of this spot. Dr. Clawbonny was more fortunate, and at a little distance from there he found a declination of 90°.

"This is exactly the magnetic pole of the earth!" he cried, stamping on the ground.

"Just here?" asked Johnson.

"Precisely here, my friend!"

"Well, then," resumed the boatswain, "we must give up all the stories of a magnetic mountain or large mass."

"Yes, Johnson," answered the doctor, laughing, "those are empty hypotheses! As you see, there is no mountain capable of attracting ships, of drawing their iron from them anchor after anchor, bolt after bolt! and your shoes here are as light as anywhere in the world."

"But how do you explain—"

"There is no explanation, Johnson; we are not wise enough for that. But what is mathematically certain is that the magnetic pole is at this very spot!"

"Ah, Dr. Clawbonny, how glad the captain would be to say as much of the North Pole!"

"He'll say it, Johnson; he'll say it!"

"God grant it!" was the answer.

The doctor and his companion raised a cairn at the spot where they tried their experiment, and the signal for their return being made, they returned to the ship at five o'clock of the evening.

CHAPTER XVII.

THE FATE OF SIR JOHN FRANKLIN.

The *Forward* succeeded, though not without difficulty, in getting by James Ross Sound, by frequent use of the ice-saws and gunpowder; the crew was very much fatigued. Fortunately the temperature was agreeable, and even thirty degrees above what James Ross found at the same time of year. The thermometer marked 34°.

Saturday they doubled Cape Felix at the northern end of King William's Land, one of the smaller islands of northern seas.

At that time the crew became very much depressed; they gazed wistfully and sadly at its far-stretching shores.

In fact, they were gazing at King William's Land, the scene of one of the saddest tragedies of modern times! Only a few miles to the west the *Erebus* and *Terror* were lost.

The sailors of the *Forward* were familiar with the attempts made to find Franklin, and the result they had obtained, but they did not know all the sad details. Now, while the doctor was following on his chart the course of the ship, many of them, Bell, Bolton, and Simpson, drew near him and began to talk with him. Soon the others followed to satisfy their curiosity; meanwhile the brig was advancing rapidly, and the bays, capes, and promontories of the coast passed before their gaze like a gigantic panorama.

Hatteras was pacing nervously to and fro on the quarter-deck; the doctor found himself on the bridge, surrounded by the men of the crew; he readily understood the interest of the situation, and the impression that would be made by an account given under those circumstances, hence he resumed the talk he had begun with Johnson.

"You know, my friends, how Franklin began: like Cook and Nelson, he was first a cabin-boy; after spending his youth in long sea-voyages, he made up his mind, in 1845, to seek the Northwest Passage; he commanded the *Erebus* and the *Terror*, two stanch vessels, which had visited the antarctic seas in 1840, under the command of James Ross. The *Erebus*, in which Franklin sailed, carried a crew of seventy men, all told, with Fitz-James as captain; Gore and Le Vesconte, lieutenants; Des Voeux, Sargent, and Couch, boatswains; and Stanley, surgeon. The *Terror* carried sixty-eight men. Crozier was the captain; the lieutenants were Little, Hodgson, and Irving; boatswains, Horesby and Thomas; the surgeon, Peddie. In the names of the bays, capes, straits, promontories, channels, and islands of these latitudes you find memorials of most of these unlucky men, of whom not one has ever again seen his home! In all one hundred and thirty-eight men! We know that the last of Franklin's letters were written from Disco Island, and dated July 12, 1845. He said, 'I hope to set sail to-night for Lancaster Sound.' What followed his departure from Disco Bay? The captains of the whalers, the *Prince of Wales* and the *Enterprise*, saw these two ships for the last time in Melville Bay, and nothing more was heard of them. Still we can follow Franklin in his course westward; he went through Lancaster and Barrow

Sounds and reached Beechey Island, where he passed the winter of 1845-46."

"But how is this known?" asked Bell, the carpenter.

"By three tombs which the Austin expedition found there in 1850. Three of Franklin's sailors had been buried there; and, moreover, by a paper found by Lieutenant Hobson of the *Fox*, dated April 25, 1848. We know also that, after leaving winter-quarters, the *Erebus* and *Terror* ascended Wellington Channel as far as latitude 77°; but instead of pushing to the north, which they doubtless found impossible, they returned towards the south—"

"And that was a fatal mistake!" uttered a grave voice. "Safety lay to the north."

Every one turned round. It was Hatteras, who, leaning on the rail of the quarter-deck, had just made that solemn remark.

"Without doubt," resumed the doctor, "Franklin intended to make his way to the American shore; but tempests beset him, and September 12, 1846, the two ships were caught in the ice, a few miles from here, to the northwest of Cape Felix; they were carried to the north-northwest of Point Victory; there," said the doctor, pointing out to the sea. "Now," he added, "the ships were not abandoned till April 22, 1848. What happened during these nineteen months? What did these poor men do? Doubtless they explored the surrounding lands, made every effort to escape, for the admiral was an energetic man; and if he did not succeed—"

"It's because his men betrayed him," said Hatteras in a deep voice.

The sailors did not dare to lift their eyes; these words made them feel abashed.

"To be brief, this paper, of which I spoke, tells us, besides, that Sir John Franklin died, worn out by his sufferings, June 11, 1847. All honor to his memory!" said the doctor, removing his hat.

The men did the same in silence.

"What became of these poor men, deprived of their leader, during the next ten months? They remained on board of their ships, and it was not till April, 1848, that they made up their mind to abandon them; one hundred and five men survived out of the hundred and thirty-eight. Thirty-three had died! Then Captains Crozier and Fitz-James erected a cairn at Point Victory, and left their last paper there. See, my friends, we are passing by that point. You can see traces of the cairn, placed, so to speak, at the farthest point reached by John Ross in 1831! There is Cape Jane Franklin! There Point Franklin! There Point Le Vesconte! There Erebus Bay, where the launch, made of pieces of one of the ships, was found on a sledge! There were found silver spoons, plenty of food, chocolate, tea, and religious books. The hundred and five survivors, under the command of Captain Crozier, set out for Great Fish River. How far did they get? Did they reach Hudson's Bay? Have any survived? What became of them after that?—"

"I will tell you what became of them," said John Hatteras in an energetic voice. "Yes, they tried to reach Hudson's Bay, and separated into several parties. They took the road to the south. In 1854 a letter from Dr. Rae states that in 1850 the Esquimaux had met in King William's Land a detachment of forty men, chasing sea-cows, travelling on the ice, dragging a boat along with them, thin, pale, and worn out with suffering and fatigue. Later, they discovered thirty corpses on the mainland and five on a neighboring island, some half buried, others left without burial; some lying beneath an overturned boat, others under the ruins of a tent; here lay an officer with his glass swung around his shoulder, and his loaded gun near him; farther on were kettles with the remains of a horrible meal. At this news, the Admiralty urged the Hudson's Bay Company to send its most skilful agents to this place. They descended Black River to its mouth. They visited Montreal and Maconochie Islands, and Point Ogle. In vain! All these poor fellows had died of misery, suffering, and starvation, after trying to prolong their lives by having recourse to cannibalism. That is what became of them along their way towards the south, which was lined with their mutilated bodies. Well, do you want to follow their path?"

"All these poor fellows had died of misery, suffering, and starvation."

Hatteras's ringing voice, passionate gestures, and glowing face produced an indescribable effect. The crew, moved by the sight of these ill-omened lands, cried with one voice,—

"To the north! to the north!"

"Well, to the north! Safety and glory await us there at the north! Heaven is declaring for us! The wind is changing! The passage is free! Prepare to go about!"

The sailors hastened to their places; the ice-streams grew slowly free; the *Forward* went about rapidly, and ran under full steam towards MacClintock's Channel.

Hatteras was justified in counting on a freer sea; on his way he retraced the probable path of Franklin; he went along the eastern side of Prince of Wales Land, which is clearly defined, while the other shore is still unknown. Evidently the clearing away of the ice towards the south took place through the eastern strait, for it appeared perfectly clear; so the *Forward* was able to make up for lost time; she was put under full steam, so that the 14th they passed Osborne Bay, and the farthest points reached by the expeditions of 1851. There was still a great deal of ice about them, but there was every indication that the *Forward* would have clear sailing-way before her.

CHAPTER XVIII.

THE WAY NORTHWARD.

The crew seemed to have returned to their habits of discipline and obedience. Their duties were slight and infrequent, so that they had plenty of leisure. The temperature never fell below the freezing-point, and the thaw removed the greatest obstacles from their path.

Duke had made friends with Dr. Clawbonny. They got on admirably together. But as in friendship one friend is always sacrificed to the other, it must be said that the doctor was not the other. Duke did with him whatever he pleased. The doctor obeyed him as a dog obeys his master. Moreover, Duke conducted himself very amicably with most of the officers and sailors; only, instinctively doubtless, he avoided Shandon; he had, too, a grudge against Pen and Foker; his hatred for them manifested itself in low growls when they came near him. They, for their part, did not dare attack the captain's dog, "his familiar spirit," as Clifton called him.

In a word, the crew had taken courage again.

"It seems to me," said James Wall one day to Richard Shandon, "that the men took the captain's words for earnest; they seem to be sure of success."

"They are mistaken," answered Shandon; "if they would only reflect, and consider our condition, they would see we are simply going from one imprudence to another."

"Still," resumed Wall, "we are in a more open sea; we are going along a well-known route; don't you exaggerate somewhat, Shandon?"

"Not a bit, Wall; the hate and jealousy, if you please, with which Hatteras inspires me, don't blind my eyes. Say, have you seen the coal-bunkers lately?"

"No," answered Wall.

"Well! go below, and you'll see how near we are to the end of our supply. By right, we ought to be going under sail, and only starting our engine to make headway against currents or contrary winds; our fuel ought to be burned only with the strictest economy, for who can say where and for how long we may be detained? But Hatteras is pushed by this mania of going forward, of reaching the inaccessible Pole, and he doesn't care for such a detail. Whether the wind is fair or foul, he goes on under steam; and if he goes on we run a risk of being very much embarrassed, if not lost."

"Is that so, Shandon? That is serious!"

"You are right, Wall, it is; not only would the engine be of no use to us if we got into a tight place, but what are we to do in the winter? We ought to take some precautions against the cold in a country where the mercury often freezes in the thermometer."

"But if I'm not mistaken, Shandon, the captain intends getting a new supply at Beechey Island; they say there is a great quantity there."

"Can any one choose where he'll go in these seas, Wall? Can one count on finding such or such a channel free of ice? And if he misses Beechey Island, or can't reach it, what is to become of us?"

"You are right, Shandon; Hatteras seems to me unwise; but why don't you say something of this sort to him?"

"No, Wall," answered Shandon, with ill-disguised bitterness, "I have made up my mind not to say a word; I am not responsible any longer for the ship; I shall await events; if I receive any commands, I obey, and I don't proclaim my opinions."

"Let me tell you you are wrong, Shandon; for the well-being of all is at stake, and the captain's imprudence may cost us all dear."

"And if I were to speak, Wall, would he listen to me?"

Wall did not dare say he would.

"But," he added, "he would perhaps listen to remonstrances of the crew."

"The crew," said Shandon, shrugging his shoulders; "but, my dear Wall, haven't you noticed that they care for everything else more than for their safety? They know they're getting near latitude 72°, and that a thousand pounds is paid for every degree of latitude beyond which is reached."

"You are right, Shandon," answered Wall, "and the captain has taken the surest means of securing his men."

"Without doubt," answered Shandon; "for the present, at least."

"What do you mean?"

"I mean that all will go very well in the absence of all dangers and fatigues, in an open sea; Hatteras has caught them by his money; but what is done for pay is ill done. But once let hardships, dangers, discomfort, sickness, melancholy, and fierce cold stare them in the face,—and we are flying towards them now,—and you will see whether they remember the pay they are to get."

"So, in your opinion, Shandon, Hatteras will fail?"

"Exactly; he will fail. In such an enterprise, there should be an identity of interests among the leaders, a sympathy which is lacking here. Besides, Hatteras is mad; his whole past proves it! But we shall see! Circumstances may arise in which the command of the ship will have to be given to a less foolhardy captain—"

"Still," said Wall, shaking his head doubtfully, "Hatteras will always have on his side—"

"He will have," interrupted Shandon,—"he will have that Dr. Clawbonny, who only cares to study; Johnson, who is a slave to discipline, and who never takes the trouble to reason; perhaps one or two besides, like Bell, the carpenter,—four at the most, and there are eighteen on board! No, Wall, Hatteras has not the confidence of the crew; he knows it well, and he tries to make up for it by bribery; he made a good use of the account of Franklin's catastrophe to create a different feeling in their excited minds; but that won't last, I tell you; and if he don't reach Beechey Island, he is lost!"

"If the crew suspected—"

"I beg of you," said Shandon, quickly, "not to say a word about this to the crew; they'll find it out for themselves. Now, at any rate, it is well to go on towards the north. But who can say whether what Hatteras takes for a step towards the Pole may not be really retracing our steps? At the end of MacClintock Channel is Melville Bay, and thence open the straits which lead back to Baffin's Bay. Hatteras had better take care! The way west is easier than the way north."∗

From these words Shandon's state of mind may be judged, and how justified the captain was in suspecting a treacherous disposition in him.

Shandon, moreover, was right when he ascribed the present satisfaction of the crew to the prospect they had of passing latitude 72°. This greed of gold seized the least audacious. Clifton had made out every one's share with great exactness. Leaving out the captain and the doctor, who could not be admitted to the division, there were sixteen men on board the *Forward*. The amount was a thousand pounds, that was £72 10s. for each man, for every degree.∗ If they should ever reach the Pole the eighteen degrees to be crossed would give each one a sum of £1,125, a fair fortune. This whim would cost the captain £18,000; but he was rich enough to pay for such a costly trip to the Pole.

These calculations aroused wonderfully the avarice of the crew, as can be readily believed, and more than one longed to pass latitude 72°, who, a fortnight before, rejoiced to be sailing southward.

The *Forward* sailed by Cape Alworth June 16th. Mount Rawlinson raised its white peaks towards the sky; the snow and mist exaggerated its size so that it appeared colossal; the temperature remained a few degrees above the freezing-point; cascades and cataracts appeared on the sides of the mountain; avalanches kept falling with a roar like that of artillery. The long stretches of glaciers made a loud echo. The contrast between this wintry scene and the thaw made a wonderful sight. The brig sailed along very near the coast; they were able to see on some sheltered rocks a few bushes bearing modest little roses, some reddish moss, and a budding dwarf willow barely rising above the ground.

At last, June 19th, in latitude 72°,∗ they doubled Point Minto, which forms one of the extremities of Ommanney Bay; the brig entered Melville Bay, called "the Sea of Money" by Bolton; this good-natured fellow used to be always jesting on this subject, much to Clawbonny's amusement.

The obstacles to their course were but few, for June 23d, in the teeth of a strong northeasterly breeze, they passed latitude 74°. This was at the middle of Melville Bay, one of the largest seas of this region. It was first crossed by Captain Parry, in his great expedition of 1819, and there it was that his crew won the £5,000 promised by act of Parliament.

Clifton contented himself with remarking that there were two degrees between latitude 72° and latitude 74°: that was £125 to his credit. But they told him that a fortune did not amount to much up there, and that a man could be called rich only when he could have a chance to drink to his wealth;

- 154 -

it seemed better to wait for the moment when they could meet at some tavern in Liverpool before rejoicing and rubbing their hands.

CHAPTER XIX.

A WHALE IN SIGHT.

Melville Bay, although perfectly navigable, was not wholly free of ice; immense ice-fields could be seen stretching to the horizon; here and there appeared a few icebergs, but they stood motionless as if anchored in the ice. The *Forward* went under full steam through broad passes where she had plenty of sailing-room. The wind shifted frequently from one point of the compass to another.

The variability of the wind in the arctic seas is a remarkable fact, and very often only a few minutes intervene between a calm and a frightful tempest. This was Hatteras's experience on the 23d of June, in the middle of this huge bay.

The steadiest winds blow generally from the ice to the open sea, and are very cold. On that day the thermometer fell several degrees; the wind shifted to the southward, and the heavy gusts, having passed over the ice, discharged themselves of their dampness under the form of a thick snow. Hatteras immediately ordered the sails which were aiding the engine to be reefed; but before this could be done his main-topsail was carried away.

Hatteras gave his orders with the utmost coolness, and did not leave the deck during the storm; he was obliged to run before the gale. The wind raised very heavy waves which hurled about pieces of ice of every shape, torn from the neighboring ice-fields; the brig was tossed about like a child's toy, and ice was dashed against its hull; at one moment it rose perpendicularly to the top of a mountain of water; its steel prow shone like molten metal; then it sank into an abyss, sending forth great whirls of smoke, while the screw revolved out the water with a fearful clatter. Rain and snow fell in torrents.

The doctor could not miss such a chance to get wet to the skin; he remained on deck, gazing at the storm with all the admiration such a spectacle cannot fail to draw forth. One standing next to him could not have heard his voice; so he said nothing, but looked, and soon he saw a singular phenomenon, one peculiar to the northern seas.

The tempest was confined to a small space of about three or four miles; in fact, the wind loses much of its force in passing over the ice, and cannot carry its violence very far; every now and then the doctor would see, through some rift in the storm, a clear sky and a quiet sea beyond the ice-fields; hence the *Forward* had only to make her way through the passes to find smooth sailing; but she ran a risk of being dashed against the moving masses which obeyed the motion of the waves. Notwithstanding, Hatteras succeeded in a few hours in carrying his vessel into smooth water, while the violence of the storm, now at its worst at the horizon, was dying away within a few cable-lengths from the *Forward*.

Melville Bay then looked very different; by the influence of the winds and waves a large number of icebergs had been detached from the shores and were now floating northward, continually crashing against one another. They could be counted by hundreds; but the bay is very broad, and the brig avoided them without difficulty. The sight of these floating masses, which seemed to be racing together, was indeed magnificent.

The doctor was wild with enthusiasm about it, when Simpson, the harpooner, came up to him and asked him to notice the changing tints of the sea, which varied from deep blue to olive green; long bands ran from north to south with edges so sharply cut that the line of division could be seen as far as the horizon. Sometimes a transparent sheet would stretch out from an opaque one.

"Well, Dr. Clawbonny, what do you think of that?" said Simpson.

"I agree, my friend, with what Scoresby said about these differently colored waters," answered the doctor, "namely, that the blue water does not contain the millions of animalcules and medusæ which the green water contains; he made a great many experiments to test it, and I am ready to agree with him."

"O, but there's something else it shows!"

"What is that?"

"Well, if the *Forward* were only a whaler, I believe we should have some sport."

"But," answered the doctor, "I don't see any whales."

"We shall very soon, though, I promise you. It's great luck for a whaler to see those green patches in these latitudes."

"Why so?" asked the doctor, whose curiosity was aroused by these remarks of a man who had had experience in what he was talking about.

"Because," answered Simpson, "it is in that green water that most of the whales are caught."

"What is the reason, Simpson?"

"Because they get more food there."

"You are sure of that?"

"O, I have seen it a hundred times in Baffin's Bay! I don't see why the same shouldn't be the case in Melville Bay."

"You must be right, Simpson."

"And see," Simpson continued as he leaned over the rail,—"see there, Doctor."

"One would say it was the track of a ship."

"Well," said Simpson, "it's an oily substance that the whale leaves behind it. Really, the whale itself can't be far off."

In fact, the atmosphere was filled with a strong fishy smell. The doctor began to examine the surface of the sea, and the harpooner's prediction was soon verified. Foker was heard shouting from aloft,—

"A whale to leeward!"

All turned their eyes in that direction; a low spout was seen rising from the sea about a mile from the brig.

"There she spouts!" shouted Simpson, whose experienced eye soon detected it.

"It's gone," said the doctor.

"We could soon find it again, if it were necessary," said Simpson, regretfully.

But to his great surprise, although no one had dared to ask it, Hatteras gave the order to lower and man the whale-boat; he was glad to give the men some distraction, and also to get a few barrels of oil. They heard the order with great satisfaction.

Four sailors took their places in the whale-boat; Johnson took the helm; Simpson stood in the bow, harpoon in hand. The doctor insisted on joining the party. The sea was quite smooth. The whale-boat went very fast, and in about ten minutes she was a mile from the brig.

The whale, having taken another breath, had dived again; but soon it came up and projected fifteen feet into the air that combination of gases and mucous fluid which escapes from its vent-holes.

"There, there!" cried Simpson, pointing to a place about eight hundred yards from the boat.

They approached it rapidly; and the brig, having also seen it, drew near slowly.

The huge monster kept appearing above the waves, showing its black back, which resembled a great rock in the sea; a whale never swims rapidly unless pursued, and this one was letting itself be rocked by the waves.

The hunters approached in silence, choosing the green water, which was so opaque as to prevent the whale from seeing them. It is always exciting to watch a frail boat attacking one of these monsters; this one was about one hundred and thirty feet long, and often between latitude 72° and 80° whales are found more than one hundred and twenty-four feet long; ancient writers have often spoken of some longer than seven hundred feet, but they are imaginary animals.

Soon the boat was very near the whale. Simpson made a sign, the men stopped rowing, and, brandishing his harpoon, he hurled it skilfully; this, with sharp barbs, sank into the thick layers of fat. The wounded whale dived rapidly. At once the four oars were unshipped; the rope which was attached to the harpoon ran out rapidly, and the boat was dragged along while Johnson steered it skilfully.

The whale swam away from the brig and hastened towards the moving icebergs; for half an hour it went on in this way; the cord had to be kept wet to prevent its taking fire from friction. When the animal seemed to go more slowly, the rope was dragged back and carefully coiled; the whale rose again to the surface, lashing violently with its tail; huge spouts of water were dashed up by it and fell in torrents on the boat, which now approached rapidly; Simpson had taken a long lance and was prepared to meet the whale face to face.

"The whale swam away from the brig and hastened towards the moving icebergs."

But it plunged rapidly into a pass between two icebergs. Further pursuit seemed dangerous.

"The devil!" said Johnson.

"Forward, forward, my friends," shouted Simpson, eager for the chase; "the whale is ours."

"But we can't follow it among the icebergs," answered Johnson, turning the boat away.

"Yes, yes!" cried Simpson.

"No, no!" said some of the sailors.

"Yes!" cried others.

During this discussion the whale had got between two icebergs which the wind and waves were driving together.

The whale-boat was in danger of being dragged into this dangerous pass, when Johnson sprang forward, axe in hand, and cut the line.

It was time; the two icebergs met with irresistible force, crushing the whale between them.

"Lost!" cried Simpson.

"Saved!" said Johnson.

"Upon my word," said the doctor, who had not flinched, "that was well worth seeing!"

The crushing power of these mountains is enormous. The whale was the victim of an accident that is very frequent in these waters. Scoresby tells us that in the course of a single summer thirty whalers have been lost in this way in Baffin's Bay; he saw a three-master crushed in one minute between two walls of ice, which drew together with fearful rapidity and sank the ship with all on board. Two other ships he himself saw cut through, as if by a long lance, by huge pieces of ice more than a hundred feet long.

A few moments later the whale-boat returned to the brig, and was hauled up to its usual place on deck.

"That's a lesson," said Shandon, aloud, "for those who are foolhardy enough to venture into the passes!"

CHAPTER XX.

BEECHEY ISLAND.

June 25th the *Forward* sighted Cape Dundas, at the northwest extremity of Prince of Wales Land. There they found more serious difficulties amid thicker ice. The channel here grows narrower, and the line of Crozier, Young, Day, and Lowther Islands ranged in a line, like forts in a harbor, drive the ice-streams nearer together. What would otherwise have taken the brig a day now detained her from June 25th to the end of the month; she was continually obliged to stop, to retreat, and to wait for a favorable chance to reach Beechey Island. Meanwhile a great deal of coal was consumed; though during the frequent halts only small fires were kept burning, sufficient to keep steam up day and night.

Hatteras knew as well as Shandon the reduced state of their supply; but feeling sure that he would find fuel at Beechey Island, he did not wish to lose a minute for the sake of economy; he had been very much delayed by running south; and, although he had taken the precaution of leaving England in April, he now found himself no farther advanced than previous expeditions had been at that time of year.

The 30th they passed Cape Walker at the northeast extremity of Prince of Wales Land; this is the farthest point seen by Kennedy and Bellot, May 3d, 1852, after an expedition across North Somerset. In 1851, Captain Ommaney of the Austin expedition had been fortunate enough to get fresh supplies there for his detachment.

This cape, which is very lofty, is remarkable for its reddish-brown color; in clear weather one can see as far as the entrance of Wellington Channel. Towards evening they saw Cape Bellot, separated from Cape Walker by MacLeon's Bay. Cape Bellot was so named in presence of that young French officer to whom the English expedition gave three cheers. At this place the coast consists of a yellowish limestone, very rough in appearance; it is protected by huge masses of ice which the north-wind collects there in the most imposing way. It was soon no longer to be seen from the *Forward's* deck, as she was making her way amid the loose ice towards Beechey Island through Barrow Strait.

Hatteras, having resolved to go on in a straight line, in order not to be carried past the island, hardly left the deck during the subsequent days; he would go aloft to the cross-trees in order to pick out the most favorable path for the brig. All that skill, coolness, boldness, and even maritime genius could do, was done by him while sailing through the strait. It is true that fortune did not favor him, for at that season he ought to have found the sea nearly open. But by dint of sparing neither steam, his men, nor himself, he succeeded in his aim.

July 3d, at eleven o'clock in the morning, the ice-master saw land to the north; Hatteras soon made it out as Beechey Island, the general rendezvous for arctic explorers. Almost all the ships which sail in these latitudes touch here. Here Franklin passed his first winter before advancing into Wellington Channel. Here Creswell, MacClure's lieutenant, after a march of four hundred and sixty miles on the ice,* rejoined the *Phoenix* and returned to

England. The last ship which anchored at Beechey Island before the *Forward* was the *Fox;* MacClintock took in supplies there, August 11, 1855, and repaired the dwellings and storehouses; that was but a short time previous. Hatteras knew all these details.

The boatswain's heart beat strongly at the sight of this island; when he had last seen it he had been quartermaster on the *Phoenix;* Hatteras asked him about the coast, the place for anchoring, the possible change of the bottom. The weather was perfect; the thermometer marked 57°.

"Well, Johnson," said the captain, "do you recognize this place?"

"Yes, Captain, it's Beechey Island! Only we ought to bear a little farther north; the coast is more easily approached there."

"But the buildings, the stores?" said Hatteras.

"O, you can't see them till you get ashore; they are hidden behind those hillocks you see there!"

"And did you carry large supplies there?"

"Yes, they were large. The Admiralty sent us here in 1853, under the command of Captain Inglefield, with the steamer *Phoenix* and a transport, the *Breadalbane*, loaded with supplies; we carried enough to revictual a whole expedition."

"But did not the commander of the *Fox* take a great deal away in 1855?" said Hatteras.

"O, don't be anxious, Captain!" answered Johnson; "there will be enough left for you; the cold keeps everything wonderfully, and we shall find everything as fresh and in as good condition as on the first day."

"I'm not so anxious about the provisions," answered Hatteras; "I have enough for several years; what I stand in need of is coal."

"Well, Captain, we left more than a thousand tons there; so you can feel easy about that."

"Let us stand nearer," resumed Hatteras, who, glass in hand, kept examining the shore.

"You see that point," said Johnson; "when we've doubled it, we shall be near our anchorage. Yes, it's from there we started for England with Lieutenant Creswell and twelve sick men of the *Investigator*. But if we were fortunate enough to be of service to Captain MacClure's lieutenant, Bellot, the officer who accompanied us on the *Phoenix*, never saw his home again! Ah, that's a sad memory! But, Captain, I think it's here we ought to anchor."

"Very well," answered Hatteras.

And he gave the proper orders. The *Forward* lay in a little harbor sheltered from the north, east, and south winds, about a cable-length from the shore.

"Mr. Wall," said Hatteras, "you will lower the launch and send six men to bring coal aboard."

"Yes, sir," answered Wall.

"I am going ashore in the gig with the doctor and the boatswain; Mr. Shandon, will you go with us?"

"At your orders," answered Shandon.

A few minutes later the doctor, with gun and baskets for any specimens he might find, took his place in the gig with his companions; ten minutes later they stepped out on a low, rocky shore.

"Lead the way, Johnson," said Hatteras; "do you remember it?"

"Perfectly, Captain; only here is a monument which I did not expect to find here."

"That," shouted the doctor, "I know what it is; let's go look at it; it will tell us of itself why it was put here."

The four men went up to it, and the doctor, baring his head, said,—

"This, my friends, is a monument raised to the memory of Franklin and his companions."

In fact, Lady Franklin having, in 1855, sent a tablet of black marble to Dr. Kane, gave another in 1858 to MacClintock to be placed on Beechey Island. MacClintock discharged his duty, and placed this tablet near a funeral pile raised to the memory of Bellot by Sir John Barrow.

This tablet bore the following inscription:—

TO THE MEMORY OF

FRANKLIN, CROZIER, FITZ-JAMES,

AND ALL THEIR GALLANT BROTHER OFFICERS AND
FAITHFUL COMPANIONS

Who have suffered and perished
in the cause of science and the service of their country.

THIS TABLET

Is erected near the spot where they passed their first arctic Winter,
and whence they issued forth to conquer difficulties or

TO DIE.

It commemorates the grief of their Admiring Countrymen and Friends,
and the anguish, subdued by Faith,
of her who has lost, in the heroic Leader of the Expedition, the Most Devoted
and Affectionate of Husbands.

"*And so he bringeth them unto the Haven where they would be.*"
1855.

This stone, on a lonely shore of these remote regions, touched every one's heart; the doctor felt the tears rising in his eyes. On the very spot whence Franklin and his men sailed, full of hope and strength, there was now merely a slab of marble to commemorate them; and in spite of this solemn warning of fate, the *Forward* was about to follow the path of the *Erebus* and *Terror*.

Hatteras was the first to rouse himself; he ascended quickly a rather high hillock, which was almost entirely bare of snow.

"Captain," said Johnson, following him, "from there we ought to see the stores."

Shandon and the doctor joined them just as they reached the top of the hill.

But their eyes saw nothing but large plains with no trace of a building.

"This is very strange," said the boatswain.

"Well, these stores?" said Hatteras, quickly.

"I don't know,—I don't see—" stammered Johnson.

"You must have mistaken the path," said the doctor.

"Still it seems to me," resumed Johnson after a moment's reflection, "that at this very spot—"

"Well," said Hatteras, impatiently, "where shall we go?"

"Let's go down again," said the boatswain, "for it's possible I've lost my way! In seven years I may have forgotten the place."

"Especially," said the doctor, "when the country is so monotonous."

"And yet—" muttered Johnson.

Shandon said not a word. After walking a few minutes, Johnson stopped.

"No," he said, "I'm not mistaken."

"Well," said Hatteras, looking around.

"What makes you say so, Johnson?" asked the doctor.

"Do you see this little rise in the earth?" asked the boatswain, pointing downwards to a mound in which three elevations could be clearly seen.

"What does that mean?" asked the doctor.

"There," answered Johnson, "are the three tombs of Franklin's sailors. I'm sure of it! I'm not mistaken, and the stores must be within a hundred paces of us, and if they're not there,—it's because—"

He durst not finish his sentence; Hatteras ran forward, and terrible despair seized him. There ought to stand those much-needed storehouses, with supplies of all sorts on which he had been counting; but ruin, pillage, and destruction had passed over that place where civilized hands had accumulated resources for battered sailors. Who had committed these depredations? Wild animals, wolves, foxes, bears? No, for they would have destroyed only the provisions; and there was left no shred of a tent, not a piece of wood, not a scrap of iron, no bit of any metal, nor—what was more serious for the men of the *Forward*—a single lump of coal.

Evidently the Esquimaux, who have often had much to do with European ships, had finally learned the value of these objects; since the visit of the *Fox* they had come frequently to this great storehouse, and had pillaged incessantly, with the intention of leaving no trace of what had been there; and now a long drift of half-melted snow covered the ground.

Hatteras was baffled. The doctor gazed and shook his head. Shandon said nothing, but an attentive observer would have noticed a wicked smile about his lips.

At this moment the men sent by Wall arrived. They took it all in at a glance. Shandon went up to the captain and said,—

"Mr. Hatteras, we need not despair; fortunately we are near the entrance to Barrow Strait, which will carry us back to Baffin's Bay."

"Mr. Shandon," answered Hatteras, "we are fortunately near the entrance of Wellington Channel, and it will lead us to the north."

"And how shall we go, Captain?"

"Under sail, sir. We have two months' fuel left, and that is more than we shall need for next winter."

"Permit me to say," began Shandon.

"I permit you to follow me to the ship, sir," was Hatteras's answer.

And turning his back on his first officer, he returned to the brig and locked himself in his cabin.

For two days the wind was unfavorable; the captain did not come on deck. The doctor profited by this forced delay to examine Beechey Island; he collected a few plants which a comparatively high temperature let grow here and there on some rocks which projected from the snow, such as heather, a few lichens, a sort of yellow ranunculus, a plant like sorrel with leaves a trifle larger, and some sturdy saxifrages.

The fauna of this country was much richer; the doctor saw large flocks of geese and cranes flying northward; partridges, eider-ducks, northern divers, numerous ptarmigans, which are delicious eating, noisy flocks of kittiwakes, and great white-bellied loons represented the winged tribe. The doctor was lucky enough to kill some gray hares, which had not yet put on their white winter coat of fur, and a blue fox, which Duke skilfully caught. A few bears, evidently accustomed to fear men, could not be approached, and the seals were very timid, probably for the same reason. The harbor was full of a very good tasting shellfish. The genus *articulata*, order *diptera*, family *culicides*, division *nemocera*, was represented by a simple mosquito, a single one, which the doctor, though much bitten, had the pleasure of catching. As a conchologist, he was less fortunate, and he was obliged to content himself with a sort of mussel and some bivalves.

CHAPTER XXI.

THE DEATH OF BELLOT.

The temperature remained at 57° during July 3d and 4th; this was the highest temperature observed. But on Thursday, the 5th, the wind shifted to the southeast, with violent snow-squalls. The thermometer fell twenty-three degrees in the preceding night. Hatteras, indifferent to the hostility of the crew, gave the order to set sail. For thirteen days, ever since passing Cape Dundas, the *Forward* had not gone a single degree farther north; hence the party represented by Clifton was dissatisfied; their wishes, it is true, coincided with those of the captain, namely, that they should make their way through Wellington Channel, and they were all glad to be off once more.

It was with difficulty that sail was set; but having in the course of the night run up the mainsail and topsails, Hatteras plunged boldly into the ice, which the current was driving towards the south. The crew became very tired of this tortuous navigation, which kept them very busy with the sails.

Wellington Channel is not very broad; it lies between North Devon on the east and Cornwallis Island on the west; for a long time this island was considered a peninsula. It was Sir John Franklin who circumnavigated it, in 1846, from the western side, going about its northern coast.

"The *Forward* in Wellington Channel."

The exploration of Wellington Channel was made in 1851, by Captain Penny, in the whale-ships *Lady Franklin* and *Sophia;* one of his lieutenants, Stewart, who reached Cape Beechey, latitude 76° 20', discovered the open sea. The open sea! It was for that Hatteras longed.

"What Stewart found, I shall find," he said to the doctor; "and I shall be able to get to the Pole under sail."

"But," answered the doctor, "don't you fear lest the crew—"

"The crew!" said Hatteras, coldly.

Then in a lower tone he murmured,—

"Poor men!" much to the doctor's surprise.

It was the first sentiment of this sort which he had ever noticed in the captain.

"No," he went on warmly, "they must follow me, and they shall."

Still, if the *Forward* need not fear collision with the ice-streams, she made but little way northward, being much delayed by contrary winds. With some difficulty they got by Capes Spencer and Innis, and Tuesday, the 10th, latitude 75° was at last reached, much to Clifton's joy.

The *Forward* was now at the very spot where the American ships, the *Rescue* and the *Advance*, commanded by Captain Haven, ran such terrible dangers. Dr. Kane accompanied this expedition; towards the end of September, 1850, these ships were caught in the ice, and carried with irresistible force into Lancaster Sound.

Shandon told James Wall about it in the presence of some of the men.

"The *Advance* and the *Rescue*," he said, "were so tossed about by ice, that they could keep no fires on board; and yet the thermometer stood at 18° below zero. During the whole winter the crews were kept imprisoned, ready to abandon their ships, and for three weeks they did not take off their clothes! It was a terrible situation; after drifting a thousand miles, they were driven to the middle of Baffin's Bay!"

One may easily judge of the effect of such a narration on a crew already discontented.

While this conversation was going on, Johnson was talking with the doctor about an event which had taken place here; the doctor, at his request, told him the exact moment when the brig reached latitude 75° 30'.

"There it is! there it is!" said Johnson, "there is that unlucky land!"

And so speaking, tears came into the boatswain's eyes.

"You mean Lieutenant Bellot's death," said the doctor.

"Yes, sir, of that brave, good man!"

"And it was here, you say, that it took place?"

"Just here, on this part of the coast of North Devon. It was very great ill-luck, and this would not have happened if Captain Pullen had come on board sooner."

"What do you mean, Johnson?"

"Listen, Doctor, and you will see by how slight a thread life is held. You know that Lieutenant Bellot had already made an expedition in search of Franklin, in 1850?"

"Yes; in the *Prince Albert*."

"Well, in 1853, having returned to France, he got permission to sail in the *Phoenix*, in which I was a sailor, under Captain Inglefield. We came with the *Breadalbane* to carry supplies to Beechey Island."

"Those which we did not find!"

"Exactly, Doctor. We arrived at Beechey Island at the beginning of August; the 10th of that month, Captain Inglefield left the *Phoenix* to rejoin Captain Pullen, who had been away for a month from his ship, the *North Star*. He intended on his return to send the Admiralty despatches to Sir Edward Belcher, who was wintering in Wellington Channel. Now, shortly after our captain's departure, Captain Pullen reached his ship. If he had only come back before Captain Inglefield had left! Lieutenant Bellot, fearing that our captain's absence might be a long one, and knowing that the Admiralty despatches were important, offered to carry them himself. He left the two ships under Captain Pullen's charge, and left August 12, with a sledge and an india-rubber canoe. He took with him Harvey, quartermaster of the *North Star*, and three sailors, Madden, David Hook, and me. We thought that Sir Edward Belcher would be somewhere near Cape Beecher, at the northern part of the channel; hence we made for that part in our sledge, keeping on the east bank. The first day we encamped three miles from Cape Innis; the next day we stopped on the ice nearly three miles from Cape Bowden. During the night, which was as bright as day, land being only three miles distant, Lieutenant Bellot determined to go and camp there; he tried to reach it in the canoe; a violent southeast breeze drove him back twice; Harvey and Madden tried in their turn, and with success; they carried a rope, and with it they established communication with the shore; three objects were carried across by it; but at the fourth attempt, we felt the ice moving away from us; Mr. Bellot shouted to his companions to loosen the rope, and we (the lieutenant, David Hook, and I) were carried to a great distance from the shore. Then a strong southeaster was blowing, and snow was falling. But we were not in any great danger, and he might have been saved, since the rest of us were saved."

Johnson stopped for a moment, and gazed at the ill-fated shore, then he went on:—

"After losing sight of our companions, we tried at first to shelter ourselves under the cover of our sledge, but in vain; then with our knives we began to cut a house in the ice. Mr. Bellot sat down for half an hour, and talked with us about the danger of our situation; I told him I was not afraid. 'With God's protection,' he said, 'not a hair of our heads shall be hurt.' I then asked him what time it was. He answered, 'About quarter past six.' It was quarter past six in the morning of Thursday, August 18th. Then Mr. Bellot bound on his books, and said he wanted to go and see how the ice was moving; he was gone only four minutes, when I went to seek him behind the floe which sheltered us; but I did not find him, and, returning to our retreat, I saw his stick on the opposite side of a crevasse about three fathoms wide, where the ice was all broken. I shouted, but there was no answer. At that time the wind was blowing very hard. I searched all around, but I could find no trace of the poor lieutenant."

"And what do you suppose became of him?" asked the doctor, who was much moved by this account.

"I suppose that when he left the shelter, the wind drove him into the crevasse, and that, being thickly clad, he could not swim to the surface. O Dr. Clawbonny, I never felt worse in my life! I could not believe it! That brave officer fell a victim to his sense of duty! For you know that it was in order to obey Captain Pullen's instructions that he was trying to reach the land before the ice began to break! He was a brave man, liked by every one, faithful, courageous! All England mourned him, and even the Esquimaux, when they heard of his death from Captain Inglefield, when he returned from Pound Bay, did nothing but weep and repeat, 'Poor Bellot! Poor Bellot!'"

"But you and your companions, Johnson," asked the doctor, much moved by this touching account,—"how did you manage to get to shore?"

"O, it was very simple! We remained twenty-four hours on the ice without food or fire, but finally we reached a firmly fastened ice-field; we sprang upon it, and with an oar we got near a floe capable of supporting us, and being controlled like a boat. In that way we reached the shore, but alone, without our brave officer."

At the end of this account the *Forward* had passed by this fatal shore, and Johnson soon lost sight of the scene of this terrible catastrophe. The next day they left Griffin's Bay on the starboard, and two days later, Capes Grinnell and Helpman; finally, July 14th, they doubled Osborne Point, and the 15th the brig anchored in Baring Bay at the end of the channel. The navigation had not been very difficult; Hatteras found a sea nearly as free as that by which Belcher profited to go and winter with the *Pioneer* and *Assistance* in latitude 77°. That was his first winter, 1852-53, for the next he spent in Baring Bay, where the *Forward* now lay at anchor.

It was in consequence of the most terrible dangers and trials that he was obliged to abandon the *Assistance* in the midst of the eternal ice.

Shandon gave a full account of this catastrophe to the demoralized sailors. Was Hatteras aware of the treachery of his first officer? It is impossible to say, but, at any rate, he said nothing about it.

At the end of Baring Bay is a narrow canal uniting Wellington Channel with Queen's Strait. There the ice had accumulated very closely. Hatteras made vain efforts to get through the passages to the north of Hamilton Island; the wind was unfavorable; hence it was necessary to go between Hamilton and Cornwallis Islands; five precious days were lost in vain attempts. The air grew colder, and, July 19th, fell as low as 26°; the next day was warmer, but this harbinger of the arctic winter warned Hatteras not to linger longer. The wind seemed to blow steadily from the west and delayed his progress. And yet he was in haste to reach the point whence Stewart saw an open sea. The 19th he resolved to enter the channel at any price; the wind blew dead against the brig, which, with her screw, could have made headway against the violent snow-squalls, but Hatteras had before all to be economical with the fuel; on the other hand, the channel was too broad to permit of the brig being towed. Hatteras, without taking into account the fatigue of his crew, made use of a device which whalers often employ under similar circumstances. He lowered the small boats to the surface of the water, not letting them free from their tackle; then they were made fast, fore and aft; oars were put out, to starboard on one side and to port on the other; the men sat on the thwarts and rowed vigorously, so as to propel the brig against the wind.

Hatteras made use of a device which whalers employ.

The *Forward* made slight headway; this method of working was very fatiguing; the men began to murmur. For four days they advanced in that way, until July 23d, when they reached Baring Island, in Queen's Channel.

The wind was still unfavorable. The crew could go no farther. The doctor found the strength of the crew much pulled down, and he thought he detected the first symptoms of scurvy; he used every precaution against this terrible disease, having abundant supplies of lime-juice and chalk-pastilles.

Hatteras soon saw there was nothing more to be got from his crew; kindness and persuasion were fruitless; he resolved to employ severity, and, if need be, to be pitiless; he distrusted especially Richard Shandon, and even James Wall, who, however, never dared to speak too loud. Hatteras had on his side the doctor, Johnson, Bell, and Simpson; these were all devoted to him body and soul. Among the uncertain were Foker, Bolton, Wolston, the gunner,

Brunton, the first engineer, who might at any moment declare against him. As to the others, Pen, Gripper, Clifton, and Warren, they openly meditated mutiny; they wanted to bring their companions over and compel the *Forward* to return to England.

Hatteras soon saw that he could get no more work from his dispirited crew, who now were worn out with fatigue from their hard work. For twenty-four hours they remained in sight of Baring Island without getting a foot forward. Still the weather grew colder, and in these high latitudes even July felt the influence of the approaching winter. The 24th, the thermometer fell to 22°. The young ice formed during the night to a depth of about half an inch; if snow should fall on it, it would soon be strong enough to bear the weight of a man. The sea soon acquired the turbid tint which indicates the formation of the first crystals.

Hatteras read aright these alarming signs; if the passes should close, he would be obliged to winter here, far from the aim of his voyage, and without even having seen that open sea which he must have got very near, according to the accounts of his predecessors. Hence he resolved to get on at any price a few degrees farther north; seeing that he could neither try rowing with his crew exhausted, nor going under sail with the wind always unfavorable, he ordered the fires to be lighted.

CHAPTER XXII.

THE FIRST SIGNS OF MUTINY.

At this unexpected command, the surprise on board of the *Forward* was very great.

"Light the fires!" said some.

"With what?" said others.

"When we have only two months' supply in the hold!" cried Pen.

"And how are we to keep warm in the winter?" asked Clifton.

"We shall have to burn the ship down to the water-line, I suppose," said Gripper.

"And cram all the masts into the stove," answered Warren, "from the foretopmast to the jib-boom."

Shandon gazed intently at Wall. The surprised engineers hesitated to go down into the engine-room.

"Did you hear what I said?" shouted the captain, angrily.

Brunton walked toward the hatchway; but he stopped before going down.

"Don't go, Brunton," some one said.

"Who spoke then?" shouted Hatteras.

"I did," said Pen, approaching the captain.

"And what is it you're saying?" asked the captain.

"I say—I say," answered Pen with many oaths,—"I say that we have had enough of this, that we are not going any farther, that we don't want to wear ourselves out with fatigue and cold during the winter, and that the fires shall not be lighted."

"Mr. Shandon," answered Hatteras, coldly, "have this man put in irons."

"But, Captain," said Shandon, "what this man said—"

"If you repeat what this man said," retorted Hatteras, "I shall order you to your cabin and confine you there. Seize that man! Do you hear?"

Johnson, Bell, and Simpson stepped towards the sailor, who was beside himself with wrath.

"The first man who lays a finger on me—" he cried, seizing a handspike, which he flourished about his head.

Hatteras walked towards him.

"Pen," he said very quietly, "if you move hand or foot, I shall blow your brains out!"

With these words he drew a revolver and aimed it at the sailor.

A murmur arose from the crew.

"Not a word from any of you," said Hatteras, "or he's a dead man."

At that moment Johnson and Bell disarmed Pen, who no longer resisted, and suffered himself to be led to the bottom of the hold.

"Now go below, Brunton," said Hatteras.

The engineer, followed by Plover and Warren, went below. Hatteras returned to the quarter-deck.

"That Pen is a worthless fellow," the doctor said to him.

"No man was ever nearer death," answered the captain, simply.

Soon there was enough steam on; the anchors of the *Forward* were raised; and the brig started eastward, heading for Point Beecher, and cutting through the newly formed ice.

A great number of islands lie between Baring Island and Point Beecher, scattered in the midst of the ice-fields; the ice-streams crowd in great numbers in the little straits into which they divide the sea; when the weather is cold they have a tendency to accumulate; here and there hummocks were forming, and it was easy to see that the floes, already harder and more crowded, would, under the influence of the first frosts, soon form an impenetrable mass.

It was with great difficulty that the *Forward* made her way through the whirling snow. Still, with the variability which is a peculiarity of these regions, the sun would appear from time to time; the air grew much milder; the ice melted as if by enchantment, and a clear expanse of water, a most welcome sight to the eyes of the crew, spread out before them where a few moments before the ice had blocked their progress. All over the horizon there spread magnificent orange tints, which rested their eyes, weary with gazing at the eternal snow.

Thursday, July 26th, the *Forward* coasted along Dundas Island, and then stood more northward; but there she found herself face to face with a thick mass of ice, eight or nine feet high, consisting of little icebergs washed away from the shore; they had to prolong the curve they were making to the west. The continual cracking of the ice, joining with the creaking of the rolling ship, sounded like a gloomy lamentation. At last the brig found a passage and advanced through it slowly; often a huge floe delayed her for hours; the fog embarrassed the steersman; at one moment he could see a mile ahead, and it was easy to avoid all obstacles; but again the snow-squalls would hide everything from their sight at the distance of a cable's length. The sea ran very high.

Sometimes the smooth clouds assumed a strange appearance, as if they were reflecting the ice-banks; there were days when the sun could not pierce the dense mist.

The birds were still very numerous, and their cries were deafening; the seals, lying lazily on the drifting ice, raised their heads without being frightened, and turned their long necks to watch the ship go by. Often, too, the brig would leave bits of sheathing on the ice against which she grazed.

Finally, after six days of this slow sailing, August 1st, Point Beecher was made, sighted in the north; Hatteras passed the last hours in the lookout; the open sea, which Stewart had seen May 30, 1851, towards latitude 76° 20', could not be far off, and yet, as far as Hatteras could see, he could make out no sign of an open polar sea. He came down without saying a word.

"Do you believe in an open sea?" asked Shandon of the second mate.

"I'm beginning to have my doubts," answered James Wall.

"Wasn't I right in considering this pretended discovery as a mere hypothesis? No one agreed with me, and you too, Wall,—you sided against me."

"They'll believe you next time, Shandon."

"Yes," he answered, "when it's too late."

And he returned to his cabin, where he had kept himself almost exclusively since his discussion with the captain.

Towards evening the wind shifted to the south. Hatteras then set his sails and had the fires put out; for many days the crew were kept hard at work; every few minutes they had to tack or bear away, or to shorten sail quickly to stop the course of the brig; the braces could not run easily through the choked-up pulleys, and added to the fatigue of the crew; more than a week was required for them to reach Point Barrow. The *Forward* had not made thirty miles in ten days.

Then the wind flew around to the north, and the engine was started once more. Hatteras still hoped to find an open sea beyond latitude 77°, such as Edward Belcher had seen.

And yet, if he believed in Penny's account, the part of the sea which he was now crossing ought to have been open; for Penny, having reached the limit of the ice, saw in a canoe the shores of Queen's Channel at latitude 77°.

Must he regard their reports as apochryphal, or had an unusually early winter fallen upon these regions?

August 15th, Mount Percy reared into the mist its peaks covered with eternal snow; a violent wind was hurling in their teeth a fierce shower of hail. The next day the sun set for the first time, terminating at last the long series of days twenty-four hours long. The men had finally accustomed themselves to this perpetual daylight; but the animals minded it very little; the Greenland dogs used to go to sleep at the usual hour, and even Duke lay down at the same hour every evening, as if the night were dark.

Still, during the nights following August 16th the darkness was never very marked; the sun, although it had set, still gave light enough by refraction.

August 19th, after taking a satisfactory observation, Cape Franklin was seen on the eastern side, and opposite it Cape Lady Franklin; at what was probably the farthest point reached by this bold explorer, his fellow-countrymen wanted the name of his devoted wife should be remembered along with his own, as an emblem of the sympathy which always united them. The doctor was much moved by this sight in this distant country.

In accordance with Johnson's advice, he began to accustom himself to enduring low temperature; he kept almost all the time on deck, braving the cold, wind, and snow. Although he had grown a little thinner, he did not suffer from the severity of the climate. Besides, he expected other dangers, and he rejoiced, almost, as he saw the winter approaching.

"See," said he one day to Johnson,—"see those flocks of birds flying south! How they fly and cry adieu!"

"Yes, Dr. Clawbonny," answered Johnson, "something has told them it was time to go, and they are off."

"More than one of our men, Johnson, would be glad to imitate them, I fancy."

"They are timid fellows, Doctor; what a bird can't do, a man ought to try! Those birds have no supply of food, as we have, and they must support themselves elsewhere. But sailors, with a good deck under the feet, ought to go to the end of the world."

"You hope, then, that Hatteras will succeed in his projects?"

"He will succeed, Doctor."

"I agree with you, Johnson, even if only one faithful man accompanies him—"

"There will be two of us!"

"Yes, Johnson," the doctor answered, pressing the brave sailor's hand.

Prince Albert's Land, along which the *Forward* was now coasting, is also called Grinnell's Land; and although Hatteras, from his dislike to Americans, never was willing to give it this name, nevertheless, it is the one by which it is generally known. This is the reason of this double title: at the same time that the Englishman Penny gave it the name of Prince Albert, the captain of the *Rescue*, Lieutenant DeHaven, named it Grinnell's Land, in honor of the American merchant who had fitted out the expedition in New York.

As the brig followed the coast it met with serious difficulties, going sometimes under sail, sometimes under steam. August 18th, Mount Britannia was sighted through the mist, and the next day the *Forward* cast anchor in Northumberland Bay. The ship was completely protected.

CHAPTER XXIII.

ATTACKED BY THE ICE.

Hatteras, after seeing to the anchorage of the ship, returned to his cabin, took out his chart, and marked his position on it very carefully; he found himself in latitude 76° 57', and longitude 99° 20', that is to say, only three minutes from latitude 77°. It was here that Sir Edward Belcher passed his first winter with the *Pioneer* and *Assistance*. It was from here that he organized his sledge and canoe expeditions; he discovered Table Island, North Cornwall, Victoria Archipelago, and Belcher Channel. Having gone beyond latitude 78°, he saw the coast inclining towards the southeast. It seemed as if it ought to connect with Jones's Strait, which opens into Baffin's Bay. But, says the report, an open sea, in the northwest, "stretched as far as the eye could reach."

Hatteras gazed with emotion at that portion of the charts where a large white space marked unknown regions, and his eyes always returned to the open polar sea.

"After so many statements," he said to himself,—"after the accounts of Stewart, Penny, and Belcher, doubt is impossible! These bold sailors saw, and with their own eyes! Can I doubt their word? No! But yet if this sea is closed by an early winter— But no, these discoveries have been made at intervals of several years; this sea exists, and I shall find it! I shall see it!"

Hatteras went upon the quarter-deck. A dense mist enveloped the *Forward;* from the deck one could hardly see the top of the mast. Nevertheless, Hatteras ordered the ice-master below, and took his place; he wanted to make use of the first break in the fog to look at the horizon in the northwest.

Shandon took occasion to say to the second mate,—

"Well, Wall, and the open sea?"

"You were right, Shandon," answered Wall, "and we have only six weeks' coal in the bunkers."

"The doctor will invent some scientific way," continued Shandon, "of heating us without fuel. I've heard of making ice with fire; perhaps he will make fire with ice."

Shandon returned to his cabin, shrugging his shoulders.

The next day, August 20th, the fog lifted for a few minutes. From the deck they saw Hatteras in his lofty perch gazing intently towards the horizon; then he came down without saying a word and ordered them to set sail; but it was easy to see that his hopes had been once more deceived.

The *Forward* heaved anchor and resumed her uncertain path northward. So wearisome was it that the main-topsail and fore-topsail yards were lowered with all their rigging; the masts were also lowered, and it was no longer possible to place any reliance on the varying wind, which, moreover, the winding nature of the passes made almost useless; large white masses were gathering here and there in the sea, like spots of oil; they indicated an approaching thaw; as soon as the wind began to slacken, the sea began to freeze again, but when the wind arose this young ice would break and disperse. Towards evening the thermometer fell to 17°.

When the brig arrived at the end of a closed pass, it rushed on at full steam against the opposing obstacle. Sometimes they thought her fairly stopped; but some unexpected motion of the ice-streams would open a new passage into which she would plunge boldly; during these stoppages the steam would escape from the safety-valves and fall on the deck in the form of snow. There was another obstacle to the progress of the brig; the ice would get caught in the screw, and it was so hard that the engine could not break it; it was then necessary to reverse the engines, turn the brig back, and send some men to free the snow with axes and levers; hence arose many difficulties, fatigues, and delays.

It went on in this way for thirteen days; the *Forward* advanced slowly through Penny Strait. The crew murmured, but obeyed; they knew that retreat was now impossible. The advance towards the north was less perilous than a return to the south; it was time to think of going into winter-quarters.

The sailors talked together about their condition, and one day they even began to talk with Shandon, who, they knew, was on their side. He so far forgot his duty as an officer as to allow them to discuss in his presence the authority of his captain.

"So you say, Mr. Shandon," asked Gripper, "that we can't go back now?"

"No, it's too late," answered Shandon.

"Then," said another sailor, "we need only look forward to going into winter-quarters?"

"It's our only resource! No one would believe me—"

"The next time," said Pen, who had returned to duty, "they will believe you."

"Since I sha'n't be in command—" answered Shandon.

"Who can tell?" remarked Pen. "John Hatteras is free to go as far as he chooses, but no one is obliged to follow him."

"Just remember," resumed Gripper, "his first voyage to Baffin's Bay and what came of it!"

"And the voyage of the *Farewell*," said Clifton, "which was lost in the Spitzenberg seas under his command."

"And from which he came back alone," added Gripper.

"Alone, but with his dog," said Clifton.

"We don't care to sacrifice ourselves for the whims of that man," continued Pen.

"Nor to lose all the wages we've earned so hard."

They all recognized Clifton by those words.

"When we pass latitude 78°," he added, "and we are not far from it, that will make just three hundred and seventy-five pounds for each man, six times eight degrees."

"But," asked Gripper, "sha'n't we lose them if we go back without the captain?"

"No," answered Clifton, "if we can prove that it was absolutely necessary to return."

"But the captain—still—"

"Don't be uneasy, Gripper," answered Pen; "we shall have a captain, and a good one, whom Mr. Shandon knows. When a captain goes mad, he is dismissed and another appointed. Isn't that so, Mr. Shandon?"

"My friends," answered Shandon, evasively, "you will always find me devoted to you. But let us wait and see what turns up."

The storm, as may be seen, was gathering over Hatteras's head; but he pushed on boldly, firm, energetic, and confident. In fact, if he had not always managed the brig as he wanted to, and carried her where he was anxious to go, he had still been very successful; the distance passed over in five months was as great as what it had taken other explorers two or three years to make. Hatteras was now obliged to go into winter-quarters, but this would not alarm men of courage, experience, and confidence. Had not Sir John Ross and MacClure spent three successive winters in the arctic regions? Could not he do what they had done?

"Yes, of course," Hatteras used to say, "and more too, if need be. Ah!" he said regretfully to the doctor, "why was I unable to get through Smith's Sound, at the north of Baffin's Bay? I should be at the Pole now!"

"Well," the doctor used invariably to answer,—if necessary he could have invented confidence,—"we shall get there, Captain, but, it is true, at the ninety-ninth meridian instead of the seventy-fifth; but what difference does that make? If every road leads to Rome, it is even surer that every meridian leads to the Pole."

August 31st, the thermometer fell to 13°. The end of the summer was evidently near; the *Forward* left Exmouth Island to starboard, and three days afterward she passed Table Island, lying in the middle of Belcher Channel. Earlier in the season it would have been possible to reach Baffin's Bay through this channel, but at this time it was impossible to think of it. This arm of the sea was completely filled with ice, and would not have offered a drop of open water to the prow of the *Forward;* for the next eight months their eyes would see nothing but boundless, motionless ice-fields.

Fortunately, they could still get a few minutes farther north, but only by breaking the new ice with huge beams, or by blowing it up with charges of powder. They especially had cause to fear calm weather while the temperature was so low, for the passes closed quickly, and they rejoiced even at contrary winds. A calm night, and everything was frozen!

Now the *Forward* could not winter where she was, exposed to the wind, icebergs, and the drift of the channel; a safe protection was the first thing to be found; Hatteras hoped to gain the coast of New Cornwall, and to find, beyond Point Albert, a bay sufficiently sheltered. Hence he persisted in crowding northward.

But, September 8, an impenetrable, continuous mass of ice lay between him and the north; the temperature fell to 10°. Hatteras, with an anxious heart, in vain sought for a passage, risking his ship a hundred times and escaping from his perils with wonderful skill. He might have been accused of imprudence, recklessness, folly, blindness, but he was one of the best of sailors.

The situation of the *Forward* became really dangerous; in fact, the sea was closing behind her, and in a few hours the ice grew so hard that men could run upon it and tow the brig in perfect safety.

Hatteras, not being able to get around this obstacle, determined to attack it boldly in front. He made use of his strongest blasting cylinders, containing eight or ten pounds of powder. The men would dig a hole in the broadest part of the ice, close the orifice with snow, after having placed the cylinder in a horizontal position, so that a greater extent of ice might be exposed to the explosion; then a fuse was lighted, which was protected by a gutta-percha tube.

In this way they tried to break the ice; it was impossible to saw it, for the fissures would close immediately. Still, Hatteras was hoping to get through the next day.

But during the night the wind blew a gale; the sea raised the crust of ice, and the terrified pilot was heard shouting,—

"Look out there aft, look out there aft!"

Hatteras turned his eyes in that direction, and what he saw in the dim light was indeed alarming.

A great mass of ice, drifting northward with the tide, was rushing towards the brig with the speed of an avalanche.

"All hands on deck!" shouted the captain.

This floating mountain was hardly half a mile away; the ice was all in confusion and crashing together like huge grains of sand before a violent tempest; the air was filled with a terrible noise.

"That, Doctor," said Johnson, "is one of the greatest perils we have yet met with."

"Yes," answered the doctor, quietly; "it is terrible enough."

"A real attack which we must repel," resumed the boatswain.

"In fact, one might well think it was an immense crowd of antediluvian animals, such as might have lived near the Pole. How they hurry on, as if they were racing!"

"Besides," added Johnson, "some carry sharp lances, of which you had better take care, Doctor."

"It's a real siege," shouted the doctor. "Well, let us run to the ramparts!"

He ran aft where the crew, provided with beams and bars, were standing ready to repel this formidable assault.

The avalanche came on, growing larger at every moment as it caught up the floating ice in its eddy; by Hatteras's orders the cannon was loaded with ball to break the threatening line. But it came on and ran towards the brig; a crash was heard, and as it came against the starboard-quarter, part of the rail had given way.

"A crash was heard, and as it came against the starboard-quarter, part of the rail had given way."

"Let no one stir!" shouted Hatteras. "Look out for the ice!"

They swarmed on board the ship with an irresistible force; lumps of ice, weighing many hundredweight, scaled the sides of the ship; the smallest, hurled as high as the yards, fell back in sharp arrows, breaking the shrouds and cutting the rigging. The men were overcome by numberless enemies, who were heavy enough to crush a hundred ships like the *Forward*. Every one tried to drive away these lumps, and more than one sailor was wounded by their sharp ends; among others, Bolton, who had his left shoulder badly torn. The noise increased immensely. Duke barked angrily at these new enemies. The darkness of the night added to the horrors of the situation, without hiding the ice which glowed in the last light of the evening.

Hatteras's orders sounded above all this strange, impossible, supernatural conflict of the men with the ice. The ship, yielding to this enormous pressure, inclined to larboard, and the end of the main-yard was already touching the ice, at the risk of breaking the mast.

Hatteras saw the danger; it was a terrible moment; the brig seemed about to be overturned, and the masts might be easily carried away.

A large block, as large as the ship, appeared to be passing along the keel; it arose with irresistible power; it came on past the quarter-deck; if it fell on the *Forward*, all was over; soon it rose even above the topmasts, and began to totter.

A cry of terror escaped from every one's lips. Every one ran back to starboard.

But at that moment the ship was relieved. They felt her lifted up, and for an instant she hung in the air, then she leaned over and fell back on the ice, and then she rolled so heavily that her planks cracked. What had happened?

Raised by this rising tide, driven by the ice which attacked her aft, she was getting across this impenetrable ice. After a minute of this strange sailing, which seemed as long as a century, she fell back on the other side of the obstacle on a field of ice; she broke it with her weight, and fell back into her natural element.

"We have got by the thick ice!" shouted Johnson, who had run forward.

"Thank God!" said Hatteras.

In fact, the brig lay in the centre of a basin of ice, which entirely surrounded her, and although her keel lay under water she could not stir; but if she were motionless, the field was drifting along.

"We are drifting, Captain!" shouted Johnson.

"All right," answered Hatteras.

Indeed, how was it possible to resist it?

Day broke, and it was evident that under the influence of a submarine current the bank of ice was floating northward with great rapidity. This floating mass carried the *Forward* with it, in the midst of the ice-field, the edge of which could not be seen; to provide for any accident that might happen, Hatteras had a large supply of provisions carried on deck, as well as materials for camping, clothing, and cover; as MacClure had done under similar circumstances, he surrounded the ship with hammocks filled with air to protect her from damage. Soon it was so cold (7°), that the ship was surrounded by a wall from which only the masts issued.

For seven days they sailed in this way; Point Albert, which forms the western extremity of New Cornwall, was seen September 10th, and soon disappeared; the ice-field was seen to be drifting eastward from that time. Where was it going? Where would it stop? Who could say?

The crew waited with folded arms. At last, September 15th, towards three o'clock in the afternoon, the ice-field, having probably run against another one, stopped suddenly; the ship was jarred violently; Hatteras, who had kept his reckoning all along, looked at his chart; he found himself in the north, with no land in sight, in longitude 95° 35', and latitude 78° 15', in the centre of the region of the unknown sea, which geographers have considered the place of greatest cold.

CHAPTER XXIV.

PREPARATIONS FOR WINTERING.

The same latitude is colder in the southern than in the northern hemisphere; but the temperature of the New World is fifteen degrees beneath that of the other parts of the world; and in America these countries, known under the name of the region of greatest cold, are the most inclement.

The mean temperature for the whole year is two degrees below zero. Physicists have explained this fact in the following way, and Dr. Clawbonny shared their opinion.

According to them, the most constant winds in the northern regions of America are from the southwest; they come from the Pacific Ocean, with an equal and agreeable temperature; but before they reach the arctic seas they are obliged to cross the great American continent, which is covered with snow; the contact chills them, and communicates to these regions their intense cold.

Hatteras found himself at the pole of cold, beyond the countries seen by his predecessors; he consequently expected a terrible winter, on a ship lost amid the ice, with a turbulent crew. He resolved to meet these dangers with his usual energy. He faced what awaited him without flinching.

He began, with Johnson's aid and experience, to take all the measures necessary for going into winter-quarters. According to his calculation the *Forward* had been carried two hundred and fifty miles from any known land, that is to say, from North Cornwall; she was firmly fixed in a field of ice, as in a bed of granite, and no human power could extricate her.

There was not a drop of open water in these vast seas chained by the fierce arctic winter. The ice-fields stretched away out of sight, but without presenting a smooth surface. Far from it. Numerous icebergs stood up in the icy plain, and the *Forward* was sheltered by the highest of them on three points of the compass; the southeast wind alone reached them. Let one imagine rock instead of ice, verdure instead of snow, and the sea again liquid, and the brig would have quietly cast anchor in a pretty bay, sheltered from the fiercest blasts. But what desolation here! What a gloomy prospect! What a melancholy view!

The brig, although motionless, nevertheless had to be fastened securely by means of anchors; this was a necessary precaution against possible thaws and submarine upheavals. Johnson, on hearing that the *Forward* was at the pole of cold, took even greater precautions for securing warmth.

"We shall have it severe enough," he had said to the doctor; "that's just the captain's luck, to go and get caught at the most disagreeable spot on the globe! Bah! you will see that we shall get out of it."

As to the doctor, at the bottom of his heart he was simply delighted. He would not have changed it for any other. Winter at the pole of cold! What good luck!

At first, work on the outside occupied the crew; the sails were kept furled on the yards instead of being placed at the bottom of the hold, as the earlier explorers did; they were merely bound up in a case, and soon the frost covered them with a dense envelope; the topmasts were not unshipped, and the crow's-nest remained in its place. It was a natural observatory; the running-rigging alone was taken down.

It became necessary to cut away the ice from the ship to relieve the pressure. That which had accumulated outside was quite heavy, and the ship did not lie as deep as usual. This was a long and laborious task. At the end of some days the ship's bottom was freed, and could be inspected; it had not suffered, thanks to its solidity; only its copper sheathing was nearly torn away. The ship, having grown lighter, drew about nine inches less than she did earlier; the ice was cut away in a slope, following the make of the hull; in this way the ice formed beneath the brig's keel and so resisted all pressure.

The doctor took part in this work; he managed the ice-cutter well; he encouraged the sailors by his good-humor. He instructed them and himself. He approved of this arrangement of the ice beneath the ship.

"That is a good precaution," he said.

"Without that, Dr. Clawbonny," answered Johnson, "resistance would be impossible. Now we can boldly raise a wall of snow as high as the gunwale; and, if we want to, we can make it ten feet thick, for there is no lack of material."

"A capital idea," resumed the doctor; "the snow is a bad conductor of heat; it reflects instead of absorbing, and the inside temperature cannot escape."

"True," answered Johnson; "we are building a fortification against the cold, and also against the animals, if they care to visit us; when that is finished, it will look well, you may be sure; in this snow we shall cut two staircases, one fore, the other aft; when the steps are cut in the snow, we shall pour water on them; this will freeze as hard as stone, and we shall have a royal staircase."

"Precisely," answered the doctor; "and it must be said it is fortunate that cold produces both snow and ice, by which to protect one's self against it. Without that, one would be very much embarrassed."

In fact, the ship was destined to disappear beneath a thick casing of ice, which was needed to preserve its inside temperature; a roof made of thick tarred canvas and covered with snow was built above the deck over its whole length; the canvas was low enough to cover the sides of the ship. The deck, being protected from all outside impressions, became their walk; it was covered with two and a half feet of snow; this snow was crowded and beaten down so as to become very hard; so it resisted the radiation of the internal heat; above it was placed a layer of sand, which as it solidified became a sort of macadamized cover of great hardness.

"A little more," said the doctor, "and with a few trees I might imagine myself at Hyde Park, or even in the hanging-gardens at Babylon."

A trench was dug tolerably near the brig; this was a circular space in the ice, a real pit, which had to be kept always open. Every morning the ice formed overnight was broken; this was to secure water in case of fire or for the baths which were ordered the crew by the doctor; in order to spare the fuel, the water was drawn from some distance below the ice, where it was less cold. This was done by means of an instrument devised by a French physicist (François Arago); this apparatus, lowered for some distance into the water, brought it up to the surface through a cylinder.

Generally in winter everything which encumbers the ship is removed, and stored on land. But what was practicable near land is impossible for a ship anchored on the ice.

Every preparation was made to fight the two great enemies of this latitude, cold and dampness; the first produces the second, which is far more dangerous. The cold may be resisted by one who succumbs to dampness; hence it was necessary to guard against it.

The *Forward*, being destined to a journey in arctic seas, contained the best arrangements for winter-quarters: the large room for the crew was well provided for; the corners, where dampness first forms, were shut off; in fact, when the temperature is very low, a film of ice forms on the walls, especially in the corners, and when it melts it keeps up a perpetual dampness. If it had been round, the room would have been more convenient; but, being heated by a large stove, and properly ventilated, it was very comfortable; the walls were lined with deerskins, not with wool, for wool absorbs the condensed moisture and keeps the air full of dampness.

Farther aft the walls of the quarter were taken down, and the officers had a larger common-room, better ventilated, and heated by a stove. This room, like that of the crew, had a sort of antechamber, which cut off all communication with the outside. In this way, the heat could not be lost, and one passed gradually from one temperature to the other. In the anterooms were left the snow-covered clothes; the shoes were cleansed on the scrapers, so as to prevent the introduction of any unwholesomeness with one into the room.

Canvas hose served to introduce air for the draught of the stoves; other pieces of hose permitted the steam to escape. In addition two condensers were placed in the two rooms, and collected this vapor instead of letting it form into water; twice a week they were emptied, and often they contained several bushels of ice. It was so much taken from the enemy.

The fire was perfectly and easily controlled, by means of the canvas hose; by use of merely a small quantity of coal it was easy to keep the temperature of 50°. Still, Hatteras, having examined the bunkers, soon saw that the greatest economy was necessary, for there was not two months' fuel on board.

A drying-room was set apart for the clothes which were to be washed; they could not be dried in the open air, for they would freeze and tear.

The delicate pieces of the machinery were carefully taken down, and the room which contained them was hermetically closed.

The life on board became the object of serious meditation; Hatteras regulated it with the utmost caution, and the order of the day was posted up in the common-room. The men arose at six o'clock in the morning; three times a week the hammocks were aired; every morning the floors were scoured with hot sand; tea was served at every meal, and the bill of fare varied as much as possible for every day of the week; it consisted of bread, farina, suet and raisins for puddings, sugar, cocoa, tea, rice, lemon-juice, potted meats, salt beef and pork, cabbages, and vegetables in vinegar; the kitchen lay outside of the living-rooms; its heat was consequently lost; but cooking is a perpetual source of evaporation and dampness.

The health of the men depends a great deal on the sort of food they get; in high latitudes, the greatest amount of animal food ought to be eaten. The doctor had supervised the sort of food to be given.

"We ought to follow the Esquimaux," he used to say; "they have received their lessons from nature, and are our masters in that; if the Arabs and Africans can content themselves with a few dates and a handful of rice, here it is important to eat, and to eat a good deal. The Esquimaux take from ten to fifteen pounds of oil a day. If that fare does not please you, we must try food rich in sugar and fat. In a word, we need carbon, so let us manufacture carbon! It is well to put coal in the stove, but don't let us forget to fill that precious stove we carry about with us."

With this bill of fare, strict cleanliness was enforced; every other day each man was obliged to bathe in the half-frozen water which the iron pump brought up, and this was an excellent way of preserving their health. The doctor set the example; he did it at first as a thing which ought to be very disagreeable; but this pretext was quickly forgotten, for he soon took real pleasure in this healthy bath.

When work or hunting or distant expeditions took the men off in the severe cold, they had to take special care not to be frost-bitten; if they were, rubbing with snow would restore the circulation. Moreover, the men, who all wore woollen clothes, put on coats of deerskin and trousers of sealskin, which perfectly resist the wind.

The different arrangements of the ship, the getting-to-rights on board, took about three weeks, and they reached October 10th without any special incident.

CHAPTER XXV.

ONE OF JAMES ROSS'S FOXES.

On that day the thermometer fell to three degrees below zero. The day was calm; the cold was very endurable in the absence of wind. Hatteras took advantage of the clearness of the air to reconnoitre the surrounding plains; he ascended one of the highest icebergs to the north, but even with his glass he could make out nothing but a series of ice-mountains and ice-fields. There was no land in sight, nothing but gloomy confusion. He returned, and tried to calculate the probable length of their imprisonment.

The hunters, and among them the doctor, James Wall, Simpson, Johnson, and Bell, kept them supplied with fresh meat. The birds had disappeared, seeking a milder climate in the south. The ptarmigans alone, a sort of rock-partridge peculiar to this latitude, did not flee the winter; it was easy to kill them, and there were enough to promise a perpetual supply of game.

Hares, foxes, wolves, ermines, and bears were plentiful; a French, English, or Norwegian hunter would have had no right to complain; but they were so shy that it was hard to approach them; besides, it was hard to distinguish them on the white plain, they being white themselves, for in winter they acquire that colored fur. In opposition to the opinions of some naturalists, the doctor held that this change was not due to the lowering of the temperature, since it took place before October; hence it was not due to any physical cause, but rather providential foresight, to secure these animals against the severity of an arctic winter.

Often, too, they saw sea-cows and sea-dogs, animals included under the name of seals; all the hunters were specially recommended to shoot them, as much for their skins as for their fat, which was very good fuel. Besides, their liver made a very good article of food; they could be counted by hundreds, and two or three miles north of the ship the ice was continually perforated by these huge animals; only they avoided the hunter with remarkable instinct, and many were wounded who easily escaped by diving under the ice.

Still, on the 19th, Simpson succeeded in getting one four hundred yards distant from the ship; he had taken the precaution to close its hole in the ice, so that it could not escape from its pursuers. He fought for a long time, and died only after receiving many bullets. He was nine feet long; his bull-dog head, the sixteen teeth in his jaw, his large pectoral fins shaped like little wings, his little tail with another pair of fins, made him an excellent specimen. The doctor wished to preserve his head for his collection of natural history, and his skin for future contingences, hence he prepared both by a rapid and economical process. He plunged the body in the hole, and thousands of little prawns removed the flesh in small pieces; at the end of half a day the work was half finished, and the most skilful of the honorable corporation of tanners at Liverpool could not have done better.

When the sun had passed the autumn equinox, that is to say, September 23d, the winter fairly begins in the arctic regions. The sun, having gradually sunk to the horizon, disappeared at last, October 23d, lighting up merely the tops of the mountains with its oblique rays. The doctor gave it his last farewell. He could not see it again till the month of February.

Still the darkness was not complete during this long absence of the sun; the moon did its best to replace it; the stars were exceedingly brilliant, the auroras were very frequent, and the refractions peculiar to the snowy horizons; besides, the sun at the time of its greatest southern declension, December 21st, approaches within thirteen degrees of the polar horizon; hence, every day there was a certain twilight for a few hours. Only the mist and snow-storms often plunged these regions in the deepest obscurity.

Still, up to this time the weather was very favorable; the partridges and hares alone had reason to complain, for the hunters gave them no rest; a great many traps were set for foxes, but these crafty animals could not be caught; very often they scraped the snow away beneath the trap and took the bait without running any risk; the doctor cursed them, being very averse to making them such a present.

October 25th, the thermometer fell as low as -4°. A violent hurricane raged; the air was filled with thick snow, which permitted no ray of light to reach the *Forward*. For several hours there was some anxiety about the fate of Bell and Simpson, who had gone some distance away hunting; they did not reach the ship till the next day, having rested for a whole day wrapped up in their furs, while the hurricane swept over them and buried them under five feet of snow. They were nearly frozen, and the doctor found it very hard to restore their circulation.

The tempest lasted eight days without interruption. No one could set foot outside. In a single day there were variations in the temperature of fifteen or twenty degrees.

During this enforced leisure every one kept to himself, some sleeping, others smoking, others again talking in a low tone and stopping at the approach of Johnson or the doctor; there was no moral tie between the men of the crew; they only met at evening prayers and at Sunday services.

Clifton knew perfectly well that when the seventy-eighth parallel was passed, his share of the pay would amount to three hundred and seventy-five pounds; he thought it a good round sum, and his ambition did not go any further. His opinion was generally shared, and all looked forward to the day when they should enjoy this hardly-earned fortune.

Hatteras kept almost entirely out of sight. He never took part in the hunts or the walks from the ship. He took no interest in the meteorological phenomena which kept the doctor in a constant state of admiration. He lived with but a single idea; it consisted of three words,—The North Pole. He only thought of when the *Forward*, free at last, should resume her bold course.

In fact, the general feeling on board was one of gloom. Nothing was so sad as the sight of this captive vessel, no longer resting in its natural element, but with its shape hidden beneath thick layers of ice; it looks like nothing; it cannot stir, though made for motion; it is turned into a wooden storehouse, a sedentary dwelling, this ship which knows how to breast the wind and the storms. This anomaly, this false situation, filled their hearts with an indefinable feeling of disquiet and regret.

During these idle hours the doctor arranged the notes he had taken, from which this book is made up; he was never out of spirits, and never lost his cheerfulness. Yet he was glad to see the end of the storm, and prepared to resume his hunting.

November 3d, at six o'clock in the morning, with a temperature of -5°, he set off in company with Johnson and Bell; the expanse of ice was unbroken; all the snow which had fallen so abundantly during the preceding days was hardened by the frost, and made good walking; the air was keen and piercing; the moon shone with incomparable purity, glistening on the least roughness in the ice; their footprints glowed like an illuminated trail, and their long shadows stood out almost black against the brilliant ice.

"The moon shone with incomparable purity, glistening on the least roughness in the ice."

The doctor had taken Duke with him; he preferred him to the Greenland dogs to hunt game, and he was right; for they are of very little use under such circumstances, and they did not appear to possess the sacred fire of the race of the temperate zone. Duke ran along with his nose on the ground, and he often stopped on the recent marks of bears. Still, in spite of his skill, the hunters did not find even a hare in two hours' walking.

"Has all the game felt it necessary to go south?" said the doctor, stopping at the foot of a hummock.

"I should fancy it must be so, Doctor," answered the carpenter.

"I don't think so," said Johnson; "the hares, foxes, and bears are accustomed to this climate; I think this last storm must have driven them away; but they will come back with the south-winds. Ah, if you were to talk about reindeer and musk-deer, that might be different!"

"And yet at Melville Island numberless animals of this sort are found," resumed the doctor; "it lies farther south, it is true, and during the winters he spent there Parry always had plenty of this magnificent game."

"We have much poorer luck," answered Bell; "if we could only get enough bear's meat, we would do very well."

"The difficulty is," said the doctor, "the bears seem to me very rare and very wild; they are not civilized enough to come within gun-shot."

"Bell is talking about the flesh of the bear," said Johnson, "but his grease is more useful than his flesh or his fur."

"You are right, Johnson," answered Bell; "you are always thinking of the fuel."

"How can I help it? Even with the strictest economy, we have only enough for three weeks!"

"Yes," resumed the doctor, "that is the real danger, for we are now only at the beginning of November, and February is the coldest month in the frigid zone; still, if we can't get bear's grease, there's no lack of seal's grease."

"But not for a very long time, Doctor," answered Johnson; "they will soon leave us; whether from cold or fright, soon they won't come upon the ice any more."

"Then," continued the doctor, "we shall have to fall back on the bear, and I confess the bear is the most useful animal to be found in these countries, for he furnishes food, clothing, light, and fuel to men. Do you hear, Duke?" he said, patting the dog's head, "we want some bears, my friend, bears! bears!"

Duke, who was sniffing at the ice at that time, aroused by the voices, and caresses of the doctor, started off suddenly with the speed of an arrow. He barked violently and, far off as he was, his loud barks reached the hunters' ears.

The extreme distance to which sound is carried when the temperature is low is an astonishing fact; it is only equalled by the brilliancy of the constellations in the northern skies; the waves of light and sound are transmitted to great distances, especially in the dry cold of the nights.

The hunters, guided by his distant barking, hastened after him; they had to run a mile, and they got there all out of breath, which happens very soon in such an atmosphere. Duke stood pointing about fifty feet from an enormous mass which was rolling about on the top of a small iceberg.

"Just what we wanted!" shouted the doctor, cocking his gun.

"A fine bear!" said Bell, following the doctor's example.

"A curious bear!" said Johnson, who intended to fire after his companions.

Duke barked furiously. Bell advanced about twenty feet, and fired; but the animal seemed untouched, for he continued rolling his head slowly.

Johnson came forward, and, after taking careful aim, he pulled the trigger.

"Good!" said the doctor; "nothing yet! Ah, this cursed refraction! We are too far off; we shall never get used to it! That bear is more than a mile away."

"Come on!" answered Bell.

The three companions hastened toward the animal, which had not been alarmed by the firing; he seemed to be very large, but, without weighing the danger, they gave themselves up already to the joy of victory. Having got within a reasonable distance, they fired; the bear leaped into the air and fell, mortally wounded, on the level ice below.

Duke rushed towards him.

"That's a bear," said the doctor, "which was easily conquered."

"Only three shots," said Bell with some scorn, "and he's down!"

"That's odd," remarked Johnson.

"Unless we got here just as he was going to die of old age," continued the doctor, laughing.

"Well, young or old," added Bell, "he's a good capture."

Talking in this way they reached the small iceberg, and, to their great surprise, they found Duke growling over the body of a white fox.

"Upon my word," said Bell, "that's too much!"

"Well," said the doctor, "we've fired at a bear, and killed a fox!"

Johnson did not know what to say.

"Well," said the doctor with a burst of laughter in which there was a trace of disappointment, "that refraction again! It's always deceiving us."

"What do you mean, Doctor?" asked the carpenter.

"Yes, my friend; it deceived us with respect to its size as well as the distance! It made us see a bear in a fox's skin! Such a mistake is not uncommon under similar circumstances! Well, our imagination alone was wrong!"

"At any rate," answered Johnson, "bear or fox, he's good eating. Let's carry him off."

But as the boatswain was lifting him to his shoulders:—

"That's odd," he said.

"What is it?" asked the doctor.

"See there, Doctor, he's got a collar around his neck."

"A collar?" asked the doctor again, examining the fox.

In fact, a half-worn-out copper collar appeared under his white fur; the doctor thought he saw letters engraved upon it; he unfastened it from the animal's neck, about which it seemed to have been for a long time.

"What does that mean?" asked Johnson.

"That means," said the doctor, "that we have just killed a fox more than twelve years old,—a fox who was caught by James Ross in 1848."

"Is it possible?" said Bell.

"There's no doubt about it. I'm sorry we killed him! While he was in winter-quarters, James Ross thought of trapping a large number of white foxes; he fastened on their necks copper collars on which was engraved the position of his ships, the *Enterprise* and *Investigator*, as well as where the supplies were left. These animals run over immense distances in search of food, and James Ross hoped that one of them might fall into the hands of one of the men of the Franklin expedition. That's the simple explanation; and this poor beast, who might have saved the life of two crews, has fallen uselessly beneath our guns."

"Well, we won't eat it," said Johnson, "especially if it's twelve years old. But we shall keep the skin as a memento."

Johnson raised it to his shoulders. The hunters made their way to the ship, guiding themselves by the stars; their expedition was not wholly without result; they were able to bring back several ptarmigans.

An hour before reaching the *Forward*, there was a singular phenomenon which greatly interested the doctor. It was a real shower of shooting-stars; they could be counted by thousands, flying over the heavens like rockets; they dimmed the light of the moon. For hours they could have stood gazing at this beautiful sight. A similar phenomenon was observed in Greenland in 1799, by the Moravians. It looked like an exhibition of fireworks. The doctor after his return to the ship spent the whole night gazing at the sight, which lasted till seven o'clock in the morning, while the air was perfectly silent.

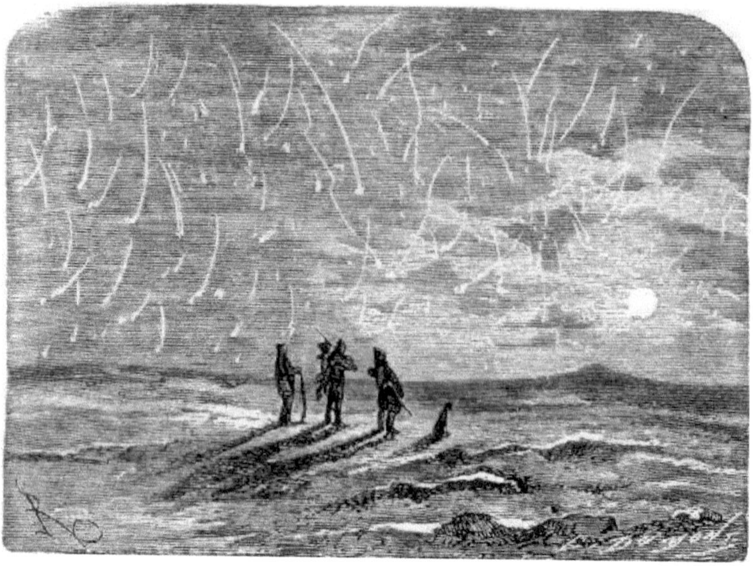

CHAPTER XXVI.

THE LAST PIECE OF COAL.

The bears, it seemed, could not be caught; a few seals were killed on the 4th, 5th, and 6th of November, and the wind shifted and the weather grew much milder; but the snow-drifts began again with incomparable severity. It became impossible to leave the ship, and it was hard to subdue the dampness. At the end of the week the condensers contained several bushels of ice.

The weather changed again November 15th, and the thermometer, under the influence of certain atmospheric conditions, sank to -24°. That was the lowest temperature they had yet observed. This cold would have been endurable in calm weather; but the wind was blowing at that time, and it seemed as if the air was filled with sharp needles.

The doctor regretted his captivity, for the snow was hardened by the wind, so as to make good walking, and he might have gone very far from the ship.

Still, it should be said that the slightest exercise in so low a temperature is very exhausting. A man can perform hardly more than a quarter of his usual work; iron utensils cannot be touched; if the hand seizes them, it feels as if it were burned, and shreds of skin cleave to the object which had been incautiously seized.

The crew, being confined to the ship, were obliged to walk on the covered deck for two hours a day, where they had leave to smoke, which was forbidden in the common-room.

There, when the fire got low, the ice used to cover the walls and the intervals between the planks; every nail and bolt and piece of metal was immediately covered with a film of ice.

The celerity of its formation astonished the doctor. The breath of the men condensed in the air, and, changing from a fluid to a solid form, it fell about them in the form of snow. A few feet from the stove it was very cold, and the men stood grouped around the fire.

Still, the doctor advised them to harden themselves, and to accustom themselves to the cold, which was not so severe as what yet awaited them; he advised them to expose their skin gradually to this intense temperature, and he himself set the example; but idleness or numbness nailed most of them to their place; they refused to stir, and preferred sleeping in that unhealthy heat.

Yet, according to the doctor, there was no danger in exposing one's self to great cold after leaving a heated room; these sudden changes only inconvenience those who are in a perspiration; the doctor quoted examples in support of his opinion, but his lessons were for the most part thrown away.

As for John Hatteras, he did not seem to mind the inclement cold. He walked to and fro silently, never faster or slower. Did not the cold affect his powerful frame? Did he possess to a very great degree the principle of natural heat which he wanted his men to possess? Was he so bound up in his meditations that he was indifferent to outside impressions? His men saw him with great astonishment braving a temperature of -24°; he would leave the ship for hours, and come back without appearing to suffer from the cold.

"He's a singular man," said the doctor to Johnson; "he astonishes me! He carries a glowing furnace within him! He is one of the strongest natures I ever saw!"

"The fact is," answered Johnson, "he goes and comes and circulates in the open air, without dressing any more thickly than in the month of June."

"O, it doesn't make much difference what one wears!" answered the doctor; "what is the use of dressing warmly if one can't produce heat within himself? It's like trying to heat ice by wrapping it up in wool! But Hatteras doesn't need it; he's built that way, and I should not be surprised if his side was as warm as the neighborhood of a glowing coal."

Johnson, who was charged with clearing away the water-hole every morning, noticed that the ice was ten feet thick.

Almost every night the doctor could observe the magnificent auroras; from four o'clock till eight of the evening, the sky in the north was slightly lighted up; then this took a regular shape, with a rim of light yellow, the ends of which seemed to touch the field of ice. Gradually the brilliancy arose in the heavens, following the magnetic meridian, and appeared striped with black bands; jets of luminosity shot with varying brightness here and there; when it reached the zenith it was often composed of several arcs bathed in waves of red, yellow, or green light. It was a dazzling sight. Soon the different curves met in a single point, and formed crowns of celestial richness. Finally the arcs all crowded together, the splendid aurora grew dim, the intense colors faded away into pale, vague, uncertain tints, and this wonderful phenomenon vanished gradually, insensibly, in the dark clouds of the south.

"Almost every night the doctor could observe the magnificent auroras."

It is difficult to realize the wonderful, magical beauty of such a spectacle in high latitudes, less than eight degrees from the pole; the auroras which are seen in the temperate zone give no idea of it; it seems as if Providence wished to reserve the greatest wonders for these regions.

Numerous mock-moons appeared also while the moon was shining, and a great many would appear in the sky, adding to the general brilliancy; often, too, simple lunar halos surrounded the moon with a circle of splendid lustre.

November 26th the tide rose very high, and the water came through the hole with great violence; the thick crust of ice seemed pushed up by the force of the sea, and the frequent cracking of the ice proclaimed the conflict that was going on beneath; fortunately the ship remained firm in her bed, but her chains worked noisily; it was as a precaution against just such an event, that Hatteras had made the brig fast.

The following days were still colder; a dense fog hid the sky; the wind tossed the snow about; it was hard to determine whether it came from the clouds or from the ice-fields; everything was in confusion.

The crew kept busy with various interior occupations, the principal one being the preparation of the grease and oil from the seal; it was frozen into blocks of ice, which had to be cut with a hatchet; it was broken into small fragments, which were as hard as marble; ten barrels full were collected. As may be seen, every vessel became nearly useless, besides the risk of its breaking when the contents froze.

The 28th the thermometer fell to -32°; there was only ten days' coal on board, and every one awaited with horror the moment when it should come to an end.

Hatteras, for the sake of economy, had the fire in the stove in the after-room put out; and from that time Shandon, the doctor, and he were compelled to betake themselves to the common-room of the crew. Hatteras was hence brought into constant communication with his men, who gazed at him with surly, dejected glances. He heard their fault-finding, their reproaches, even their threats, without being able to punish them. However, he seemed deaf to every remark. He never went near the fire. He remained in a corner, with folded arms, without saying a word.

In spite of the doctor's recommendations, Pen and his friends refused to take the slightest exercise; they passed whole days crouching about the stove or under their bedclothes; hence their health began to suffer; they could not react against the rigor of the climate, and scurvy soon made its appearance on board.

The doctor had long since begun to distribute, every morning, lemon-juice and lime pastilles; but these precautions, which were generally so efficacious, did very little good to the sick; and the disease, following its usual course, soon showed its most horrible symptoms.

Terrible indeed it was to see those wretches with their nerves and muscles contracted with pain! Their legs were fearfully swollen, and were covered with large bluish-black patches; their bleeding gums, their swollen lips, permitted them to utter only inarticulate sounds; their blood was poisoned, deprived of fibrine, and no longer carried life to the extremities.

Clifton was the first to be attacked by this cruel malady; soon Gripper, Brunton, and Strong had to keep to their hammocks. Those whom the illness spared could not avoid the sight of the sufferings of their friends; the common-room was the only place where they could stay; so it was soon transformed into a hospital, for of the eighteen sailors of the *Forward*, thirteen were soon down with scurvy. It seemed as if Pen would escape the contagion; his strong constitution preserved him; Shandon felt the first symptoms, but it went no further with him, and plenty of exercise soon restored him to good health.

The doctor tended his patients with the greatest devotion, and his heart would bleed at the sight of the sufferings he could not assuage. Still, he inspired as much cheerfulness as he could in the lonely crew; his words, his consolations, his philosophical reflections, his fortunate inventions, broke the monotony of those long days of suffering; he would read aloud to them; his wonderful memory kept him supplied with amusing anecdotes, while the men who were well stood pressing closely around the stove; but the groans of the sick, their complaints, and their cries of despair would continually interrupt him, and, breaking off in the middle of a story, he would become the devoted and attentive physician.

Besides, his health remained good; he did not grow thin; his corpulence stood him in better stead than the thickest raiment, and he used to say he was as well clad as a seal or a whale, who, thanks to their thick layers of fat, easily support the rigors of the winter.

Hatteras did not suffer physically or morally. The sufferings of the crew did not seem to depress him. Perhaps he would not let his emotions appear on his face, while an acute observer would have detected the heart of a man beneath this mask of iron.

The doctor analyzed him, studied him, and could not classify this strange organization, this unnatural temperament.

The thermometer fell still lower; the deck was entirely deserted; the Esquimaux dogs alone walked up and down it, barking dismally.

There was always a man on guard near the stove, who superintended putting on the coal; it was important not to let it go out; when the fire got low the cold crept into the room, formed on the walls, and the moisture suddenly condensed and fell in the form of snow on the unfortunate occupants of the brig.

It was among these terrible sufferings that they reached December 8th; that morning the doctor went as usual to look at the thermometer. He found the mercury entirely frozen in the bulb.

"Forty-four degrees below zero!" he said with terror.

And on that day the last piece of coal on board was thrown into the stove.

CHAPTER XXVII.

THE GREAT COLD AT CHRISTMAS.

For a moment he had a feeling of despair. The thought of death, and death by cold, appeared in all its horror; this last piece of coal burned with an ominous splutter; the fire seemed about to go out, and the temperature of the room fell noticeably. But Johnson went to get some of the new fuel which the marine animals had furnished to them, and with it he filled the stove; he added to it some tow filled with frozen oil, and soon obtained sufficient heat. The odor was almost unendurable; but how get rid of it? They had to get used to it. Johnson agreed that his plan was defective, and that it would not be considered a success in Liverpool.

"And yet," he added, "this unpleasant smell will, perhaps, produce good results."

"What are they?" asked the carpenter.

"It will doubtless attract the bears this way, for they are fond of the smell."

"Well," continued Bell, "what is the need of having bears?"

"Bell," replied Johnson, "we can't count on seals any longer; they're gone away, and for a long time; if bears don't come in their place to supply us with their share of fuel, I don't know what is to become of us."

"True, Johnson, our fate is very uncertain; our position is a most alarming one. And if this sort of fuel gives out, I don't see how—"

"There might be another—"

"Another?" asked Bell.

"Yes, Bell! in despair on account of—but the captain would never—but yet we shall perhaps have to come to it."

And Johnson shook his head sadly, and fell to thinking gloomily. Bell did not interrupt him. He knew that the supply of fat, which it had been so hard to acquire, would only last a week, even with the strictest economy.

The boatswain was right. A great many bears, attracted by the scent, were seen to leeward of the *Forward;* the healthy men gave chase; but these animals are very swift of foot, and crafty enough to escape most stratagems; it was impossible to get near them, and the most skilful gunners could not hit them.

The crew of the brig was in great danger of dying from the cold; it could not withstand, for forty-eight hours, such a temperature as would exist in the common-room. Every one looked forward with terror to getting to the end of the fuel.

Now this happened December 20th, at three o'clock in the afternoon; the fire went out; the sailors, grouped about the empty stove, gazed at one another with haggard eyes. Hatteras remained without moving in his corner; the doctor, as usual, paced up and down excitedly; he did not know what was to be done.

The temperature in the room fell at once to -7°.

But if the doctor was baffled and did not know what they should turn their hands to, others knew very well. So Shandon, cold and resolute, Pen, with wrath in his eyes, and two or three of his companions, such as he could induce to accompany him, walked towards Hatteras.

"Captain!" said Shandon.

Hatteras, absorbed in his thoughts, did not hear him.

"Captain!" repeated Shandon, touching him with his hand.

Hatteras arose.

"Sir," he said.

"Captain, the fire is out."

"Well?" continued Hatteras.

"If you intend that we shall freeze to death," Shandon went on with grim irony, "we should be glad if you would tell us."

"My intention," answered Hatteras with a deep voice, "is that every man shall do his duty to the end."

"There's something superior to duty, Captain," answered his first officer, "and that is the right of self-preservation. I repeat it, we have no fire; and if this goes on, in two days not one of us will be alive."

"I have no wood," answered Hatteras, gloomily.

"Well," shouted Pen, violently, "when the wood gives out, we must go cut it where it grows!"

Hatteras grew pale with anger.

"Where is that?" he asked.

"On board," answered the sailor, insolently.

"On board!" repeated the captain, with clinched fists and sparkling eyes.

"Of course," answered Pen, "when the ship can't carry the crew, the ship ought to be burned."

At the beginning of this sentence Hatteras had grasped an axe; at its end, this axe was raised above Pen's head.

"Wretch!" he cried.

The doctor sprang in front of Pen, and thrust him back; the axe fell on the floor, making a deep gash. Johnson, Bell, and Simpson gathered around Hatteras, and seemed determined to support him. But plaintive, grievous cries arose from the berths, transformed into death-beds.

"Fire, fire!" they cried, shivering beneath their now insufficient covering.

Hatteras by a violent effort controlled himself, and after a few moments of silence, he said calmly,—

"If we destroy the ship, how shall we get back to England?"

"Sir," answered Johnson, "perhaps we can without doing any material damage burn the less important parts, the bulwarks, the nettings—"

"The small boats will be left," said Shandon; "and besides, why might we not make a smaller vessel out of what is left of the old one?"

"Never!" answered Hatteras.

"But—" interposed many of the men, shouting together.

"We have a large quantity of spirits of wine," suggested Hatteras; "burn all of that."

"All right; we'll take the spirits of wine!" answered Johnson, assuming an air of confidence which he was far from feeling.

And with the aid of long wicks, dipped into this liquid of which the pale flame licked the walls of the stove, he was able to raise the temperature of the room a few degrees.

In the following days the wind came from the south again and the thermometer rose; the snow, however, kept falling. Some of the men were able to leave the ship for the driest hours of the day; but ophthalmia and scurvy kept most of them on board; besides, neither hunting nor fishing was possible.

But this was only a respite in the fearful severity of the cold, and on the 25th, after a sudden change of wind, the frozen mercury disappeared again in the bulb of the instrument; then they had to consult the spirit-thermometer, which does not freeze even in the most intense colds.

The doctor, to his great surprise, found it marking -66°. Seldom has man been called upon to endure so low a temperature.

The ice stretched in long, dark lines upon the floor; a dense mist filled the room; the dampness fell in the form of thick snow; the men could not see one another; their extremities grew cold and blue; their heads felt as if they wore an iron band; and their thoughts grew confused and dull, as if they were half delirious. A terrible symptom was that their tongues refused to articulate a sound.

From the day the men threatened to burn the ship, Hatteras would walk for hours upon the deck, keeping watch. This wood was flesh and blood to him. Cutting a piece from it would have been like cutting off a limb. He was armed, and he kept constant guard, without minding the cold, the snow, or the ice, which stiffened his clothing as if it covered it with a granite cuirass. Duke understood him, and followed him, barking and howling.

"He was armed, and he kept constant guard, without minding the cold, the snow, or the ice."

Nevertheless, December 25th he went down into the common-room. The doctor, with all the energy he had left, went up to him and said,—

"Hatteras, we are going to die from want of fire!"

"Never!" said Hatteras, knowing very well what request he was refusing.

"We must," continued the doctor, mildly.

"Never!" repeated Hatteras more firmly; "I shall never give my consent! Whoever wishes, may disobey me."

Thus was permission given them. Johnson and Bell hastened to the deck. Hatteras heard the wood of the brig crashing under the axe, and wept.

That was Christmas Day, the great family festival in England, one specially devoted to the amusement of the children. What a painful recollection was that of the happy children gathered about the green Christmas tree! Every one recalled the huge pieces of roast meat, cut from the fattened ox, and the tarts, the mince-pies, and other luxuries so dear to the English heart! But here was nothing but suffering, despair, and wretchedness, and for the Christmas log, these pieces of a ship lost in the middle of the frigid zone!

Nevertheless, under the genial influence of the fire, the spirits and strength of the men returned; the hot tea and coffee brought great and immediate consolation, and hope is so firm a friend of man, that they even began to hope for some luckier fate. It was thus that the year 1860 passed away, the early winter of which had so interfered with Hatteras's plans.

Now it happened that this very New Year's Day was marked by an unexpected discovery. It was a little milder than the previous days had been; the doctor had resumed his studies; he was reading Sir Edward Belcher's account of his expedition in the polar regions. Suddenly, a passage which he had never noticed before filled him with astonishment; he read it over again; doubt was no longer possible.

Sir Edward Belcher states that, having come to the end of Queen's Channel, he found there many traces of the presence of men. He says:—

"There are remains of dwellings far superior to what can be attributed to the savage habits of the wandering tribes of Esquimaux. The walls are firmly placed on deep-dug foundations; the inside, covered with a thick layer of gravel, has been paved. Skeletons of moose, reindeer, and seals abound. We found coal there."

At these last words an idea occurred to the doctor; he took his book and ran to tell Hatteras.

"Coal!" shouted the captain.

"Yes, Hatteras, coal; that is to say, our preservation!"

"Coal, on this lonely shore!" continued Hatteras; "no, that's impossible!"

"How can you doubt it, Hatteras? Belcher would not have mentioned it if he had not been sure, without having seen it with his own eyes."

"Well, what then, Doctor?"

"We are not a hundred miles from the place where Belcher saw this coal! What is a journey of a hundred miles? Nothing. Longer expeditions have often been made on the ice, and with the cold as intense. Let us go after it, Captain!"

"We'll go!" said Hatteras, who had made up his mind quickly; and with his active imagination he saw the chance of safety.

Johnson was informed of the plan, of which he approved highly; he told his companions; some rejoiced, others heard of it with indifference.

"Coal on these shores!" said Wall from his sick-bed.

"We'll let them go," answered Shandon, mysteriously.

But before they had begun to make preparations for the trip, Hatteras wanted to fix the position of the *Forward* with the utmost exactitude. The importance of this calculation it is easy to see. Once away from the ship, it could not be found again without knowing its position precisely.

So Hatteras went up on deck; he took observations at different moments of several lunar distances, and the altitude of the principal stars. He found, however, much difficulty in doing this, for when the temperature was so low, the glass and the mirrors of the instrument were covered with a crust of ice from Hatteras's breath; more than once his eyelids were burned by touching the copper eye-pieces. Still, he was able to get very exact bases for his calculations, and he returned to the common-room to work them out. When he had finished, he raised his head with stupefaction, took his chart, marked it, and looked at the doctor.

"Well?" asked the latter.

"What was our latitude when we went into winter-quarters?"

"Our latitude was 78° 15', and the longitude 95° 35', exactly the pole of cold."

"Well," added Hatteras in a low voice, "our ice-field is drifting! We are two degrees farther north and farther west,—at least three hundred miles from your coal-supply!"

"And these poor men who know nothing about it!" cried the doctor.

"Not a word!" said Hatteras, raising his finger to his lips.

CHAPTER XXVIII.

PREPARATIONS FOR DEPARTURE.

Hatteras did not wish to let his crew know about this new condition of affairs. He was right. If they had known that they were being driven towards the north with irresistible force, they would have given way to despair. The doctor knew this, and approved of the captain's silence.

Hatteras had kept to himself the impressions which this discovery had caused within him. It was his first moment of joy during these long months of struggle with the hostile elements. He was one hundred and fifty miles farther north; hardly eight degrees from the Pole! But he hid his joy so well that the doctor did not even suspect it; he asked himself why Hatteras's eye shone with so unusual a lustre; but that was all, and the natural reply to this question did not enter his head.

The *Forward*, as it approached the Pole, had drifted away from the coal which had been seen by Sir Edward Belcher; instead of a hundred miles, it would have to be sought two hundred and fifty miles farther south. Still, after a short discussion between Hatteras and Clawbonny, they determined to make the attempt.

If Belcher was right, and his accuracy could not be doubted, they would find everything just at he had left it. Since 1853, no new expedition had visited these remote continents. Few, if any, Esquimaux are found in this latitude. The disaster which had befallen at Beechey Island could not be repeated on the shores of North Cornwall. Everything seemed to favor an excursion across the ice.

They estimated that they would be gone forty days at the outside, and preparations were made by Johnson for that time of absence.

In the first place, he saw about the sledge; it was of the shape of those used in Greenland, thirty-five inches broad and twenty-four feet long. The Esquimaux sometimes make them fifty feet long. It was built of long planks, bent at each end, and kept in position by two strong cords. This shape adapted it to resist violent shocks. The sledge ran easily upon the ice; but before the snow had hardened, it was necessary to place two vertical frames near together, and being raised in this way, it could run on without cutting too much into the snow. Besides, by rubbing it with a mixture of sulphur and snow in the Esquimaux fashion, it ran very easily.

It was drawn by six dogs; they were strong in spite of their thinness, and did not appear to be injured by the severity of the winter; the harnesses of deerskin were in good condition; perfect reliance could be placed on the equipment, which the Greenlanders at Upernavik had sold in conscience. These six animals alone could draw a weight of two thousand pounds without inordinate fatigue.

They carried with them a tent, in case it should be impossible to build a snow-house; a large sheet of mackintosh to spread over the snow, so that it should not melt at contact with their bodies; and, last of all, many coverings of wool and buffalo-skin. In addition, they carried the Halkett-boat.

Their provisions consisted of five chests of pemmican, weighing four hundred and fifty pounds; a pound of pemmican was allotted for each man and dog; of the latter there were seven, including Duke; there were to be four men. They carried, besides, twelve gallons of spirits of wine, weighing nearly a hundred and fifty pounds; tea and biscuit, in proper amounts; a little portable kitchen, with a great many wicks; and much tow, ammunition, and four double-barrelled guns. The men of the party made use of Captain Parry's invention, and wore girdles of india-rubber in which the heat of the body and the motion in walking could keep tea, coffee, and water in a liquid state.

Johnson took special care of the preparation of snow-shoes, with their wooden frames and leathern straps; they served as skates; on thoroughly frozen spots deerskin moccasins could be worn with comfort; every man carried two pairs of each.

These preparations, which were so important because the omission of a single detail might have caused the ruin of the whole expedition, required four whole days. Every day at noon Hatteras took an observation of the ship's position; it was no longer drifting, and this had to be perfectly sure in order to secure their return.

Hatteras undertook to choose the four men who were to accompany him. It was not an easy decision to take; some it was not advisable to take, but then the question of leaving them on board had also to be considered. Still, the common safety demanded the success of this trip, and the captain deemed it right to choose sure and experienced men.

Hence Shandon was left out, but not much to his regret. James Wall was too ill to go. The sick grew no worse; their treatment consisted of repeated rubbing and strong doses of lemon-juice; this was easily seen to without the presence of the doctor being essential. Hence he enrolled himself among those who should go, and no voice was raised against it. Johnson would have gladly gone with the captain in his dangerous expedition; but Hatteras drew him to one side and said to him in an affectionate, almost weeping voice,—

"Johnson, you are the only man I can trust. You are the only officer with whom I can leave the ship. I must know that you are here to keep an eye on Shandon and the others. They are kept to the ship by the winter; but who can say what plans they are not capable of forming? You shall receive my formal instructions, which shall place the command in your hands. You shall take my place. We shall be absent four or five weeks at the most, and I shall be at ease having you here where I cannot be. You need wood, Johnson. I know it! But, as much as possible, spare my ship. Do you understand, Johnson?"

"I understand, Captain," answered the old sailor, "and I will remain if you prefer it."

"Thanks!" said Hatteras, pressing the boatswain's hand; and he added, "In case we don't come back, Johnson, wait till the next thaw, and try to push on to the Pole. If the rest refuse, don't think of us, but take the *Forward* back to England."

"That is your wish, Captain?"

"It is," answered Hatteras.

"Your orders shall be obeyed," said Johnson, quietly.

The doctor regretted that his friend was not going to accompany him, but he was obliged to recognize the wisdom of Hatteras's plan.

His two other companions were Bell the carpenter, and Simpson. The first, who was sturdy, brave, and devoted, would be of great service in their camping in the snow; the other, although less resolute, nevertheless determined to take part in this expedition in which he might be of use as hunter and fisher.

So this detachment consisted of Hatteras, Clawbonny, Bell, Simpson, and the faithful Duke, making in all four men and seven dogs to be fed. A suitable amount of provisions was made ready.

During the early days of January the mean temperature was -33°. Hatteras waited impatiently for milder weather; he frequently consulted the barometer, but no confidence could be placed in this instrument, which in these high latitudes seems to lose some of its customary accuracy; in these regions there are many exceptions to the general laws of nature: for instance, a clear sky was not always accompanied by cold, nor did a fall of snow raise the temperature; the barometer was uncertain, as many explorers in these seas have noticed; it used to fall when the wind was from the north or east; when low it foretold fine weather; when high, rain or snow. Hence its indications could hardly be relied on.

Finally, January 5th an easterly breeze brought with it a rise in the thermometer of fifteen degrees, so that it stood at -18°. Hatteras resolved to start the next day; he could no longer endure seeing his ship torn to pieces before his eyes; the whole quarter-deck had been burned up.

So, January 6th, amid squalls of snow, the order to depart was given; the doctor gave his last words of advice to the sick; Bell and Simpson shook hands silently with their companions. Hatteras wanted to make a farewell speech to the men, but he saw nothing but angry faces around him. He fancied he saw an ironical smile playing about Shandon's lips. He held his peace. Perhaps he had a momentary pang at parting as he gazed at the *Forward*.

But it was too late for him to change his mind; the sledge, loaded and harnessed, was waiting on the ice; Bell was the first to move; the others followed. Johnson accompanied the travellers for a quarter of a mile; then Hatteras asked him to return, which he did after a long leave-taking. At that moment, Hatteras, turning for the last time towards the brig, saw the tops of her masts disappearing in the dark snow-clouds.

CHAPTER XXIX.

ACROSS THE ICE-FIELDS.

The little band made their way towards the southeast. Simpson drove the sledge. Duke aided him much, without being disturbed at the occupation of his mates. Hatteras and the doctor followed behind on foot, while Bell, who was charged with making a road, went on in advance, testing the ice with the iron point of his stick.

"The little band made their way towards the southeast."

The rise in the thermometer foretold a fall of snow, and soon it came, beginning in large flakes. This added to the hardships of their journey; they kept straying from a straight line; they could not go quickly; nevertheless, they averaged three miles an hour.

The ice-field, under the pressure of the frost, presented an unequal surface; the sledge was often nearly turned over, but they succeeded in saving it.

Hatteras and his companions wrapped themselves up in their fur clothes cut in the Greenland fashion; they were not cut with extraordinary neatness, but they suited the needs of the climate; their faces were enclosed in a narrow hood which could not be penetrated by the snow or wind; their mouths, noses, and eyes were alone exposed to the air, and they did not need to be protected against it; nothing is so inconvenient as scarfs and nose-protectors, which soon are stiff with ice; at night they have to be cut away, which, even in the arctic seas, is a poor way of undressing. It was necessary to leave free passage for the breath, which would freeze at once on anything it met.

The boundless plain stretched out with tiresome monotony; everywhere there appeared heaped-up ice-hills, hummocks, blocks, and icebergs, separated by winding valleys; they walked staff in hand, saying but little. In this cold atmosphere, to open the mouth was painful; sharp crystals of ice suddenly formed between the lips, and the heat of the breath could not melt them. Their progress was silent, and every one beat the ice with his staff. Bell's footsteps were visible in the fresh snow; they followed them mechanically, and where he had passed, the others could go safely.

Numerous tracks of bears and foxes crossed one another everywhere; but during this first day not one could be seen; to chase them would have been dangerous and useless: they would only have overloaded the already heavy sledge.

Generally, in excursions of this sort, travellers take the precaution of leaving supplies along their path; they hide them from the animals, in the snow, thus lightening themselves for their trip, and on their return they take the supplies which they did not have the trouble of carrying with them.

Hatteras could not employ this device on an ice-field which perhaps was moving; on firm land it would have been possible; and the uncertainty of their route made it doubtful whether they would return by the same path.

At noon, Hatteras halted his little troop in the shelter of an ice-wall; they dined off pemmican and hot tea; the strengthening qualities of this beverage produced general comfort, and the travellers drank a large quantity. After an hour's rest they started on again; in the first day they walked about twenty miles; that evening men and dogs were tired out.

Still, in spite of their fatigue, they had to build a snow-house in which to pass the night; the tent would not have been enough. This took them an hour and a half. Bell was very skilful; the blocks of ice, which were cut with a knife, were placed on top of one another with astonishing rapidity, and they took the shape of a dome, and a last piece, the keystone of the arch, established the solidity of the building; the soft snow served as mortar in the interstices; it soon hardened and made the whole building of a single piece.

Access was had into this improvised grotto by means of a narrow opening, through which it was necessary to crawl on one's hands and knees; the doctor found some difficulty in entering, and the others followed. Supper was soon prepared on the alcohol cooking-stove. The temperature inside was very comfortable; the wind, which was raging without, could not get in.

"Sit down!" soon shouted the doctor in his most genial manner.

And this meal, though the same as the dinner, was shared by all. When it was finished their only thought was sleep; the mackintoshes, spread out upon the snow, protected them from the dampness. At the flame of the portable stove they dried their clothes; then three of them, wrapped up in their woollen coverings, fell asleep, while one was left on watch; he had to keep a lookout on the safety of all, and to prevent the opening from being closed, otherwise they ran a risk of being buried alive.

Duke shared their quarters; the other dogs remained without, and after they had eaten their supper they lay down and were soon hidden by the snow.

Their fatigue soon brought sound sleep. The doctor took the watch until three of the morning. In the night the hurricane raged furiously. Strange was the situation of these lonely men lost in the snow, enclosed in this vault with its walls rapidly thickening under the snow-fall.

The next morning at six o'clock their monotonous march was resumed; there were ever before them the same valleys and icebergs, a uniformity which made the choice of a path difficult. Still, a fall of several degrees in the temperature made their way easier by hardening the snow. Often they came across little elevations, which looked like cairns or storing-places of the Esquimaux; the doctor had one destroyed to satisfy his curiosity, but he found nothing except a cake of ice.

"What do you expect to find, Clawbonny?" asked Hatteras; "are we not the first men to penetrate into this part of the globe?"

"Probably," answered the doctor, "but who knows?"

"Don't let us waste our time in useless searching," resumed the captain; "I am in a hurry to rejoin the ship, even if this long-wanted fuel should not be found."

"I have great hopes of finding it," said the doctor.

"Doctor," Hatteras used to say frequently, "I did wrong to leave the *Forward;* it was a mistake! The captain's place is on board, and nowhere else."

"Johnson is there."

"Yes! but—let us hurry on!"

They advanced rapidly; Simpson's voice could be heard urging on the dogs; they ran along on a brilliant surface, all aglow with a phosphorescent light, and the runners of the sledge seemed to toss up a shower of sparks. The doctor ran on ahead to examine this snow, when suddenly, as he was trying to jump upon a hummock, he disappeared from sight. Bell, who was near him, ran at once towards the place.

"Well, Doctor," he cried anxiously, while Hatteras and Simpson joined him, "where are you?"

"Doctor!" shouted the captain.

"Down here, at the bottom of a hole," was the quiet answer. "Throw me a piece of rope, and I'll come up to the surface of the globe."

They threw a rope down to the doctor, who was at the bottom of a pit about ten feet deep; he fastened it about his waist, and his three companions drew him up with some difficulty.

"Are you hurt?" asked Hatteras.

"No, there's no harm done," answered the doctor, wiping the snow from his smiling face.

"But how did it happen?"

"O, it was in consequence of the refraction," he answered, laughing; "I thought I had about a foot to step over, and I fell into this deep hole! These optical illusions are the only ones left me, my friends, and it's hard to escape from them! Let that be a lesson to us all never to take a step forward without first testing the ice with a staff, for our senses cannot be depended on. Here our ears hear wrong, and our eyes deceive us! It's a curious country!"

"Can you go on?" asked the captain.

"Go on, Hatteras, go on! This little fall has done me more good than harm."

They resumed their march to the southeast, and at evening they halted, after walking about twenty-five miles; they were all tired, but still the doctor had energy enough to ascend an ice-mountain while the snow-hut was building.

"The doctor had energy enough to ascend an ice-mountain while the snow-hut was building."

The moon, which was nearly at its full, shone with extraordinary brilliancy in a clear sky; the stars were wonderfully brilliant; from the top of the iceberg a boundless plain could be seen, which was covered with strangely formed hillocks of ice; in the moonlight they looked like fallen columns or overthrown tombstones; the scene reminded the doctor of a huge, silent graveyard barren of trees, in which twenty generations of human beings might be lying in their long sleep.

In spite of the cold and fatigue, Clawbonny remained for a long time in a revery, from which it was no easy task for his companions to arouse him; but they had to think of resting; the snow-hut was completed; the four travellers crawled in like moles, and soon were all asleep.

The following days went on without any particular incident; at times they went on slowly, at times quickly, with varying ease, according to the changes in the weather; they wore moccasins or snow-shoes, as the nature of the ice demanded.

In this way they went on till January 15th; the moon, now in its last quarter, was hardly visible; the sun, although always beneath the horizon, gave a sort of twilight for six hours every day, but not enough to light up the route, which had to be directed by the compass. Then Bell went on ahead; Hatteras followed next; Simpson and the doctor sought also to keep in a straight line behind, with their eyes on Hatteras alone; and yet, in spite of all their efforts, they often got thirty or forty degrees from the right way, much to their annoyance.

Sunday, January 15th, Hatteras judged that they had come about one hundred miles to the south; this morning was set aside to mending their clothes and materials; the reading of divine service was not forgotten.

At noon they started again; the temperature was very low; the thermometer marked only -22°; the air was very clear.

Suddenly, without warning, a frozen vapor arose into the air from the ice, to a height of about ninety feet, and hung motionless; no one could see a foot before him; this vapor formed in long, sharp crystals upon their clothing.

The travellers, surprised by this phenomenon, which is called frost-rime, only thought of getting together; so immediately various shouts were heard:—

"O Simpson!"

"Bell, this way!"

"Dr. Clawbonny!"

"Doctor!"

"Captain, where are you?"

They began to look for one another with outstretched arms, wandering through the fog which their eyes could not pierce. But to their disappointment they could hear no answer; the vapor seemed incapable of carrying sound.

Each one then thought of firing his gun as a signal to the others. But if their voices were too feeble, the reports of the fire-arms were too loud; for the echoes, repeated in every direction, made but a confused roar, in which no particular direction could be perceived.

Then they began to act, each one as he thought best. Hatteras stood still and folded his arms. Simpson contented himself with stopping the sledge. Bell retraced his steps, feeling them with his hand. The doctor, stumbling over the blocks of ice, wandered here and there, getting more and more bewildered.

At the end of five minutes he said to himself,—

"This can't last long! Singular climate! This is too much! There is nothing to help us, without speaking of these sharp crystals which cut my face. Halloo, Captain!" he shouted again.

But he heard no answer; he fired his gun, but in spite of his thick gloves the iron burned his hands. Meanwhile he thought he saw a confused mass moving near him.

"There's some one," he said. "Hatteras! Bell! Simpson! Is that you? Come, answer!"

A dull roar was alone heard.

"Ah!" thought the doctor, "what is that?"

The object approached; it lost its first size and appeared in more definite shape. A terrible thought flashed into the doctor's mind.

"A bear!" he said to himself.

In fact, it was a huge bear; lost in the fog, it came and went with great danger to the men, whose presence it certainly did not suspect.

"Matters are growing complicated!" thought the doctor, standing still.

Sometimes he felt the animal's breath, which was soon lost in the frost-rime; again he would see the monster's huge paws beating the air so near him that his clothes were occasionally torn by its sharp claws; he jumped back, and the animal disappeared like a phantasmagoric spectre.

But as he sprang back he found an elevation beneath his feet; he climbed up first one block of ice, then another, feeling his way with his staff.

"An iceberg!" he said to himself; "if I can get to the top I am safe."

With these words he climbed up an elevation of about ninety feet with surprising agility; he arose above the frozen mist, the top of which was sharply defined.

"Good!" he said to himself; and looking about him he saw his three companions emerging from the vapor.

"Hatteras!"

"Dr. Clawbonny!"

"Bell!"

"Simpson!"

These names were shouted out almost at the same time; the sky, lit up by a magnificent halo, sent forth pale rays which colored the frost-rime as if it were a cloud, and the top of the icebergs seemed to rise from a mass of molten silver. The travellers found themselves within a circle of less than a hundred feet in diameter. Thanks to the purity of the air in this upper layer in this low temperature, their words could be easily heard, and they were able to talk on the top of this iceberg. After the first shots, each one, hearing no answer, had only thought of climbing above the mist.

"The sledge!" shouted the captain.

"It's eighty feet beneath us," answered Simpson.

"Is it all right?"

"All right."

"And the bear?" asked the doctor.

"What bear?" said Bell.

"A bear!" said Hatteras; "let's go down."

"No!" said the doctor; "we shall lose our way, and have to begin it all over again."

"And if he eats our dogs—" said Hatteras.

At that moment Duke was heard barking, the sound rising through the mist.

"That's Duke!" shouted Hatteras; "there's something wrong. I'm going down."

All sorts of howling arose to their ears; Duke and the dogs were barking furiously. The noise sounded like a dull murmur, like the roar of a crowded, noisy room. They knew that some invisible struggle was going on below, and the mist was occasionally agitated like the sea when marine monsters are fighting.

"Duke, Duke!" shouted the captain, as he made ready to enter again into the frost-rime.

"Wait a moment, Hatteras,—wait a moment! It seems to me that the fog is lifting."

It was not lifting, but sinking, like water in a pool; it appeared to be descending into the ground from which it had risen; the summits of the icebergs grew larger; others, which had been hidden, arose like new islands; by an optical illusion, which may be easily imagined, the travellers, clinging to these ice-cones, seemed to be rising in the air, while the top of the mist sank beneath them.

Soon the top of the sledge appeared, then the harnessed dogs, and then about thirty other animals, then great objects moving confusedly, and Duke leaping about with his head alternately rising and sinking in the frozen mist.

"Foxes!" shouted Bell.

"Bears!" said the doctor; "one, two, three."

"Our dogs, our provisions!" cried Simpson.

A troop of foxes and bears, having come across the sledge, were ravaging the provisions. Their instinct of pillaging united them in perfect harmony; the dogs were barking furiously, but the animals paid no heed, but went on in their work of destruction.

"Fire!" shouted the captain, discharging his piece.

"'Fire!' shouted the captain, discharging his piece."

His companions did the same. But at the combined report the bears, raising their heads and uttering a singular roar, gave the signal to depart; they fell into a little trot which a galloping horse could not have kept up with, and, followed by the foxes, they soon disappeared amid the ice to the north.

CHAPTER XXX.

THE CAIRN.

This phenomenon, which is peculiar to the polar regions, had lasted three quarters of an hour; the bears and foxes had had plenty of time; these provisions arrived opportunely for these animals, who were nearly starved during the inclement weather; the canvas cover of the sledge was torn by their strong claws, the casks of pemmican were opened and emptied; the biscuit-sacks pillaged, the tea spilled over the snow, a barrel of alcohol torn open and its contents lost, their camping materials scattered and damaged, bore witness to the ferocity of these wild beasts, and their greediness.

"This is a misfortune," said Bell, gazing at this scene of ruin.

"Which is probably irreparable," said Simpson.

"Let us first estimate the loss," interrupted the doctor, "and we'll talk about it afterwards."

Hatteras, without saying a word, began to gather the scattered boxes and sacks; they collected the pemmican and biscuits which could be eaten; the loss of part of their alcohol was much to be regretted; for if that was gone there would be nothing warm to drink; no tea, no coffee. In making an inventory of the supplies left, the doctor found two hundred pounds of pemmican gone, and a hundred and fifty pounds of biscuit; if their journey continued they would have to subsist on half-rations.

They then began to discuss what should be done, whether they should return to the ship and start out again. But how could they make up their minds to lose the hundred and fifty miles they had already made? To return without fuel would have a depressing effect upon the spirits of the crew. Could men be found again to resume their march across the ice?

Evidently it was better to push on, even at the risk of severe privations.

The doctor, Hatteras, and Bell were of this opinion; Simpson wanted to go back; the fatigue of the journey had worn upon his health; he was visibly weaker; but finding himself alone of this opinion, he resumed his place at the head of the sledge, and the little caravan continued its journey to the south.

During the three next days, from the 15th to the 17th of January, all the monotonous incidents of the voyage were repeated; they advanced more slowly, and with much fatigue; their legs grew tired; the dogs dragged the sledge with difficulty; their diminished supply of food could not comfort men or beasts. The weather was very variable, changing from intense, dry cold to damp, penetrating mists.

January 18th the aspect of the ice-fields changed suddenly; a great number of peaks, like sharp-pointed pyramids, and very high, appeared at the horizon; the ground in certain places came through the snow; it seemed formed of gneiss, schist, and quartz, with some appearance of limestone. The travellers at last touched earth again, and this land they judged to be that called North Cornwall.

The doctor could not help striking the earth with joy; they had now only a hundred miles to go before reaching Cape Belcher, but their fatigue increased strangely on this soil, covered with sharp rocks, and interspersed with dangerous points, crevasses, and precipices; they had to go down into the depths of these abysses, climb steep ascents, and cross narrow gorges, in which the snow was drifted to the depth of thirty or forty feet.

The travellers soon regretted the almost easy journey over the ice-fields, which so well suited the sledge; now it had to be dragged by main force; the weary dogs were insufficient; the men, compelled to take their place alongside of them, wore themselves out with hauling; often they had to take off the whole load to get over some steep hills; a place only ten feet wide often kept them busy for hours; so in this first day they made only five miles in North Cornwall, which is certainly well named, for it exhibits all the roughness, the sharp points, the steep gorges, the confused rockiness, of the southwest coast of England.

- 243 -

The next day the sledge reached the top of the hills near the shore; the exhausted travellers, being unable to make a snow-hut, were obliged to pass the night under the tent, wrapped up in buffalo-skins, and drying their wet stockings by placing them about their bodies. The inevitable consequences of such conduct are easily comprehended; that night the thermometer fell below -44°, and the mercury froze.

Simpson's health caused great anxiety; a persistent cough, violent rheumatism, and intolerable pain obliged him to lie on the sledge which he could no longer guide. Bell took his place; he too was suffering, but not so much as to be incapacitated. The doctor also felt the consequences of this trip in this terrible weather; but he uttered no complaint; he walked on, resting on his staff; he made out the way and helped every one. Hatteras, impassible, and as strong as on the first day, followed the sledge in silence.

January 20th the weather was so severe that the slightest effort produced complete prostration. Still, the difficulties of the way were so great, that Hatteras, the doctor, and Bell harnessed themselves with the dogs; sudden shocks had broken the front of the sledge, and they had to stop to repair it. Such delays were frequent every day.

The travellers followed a deep ravine, up to their waists in snow, and perspiring violently in spite of the intense cold. They did not say a word. Suddenly Bell, who was near the doctor, looked at him with some alarm; then, without uttering a word, he picked up a handful of snow and began rubbing his companion's face violently.

"Well, Bell!" said the doctor, resisting.

- 244 -

But Bell continued rubbing.

"Come, Bell," began the doctor again, his mouth, nose, and eyes full of snow, "are you mad? What's the matter?"

"If you have a nose left," answered Bell, "you ought to be grateful to me."

"A nose!" answered the doctor, quickly, clapping his hand to his face.

"Yes, Doctor, you were frost-bitten; your nose was white when I looked at you, and if I had not done as I did, you would have lost that ornament which is in the way on a journey, but agreeable to one's existence."

In fact, the doctor's nose was almost frozen; the circulation of the blood was restored in time, and, thanks to Bell, all danger was gone.

"Thanks, Bell!" said the doctor; "I'll be even with you yet."

"I hope so, Doctor," the carpenter answered; "and may Heaven protect us from worse misfortunes!"

"Alas, Bell," continued the doctor, "you mean Simpson! The poor fellow is suffering terribly."

"Do you fear for his life?" asked Hatteras, quickly.

"Yes, Captain," answered the doctor.

"And why?"

"He has a violent attack of scurvy; his legs have begun to swell, and his gums too; the poor fellow lies half frozen on the sledge, and every movement redoubles his suffering. I pity him, Hatteras, and I can't do anything to relieve him."

"Poor Simpson!" murmured Bell.

"Perhaps we shall have to halt for a day or two," resumed the doctor.

"Halt!" shouted Hatteras, "when the lives of eighteen men are hanging on our return!"

"Still—" said the doctor.

"Clawbonny, Bell, listen to me," said Hatteras; "we have food for only twenty days! Judge for yourselves whether we can stop for a moment!"

Neither the doctor nor Bell made any reply, and the sledge resumed its progress, which had been delayed for a moment. That evening they stopped beneath a hillock of ice, in which Bell at once cut a cavern; the travellers entered it; the doctor passed the night attending to Simpson; the scurvy had already made fearful ravages, and his sufferings caused perpetual laments to issue from his swollen lips.

"Ah, Dr. Clawbonny!"

"Courage, my dear fellow!" said the doctor.

"I shall never get well! I feel it! I'd rather die!"

The doctor answered these despairing words by incessant cares; although worn out by the fatigue of the day, he spent the night in composing a soothing potion for his patient; but the lime-juice was ineffectual, and continual friction could not keep down the progress of the scurvy.

The next day he had to be placed again upon the sledge, although he besought them to leave him behind to die in peace; then they resumed their dreary and difficult march.

The frozen mists penetrated the three men to the bone; the snow and sleet dashed against them; they were working like draught-horses, and with a scanty supply of food.

Duke, like his master, kept coming and going, enduring every fatigue, always alert, finding out by himself the best path; they had perfect confidence in his wonderful instinct.

During the morning of January 23d, amid almost total darkness, for the moon was new, Duke had run on ahead; for many hours he was not seen;

Hatteras became uneasy, especially because there were many traces of bears to be seen; he was uncertain what to do, when suddenly a loud barking was heard.

Hatteras urged on the sledge, and soon he found the faithful animal at the bottom of a ravine. Duke stood as motionless as if turned to stone, barking before a sort of cairn made of pieces of limestone, covered with a cement of ice.

"This time," said the doctor, detaching his harness, "it's a cairn, there's no doubt of that."

"What's that to us?" asked Hatteras.

"Hatteras, if it is a cairn, it may contain some document of value for us; perhaps some provisions, and it would be worth while to see."

"What European could have come as far as this?" asked Hatteras, shrugging his shoulders.

"But in lack of Europeans," answered the doctor, "cannot Esquimaux have made it here to contain what they have fished or shot? It's their habit, I think."

"Well, go and look at it," continued Hatteras; "but I'm afraid it will be hardly worth your while."

Clawbonny and Bell walked to the cairn with picks in their hands. Duke continued barking furiously. The limestones were firmly fastened together by the ice; but a few blows scattered them on the ground.

"There's something there, evidently," said the doctor.

"I think so," answered Bell.

They rapidly destroyed the cairn. Soon they found a bundle and in it a damp paper. The doctor took it with a beating heart. Hatteras ran forward, seized the paper, and read:—

"Altam..., *Porpoise*, December 13, 1860, longitude 12..°, latitude 8..° 35'."

"The *Porpoise?*" said the doctor.

"The *Porpoise!*" replied Hatteras. "I never heard of a ship of this name in these seas."

"It is clear," resumed the doctor, "that travellers, perhaps shipwrecked sailors, have been here within two months."

"That is sure," said Bell.

"What are we going to do?" asked the doctor.

"Push on," answered Hatteras, coldly. "I don't know anything about any ship called the *Porpoise*, but I know that the brig *Forward* is waiting for our return."

CHAPTER XXXI.

THE DEATH OF SIMPSON.

They resumed their journey; the mind of every one was filled with new and unexpected ideas, for to meet any one in these regions is about the most remarkable event that can happen. Hatteras frowned uneasily.

"The *Porpoise!*" he kept saying to himself; "what ship is that? And what is it doing so near the Pole?"

At the thought, he shuddered. The doctor and Bell only thought of the two results which might follow the discovery of this document, that they might be of service in saving some one, or, possibly, that they might be saved by them. But the difficulties, obstacles, and dangers soon returned, and they could only think of their perilous position.

"They could only think of their perilous position."

Simpson's condition grew worse; the doctor could not be mistaken about the symptoms of a speedy death. He could do nothing; he was himself suffering from a painful ophthalmia, which might be accompanied by deafness if he did not take care. The twilight at that time gave light enough, and this light, reflected by the snow, was bad for the eyes; it was hard to protect them from the reflection, for glasses would be soon covered with a layer of ice which rendered them useless. Hence they had to guard carefully against accident by the way, and they had to run the risk of ophthalmia; still, the doctor and Bell covered their eyes and took turns in guiding the sledge.

It ran far from smoothly on its worn runners; it became harder and harder to drag it; their path grew more difficult; the land was of volcanic origin, and all cut up with craters; the travellers had been compelled gradually to ascend fifteen hundred feet to reach the top of the mountains. The temperature was lower, the storms were more violent, and it was a sorry sight to see these poor men on these lonely peaks.

They were also made sick by the whiteness of everything; the uniform brilliancy tired them; it made them giddy; the earth seemed to wave beneath their feet with no fixed point on the immense white surface; they felt as one does on shipboard when the deck seems to be giving way beneath the foot; they could not get over the impression, and the persistence of the feeling wearied their heads. Their limbs grew torpid, their minds grew dull, and often they walked like men half asleep; then a slip or a sudden fall would rouse them for a few moments from their sluggishness.

January 25th they began to descend the steep slopes, which was even more fatiguing; a false step, which it was by no means easy to avoid, might hurl them down into deep ravines where they would certainly have perished. Towards evening a violent tempest raged about the snowy summit; it was impossible to withstand the force of the hurricane; they had to lie down on the ground, but so low was the temperature that they ran a risk of being frozen to death at once.

Bell, with Hatteras's aid, built with much difficulty a snow-house, in which the poor men sought shelter; there they partook of a few fragments of pemmican and a little hot tea; only four gallons of alcohol were left; and they had to use this to allay their thirst, for snow cannot be absorbed if taken in its natural state; it has to be melted first. In the temperate zone, where the cold hardly ever sinks much below the freezing-point, it can do no harm; but beyond the Polar Circle it is different; it reaches so low a temperature that the bare hand can no more touch it than it can iron at a white heat, and this, although it is a very poor conductor of heat; so great is the difference of temperature between it and the stomach that its absorption produces real suffocation. The Esquimaux prefer severe thirst to quenching it with this snow, which does not replace water, and only augments the thirst instead of appeasing it. The only way the travellers could make use of it was by melting it over the spirit-lamp.

At three in the morning, when the tempest was at its height, the doctor took his turn at the watch; he was lying in a corner of the hut when a groan of distress from Simpson attracted his attention; he arose to see to him, but in rising he hit his head sharply against the icy roof; without paying any attention to that, he bent over Simpson and began to rub his swollen, discolored legs; after doing this for a quarter of an hour he started to rise, and bumped his head again, although he was on his knees.

"That's odd," he said to himself.

He raised his hand above his head; the roof was perceptibly sinking.

"Great God!" he cried; "wake up, my friends!"

At his shouts Hatteras and Bell arose quickly, striking their heads against the roof; they were in total darkness.

"We shall be crushed!" said the doctor; "let's get out!"

And all three, dragging Simpson after them, abandoned their dangerous quarters; and it was high time, for the blocks of ice, ill put together, fell with a loud crash.

The poor men found themselves then without shelter against the hurricane. Hatteras attempted to raise the tent, but it was impossible, so severe was the wind, and they had to shelter themselves beneath the canvas, which was soon covered with a thick layer of snow; but this snow prevented the radiation of their warmth and kept them from being frozen to death.

The storm lasted all night; Bell, when he was harnessing the half-starved dogs, noticed that three of them had begun to eat the leather straps; two were very sick and seemed unable to go on. Still, they set out as well as they could; they had sixty miles between them and the point they wished to reach.

On the 26th, Bell, who was ahead, shouted suddenly to his companions. They ran towards him, and he pointed with astonishment to a gun resting on a piece of ice.

"A gun!" cried the doctor.

Hatteras took it; it was in good condition, and loaded.

"The men of the *Porpoise* can't be far off."

Hatteras, as he was examining the gun, noticed that it was of American make; his hands clinched nervously its barrel.

"Forward!" he said calmly.

They continued to descend the mountains. Simpson seemed deprived of all feeling; he had not even strength left to moan.

The tempest continued to rage; the sledge went on more and more slowly; they made but a few miles in twenty-four hours, and, in spite of the strictest economy, their supplies threatened to give out; but so long as enough was left to carry them back, Hatteras pushed on.

On the 27th they found, partly buried beneath the snow, a sextant and then a flask, which contained brandy, or rather a piece of ice, in the middle of which all the spirit of the liquor had collected in the form of snow; it was of no use.

Evidently, without meaning it, Hatteras was following in the wake of some great disaster; he went on by the only possible route, collecting the traces of some terrible shipwreck. The doctor kept a sharp lookout for other cairns, but in vain.

Sad thoughts beset him: in fact, if he should discover these wretches, of what service could he be to them? He and his companions were beginning to lack everything; their clothing was torn, their supplies were scanty. If the survivors were many, they would all starve to death. Hatteras seemed inclined to flee from them! Was he not justified, since the safety of the crew depended upon him? Ought he to endanger the safety of all by bringing strangers on board?

But then strangers were men, perhaps their countrymen! Slight as was their chance of safety, ought they to be deprived of it? The doctor wanted to get Bell's opinion; but Bell refused to answer. His own sufferings had hardened his heart. Clawbonny did not dare ask Hatteras: so he sought aid from Providence.

Towards the evening of that day, Simpson appeared to be failing fast; his cold, stiff limbs, his impeded breathing, which formed a mist about his head, his convulsive movements, announced that his last hour had come. His expression was terrible to behold; it was despairing, with a look of impotent rage at the captain. It contained a whole accusation, mute reproaches which were full of meaning, and perhaps deserved.

Hatteras did not go near the dying man. He avoided him, more silent, more shut into himself than ever!

The following night was a terrible one; the violence of the tempest was doubled; three times the tent was thrown over, and snow was blown over the suffering men, blinding them, and wounding them with the pieces torn from the neighboring masses. The dogs barked incessantly. Simpson was exposed to all the inclemency of the weather. Bell succeeded in again raising the canvas, which, if it did not protect them from the cold, at least kept off the snow. But a sudden squall blew it down for the fourth time and carried it away with a fierce blast.

"Ah, that is too much!" shouted Bell.

"Courage, courage!" answered the doctor, stooping down to escape being blown away.

Simpson was gasping for breath. Suddenly, with a last effort, he half rose, stretched his clinched fist at Hatteras, who was gazing steadily at him, uttered a heart-rending cry, and fell back dead in the midst of his unfinished threat.

"Suddenly, with a last effort, he half rose."

"Dead!" said the doctor.

"Dead!" repeated Bell.

Hatteras, who was approaching the corpse, drew back before the violence of the wind.

He was the first of the crew who succumbed to the murderous climate, the first to offer up his life, after incalculable sufferings, to the captain's persistent obstinacy. This man had considered him an assassin, but Hatteras did not quail before the accusation. But a tear, falling from his eyes, froze on his pale cheek.

The doctor and Bell looked at him in terror. Supported by his long staff, he seemed like the genius of these regions, straight in the midst of the fierce blast, and terrible in his stern severity.

He remained standing, without stirring, till the first rays of the twilight appeared, bold and unconquerable, and seeming to defy the tempest which was roaring about him.

CHAPTER XXXII.

THE RETURN TO THE FORWARD.

Toward six o'clock in the morning the wind fell, and, shifting suddenly to the north, it cleared the clouds from the sky; the thermometer stood at -33°. The first rays of the twilight appeared on the horizon above which it would soon peer.

Hatteras approached his two dejected companions and said to them, sadly and gently,—

"My friends, we are more than sixty miles from the point mentioned by Sir Edward Belcher. We have only just enough food left to take us back to the ship. To go farther would only expose us to certain death, without our being of service to any one. We must return."

"That is a wise decision, Hatteras," answered the doctor; "I should have followed you anywhere, but we are all growing weaker every day; we can hardly set one foot before the other; I approve of returning."

"Is that your opinion, Bell?" asked Hatteras.

"Yes, Captain," answered the carpenter.

"Well," continued Hatteras, "we will take two days for rest. That's not too much. The sledge needs a great many repairs. I think, too, we ought to build a snow-house in which we can repose."

This being decided, the three men set to work energetically. Bell took the necessary precautions to insure the solidity of the building, and soon a satisfactory retreat arose at the bottom of the ravine where they had last halted.

It was doubtless after a hard struggle that Hatteras had decided to discontinue his journey. So much effort and fatigue thrown away! A useless trip, entailing the death of one of his men! To return without a scrap of coal: what would the crew say? What might it not do under the lead of Shandon? But Hatteras could not continue the struggle any longer.

He gave all his attention to their preparations for returning; the sledge was repaired; its load, too, had become much lighter, and only weighed two hundred pounds. They mended their worn-out, torn clothes, all soaked through and through by the snow; new moccasins and snow-shoes replaced those which were no longer serviceable. This kept them busy the whole of the 29th and the morning of the 30th; then they all sought what rest they could get, and prepared for what was before them.

During the thirty-six hours spent in or near the snow-house, the doctor had been noticing Duke, whose singular behavior did not seem to him to be natural; the dog kept going in circles which seemed to have a common centre; there was a sort of elevation in the soil, produced by accumulated layers of ice; Duke, as he ran around this place, kept barking gently and wagging his tail impatiently, looking at his master as if asking something.

The doctor, after reflecting a moment, ascribed this uneasiness to the presence of Simpson's corpse, which his companions had not yet had time to bury. Hence he resolved to proceed to this sad ceremony on that very day; the next morning they were to start. Bell and the doctor, picks in hand, went to the bottom of the ravine; the elevation which Duke had noticed offered a suitable place for the grave, which would have to be dug deep to escape the bears.

The doctor and Bell began by removing the soft snow, then they attacked the solid ice; at the third blow of his pick the doctor struck against some hard body; he picked up the pieces and found them the fragments of a glass bottle. Bell brought to light a stiffened bag, in which were a few crumbs of fresh biscuit.

"What's this?" said the doctor.

"What can it be?" asked Bell, stopping his work.

The doctor called to Hatteras, who came at once.

Duke barked violently, and with his paws tried to tear up the ice.

"Have we by any possibility come across a supply of provisions?" said the doctor.

"It looks like it," answered Bell.

"Go on!" said Hatteras.

A few bits of food were found and a box quarter full of pemmican.

"If we have," said Hatteras, "the bears have visited it before we did. See, these provisions have been touched already."

"It is to be feared," answered the doctor, "for—"

He did not finish his sentence; a cry from Bell interrupted him; he had turned over a tolerably large piece of ice and showed a stiff, frozen human leg in the ice.

"A corpse!" cried the doctor.

"It's a grave," said Hatteras.

It was the body of a sailor about thirty years old, in a perfect state of preservation; he wore the usual dress of Arctic sailors; the doctor could not say how long he had been dead.

After this, Bell found another corpse, that of a man of fifty, exhibiting traces of the sufferings that had killed him.

"They were never buried," cried the doctor; "these poor men were surprised by death as we find them."

"You are right, Doctor," said Bell.

"Go on, go on!" said Hatteras.

Bell hardly dared. Who could say how many corpses lay hidden here?

"They were the victims of just such an accident as we nearly perished by," said the doctor; "their snow-house fell in. Let us see if one may not be breathing yet!"

The place was rapidly cleared away, and Bell brought up a third body, that of a man of forty; he looked less like a corpse than the others; the doctor bent over him and thought he saw some signs of life.

"He's alive!" he shouted.

Bell and he carried this body into the snow-house, while Hatteras stood in silence, gazing at the sunken dwelling.

The doctor stripped the body; it bore no signs of injury; with Bell's aid he rubbed it vigorously with tow dipped in alcohol, and he saw life gradually reviving within it; but the man was in a state of complete prostration, and unable to speak; his tongue clove to his palate as if it were frozen.

The doctor examined his patient's pockets; they were empty. No paper. He let Bell continue rubbing, and went out to Hatteras.

He found him in the ruined snow-house, clearing away the floor; soon he came out, bearing a half-burned piece of an envelope. A few words could be deciphered:—

....tamont
....*orpoise*
....w York.

"Altamont!" shouted the doctor, "of the *Porpoise!* of New York!"

"An American!" said Hatteras.

"I shall save him," said the doctor; "I'll answer for it, and we shall find out the explanation of this puzzle."

He returned to Altamont, while Hatteras remained pensive. The doctor succeeded in recalling the unfortunate man to life, but not to consciousness; he neither saw, heard, nor spoke, but at any rate he was alive!

The next morning Hatteras said to the doctor,—

"We must start."

"All right, Hatteras! The sledge is not loaded; we shall carry this poor fellow back to the ship with us."

"Very well," said Hatteras. "But first let us bury these corpses."

The two unknown sailors were placed beneath the ruins of the snow-house; Simpson's body took the place of Altamont's.

The three travellers uttered a short prayer over their companion, and at seven o'clock in the morning they set off again for the ship.

Two of the dogs were dead. Duke volunteered to drag the sledge, and he worked as resolutely as a Greenland dog.

For twenty days, from January 31st to February 19th, the return was very much like the first part of the journey. Save that it was in the month of February, the coldest of the whole year, and the ice was harder; the travellers suffered terribly from the cold, but not from the wind or snow-storm.

The sun reappeared for the first time January 31st; every day it rose higher above the horizon. Bell and the doctor were at the end of their strength, almost blind and quite lame; the carpenter could not walk without crutches. Altamont was alive, but continued insensible; sometimes his life was despaired of, but unremitting care kept him alive! And yet the doctor needed to take the greatest care of himself, for his health was beginning to suffer.

Hatteras thought of the *Forward!* In what condition was he going to find it? What had happened on board? Had Johnson been able to withstand Shandon and his allies? The cold had been terrible! Had they burned the ship? Had they spared her masts and keel?

While thinking of this, Hatteras walked on as if he had wished to get an early view of the *Forward*.

February 24th, in the morning, he stopped suddenly. Three hundred paces before him appeared a reddish glow, above which rose an immense column of black smoke, which was lost in the gray clouds of the sky.

"See that smoke!" he shouted.

His heart beat as if it would burst.

"See that smoke!" he said to his companions. "My ship is on fire!"

"But we are more than three miles from it," said Bell. "It can't be the *Forward!*"

"Yes, but it is," answered the doctor; "the mirage makes it seem nearer."

"Let us run!" cried Hatteras.

They left the sledge in charge of Duke, and hastened after the captain. An hour later they came in sight of the ship. A terrible sight! The brig was burning in the midst of the ice, which was melting about her; the flames were lapping her hull, and the southerly breeze brought to Hatteras's ears unaccustomed sounds.

Five hundred feet from the ship stood a man raising his hands in despair; he stood there, powerless, facing the fire which was destroying the *Forward*.

The man was alone; it was Johnson.

Hatteras ran towards him.

"My ship! my ship!" he cried.

"You! Captain!" answered Johnson; "you! stop! not a step farther!"

"Well?" asked Hatteras with a terrible air.

"The wretches!" answered Johnson, "they've been gone forty-eight hours, after firing the ship!"

"Curse them!" groaned Hatteras.

Then a terrible explosion was heard; the earth trembled; the icebergs fell; a column of smoke rose to the clouds, and the *Forward* disappeared in an abyss of fire.

"Then a terrible explosion was heard."

At that moment the doctor and Bell came up to Hatteras. He roused himself suddenly from his despair.

"My friends," he said energetically, "the cowards have taken flight! The brave will succeed! Johnson, Bell, you are bold; Doctor, you are wise; as for me, I have faith! There is the North Pole! Come, to work!"

Hatteras's companions felt their hearts glow at these brave words.

And yet the situation was terrible for these four men and the dying man, abandoned without supplies, alone at the eighty-fourth degree of latitude, in the very heart of the polar regions.

END OF PART I.

PART II.
THE DESERT OF ICE.

CHAPTER I.

THE DOCTOR'S INVENTORY.

The design which Captain Hatteras had formed of exploring the North, and of giving England the honor of discovering the Pole, was certainly a bold one. This hardy sailor had just done all that human skill could do. After struggling for nine months against contrary winds and seas, after destroying icebergs and ice-fields, after enduring the severity of an unprecedentedly cold winter, after going over all that his predecessors had done, after carrying the *Forward* beyond the seas which were already known, in short, after completing half his task, he saw his grand plans completely overthrown. The treachery, or rather the demoralization of his wearied crew, the criminal folly of some of the ringleaders, left him in a terrible situation; of the eighteen men who had sailed in the brig, four were left, abandoned without supplies, without a boat, more than twenty-five hundred miles from home!

The explosion of the *Forward*, which had just blown up before their eyes, took from them their last means of subsistence. Still, Hatteras's courage did not abandon him at this terrible crisis. The men who were left were the best of the crew; they were genuine heroes. He made an appeal to the energy and wisdom of Dr. Clawbonny, to the devotion of Johnson and Bell, to his own faith in the enterprise; even in these desperate straits he ventured to speak of hope; his brave companions listened to him, and their courage in the past warranted confidence in their promises for the future.

The doctor, after listening to the captain's words, wanted to get an exact idea of their situation; and, leaving the others about five hundred feet from the ship, he made his way to the scene of the catastrophe.

Of the *Forward*, which had been built with so much care, nothing was left; pieces of ice, shapeless fragments all blackened and charred, twisted pieces of iron, ends of ropes still burning like fuse, and scattered here and there on the ice-field, testified to the force of the explosion. The cannon had been hurled to some distance, and was lying on a piece of ice that looked like a gun-carriage. The surface of the ice, for a circle of six hundred feet in diameter, was covered with fragments of all sorts; the brig's keel lay under a mass of ice; the icebergs, which had been partly melted by the fire, had already recovered their rock-like hardness.

The doctor then began to think of his ruined cabin, of his lost collections, of his precious instruments destroyed, his books torn, burned to ashes. So much that was valuable gone! He gazed with tearful eyes at this vast disaster, thinking not of the future, but of the irreparable misfortune which dealt him so severe a blow. He was immediately joined by Johnson; the old sailor's face bore signs of his recent sufferings; he had been obliged to struggle against his revolted companions, defending the ship which had been intrusted to his care. The doctor sadly pressed the boatswain's hand.

"Well, my friend, what is going to become of us?" asked the doctor.

"Who can say?" answered Johnson.

"At any rate," continued the doctor, "don't let us give way to despair; let us be men!"

"Yes, Doctor," answered the old sailor, "you are right; it's when matters look worst that we most need courage; we are in a bad way; we must see how we can best get out of it."

"Poor ship!" said the doctor, sighing; "I had become attached to it; I had got to look on it as on my own home, and there's not left a piece that can be recognized!"

"Who would think, Doctor, that this mass of dust and ashes could be so dear to our heart?"

"And the launch," continued the doctor, gazing around, "was it destroyed too?"

"No, Doctor; Shandon and the others, who left, took it with them."

"And the gig?"

"Was broken into a thousand pieces. See, those sheets of tin are all that's left of her."

"Then we have nothing but the Halkett-boat?"*

> * Made of india-rubber, and capable of being inflated at pleasure.

"That is all, and it is because you insisted on our taking it, that we have that."

"It's not of much use," said the doctor.

"They were a pack of miserable, cowardly traitors who ran away!" said Johnson. "May they be punished as they deserve!"

"Johnson," answered the doctor, mildly, "we must remember that their suffering had worn upon them very much. Only exceptional natures remain stanch in adversity, which completely overthrows the weak. Let us rather pity than curse them!"

After these words the doctor remained silent for a few minutes, and gazed around uneasily.

"What is become of the sledge?" asked Johnson.

"We left it a mile back."

"In care of Simpson?"

"No, my friend; poor Simpson sank under the toil of the trip."

"Dead!" cried the boatswain.

"Dead!" answered the doctor.

"Poor fellow!" said Johnson; "but who knows whether we may not soon be reduced to envying his fate?"

"But we have brought back a dying man in place of the one we lost," answered the doctor.

"A dying man?"

"Yes, Captain Altamont."

The doctor gave the boatswain in a few words an account of their finding him.

"An American!" said Johnson, thoughtfully.

"Yes; everything seems to point that way. But what was this *Porpoise* which had evidently been shipwrecked, and what was he doing in these waters?"

"He came in order to be lost," answered Johnson; "he brought his crew to death, like all those whose foolhardiness leads them here. But, Doctor, did the expedition accomplish what it set out for?"

"Finding the coal?"

"Yes," answered Johnson.

The doctor shook his head sadly.

"None at all?" asked the old sailor.

"None; our supplies gave out, fatigue nearly conquered us. We did not even reach the spot mentioned by Edward Belcher."

"So," continued Johnson, "you have no fuel?"

"No."

"Nor food?"

"No."

"And no boat with which to reach England?"

They were both silent; they needed all their courage to meet this terrible situation.

"Well," resumed the boatswain, "there can be no doubts about our condition! We know what we have to expect! But the first thing to do, when the weather is so cold, is to build a snow-house."

"Yes," answered the doctor, "with Bell's aid that will be easy; then we'll go after the sledge, we'll bring the American here, and then we'll take counsel with Hatteras."

"Poor captain!" said Johnson, forgetting his own griefs; "he must suffer terribly."

With these words they returned to their companions. Hatteras was standing with folded arms, as usual, gazing silently into space. His face wore its usual expression of firmness. Of what was this remarkable man thinking? Of his desperate condition and shattered hopes? Was he planning to return, since both men and the elements had combined against his attempt?

No one could have read his thoughts, which his face in no way expressed. His faithful Duke was with him, braving a temperature of -32°.

Bell lay motionless on the ice; his insensibility might cost him his life; he was in danger of being frozen to death. Johnson shook him violently, rubbed him with snow, and with some difficulty aroused him from his torpor.

"Come, Bell, take courage!" he said; "don't lose heart; get up; we have to talk matters over, and we need a shelter. Have you forgotten how to make a snow-house? Come, help me, Bell! There's an iceberg we can cut into! Come, to work! That will give us what we need, courage!"

Bell, aroused by these words, obeyed the old sailor.

"Meanwhile," Johnson went on, "the doctor will be good enough to go to the sledge and bring it back with the dogs."

"I am ready," answered the doctor; "in an hour I shall be back."

"Shall you go too, Captain?" added Johnson, turning to Hatteras.

Although he was deep in thought, the captain heard the boatswain's question, for he answered gently,—

"No, my friend, if the doctor is willing to go alone. We must form some plan of action, and I want to be alone to think matters over. Go. Do what you think right for the present. I will be thinking of the future."

Johnson turned to the doctor.

"It's singular," he said; "the captain seems to have forgotten his anger; his voice never was so gentle before."

"Well!" answered the doctor; "he has recovered his presence of mind. Mark my words, Johnson, that man will be able to save us!"

Thereupon the doctor wrapped himself up as well as he could, and, staff in hand, walked away towards the sledge in the midst of a fog which the moonlight made almost bright. Johnson and Bell set to work immediately; the old sailor encouraged the carpenter, who wrought on in silence; they did not need to build, but to dig into the solid ice; to be sure it was frozen very hard, and so rendered the task difficult, but it was thereby additionally secure; soon Johnson and Bell could work comfortably in the orifice, throwing outside all that they took from the solid mass.

From time to time Hatteras would walk fitfully, stopping suddenly every now and then; evidently he did not wish to reach the spot where his brig had been. As he had promised, the doctor was soon back; he brought with him Altamont, lying on the sledge beneath all the coverings; the Greenland dogs, thin, tired, and half starved, could hardly drag the sledge, and were gnawing at their harness; it was high time that men and beasts should take some rest.

While they were digging the house, the doctor happened to stumble upon a small stove which had not been injured by the explosion, and with a piece of chimney that could be easily repaired: the doctor carried it away in triumph. At the end of three hours the house was inhabitable; the stove was set in and filled with pieces of wood; it was soon roaring and giving out a comfortable warmth.

The American was brought in and covered up carefully; the four Englishmen sat about the fire. The last supplies of the sledge, a little biscuit and some hot tea, gave them some comfort. Hatteras did not speak; every one respected his silence. When the meal was finished the doctor made a sign for Johnson to follow him outside.

"Now," he said, "we are going to make an inventory of what is left. We must know exactly what things we have; they are scattered all about; we must pick them up; it may snow at any moment, and then it would be impossible to find a scrap."

"Don't let us lose any time, then," answered Johnson; "food and wood is what we need at once."

"Well, let us each take a side," answered the doctor, "so as to cover the whole ground; let us begin at the centre and go out to the circumference."

They went at once to the bed of ice where the *Forward* had lain; each examined with care all the fragments of the ship beneath the dim light of the moon. It was a genuine hunt; the doctor entered into this occupation with all the zest, not to say the pleasure, of a sportsman, and his heart beat high when he discovered a chest almost intact; but most were empty, and their fragments were scattered everywhere.

The violence of the explosion had been considerable; many things were but dust and ashes; the large pieces of the engine lay here and there, twisted out of shape; the broken flanges of the screw were hurled twenty fathoms from the ship and buried deeply in the hardened snow; the bent cylinders had been torn from their pivots; the chimney, torn nearly in two, and with chains still hanging to it, lay half hid under a large cake of ice; the bolts, bars, the iron-work of the helm, the sheathing, all the metal-work of the ship, lay about as if it had been fired from a gun.

"The large pieces of the engine lay here and there, twisted out of shape."

But this iron, which would have made the fortune of a tribe of Esquimaux, was of no use under the circumstances; before anything else food had to be found, and the doctor did not discover a great deal.

"That's bad," he said to himself; "it is evident that the store-room, which was near the magazine, was entirely destroyed by the explosion; what wasn't burned was shattered to dust. It's serious; and if Johnson is not luckier than I am, I don't see what's going to become of us."

Still, as he enlarged his circles, the doctor managed to collect a few fragments of pemmican, about fifteen pounds, and four stone bottles, which had been thrown out upon the snow and so had escaped destruction; they held five or six pints of brandy.

Farther on he picked up two packets of grains of cochlearia, which would well make up for the loss of their lime-juice, which is so useful against the scurvy.

Two hours later the doctor and Johnson met. They told one another of their discoveries; unfortunately they had found but little to eat: some few pieces of salt pork, fifty pounds of pemmican, three sacks of biscuit, a little chocolate, some brandy, and about two pounds of coffee, picked up berry by berry on the ice.

No coverings, no hammocks, no clothing, were found; evidently the fire had destroyed all. In short, the doctor and boatswain had found supplies for three weeks at the outside, and with the strictest economy; that was not much for them in their state of exhaustion. So, in consequence of these disasters, Hatteras found himself not only without any coal, but also short of provisions.

As to the fuel supplied by the fragments of the ship, the pieces of the masts and the keel, they might hold out about three weeks; but then the doctor, before using it to heat their new dwelling, asked Johnson whether out of it they might not build a new ship, or at least a launch.

"No, Doctor," answered the boatswain, "it's impossible; there's not a piece of wood large enough; it's good for nothing except to keep us warm for a few days and then—"

"Then?" asked the doctor.

"God alone knows," answered the sailor.

Having made out their list, the doctor and Johnson went after the sledge; they harnessed the tired dogs, returned to the scene of the explosion, packed up the few precious objects they had found, and carried them to their new house; then, half frozen, they took their place near their companions in misfortune.

"They harnessed the tired dogs."

CHAPTER II.

ALTAMONT'S FIRST WORDS.

Towards eight o'clock in the evening the snow-clouds cleared away for a few minutes; the constellations shone brilliantly in the clear air. Hatteras made use of this change to get the altitude of some stars; he went out without saying a word, carrying his instruments with him. He wished to ascertain his position and see if the ice-field had not been drifting again. After an absence of half an hour he came back, lay down in a corner, and remained perfectly still, although not asleep.

The next day snow began to fall heavily; the doctor could not help being glad that he had made his examination the day before, for a white curtain soon covered the whole expanse, and every trace of the explosion was hidden under three feet of snow.

On that day they could not set foot outside; fortunately their quarters were comfortable, or at least seemed so to the exhausted travellers. The little stove worked well, except occasionally when violent gusts drove the smoke into the room; with its heat they could make coffee and tea, which are both so serviceable beverages when the temperature is low.

The castaways, for they deserve the name, found themselves more comfortable than they had been for a long time; hence they only thought of the present, of the agreeable warmth, of the brief rest, forgetting, or even indifferent to the future, which threatened with speedy death.

The American suffered less, and gradually returned to life; he opened his eyes, but he did not say anything; his lips bore traces of the scurvy, and could not utter a sound; he could hear, and was told where he was and how he got there. He moved his head as a sign of gratitude; he saw that he had been saved from burial beneath the snow; the doctor forbore telling him how very short a time his death had been delayed, for, in a fortnight or three weeks at the most, their supply of food would be exhausted.

Towards midday Hatteras arose and went up to the doctor, Johnson, and Bell.

"My friends," he said to them, "we are going to take a final resolution as to the course we must follow. In the first place, I must ask Johnson to tell me under what circumstances this act of treachery came to pass."

"Why should we know?" said the doctor; "the fact is certain, we need give it no more thought."

"I am thinking of it, all the same," answered Hatteras. "But after I've heard what Johnson has to say, I shall not think of it again."

Johnson's Story.

"This is the way it happened," went on the boatswain; "I did all I could to prevent the crime—"

"I am sure of that, Johnson, and I will add that the leaders had been plotting it for some time."

"So I thought," said the doctor.

"And I too," continued Johnson; "for very soon after your departure, Captain, on the very next day, Shandon, who was angry with you and was egged on by the others, took command of the ship; I tried to resist, but in vain. After that, every one acted as he saw fit; Shandon did not try to control them; he wanted to let the crew see that the time of suffering and privation had gone by. Hence there was no economy; a huge fire was lighted in the stove; they began to burn the brig. The men had the provisions given them freely, and the spirits too, and you can easily imagine the abuse they made of them after their long abstinence. Things went on in this way from the 7th to the 15th of January."

"So," said Hatteras, in a grave voice, "it was Shandon who incited the men to revolt?"

"Yes, Captain."

"Say nothing more about him. Go on, Johnson."

"It was towards January 24th or 25th, that the plan of leaving the ship was formed. They determined to reach the western coast of Baffin's Bay; from there, in the launch, they could meet whalers, or, perhaps, the settlements on the eastern side. Their supplies were abundant; the sick grew better with the hope of reaching home. So they made their plans for leaving; they built a sledge for the transport of their food, fuel, and the launch; the men were to drag it themselves. This occupied them until February 15th. I kept anxiously awaiting your return, Captain, and yet I feared having you present; you would have had no influence over the crew, who would rather have killed you than have remained on board. They were wild with the hope of escape. I took all my companions aside and spoke to them, I besought them to stay; I pointed out all the dangers of such a journey, as well as the cowardliness of abandoning you. I could get nothing, even from the best. They chose February 22d for leaving. Shandon was impatient. They heaped upon the sledge all the food and liquor it could hold; they took a great deal of wood; the whole larboard side had been cut away to the water-line. The last day they passed carousing; they ravaged and stole everything, and it was during this drunkenness that Pen and two or three others set fire to the ship. I resisted, and struggled against them; they threw me down and struck me; at last, these villains, with Shandon at their head, fled to the east, and disappeared from my sight. I remained alone; what could I do against this fire which was seizing the whole ship? The water-hole was frozen over; I hadn't a drop of water. For two days the *Forward* was wrapped in flames, and you know the rest."

Having finished this account, a long silence prevailed in this ice-house; the gloomy tale of the burning of the ship, the loss of their precious brig, appeared so vividly before the minds of the castaways; they found themselves before an impossibility, and that was a return to England. They did not dare to look at one another, for fear of seeing on each other's faces blank despair. There was nothing to be heard save the hasty breathing of the American.

At last Hatteras spoke.

"Johnson," said he, "I thank you; you have done all you could to save my ship. But you could not do anything alone. Again I thank you, and now don't let us speak again of this misfortune. Let us unite our efforts for the common safety. There are four of us here, four friends, and the life of one is of no more worth than the life of another. Let each one give his opinion on what should be done."

"Ask us, Hatteras," answered the doctor; "we are all devoted to you, our answers shall be sincere. And, in the first place, have you any plan?"

"I can't have any alone," said Hatteras, sadly. "My opinion might seem interested; I want to hear your opinion first."

"Captain," said Johnson, "before speaking on such weighty matters, I have an important question to ask you."

"What is it?"

"You ascertained our position yesterday; well, has the ice-field drifted any more, or are we in just the same place?"

"It has not stirred," answered Hatteras. "The latitude before we left was 80° 15', and longitude 97° 35'."

"And," said Johnson, "how far are we from the nearest sea to the west?"

"About six hundred miles," answered Hatteras.

"And this water is—"

"Smith's Sound."

"The same which we could not cross last April?"

"The same."

"Well, Captain, now we know where we are, and we can make up our minds accordingly."

"Speak, then," said Hatteras, letting his head sink into his hands.

In that way he could hear his friends without looking at them.

"Well, Bell," said the doctor, "what do you think is the best course to follow?"

"It isn't necessary to reflect a long time," answered the carpenter; "we ought to return, without wasting a day or an hour, either to the south or the west, and reach the nearest coast, even if it took us two months!"

"We have supplies for only three weeks," answered Hatteras, without raising his head.

"Well," continued Johnson, "we must make that distance in three weeks, since it's our only chance of safety; if we have to crawl on our knees at the end, we must leave, and arrive in twenty-five days."

"This part of the northern continent is not known," answered Hatteras. "We may meet obstacles, such as mountains and glaciers, which will completely bar our progress."

"I don't consider that," answered the doctor, "a sufficient reason for not attempting the journey; evidently, we shall suffer a great deal; we ought to reduce our daily supply to the minimum, unless luck in hunting—"

"There's only half a pound of powder left," answered Hatteras.

"Come, Hatteras," resumed the doctor, "I know the weight of all your objections, and I don't nourish any vain hopes. But I think I can read your thoughts; have you any practicable plan?"

"No," answered the captain, after a few moments' hesitation.

"You do not doubt our courage," continued the doctor; "we are willing to follow you to the last, you know very well; but should we not now abandon all hope of reaching the Pole? Mutiny has overthrown your plans; you fought successfully against natural obstacles, but not against the weakness and perfidy of men; you have done all that was humanly possible, and I am sure you would have succeeded; but, in the present condition of affairs, are you not compelled to give up your project, and in order to take it up again, should you not try to reach England without delay?"

"Well, Captain?" asked Johnson, when Hatteras had remained a long time silent.

At last the captain raised his head, and said in a constrained tone,—

"Do you think you are sure of reaching the shore of the sound, tired as you are, and almost without food?"

"No," answered the doctor; "but it's sure the shore won't come to us; we must go to it. Perhaps we shall find to the south tribes of Esquimaux who may aid us."

"Besides," added Johnson, "may we not find in the sound some ship that has been forced to winter there."

"And if need be," continued the doctor, "when we've reached the sound, may we not cross it, and reach the west coast of Greenland, and then, either by Prudhoe's Land, or Cape York, get to some Danish settlement? Nothing of that sort is to be found on the ice-field. The way to England is down there to the south, and not here to the north!"

"Yes," said Bell, "Dr. Clawbonny is right; we must go, and go at once. Hitherto we have forgotten home too much, and those who are dear to us."

"Do you agree, Johnson?" Hatteras asked again.

"Yes, Captain."

"And you, Doctor?"

"Yes, Hatteras."

Hatteras still remained silent; in spite of all he could do, his face expressed his agitation. His whole life depended on the decision he should take; if he should return, it was all over with his bold plans; he could not hope to make the attempt a fourth time.

The doctor, seeing the captain was silent, again spoke.

"I ought to add, Hatteras," he said, "that we ought not to lose an instant; we ought to load the sledge with all our provisions, and take as much wood as possible. A journey of six hundred miles under such circumstances is long, I confess, but not insuperable; we can, or rather we ought, to make twenty miles a day, which would bring us to the coast in a month, that is to say, towards March 26th."

"But," said Hatteras, "can't we wait a few days?"

"What do you hope for?" answered Johnson.

"I don't know. Who can foretell the future? Only a few days yet! It's hardly enough to rest your wearied bodies. We couldn't go two stages without dropping from weariness, without any snow-house to shelter us!"

"But a terrible death certainly awaits us here!" cried Bell.

"My friends," continued Hatteras in a tone almost of entreaty, "you are despairing too soon! I should propose to seek safety to the north, were it not that you would refuse to follow me. And yet are there not Esquimaux near the Pole, as well as at Smith's Sound? That open sea, of which the existence is uncertain, ought to surround a continent. Nature is logical in everything it does. Well, we ought to believe that vegetation appears when the greatest cold ceases. Is there not a promised land awaiting us at the north, and which you want to fly from without hope of return?"

Hatteras warmed as he spoke; his heated imagination called up enchanting visions of these countries, whose existence was still so problematical.

"One more day," he repeated, "a single hour!"

Dr. Clawbonny, with his adventurous character and his glowing imagination, felt himself gradually aroused; he was about to yield; but Johnson, wiser and colder, recalled him to reason and duty.

"Come, Bell," he said, "to the sledge!"

"Come along!" answered Bell.

The two sailors turned towards the door of the snow-house.

"O Johnson! you! you!" shouted Hatteras. "Well, go! I shall stay!"

"Captain!" said Johnson, stopping in spite of himself.

"I shall stay, I say! Go! leave me like the rest! Go!—Come, Duke, we two shall stay!"

The brave dog joined his master, barking. Johnson looked at the doctor. He did not know what to do; the best plan was to calm Hatteras, and to sacrifice a day to his fancies. The doctor was about making up his mind to this effect, when he felt some one touch his arm.

He turned round. The American had just left the place where he had been lying; he was crawling on the floor; at last he rose to his knees, and from his swollen lips a few inarticulate sounds issued.

The doctor, astonished, almost frightened, gazed at him silently. Hatteras approached the American, and examined him closely. He tried to make out the words which the poor fellow could not pronounce. At last, after trying for five minutes, he managed to utter this word:—

"*Porpoise.*"

"The *Porpoise?*" asked the captain.

The American bowed affirmatively.

"In these seas?" asked Hatteras with beating heart.

The same sign from the sick man.

"To the north?"

"Yes."

"And you know where it lies?"

"Yes."

"Exactly?"

There was a moment's silence. The bystanders were all excited.

"Now, listen carefully," said Hatteras to the sick man; "we must know where this ship lies. I am going to count the degrees aloud; you will stop me by a sign."

The American bowed his head to show that he understood.

"Come," said Hatteras, "we'll begin with the longitude. One hundred and five? No.—Hundred and six? Hundred and seven? Hundred and eight? Far to the west?"

"Yes," said the American.

"Let us go on. Hundred and nine? Ten? Eleven? Twelve? Fourteen? Sixteen? Eighteen? Nineteen? Twenty?"

"Yes," answered Altamont.

"Longitude one hundred and twenty?" said Hatteras. "And how many minutes? I shall count."

Hatteras began at number one. At fifteen Altamont made a sign for him to stop.

"All right!" said Hatteras. "Now for the latitude. You understand? Eighty? Eighty-one? Eighty-two? Eighty-three?"

The American stopped him with a gesture.

"Well! And the minutes? Five? Ten? Fifteen? Twenty? Twenty-five? Thirty? Thirty-five?"

Another sign from Altamont, who smiled slightly.

"So," continued Hatteras, in a deep voice, "the *Porpoise* lies in longitude 120° 15', and 83° 35' latitude?"

"Yes!" said the American, as he fell fainting into the doctor's arms. This exertion had exhausted him.

"'Yes!' said the American."

"My friends," cried Hatteras, "you see that safety lies to the north, always to the north! We shall be saved!"

But after these first words of joy, Hatteras seemed suddenly struck by a terrible thought. His expression changed, and he felt himself stung by the serpent of jealousy.

Some one else, an American, had got three degrees nearer the Pole! And for what purpose?

CHAPTER III.

SEVENTEEN DAYS OF LAND JOURNEY.

This new incident, these first words which Altamont uttered, had completely altered the situation of the castaways; but just now they had been far from any possible aid, without a reasonable chance of reaching Baffin's Bay, threatened with starvation on a journey too long for their wearied bodies, and now, within four hundred miles from their snow-house, there was a ship which offered them bounteous supplies, and perhaps the means of continuing their bold course to the Pole. Hatteras, the doctor, Johnson, and Bell, all began to take heart after having been so near despair; they were nearly wild with joy.

But Altamont's account was still incomplete, and, after a few moments' repose, the doctor resumed his talk with him; he framed his questions in such a way that a simple sign of the head or a motion of the eyes would suffice for an answer.

Soon he made out that the *Porpoise* was an American bark from New York, that it had been caught in the ice with a large supply of food and fuel; and, although she lay on her beam-ends, she must have withstood the ice, and it would be possible to save her cargo.

Two months before, Altamont and the crew had abandoned her, carrying the launch upon a sledge; they wanted to get to Smith's Sound, find a whaling-vessel, and be carried in her to America; but gradually fatigue and disease had fallen upon them, and they fell aside on the way. At last only the captain and two sailors were left of a crew of thirty men, and Altamont's life was the result of what was really a miracle.

Hatteras wanted to find out from the American what he was doing in these high latitudes.

Altamont managed to make him understand that he had been caught in the ice and carried by it without possibility of resisting it.

Hatteras asked him anxiously for what purpose he was sailing.

Altamont gave them to understand that he had been trying the Northwest Passage.

Hatteras did not persist, and asked no other question of the sort.

The doctor then began to speak.

"Now," he said, "all our efforts should be directed to finding the *Porpoise;* instead of struggling to Baffin's Bay, we may, by means of a journey only two thirds as long, reach a ship which will offer us all the resources necessary for wintering."

"There's nothing more to be done," said Bell.

"I should add," said the boatswain, "that we should not lose a moment; we should calculate the length of our journey by the amount of our supplies, instead of the other and usual way, and be off as soon as possible."

"You are right, Johnson," said the doctor; "if we leave to-morrow, Tuesday, February 26th, we ought to reach the *Porpoise* March 15th, at the risk of starving to death. What do you think of that, Hatteras?"

"Let us make our preparations at once," said the captain, "and be off. Perhaps we shall find the way longer than we suppose."

"Why so?" asked the doctor. "This man seemed certain of the situation of his ship."

"But," answered Hatteras, "supposing the *Porpoise* has been drifting as the *Forward* did?"

"True," said the doctor, "that's not unlikely."

Johnson and Bell had nothing to urge against the possibility of a drift of which they had themselves been victims.

But Altamont, who was listening to the conversation, gave the doctor to understand that he wished to speak. After an effort of about a quarter of an hour, Clawbonny made out that the *Porpoise* was lying on a bed of rocks, and so could not have drifted away. This information calmed the anxiety of the Englishmen; still it deprived them of their hope of returning to Europe, unless Bell should be able to build a small boat out of the timbers of the *Porpoise*. However that might be, it was now of the utmost importance that they should reach the wreck.

The doctor put one more question to the American, namely, whether he had found an open sea at latitude 83°.

"No," answered Altamont.

There the conversation stopped. They began at once to prepare for departure; Bell and Johnson first began to see about the sledge, which needed complete repairing. Since they had plenty of wood, they made the uprights stronger, availing themselves of the experience of their southern trip. They had learned the dangers of this mode of transport, and since they expected to find plenty of deep snow, the runners were made higher.

On the inside Bell made a sort of bed, covered with the canvas of the tent, for the American; the provisions, which were unfortunately scanty, would not materially augment the weight of the sledge, but still they made up for that by loading it with all the wood it could carry.

The doctor, as he packed all the provisions, made out a very careful list of their amount; he calculated that each man could have three quarters of a ration for a journey of three weeks. A whole ration was set aside for the four dogs which should draw it. If Duke aided them, he was to have a whole ration.

These preparations were interrupted by the need of sleep and rest, which they felt at seven o'clock in the evening; but before going to bed they gathered around the stove, which was well filled with fuel, and these poor men luxuriated in more warmth than they had enjoyed for a long time; some pemmican, a few biscuits, and several cups of coffee soon put them in good-humor, especially when their hopes had been so unexpectedly lighted up. At seven in the morning they resumed work, and finished it at three in the afternoon. It was already growing dark. Since January 31st the sun had appeared above the horizon, but it gave only a pale and brief light; fortunately the moon would rise at half past six, and with this clear sky it would make their path plain. The temperature, which had been growing lower for several days, fell at last to -33°.

The time for leaving came. Altamont received the order with joy, although the jolting of the sledge would increase his sufferings; he told the doctor that medicine against the scurvy would be found on board of the *Porpoise*. He was carried to the sledge and placed there as comfortably as possible; the dogs, including Duke, were harnessed in; the travellers cast one last glance at the spot where the *Forward* had lain. A glow of rage passed over Hatteras's face, but he controlled it at once, and the little band set out with the air very dry at first, although soon a mist came over them.

Each one took his accustomed place, Bell ahead pointing out the way, the doctor and Johnson by the sides of the sledge, watching and lending their aid when it was necessary, and Hatteras behind, correcting the line of march.

They went along tolerably quickly; now that the temperature was so low, the ice was hard and smooth for travel; the five dogs easily drew the sledge, which weighed hardly more than nine hundred pounds. Still, men and beasts panted heavily, and often they had to stop to take breath.

Towards seven o'clock in the evening, the moon peered through mist on the horizon. Its rays threw out a light which was reflected from the ice; towards the northwest the ice-field looked like a perfectly smooth plain; not a hummock was to be seen. This part of the sea seemed to have frozen smooth like a lake.

It was an immense, monotonous desert.

Such was the impression that this spectacle made on the doctor's mind, and he spoke of it to his companion.

"You are right, Doctor," answered Johnson; "it is a desert, but we need not fear dying of thirst."

"A decided advantage," continued the doctor; "still, this immensity proves one thing to me, and that is that we are far distant from any land; in general, the proximity of land is indicated by a number of icebergs, and not one is to be seen near us."

"We can't see very far for the fog," said Johnson.

"Without doubt; but since we started we have crossed a smooth field of which we cannot see the end."

"Do you know, Doctor, it's a dangerous walk we are taking! We get used to it and don't think of it, but we are walking over fathomless depths."

"You are right, my friend, but we need not fear being swallowed; with such cold as this the ice is very strong. Besides, it has a constant tendency to get thicker, for snow falls nine days out of ten, even in April, May, and June, and I fancy it must be something like thirty or forty feet thick."

"That is a comfort," said Johnson.

"In fact, we are very much better off than those who skate on the Serpentine, and who are in constant dread of falling through; we have no such fear."

"Has the resistance of ice been calculated?" asked the old sailor, who was always seeking information from the doctor.

"Yes," the latter answered: "everything almost that can be measured is now known, except human ambition! and is it not that which is carrying us towards the North Pole? But to return to your question, my answer is this. Ice two inches thick will bear a man; three and a half inches thick, a horse and rider; five inches thick, an eight-pound cannon; eight inches, a fully harnessed artillery-piece; and ten inches, an army, any number of men! Where we are now, the Liverpool Custom House or the Halls of Parliament in London could be built."

"One can hardly imagine such strength," said Johnson; "but just now, Doctor, you spoke of snow falling nine days out of ten; that is true, but where does all the snow come from? The sea is all frozen, and I don't see how the vapor can rise to form the clouds."

"A very keen observation, Johnson; but, in my opinion, the greatest part of the snow or rain which we receive in the polar regions is formed from the water of the seas in the temperate zones. One flake arose into the air under the form of vapor from some river in Europe, it helped make a cloud, and finally came here to be condensed; it is not impossible that we who drink it may be quenching our thirst at the rivers of our own country."

"That is true," answered Johnson.

At that moment Hatteras's voice was heard directing their steps and interrupting their conversation. The fog was growing thicker, and making a straight line hard to follow.

Finally the little band halted at about eight o'clock in the evening, after walking nearly fifteen miles; the weather was dry; the tent was raised, the fire lighted, supper cooked, and all rested peacefully.

Hatteras and his companions were really favored by the weather. The following days brought no new difficulties, although the cold became extremely severe and the mercury remained frozen in the thermometer. If the wind had risen, no one could have withstood the temperature. The doctor was able to corroborate Parry's observations, which he made during his journey to Melville Island; he said that a man comfortably dressed could walk safely in the open air exposed to great cold, if the air were only calm; but as soon as the slightest wind arose, a sharp pain was felt in the face, and an extreme headache which is soon followed by death. The doctor was very anxious, for a slight wind would have frozen the marrow in their bones.

March 5th he observed a phenomenon peculiar to these latitudes: the sky was clear and thick with stars, and thick snow began to fall without any cloud being visible; the constellations shone through the flakes which fell regularly on the ice-field. This went on for about two hours, and stopped before the doctor had found a satisfactory explanation of its fall.

The last quarter of the moon had then disappeared; total darkness reigned for seventeen hours out of the twenty-four; the travellers had to tie themselves together by a long cord, to avoid being separated; it was almost impossible for them to go in a straight line.

Still, these bold men, although animated by an iron will, began to grow weary; their halts were more frequent, and yet they ought not to lose an hour, for their supplies were rapidly diminishing. Hatteras would often ascertain their position by observation of the moon and stars. As he saw the days pass by and the destination appear as remote as before, he would ask himself sometimes if the *Porpoise* really existed, whether the American's brain might not have been deranged by his sufferings, or whether, through hate of the English, and seeing himself without resources, he did not wish to drag them with him to certain death.

He expressed his fears to the doctor, who discouraged them greatly, but he readily understood the lamentable rivalry which existed between the American and English captains.

"They are two men whom it will be hard to make agree," he said to himself.

March 14th, after journeying for sixteen days, they had only reached latitude 82°; their strength was exhausted, and they were still a hundred miles from the ship; to add to their sufferings, they had to bring the men down to a quarter-ration, in order to give the dogs their full supply.

They could not depend on their shooting for food, for they had left only seven charges of powder and six balls; they had in vain fired at some white hares and foxes, which besides were very rare. None had been hit.

Nevertheless, on the 18th, the doctor was fortunate enough to find a seal lying on the ice; he wounded him with several balls; the animal, not being able to escape through his hole in the ice, was soon slain. He was of very good size. Johnson cut him up skilfully, but he was so very thin that he was of but little use to the men, who could not make up their minds to drink his oil, like the Esquimaux. Still the doctor boldly tried to drink the slimy fluid, but he could not do it. He preserved the skin of the animal, for no special reason, by a sort of hunter's instinct, and placed it on the sledge.

"The doctor was fortunate enough to find a seal."

The next day, the 16th, they saw a few icebergs on the horizon. Was it a sign of a neighboring shore, or simply a disturbance of the ice? It was hard to say.

When they had reached one of these hummocks, they dug in it with a snow-knife a more comfortable retreat than that afforded by the tent, and after three hours of exertion they were able to rest about their glowing stove.

CHAPTER IV.

THE LAST CHARGE OF POWDER.

Johnson had admitted the tired dogs into the snow-house; when the snow is falling heavily it serves as a covering to the animals, preserving their natural heat. But in the open air, with a temperature of -40°, they would soon have frozen to death.

Johnson, who made an excellent dog-driver, tried feeding the dogs with the dark flesh of the seals which the travellers could not swallow, and to his great surprise they made a rich feast out of it; the old sailor in his delight told the doctor. He, however, was not in the least surprised; he knew that in the north of America the horses make fish their main article of food, and what a herbivorous horse could content himself with would certainly satisfy an omnivorous dog.

Before going to rest, although sleep became an imperious necessity for men who had walked fifteen miles on the ice, the doctor wished to have a few serious words with his companions about the dangers of their situation.

"We are only at latitude 82°," he said, "and our supplies are already running short."

"A reason for losing no time," answered Hatteras; "we must push on; the strong can draw the feeble."

"Shall we find a ship when we get there?" asked Bell, who was much depressed by the fatigue of the journey.

"Why doubt it?" said Johnson; "the American's safety depends on ours."

To make sure, the doctor was anxious to question Altamont again. He could speak easily, although his voice was weak; he confirmed all the statements he had already made; he repeated that the ship was aground on some granite rocks, where it could not stir, and that it lay in longitude 120° 15', and latitude 83° 35'.

"We can't doubt this statement," resumed the doctor; "the difficulty is not whether the *Porpoise* is there, but the way of getting to her."

"How much food have we left?" asked Hatteras.

"Enough for three days at the outside," answered the doctor.

"Well, we must get to her in three days," said the captain, firmly.

"We must indeed," continued the doctor, "and if we succeed we shall have no need to complain, for we shall have been favored by faultless weather; the snow has given us a fortnight's respite, and the sledge has glided easily on the hardened ice! Ah, if it only carried two hundred pounds of food! Our dogs could have managed it easily enough. But still we can't help it!"

"With luck and skill," said Johnson, "we might put to some use the few charges of powder which are left us. If we should kill a bear we should be supplied for all the rest of the journey."

"Without doubt," answered the doctor, "but these animals are rare and shy; and then, when one thinks of the importance of a shot, his hand will shake and his aim be lost."

"But you are a good shot," answered Bell.

"Yes, when four men's dinners do not depend on my hitting; still, I will do my best if I get a chance. Meanwhile let us try to satisfy ourselves with this thin soup of scraps of pemmican, then go to sleep, and to-morrow early we'll start forth again."

A few moments later excessive fatigue outweighed every other feeling, and they all sank into a heavy sleep. Early on Saturday Johnson awoke his companions; the dogs were harnessed to the sledge, and they took up again their journey northward.

The heavens were magnificent, the air was very clear, the temperature very low; when the sun appeared above the horizon it appeared like an elongated ellipse; its horizontal diameter appeared, in consequence of refraction, to be double its vertical diameter. It sent forth its clear, cold rays over the vast icy plain. This return to light, if not to heat, rejoiced them all.

The doctor, gun in hand, walked off for a mile or two, braving the cold and solitude; before going he measured the supply carefully; only four charges of powder were left, and three balls; that was a small supply when one remembers that a strong animal like the polar bear often falls only after receiving ten or twelve shots. Hence the doctor did not go in search of so fierce game; a few hares or two or three foxes would have satisfied him and given him plenty of provisions. But during that day, if he saw one, or could not approach one, or if he were deceived by refraction, he would lose his shot; and this day, as it was, cost him a charge of powder and a ball. His companions, who trembled with hope at the report of his gun, saw him returning with downcast looks; they did not say anything; that evening they went to sleep as usual, after putting aside two quarter-rations reserved for the two following days. The next day their journey seemed more laborious; they hardly walked, they rather dragged along; the dogs had eaten even the entrails of the seal, and they were beginning to gnaw their harness.

A few foxes passed at some distance from the sledge, and the doctor, having missed another shot as he chased them, did not dare to risk his last ball and his last charge save one of powder.

That evening they halted early, unable to set one foot before the other, and, although their way was lighted by a brilliant aurora, they could not go on. This last meal, eaten Sunday evening under their icy tent, was very melancholy. If Heaven did not come to their aid, they were lost. Hatteras did not speak, Bell did not even think, Johnson reflected in silence, but the doctor did not yet despair.

Johnson thought of setting some traps that night; but since he had no bait, he had very little hope of success, and in the morning he found, as he expected, that, although a great many foxes had left their marks around, yet not one had been caught. He was returning much disappointed, when he saw an enormous bear sniffing the air at about thirty yards from the sledge. The old sailor thought Providence had sent this animal to him to be slain; without awakening his companions he seized the doctor's gun and made his way towards the bear.

Having got quite near he took aim, but just as he was about to pull the trigger he felt his arm trembling; his large fur gloves were in his way; he took them off quickly, and seized his gun with a firmer hand. Suddenly, a cry of pain escaped him; the skin of his fingers, burned by the cold of the gun-barrel, remained clinging to it, while the gun fell to the ground, and went off from the shock, sending the last ball off into space. At the sound of the report the doctor ran; he understood everything at a glance; he saw the animal trot quickly away; Johnson was in despair, and thought no more of the pain.

"I'm as tender as a baby," he cried, "not to be able to endure that pain! And an old man like me!"

"Come back, Johnson," the doctor said to him, "you'll get frozen; see, your hands are white already; come back, come!"

"I don't deserve your attentions, Doctor," answered the boatswain; "leave me!"

"Come along, you obstinate fellow! Come along! It will soon be too late!"

And the doctor, dragging the old sailor under the tent, made him plunge his hands into a bowl of water, which the heat of the stove had kept liquid, although it was not much above the freezing-point; but Johnson's hands had no sooner touched it than it froze at once.

"You see," said the doctor, "it was time to come back, otherwise I should have had to amputate your hands."

Thanks to his cares, all danger was gone in an hour; but it was no easy task, and constant friction was necessary to recall the circulation into the old sailor's fingers. The doctor urged him to keep his hands away from the stove, the heat of which might produce serious results.

That morning they had to go without breakfast; of the pemmican and the salt meat nothing was left. There was not a crumb of biscuit, and only half a pound of coffee. They had to content themselves with drinking this hot, and then they set out.

"There's nothing more!" said Bell to Johnson, in a despairing accent.

"Let us trust in God," said the old sailor; "he is able to preserve us!"

"This Captain Hatteras!" continued Bell; "he was able to return from his first expeditions, but he'll never get back from this one, and we shall never see home again!"

"Courage, Bell! I confess that the captain is almost foolhardy, but there is with him a very ingenious man."

"Dr. Clawbonny?" said Bell.

"Yes," answered Johnson.

"What can he do in such circumstances?" retorted Bell, shrugging his shoulders. "Can he change these pieces of ice into pieces of meat? Is he a god, who can work by miracles?"

"Who can say?" the boatswain answered his companion's doubts; "I trust in him."

Bell shook his head, and fell into a silent apathy, in which he even ceased to think.

That day they made hardly three miles; at evening they had nothing to eat; the dogs threatened to devour one another; the men suffered extremely from hunger. Not a single animal was to be seen. If there had been one, of what use would it have been? They could not go hunting with a knife. Only Johnson thought he recognized a mile to leeward the large bear, who was following the ill-fated little party.

"It is spying us!" he said to himself; "it sees a certain prey in us!"

But Johnson said no word to his companions; that evening they made their accustomed halt, and their supper consisted only of coffee. They felt their eyes growing haggard, their brain growing confused, and, tortured by hunger, they could not get an hour's sleep; strange and painful dreams took possession of their minds.

At a latitude in which the body imperiously demands refreshment, these poor men had not eaten solid food for thirty-six hours, when Tuesday morning came. Nevertheless, inspired by superhuman energy, they resumed their journey, pushing on the sledge which the dogs were unable to draw. At the end of two hours they fell, exhausted. Hatteras wanted to push on. He, still strong, besought his companions to rise, but they were absolutely unable. Then, with Johnson's assistance, he built a resting-place in an iceberg. It seemed as if they were digging their own graves.

"At the end of two hours they fell, exhausted."

"I am willing to die of hunger," said Hatteras, "but not of cold."

After much weariness the house was ready, and they all entered it.

So that day passed. In that evening, while his companions lay inert, Johnson had a sort of hallucination; he dreamed of an immense bear. That word, which he kept repeating, attracted the doctor's attention, so that he shook himself free from his stupor, and asked the old sailor why he kept talking about a bear, and what bear he meant.

"The bear which is following us," answered Johnson.

"The bear which is following us?" repeated the doctor.

"Yes, the last two days."

"The last two days! Have you seen him?"

"Yes, he's a mile to leeward."

"And you didn't tell us, Johnson?"

"What was the use?"

"True," said the doctor; "we have no ball to fire at him."

"Not a slug, a bit of iron, nor a bolt!" said the old sailor.

The doctor was silent, and began to think intently. Soon he said to the boatswain,—

"You are sure the bear is following us?"

"Yes, Doctor, he's lying in wait to eat us. He knows we can't escape him!"

"Johnson!" said the doctor, touched by the despairing accent of his companion.

"His food is sure," continued the poor man, who was beginning to be delirious; "he must be half famished, and I don't see why we need keep him waiting any longer!"

"Be quiet, Johnson!"

"No, Doctor; if we've got to come to it, why should we prolong the animal's sufferings? He's hungry as we are; he has no seal to eat! Heaven sends him us men; well, so much the better for him!"

Thereupon Johnson went out of his mind; he wanted to leave the snow-house. The doctor had hard work to prevent him, and he only succeeded by saying, as if he meant it,—

"To-morrow I shall kill that bear!"

"To-morrow!" said Johnson, as if he had awakened from a bad dream.

"Yes, to-morrow."

"You have no ball!"

"I shall make one."

"You have no lead!"

"No, but I have some quicksilver."

Thereupon the doctor took the thermometer; it marked +50°. He went outside, placed the instrument on the ice, and soon returned. The outside temperature was -50°. Then he said to the old sailor,—

"Now go to sleep, and wait till to-morrow."

That night they endured the horrors of hunger; only the doctor and the boatswain were able to temper them with a little hope. The next morning, at dawn, the doctor rushed out, followed by Johnson, and ran to the thermometer; all the mercury had sunk into the bulb, in the form of a compact cylinder. The doctor broke the instrument, and seized in his gloved fingers a piece of very hard metal. It was a real bullet.

"Ah, Doctor," shouted the old sailor, "that's a real miracle! You are a wonderful man!"

"No, my friend," answered the doctor, "I am only a man with a good memory, who has read a good deal."

"Why, what do you mean?"

"I happened to remember something Captain Ross related in the account of his voyage: he said he shot through an inch plank with a bullet of frozen mercury; if I had any oil it would amount to nearly the same thing, for he speaks of a ball of sweet almond, which was fired against a post and fell back to the ground unbroken."

"That is hardly credible!"

"But it is true, Johnson; this piece of metal may save our lives; let us leave it here in the air before we take it, and go and see whether the bear is still following us."

At that moment Hatteras came out of the hut; the doctor showed him the bullet, and told him what he thought of doing; the captain pressed his hand, and the three went off to inspect. The air was very clear. Hatteras, who was ahead of his companions, discovered the bear about a half-mile off. The animal, seated on his hind quarters, was busily moving his head about, sniffing towards these new arrivals.

"There he is!" shouted the captain.

"Silence!" said the doctor.

But the huge beast did not stir when he saw the hunters. He gazed at them without fear or anger. Still, it would be found hard to approach him.

"My friends," said Hatteras, "we have not come out for sport, but to save our lives. Let us act cautiously."

"Yes," answered the doctor; "we can only have one shot, and we must not miss; if he were to run away, he would be lost, for he can run faster than a hare."

"Well, we must go straight for him," said Johnson; "it is dangerous, but what does it matter? I am willing to risk my life."

"No, let me go!" cried the doctor.

"No, I shall go," answered Hatteras, quietly.

"But," said Johnson, "are not you of more use to the others than I should be?"

"No, Johnson," answered the captain, "let me go; I shall run no needless risk; perhaps, too, I shall call on you to help me."

"Hatteras," asked the doctor, "are you going to walk straight towards the bear?"

"If I were sure of hitting him, I would do so, even at the risk of having my head torn open, but he would flee at my approach. He is very crafty; we must try to be even craftier."

"What do you intend to do?"

"To get within ten feet of him without his suspecting it."

"How are you going to do it?"

"By a simple but dangerous method. You kept, did you not, the skin of the seal you shot?"

"Yes, it is on the sledge."

"Well, let us go back to the snow-house, while Johnson stays here on watch."

The boatswain crept behind a hummock which hid him entirely from the sight of the bear, who stayed in the same place, continually sniffing the air.

CHAPTER V.

THE SEAL AND THE BEAR.

Hatteras and the doctor went back to the house.

"You know," said the captain, "that the polar bears chase seals, which are their principal food. They watch for days at their breathing-holes, and seize them the moment they come upon the ice. So a bear will not be afraid of a seal; far from it."

"I understand your plan," said the doctor, "but it's dangerous."

"But there is a chance of success," answered the captain, "and we must try it. I am going to put on the sealskin and crawl over the ice. Let us lose no time. Load the gun and give it to me."

The doctor had nothing to say; he would himself have done what his companion was about to try; he left the house, carrying two axes, one for Johnson, the other for himself; then, accompanied by Hatteras, he went to the sledge.

There Hatteras put on the sealskin, which very nearly covered him. Meanwhile, Hatteras loaded the gun with the last charge of powder, and dropped in it the quicksilver bullet, which was as hard as steel and as heavy as lead. Then he handed Hatteras the gun, which he hid beneath the sealskin. Then he said to the doctor,—

"You go and join Johnson; I shall wait a few moments to puzzle the enemy."

"Courage, Hatteras!" said the doctor.

"Don't be uneasy, and above all don't show yourselves before you hear my gun."

The doctor soon reached the hummock which concealed Johnson.

"Well?" the latter asked.

"Well, we must wait. Hatteras is doing all this to save us."

The doctor was agitated; he looked at the bear, which had grown excited, as if he had become conscious of the danger which threatened him. A quarter of an hour later the seal was crawling over the ice; he made a circuit of a quarter of a mile to baffle the bear; then he found himself within three hundred feet of him. The bear then saw him, and settled down as if he were trying to hide. Hatteras imitated skilfully the movements of a seal, and if he had not known, the doctor would certainly have taken him for one.

"That's true!" whispered Johnson.

The seal, as he approached the bear, did not appear to see him; he seemed to be seeking some hole through which to reach the water. The bear advanced towards him over the ice with the utmost caution; his eager eyes betrayed his excitement; for one or perhaps two months he had been fasting, and fortune was now throwing a sure prey before him. The seal had come within ten feet of his enemy; the bear hastened towards him, made a long leap, and stood stupefied three paces from Hatteras, who, casting aside the sealskin, with one knee resting on the ground, was aiming at the bear's heart.

The report was sounded, and the bear rolled over on the ice.

"Forward!" shouted the doctor. And, followed by Johnson, he hastened to the scene of combat. The huge beast rose, and beat the air with one paw while with the other he tore up a handful of snow to stanch the wound. Hatteras did not stir, but waited, knife in hand. But his aim had been accurate, and his bullet had hit its mark; before the arrival of his friends he had plunged his knife into the beast's throat, and it fell, never to rise.

"He plunged his knife into the beast's throat."

"Victory!" shouted Johnson.

"Hurrah! hurrah! hurrah!" cried the doctor.

Hatteras, with folded arms, was gazing calmly at the corpse of his foe.

"It's now my turn," said Johnson; "it's very well to have killed it, but there is no need of waiting till it's frozen as hard as a stone, when teeth and knife will be useless for attacking it."

Johnson began by skinning the bear, which was nearly as large as an ox; it was nine feet long and six feet in circumference; two huge tusks, three inches long, issued from his mouth. On opening him, nothing was found in his stomach but water; the bear had evidently eaten nothing for a long time; nevertheless, he was very fat, and he weighed more than fifteen hundred pounds; he was divided into four quarters, each one of which gave two hundred pounds of meat, and the hunters carried this flesh back to the snow-house, without forgetting the animal's heart, which went on beating for three hours.

The others wanted to eat the meat raw, but the doctor bade them wait until it should be roasted. On entering the house he was struck by the great cold within it; he went up to the stove and found the fire out; the occupations as well as the excitement of the morning had made Johnson forget his customary duty. The doctor tried to rekindle the fire, but there was not even a spark lingering amid the cold ashes.

"Well, we must have patience!" he said to himself. He then went to the sledge to get some tinder, and asked Johnson for his steel, telling him that the fire had gone out. Johnson answered that it was his fault, and he put his hand in his pocket, where he usually kept it; he was surprised not to find it there. He felt in his other pockets with the same success; he went into the snow-house and examined carefully the covering under which he had slept in the previous night, but he could not find it.

"Well?" shouted the doctor.

Johnson came back, and stared at his companions.

"And haven't you got the steel, Dr. Clawbonny?" he asked.

"No, Johnson."

"Nor you, Captain?"

"No," answered Hatteras.

"You have always carried it," said the doctor.

"Well, I haven't got it now—" murmured the old sailor, growing pale.

"Not got it!" shouted the doctor, who could not help trembling. There was no other steel, and the loss of this might bring with it terrible consequences.

"Hunt again!" said the doctor.

Johnson ran to the piece of ice behind which he had watched the bear, then to the place of combat, where he had cut him up; but he could not find anything. He returned in despair. Hatteras looked at him without a word of reproach.

"This is serious," he said to the doctor.

"Yes," the latter answered.

"We have not even an instrument, a glass from which we might take the lens to get fire by means of it!"

"I know it," answered the doctor; "and that is a great pity, because the rays of the sun are strong enough to kindle tinder."

"Well," answered Hatteras, "we must satisfy our hunger with this raw meat; then we shall resume our march and we shall try to reach the ship."

"Yes," said the doctor, buried in reflection; "yes, we could do that if we had to. Why not? We might try—"

"What are you thinking of?" asked Hatteras.

"An idea which has just occurred to me—"

"An idea," said Johnson; "one of your ideas! Then we are saved!"

"It's a question," answered the doctor, "whether it will succeed."

"What is your plan?" said Hatteras.

"We have no lens; well, we will make one."

"How?" asked Johnson.

"With a piece of ice which we shall cut out."

"Why, do you think—"

"Why not? We want to make the sun's rays converge to a common focus, and ice will do as much good as crystal."

"Is it possible?" asked Johnson.

"Yes, only I should prefer fresh to salt water; it is more transparent, and harder."

"But, if I am not mistaken," said Johnson, pointing to a hummock a hundred paces distant, "that dark green block shows—"

"You are right; come, my friends; bring your hatchet, Johnson."

The three men went towards the block which, as they supposed, was formed of fresh water.

The doctor had a piece, a foot in diameter, cut through, and he began to smooth it with the hatchet; then he equalized the surface still further with his knife; then he polished it with his hand, and he obtained soon a lens as transparent as if it had been made of the most magnificent crystal. Then he returned to the snow-house, where he took a piece of tinder and began his experiment. The sun was shining brightly; the doctor held the lens so that the rays should be focused on the tinder, which took fire in a few seconds.

"Hurrah! hurrah!" cried Johnson, who could hardly trust his eyes. "O Doctor, Doctor!"

The old sailor could not restrain his joy; he was coming and going like a madman. The doctor had returned to the house; a few minutes later the stove was roaring, and soon a delicious odor of cooking aroused Bell from his torpor. It may be easily imagined how the feast was enjoyed; still the doctor advised his friends to partake in moderation; he set an example, and while eating he again began to talk.

"To-day is a lucky day," he said; "we have food enough for our journey. But we mustn't fall asleep in the delights of Capua, and we'd better start out again."

"We can't be more than forty-eight hours from the *Porpoise*," said Altamont, who could now begin to speak once more.

"I hope," said the doctor, smiling, "that we shall find material for a fire there."

"Yes," said the American.

"For, if my ice lens is good," continued the doctor, "there would still be something desired on cloudy days, and there are many of them less than four degrees from the Pole."

"True!" said Altamont with a sigh, "less than four degrees! My ship has gone nearer than any yet has been!"

"Forward!" said Hatteras, quickly.

"Forward!" repeated the doctor, gazing uneasily at the two captains.

The strength of the travellers soon returned; the dogs had eaten freely of the bear's flesh, and they continued their journey northward. During their walk the doctor tried to draw from Altamont the object of his expedition, but the American gave only evasive answers.

"There are two men to be watched," he whispered to the boatswain.

"Yes," answered Johnson.

"Hatteras never says a word to the American, and the American seems to show very little gratitude. Fortunately I am here."

"Dr. Clawbonny," answered Johnson, "since this Yankee has returned to life, I don't like his face much."

"Either I'm mistaken," answered the doctor, "or he suspects Hatteras's plans."

"Do you think that the stranger has the same plans?"

"Who can tell? The Americans are bold; an American may well try what an Englishman tries!"

"You think that Altamont—"

"I don't think anything about it," answered the doctor; "but the situation of this ship on the way to the Pole gives one material for thought."

"But Altamont said he had drifted there."

"He said so! Yes, but he was smiling in a very strange way."

"The devil, Dr. Clawbonny; it would be unfortunate if there should be any rivalry between two such men."

"Heaven grant that I may be mistaken, Johnson, for this misfortune might produce serious complications, if not some catastrophe."

"I hope Altamont will not forget that we saved his life."

"But isn't he going to save us? I confess that without us he would not be alive; but what would become of us without him, without his ship, without its resources?"

"Well, Doctor, you are here, and I hope with your aid all will go well."

"I hope so, Johnson."

The voyage went on without incident; there was no lack of bear's flesh, and they made copious meals of it; there was a certain good-humor in the little band, thanks to the jests of the doctor and his pleasant philosophy; this worthy man always had some scrap of information to give to his companions. His health continued good; he had not grown very thin, in spite of his fatigues and privations; his friends at Liverpool would have recognized him without difficulty; especially would they have recognized his unaltered good-humor.

During the morning of Saturday the appearance of the plain of ice changed materially; the perturbed fragments, the frequent packs, the hummocks, showed that the ice-field was enduring some severe pressure; evidently some unknown continent, some new island, might have caused this by narrowing the passes. Blocks of fresh water, more frequent and larger, indicated the coast to be near. Hence, there was near them a new land, and the doctor yearned with a desire to add to the charts of the northern regions. Great is the pleasure of ascertaining the line of these unknown coasts, and of tracing it with a pencil; that was the doctor's aim, while that of Hatteras was merely to place his foot upon the Pole, and he took pleasure in advance in thinking of the names he was going to give to the seas, straits, bays, and slightest promontories in these new continents; certainly he would not forget the names of his companions, his friends, nor her Gracious Majesty, nor the royal family; and he foresaw a certain "Cape Clawbonny" with great satisfaction.

These thoughts kept him busy all day; that evening they encamped as usual, and each one took his turn at watching near these unknown lands. The next day, Sunday, after a heavy breakfast of bear's paws, which were very good, the travellers pushed on to the north, inclining a little to the west; the road grew difficult, but yet they advanced rapidly. Altamont, from the top of the sledge, scanned the horizon with feverish attention; his companions were the victims of involuntary uneasiness. The last solar observations gave them latitude 83° 35', and longitude 120° 15'; that was the place where the American ship was said to be lying; the question of life and death was to be solved that day. At last, at about half past two in the afternoon, Altamont stood straight, stopped the little band by a loud cry, and, pointing with his hand to a white mass, which all the rest had taken for an iceberg, he cried with a loud voice,—

"The *Porpoise!*"

CHAPTER VI.

THE PORPOISE.

March 24th was Palm Sunday,—that day when the streets of the towns and villages of Europe are filled with flowers and leaves; bells are ringing, and the air is filled with rich perfumes. But here, in this desolate country, what sadness and silence! The wind was keen and bitter; not a leaf of foliage was to be seen! But still, this Sunday was a day of rejoicing for our travellers, for at last they were about to find supplies which would save them from certain death. They hastened their steps; the dogs drew the sledge briskly, Duke barked joyously, and they all soon reached the American ship. The *Porpoise* was wholly buried beneath the snow; there was no sign of mast, yard, or rigging; all had been lost at the time of the shipwreck; the ship lay on a bed of rocks now completely hidden. The *Porpoise* was careened to one side by the violence of the shock, her bottom was torn open, so that the ship seemed uninhabitable. This was soon seen by the captain, the doctor, and Johnson, after they had entered the vessel; they had to cut away fifteen feet of ice to get to the hatchway; but to their great joy they saw that the animals, many traces of which were to be seen, had spared the supplies.

"If we have here," said Johnson, "plenty of food and fuel, this hull does not seem inhabitable."

"Well, we must build a snow-house," answered Hatteras, "and make ourselves as comfortable as possible on the mainland."

"Without doubt," continued the doctor; "but don't let us hurry; let us do things carefully; if need be we can fit out some quarters in the ship; meanwhile we can build a strong house, capable of protecting us against the cold and wild beasts. I am willing to be the architect, and you'll see what I can do."

"I don't doubt your skill, Doctor," answered Johnson; "we'll make ourselves as comfortable as possible here, and we'll make an inventory of all that the ship contains; unfortunately, I don't see any launch, or boat, and these ruins are in too bad a state to permit of our making a small boat."

"Who can say?" answered the doctor. "With time and thought a great deal can be done; now we have not to trouble ourselves about navigation, but about a house to live in; I propose not to form any other plans, and to let everything have its turn."

"That is wise," answered Hatteras; "let us begin with the beginning."

The three companions left the ship, returned to the sledge, and announced their determination to Bell and the American; Bell said he was ready to work; the American shook his head, on learning that nothing could be done with his ship; but since all discussion would have been idle, they determined at first to take refuge in the *Porpoise*, and to build a large building on the shore.

At four o'clock in the afternoon the five travellers were installed as comfortably as possible between decks; by means of spars and fragments of masts, Bell had made a nearly level floor; there they placed coverings stiffened by the frost, which the heat of the stove soon brought back to their natural state; Altamont, leaning on the doctor, was able to make his way to the corner which had been set aside for him; on setting foot on his ship, he had sighed with a feeling of relief, which did not encourage the boatswain.

"He feels at home," the old sailor thought, "and one would say that he had invited us here."

The rest of the day was devoted to repose; the weather threatened to change under the influence of the westerly winds; the thermometer outside stood at -26°. In fact, the *Porpoise* lay beyond the pole of cold, at a latitude relatively less severe, though farther to the north. On that day they finished the bear, with some biscuits they found on the ship, and a few cups of tea; then fatigue overcame them, and each one sank into a sound sleep.

The next morning they all awoke rather late; they soon recalled the difference in their situation; they were no longer perplexed with uncertainty about the morrow; they only thought of establishing themselves comfortably. These castaways looked at themselves as colonists who had reached their destination, and, forgetting the sufferings of their long march, they had no other thought than that of securing a comfortable future.

"These castaways looked at themselves as colonists who had reached their destination."

"Well," said the doctor, stretching his arms, "it's something not to have to wonder where one will sleep to-night and what one will have to eat to-morrow."

"Let us first make an inventory of the ship," answered Johnson.

The *Porpoise* had been carefully equipped for a long voyage.

The inventory, when complete, indicated the following supplies:—

6,150 lbs. of flour, fat and raisins for puddings;

2,000 " " beef and salt pork;

1,500 " " pemmican;

700 " " sugar;

700 " " chocolate;

500 " " rice;

1½ chests of tea, weighing 87 lbs;

many barrels of canned fruits and vegetables, lime-juice in abundance, cochlearia, sorrel and water-cresses, and three hundred gallons of rum and brandy; in the hold there was a large supply of ammunition; there was plenty of coal and wood. The doctor collected carefully the nautical instruments, and he also found a Bunsen's Pile, which had been carried for electrical tests and experiments. In short, they had supplies enough to keep five men on whole rations for two years; all fear of starving or freezing to death was hence wholly removed.

"Our means of living are certain," said the doctor to the captain, "and there is nothing to prevent our reaching the Pole."

"The Pole!" answered Hatteras, trembling with excitement.

"Certainly," continued the doctor; "what's to prevent our pushing on during the summer across the land?"

"Across the land! true! But how about the sea?"

"Can't we build a small boat out of the timber of the *Porpoise?*"

"An American boat, you mean," answered Hatteras, scornfully, "and commanded by this American!"

The doctor understood the captain's repugnance, and judged it best to change the conversation.

"Now that we know what our supplies are," he went on, "we must build some safe place for them, and a house for ourselves. We have plenty of material, and we can settle ourselves very comfortably. I hope, Bell," he added, turning to the carpenter, "that you are going to distinguish yourself; I may be able to help you too, I trust."

"I'm ready, Doctor," answered Bell; "if it were necessary I could easily build a whole city with houses and streets out of these blocks of ice—"

"We sha'n't need as much as that; let us follow the example of the agents of the Hudson's Bay Company; they build forts which protect them from the wild beasts and the Indians; that is all we need; let us make it no larger than necessary; on one side the dwelling, on the other the stores, with a sort of curtain, and two bastions. I'll try to rub up what I know about fortification."

"Upon my word, Doctor," said Johnson, "I don't doubt that we shall make something very fine under your direction."

"Well, my friends, we must first choose a site; a good engineer should first study the lay of the land. Will you come with me, Hatteras?"

"I shall trust to you, Doctor," answered the captain. "You see about that, while I explore the coast."

Altamont, who was still too feeble to get to work, was left on board of his ship, and the two Englishmen set foot on the mainland. The weather was thick and stormy; at noon the thermometer stood at -11°, but, there being no wind, that temperature was comfortable. Judging from the outline of the shore, a large sea, at that time wholly frozen, stretched out farther than eye could reach in the west; on the east it was limited by a rounded coast, cut into by numerous estuaries, and rising suddenly about two hundred yards from the shore; it formed a large bay, full of dangerous rocks, on which the *Porpoise* had been wrecked; far off on the land rose a mountain, which the doctor conjectured to be about three thousand feet high. Towards the north a promontory ran into the sea, after hiding a part of the bay. An island of moderate size rose from the field of ice, three miles from the mainland, so that it offered a safe anchorage to any ship that could enter the bay. In a hollow cut of the shore was a little inlet, easily reached by ships, if this part of the arctic seas was ever open. Yet, according to the accounts of Beecher and Penny, this whole sea was open in the summer months.

In the middle of the coast the doctor noticed a sort of plateau about two hundred feet in diameter; on three sides it was open to the bay; the fourth was enclosed by an elevation about a hundred and twenty feet high; this could be ascended only by steps cut in the ice. This seemed a proper place for a solid building, and it could be easily fortified; nature had adapted it for the purpose; it was only necessary to make use of the place. The doctor, Bell, and Johnson reached this place by means of steps cut in the ice. As soon as the doctor saw the excellence of the place, he determined to dig away the ten feet of hardened snow which covered it; the buildings had to be built on a solid foundation.

During Monday, Tuesday, and Wednesday, work went on without relaxation; at last the ground appeared; it consisted of a hard, dense granite, with the angles as sharp as glass; it contained, moreover, garnets and large crystals of feldspar, against which the pickaxe struck fire.

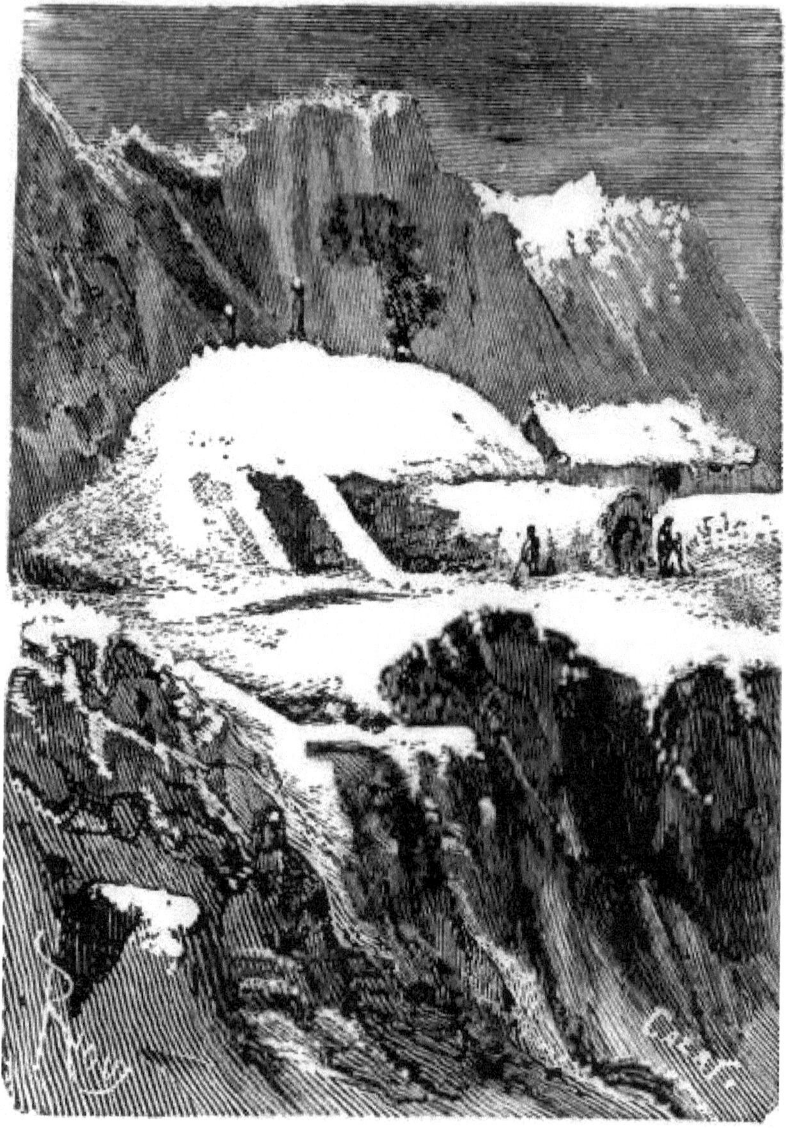

The doctor then gave them the dimensions and plan of the snow-house; it was to be forty feet long, twenty broad, and ten deep; it was divided into three rooms, a sitting-room, a bedroom, and a kitchen; more was not needed. To the left was the kitchen, to the right the bedroom, in the middle the sitting-room. For five days they worked busily. There was no lack of material; the ice walls were thick enough to resist thawing, for they could not risk being wholly without protection, even in summer. In proportion as the house rose, it became agreeable to see; there were four front windows, two in the sitting-room, one in the kitchen, another in the bedroom; for panes of glass they substituted large sheets of ice, in the Esquimaux fashion, which served as well as unpolished glass for the passage of light. In front of the sitting-room, between two windows, there ran a long entry like a tunnel, which gave admission to the house; a solid door, brought from the *Porpoise*, closed it hermetically. When the house was finished, the doctor was delighted with his handiwork; it would have been impossible to say to what school of architecture the building belonged, although the architect would have avowed his preferences for the Saxon Gothic, so common in England; but the main point was, that it should be solid; therefore the doctor placed on the front short uprights; on top a sloping roof rested against the granite wall. This served to support the stove-pipes, which carried the smoke away. When the task was completed, they began to arrange the interior. They carried into the bedroom the sleeping-accommodations from the *Porpoise;* they were arranged in a circle about a large stove. Benches, chairs, sofas, tables, wardrobes, were arranged in the sitting-room, which was also used as a dining-room; the kitchen received the cooking-stoves of the ship, and the various utensils. Sails, stretched on the floor, formed the carpet, and also served as hangings to the inner doors, which had no other way of closing. The walls of the house averaged five feet in thickness, and the recesses for the windows looked like embrasures in a fort. It was all built with great solidity; what more was to be desired? Ah, if they had listened to the doctor, there is no knowing what they would not have made of this ice and snow, which can be so easily manipulated! He all day long would ponder over plans which he never hoped to bring about, but he thereby lightened the dull work of all by the ingenuity of his suggestions. Besides, he had come across, in his wide reading, a rather rare book by one Kraft, entitled "Detailed Description of the Snow-Palace built at St. Petersburg, in January, 1740, and of all the Objects it contained." The recollection of this book impressed him. One evening he gave his companions a full account of the wonders of that snow-palace.

"Why couldn't we do here," he asked, "what they did at St. Petersburg? What do we need? Nothing, not even imagination!"

"So it was very handsome?" said Johnson.

"It was fairy-like, my friend. The house, built by order of the Empress Anna, and in which she had celebrated the marriage of one of her buffoons in 1740, was nearly as large as ours; but in front stood six cannons of ice; they were often fired without bursting; there were also mortars to hold sixty-pound shells; so we could have some formidable artillery; the bronze is handy, and falls even from heaven. But the triumph of taste and art was on the front of the palace, which was adorned with handsome statues; the steps were garnished with vases of flowers of the same material; on the right stood an enormous elephant, who played water through his trunk by day, and burning naphtha by night. What a menagerie we might have if we only wanted to!"

"As for animals," answered Johnson, "we sha'n't lack them, I fancy, and they won't be any the less interesting for not being made of ice."

"Well," said the doctor, "we shall be able to defend ourselves against their attacks; but to return to the palace, I should add that inside there were mirrors, candelabra, beds, mattresses, pillows, curtains, clocks, chairs, playing-cards, wardrobes well furnished, and all cut out of ice; in fact, nothing was lacking."

"It was then a true palace?" said Bell.

"A splendid palace, worthy of a sovereign! Ice! It was kind of Providence to invent it, since it lends itself to so many miracles and accommodates so readily to the needs of castaways!"

It took them until March 31st to get the house ready; this was Easter Sunday, and the day was set aside for rest; the whole day was spent in the sitting-room, where divine service was read, and each was able to judge of the excellent arrangements of the snow-house.

The next morning they set about building stores and a magazine; this took them about a week, including the time employed for emptying the *Porpoise*, which was not done without difficulty, for the low temperature did not permit them to work very long. At last, April 8th, provisions, food, and supplies were safely sheltered on land; the stores were placed to the north, and the powder-house to the south, about sixty feet from the end of the house; a sort of dog-kennel was built near the stores; it was destined for the Greenland dogs, and the doctor honored it with the title of "Dog-Palace." Duke partook of the common quarters.

Then the doctor passed to the means of defence of the place. Under his direction the plateau was surrounded by a real fortification of ice which secured it against every invasion; its height made a natural protection, and as there was no salient, it was equally strong on all sides. The doctor's system of defence recalled strongly the method of Sterne's Uncle Toby, whose gentleness and good-humor he also shared. He was a pleasant sight when he was calculating the inclination of the platform and the breadth of the causeway; but this task was so easy with the snow, that he enjoyed it, and he was able to make the wall seven feet thick; besides the plateau overlooking the bay, he had to build neither counterscarp nor glacis; the parapet of snow, after following the outlines of the plateau, joined the rock on the other side.

The work of fortification was finished April 15th. The fort was completed, and the doctor seemed very proud of his work.

The fort was completed.

In truth, this fortified enclosure could have withstood for a long time against a tribe of Esquimaux, if such enemies were met under that latitude; but there was no trace of human beings there; Hatteras, in making out the outline of the bay, did not see any ruins of the huts which are so commonly found in the places resorted to by Greenland tribes; the castaways of the *Forward* and the *Porpoise* appeared to be the first ever to set foot on this unknown shore. But if they need not fear men, animals were to be dreaded, and the fort, thus defended, would have to protect the little garrison against their attacks.

CHAPTER VII.

A DISCUSSION ABOUT CHARTS.

During these preparations for going into winter-quarters, Altamont had entirely recovered his health and strength; he was even able to aid in unloading the ship. His vigorous constitution at last carried the day, and his pallor soon gave way before the vigor of his blood.

They saw in him a sanguine, robust citizen of the United States, an intelligent, energetic man with a resolute character, a bold, hardy American ready for everything; he was originally from New York, and had been a sailor from infancy, as he told his companions; his ship, the *Porpoise*, had been equipped and sent out by a society of wealthy American merchants, at the head of whom was the famous Mr. Grinnell.

There was a certain similarity between his disposition and that of Hatteras, but their sympathies were different. This similarity did not incline them to become friends; indeed, it had the opposite effect. A close observer would have detected serious discordances between them; and this, although they were very frank with one another. Altamont was less so, however, than Hatteras; with greater ease of manner, he was less loyal; his open character did not inspire as much confidence as did the captain's gloomy temperament. Hatteras would say what he had to say, and then he held his peace. The other would talk a great deal, but say very little. Such was the doctor's reading of the American's character, and he was right in his presentiment of a future disagreement, if not hatred, between the captains of the *Porpoise* and the *Forward*.

And yet only one could command. To be sure, Hatteras had all the right of commanding, by virtue of anterior right and superior force. But if one was at the head of his own men, the other was on board of his own ship. And that was generally felt. Either from policy or instinctively, Altamont was at first attracted towards the doctor; it was to him he owed his life, but it was sympathy rather than gratitude which moved him. This was the invariable effect of Clawbonny's nature; friends grew about him like wheat under the summer sun. Every one has heard of people who rise at five o'clock in the morning to make enemies; the doctor could have got up at four without doing it. Nevertheless, he resolved to profit by Altamont's friendship to the extent of learning the real reason of his presence in the polar seas. But with all his wordiness the American answered without answering, and kept repeating what he had to say about the Northwest Passage. The doctor suspected that there was some other motive for the expedition, the same, namely, that Hatteras suspected. Hence he resolved not to let the two adversaries discuss the subject; but he did not always succeed. The simplest conversations threatened to wander to that point, and any word might kindle a blaze of controversy. It happened soon. When the house was finished, the doctor resolved to celebrate the fact by a splendid feast; this was a good idea of Clawbonny's, who wanted to introduce in this continent the habits and pleasures of European life. Bell had just shot some ptarmigans and a white rabbit, the first harbinger of spring. This feast took place April 14, Low Sunday, on a very pleasant day; the cold could not enter the house, and if it had, the roaring stoves would have soon conquered it. The dinner was good; the fresh meat made an agreeable variety after the pemmican and salt meat; a wonderful pudding, made by the doctor's own hand, was much admired; every one asked for another supply; the head cook himself, with an apron about his waist and a knife hanging by his side, would not have disgraced the kitchen of the Lord High Chancellor of England. At dessert, liquors appeared; the American was not a teetotaler; hence there was no reason for his depriving himself of a glass of gin or brandy; the other guests, who were never in any way intemperate, could permit themselves this infraction of their rule; so, by the doctor's command, each one was able to drain a glass at the end of the merry meal. When a toast was drunk to the United States, Hatteras was simply silent. It was then that the doctor brought forward an interesting subject.

"My friends," he said, "it is not enough that we have crossed the waters and ice and have come so far; there is one thing left for us to do. Hence I propose that we should give names to this hospitable land where we have found safety and rest; that is the course pursued by all navigators, and there is not one who has neglected it; therefore we ought to carry back with us not only a map of the shores, but also the names of the capes, bays, points, and promontories which we find. That is absolutely necessary."

"Good!" cried Johnson; "besides, when one can give all these lands their own names, it looks like genuine work, and we can't consider ourselves as cast away on an unknown shore."

"Besides," added Bell, "that simplifies instructions and facilitates the execution of orders; we may be compelled to separate during some expedition or in hunting, and the best way for finding our way back is to know the names of the places."

"Well," said the doctor, "since we are all agreed, let us try to settle on some names without forgetting our country and friends."

"You are right, Doctor," answered the American, "and you give what you say additional value by your warmth."

"Well," continued the doctor, "let us go on in order."

Hatteras had not taken part in the conversation; he was thinking. Still the eyes of his companions were fastened on him; he rose and said,—

"If you are all willing, and I don't think any one will dissent,"—at those words Hatteras looked at Altamont,—"it seems to me proper to name this house after its skilful architect, and to call it 'Doctor's House.'"

"That's true," said Bell.

"Good!" shouted Johnson; "Doctor's House!"

"Couldn't be better," added Altamont. "Hurrah for Dr. Clawbonny!"

Three cheers were then given, to which Duke added an approving bark.

"So," resumed Hatteras, "let this house bear that name until some new land is discovered to bear the name of our friend."

"Ah!" said Johnson, "if the earthly Paradise were to be named over again, the name of Clawbonny would suit it to a miracle!"

The doctor, much moved, wanted to defend himself by modesty, but he was unable. It was then formally agreed that the feast had been eaten in the grand dining-hall of Doctor's House, after being cooked in the kitchen of Doctor's House, and that they would go comfortably to bed in the chamber of Doctor's House.

"Now," said the doctor, "let us take the more important points of our discoveries."

"There is," said Hatteras, "this immense sea which surrounds us, and in which no ship has ever floated."

"No ship!" interrupted Altamont; "it seems to me the *Porpoise* should not be forgotten, unless indeed it came by land," he added jestingly.

"One might think it had," retorted Hatteras, "to see the rocks on which it is now resting."

"Indeed, Hatteras," answered Altamont with some vexation; "but, on the whole, isn't even that better than blowing up as the *Forward* did!"

Hatteras was about to make some angry reply, when the doctor interrupted him.

"My friends," he said, "we are not talking about ships, but about the new sea—"

"It is not new," interrupted Altamont. "It already bears a name on all the charts of the Pole. It is the Arctic Ocean, and I don't see any reason for changing its name; if we should find out in the future that it is only a sound or gulf, we can see what is to be done."

"Very well," said Hatteras.

"Agreed," said the doctor, regretting that he had aroused a discussion between rival nationalities.

"Let us come to the land which we are now in," resumed Hatteras. "I am not aware that it bears any name on the most recent maps."

"I am not aware that it bears any name on the most recent maps."

At these words he turned to Altamont, who did not lower his eyes, but answered,—

"You may be mistaken again, Hatteras."

"Mistaken! this unknown land, this new country—"

"Has a name already," answered the American, quietly.

Hatteras was silent. His lips trembled.

"And what is its name?" asked the doctor, a little surprised at the American's statement.

"My dear Clawbonny," answered Altamont, "it is the custom, not to say the habit, of every explorer to give a name to the continent which he has discovered. It seems to me that on this occasion it was in my power and that it was my duty to use this indisputable right—"

"Still—" said Johnson, whom Altamont's coolness annoyed.

"It seems to me hard to pretend," the American resumed, "that the *Porpoise* did not discover this coast, and even on the supposition that it came by land," he added, glancing at Hatteras, "there can't be any question."

"That is a claim I can't admit," answered Hatteras, gravely, forcibly restraining himself. "To give a name, one should be the discoverer, and that I fancy you were not. Without us, besides, where would you be, sir, you who presume to impose conditions upon us? Twenty feet under the snow!"

"And without me, sir," replied the American, "without my ship, where would you be at this moment? Dead of cold and hunger?"

"My friends," said the doctor, intervening for the best, "come, a little calm, it can all settle itself. Listen to me!"

"That gentleman," continued Altamont, pointing to the captain, "can give a name to all the lands he discovers, if he discovers any; but this continent belongs to me! I cannot admit of its bearing two names, like Grinnell Land and Prince Albert's Land, because an Englishman and American happened to find it at the same time. Here it's different. My rights of precedence are beyond dispute! No ship has ever touched this shore before mine. No human being before me has ever set foot upon it; now, I have given it its name, and it shall keep it."

"And what is its name?" asked the doctor.

"New America," answered Altamont.

Hatteras clinched his fists on the table. But with a violent effort he controlled himself.

"Can you prove to me," Altamont went on, "that any Englishman has ever set foot on this soil before me?"

Johnson and Bell were silent, although they were no less angry than the captain at the haughty coolness of their opponent. But there was nothing to be said. The doctor began again after a few moments of painful silence.

"My friends," he said, "the first law of humanity is justice; it embraces all the rest. Let us then be just, and not give way to evil feelings. Altamont's priority appears to me incontestable. There is no question about it; we shall have our revenge later, and England will have a good share in future discoveries. Let us leave to this land, then, the name of New America. But Altamont, in giving it this name, has not, I imagine, disposed of the bays, capes, points, and promontories which it encloses, and I don't see anything to prevent our calling it Victoria Bay."

"None at all," answered Altamont, "provided that the cape jutting into the sea over there is named Cape Washington."

"You might have chosen, sir," cried Hatteras, beside himself, "a name less offensive to an English ear."

"But none dearer to an American ear," answered Altamont, with much pride.

"Come, come," continued the doctor, who found it hard to keep the peace in this little world, "no discussion about that! Let an American be proud of his great men! Let us honor genius wherever it is found, and since Altamont has made his choice, let us now speak for ourselves and our friends. Let our captain—"

"Doctor," answered Hatteras, "since this is an American land, I don't care to have my name figure here."

"Is that opinion unchangeable?" asked the doctor.

"It is," answered Hatteras.

The doctor did not insist any further.

"Well, then, it's our turn," he said, addressing the old sailor and the carpenter; "let us leave a trace of our passage here. I propose that we call that island about three miles from here Johnson Island, in honor of our boatswain."

"O," said the latter, a little embarrassed, "O doctor!"

"As to the mountain which we have seen in the west, we shall call it Bell Mountain, if our carpenter is willing."

"It's too much honor for me," answered Bell.

"It's only fair," said the doctor.

"Nothing better," said Altamont.

"Then we have only to name our fort," resumed the doctor; "there need be no discussion about that; it's neither to Her Royal Highness Queen Victoria nor to Washington that we owe our protection in it at this moment, but to God, who brought us together and saved us all. Let it be called Fort Providence!"

"A capital plan!" answered Altamont.

"Fort Providence," added Johnson, "that sounds well! So, then, in returning from our excursions in the north, we shall start from Cape Washington to reach Victoria Bay, and from there to Fort Providence, where we shall find rest and plenty in Doctor's House."

"Then that's settled," answered the doctor; "later, as we make discoveries, we shall have other names to give, which I hope will not give rise to discussion; for, my friends, we ought to stand by one another and love one another; we represent humanity on this distant shore; let us not give ourselves up to the detestable passions which infest society; let us rather remain unattackable by adversity. Who can say what dangers Heaven has in store for us, what sufferings we may not have to support before we return to our own country? Let us five be like one man, and leave on one side the rivalry which is wrong anywhere, and especially here. You understand me, Altamont? And you, Hatteras?"

The two men made no reply, but the doctor did not seem to notice their silence. Then they talked about other things; about hunting, so as to get a supply of fresh meat; with the spring, hares, partridges, even foxes, would return, as well as bears; they resolved accordingly not to let a favorable day pass without exploring the land of New America.

CHAPTER VIII.

EXCURSION TO THE NORTH OF VICTORIA BAY.

The next morning, as soon as the sun appeared, Clawbonny ascended the wall of rock which rose above Doctor's House; it terminated suddenly in a sort of truncated cone; the doctor reached the summit with some little difficulty, and from there his eye beheld a vast expanse of territory which looked as if it were the result of some volcanic convulsion; a huge white canopy covered land and sea, rendering them undistinguishable the one from the other. The doctor, when he saw that this rock overlooked all the surrounding plain, had an idea,—a fact which will not astonish those who are acquainted with him. This idea he turned over, pondered, and made himself master of by the time he returned to the house, and then he communicated it to his companions.

"The doctor reached the summit with some little difficulty."

"It has occurred to me," he said to them, "to build a lighthouse at the top of the cone up there."

"A lighthouse?" they cried.

"Yes, a lighthouse; it will be of use to show us our way back at night when we are returning from distant excursions, and to light up the neighborhood in the eight months of winter."

"Certainly," answered Altamont, "such an apparatus would be useful; but how will you build it?"

"With one of the *Porpoise's* lanterns."

"Very good; but with what will you feed the lamp? With seal-oil?"

"No; it doesn't give a bright enough light; it could hardly pierce the fog."

"Do you think you can get hydrogen from our coal and make illuminating gas?"

"Well, that light would not be bright enough, and it would be wrong to use up any of our fuel."

"Then," said Altamont, "I don't see—"

"As for me," answered Johnson, "since the bullet of mercury, the ice lens, the building of Fort Providence, I believe Dr. Clawbonny is capable of anything."

"Well," resumed Altamont, "will you tell us what sort of a light you are going to have?"

"It's very simple," answered the doctor; "an electric light."

"An electric light!"

"Certainly; didn't you have on board of the *Porpoise* a Bunsen's pile in an uninjured state?"

"Yes," answered the American.

"Evidently, when you took it, you intended to make some experiments, for it is complete. You have the necessary acid, and the wires isolated, hence it would be easy for us to get an electric light. It will be more brilliant, and will cost nothing."

"That is perfect," answered the boatswain, "and the less time we lose—"

"Well, the materials are there," answered the doctor, "and in an hour we shall have a column ten feet high, which will be enough."

The doctor went out; his companions followed him to the top of the cone; the column was promptly built and was soon surmounted by one of the *Porpoise's* lanterns. Then the doctor arranged the conducting wires which were connected with the pile; this was placed in the parlor of the ice-house, and was preserved from the frost by the heat of the stoves. From there the wires ran to the lantern. All this was quickly done, and they waited till sunset to judge of the effect. At night the two charcoal points, kept at a proper distance apart in the lantern, were brought together, and flashes of brilliant light, which the wind could neither make flicker nor extinguish, issued from the lighthouse. It was a noteworthy sight, these sparkling rays, rivalling the brilliancy of the plains, and defining sharply the outlines of the surrounding objects. Johnson could not help clapping his hands.

"Dr. Clawbonny," he said, "has made another sun!"

"One ought to do a little of everything," answered the doctor, modestly.

The cold put an end to the general admiration, and each man hastened back to his coverings.

After this time life was regularly organized. During the following days, from the 15th to the 20th of April, the weather was very uncertain; the temperature fell suddenly twenty degrees, and the atmosphere experienced severe changes, at times being full of snow and squally, at other times cold and dry, so that no one could set foot outside without precautions. However, on Saturday, the wind began to fall; this circumstance made an expedition possible; they resolved accordingly to devote a day to hunting, in order to renew their provisions. In the morning, Altamont, the doctor, Bell, each one taking a double-barrelled gun, a proper amount of food, a hatchet, a snow-knife in case they should have to dig a shelter, set out under a cloudy sky. During their absence Hatteras was to explore the coast and take their bearings. The doctor took care to start the light; its rays were very bright; in fact, the electric light, being equal to that of three thousand candles or three hundred gas-jets, is the only one which at all approximates to the solar light.

The cold was sharp, dry, and still. The hunters set out towards Cape Washington, finding their way made easier over the hardened snow. In about half an hour they had made the three miles which separated the cape from Fort Providence. Duke was springing about them. The coast inclined to the east, and the lofty summits of Victoria Bay tended to grow lower toward the north. This made them believe that New America was perhaps only an island; but they did not have then to concern themselves with its shape. The hunters took the route by the sea and went forward rapidly. There was no sign of life, no trace of any building; they were walking over a virgin soil. They thus made about fifteen miles in the first three hours, eating without stopping to rest; but they seemed likely to find no sport. They saw very few traces of hare, fox, or wolf. Still, a few snow-birds flew here and there, announcing the return of spring and the arctic animals. The three companions had been compelled to go inland to get around some deep ravines and some pointed rocks which ran down from Bell Mountain; but after a few delays they succeeded in regaining the shore; the ice had not yet separated. Far from it. The sea remained fast; still a few traces of seals announced the beginning of their visit, and that they were already come to breathe at the surface of the ice-field. It was evident from the large marks, the fresh breaking of the ice, that many had very recently been on the land. These animals are very anxious for the rays of the sun, and they like to bask on the shore in the sun's heat. The doctor called his companions' attention to these facts.

"Let us notice this place," he said. "It is very possible that in summer we shall find hundreds of seals here; they can be approached and caught without difficulty, if they are unfamiliar with men. But we must take care not to frighten them, or they will disappear as if by magic and never return; in that way, careless hunters, instead of killing them one by one, have often attacked them in a crowd, with noisy cries, and have thereby driven them away."

"Are they only killed for their skin and oil?" asked Bell.

"By Europeans, yes, but the Esquimaux eat them; they live on them, and pieces of seal's flesh, which they mix with blood and fat, are not at all unappetizing. After all, it depends on the way it's treated, and I shall give you some delicate cutlets if you don't mind their dark color."

"We shall see you at work," answered Bell; "I'll gladly eat it, Doctor."

"My good Bell, as much as you please. But, however much you eat, you will never equal a Greenlander, who eats ten or fifteen pounds of it a day."

"Fifteen pounds!" said Bell. "What stomachs!"

"Real polar stomachs," answered the doctor; "prodigious stomachs which can be dilated at will, and, I ought to add, can be contracted in the same way, so that they support starving as well as gorging. At the beginning of his dinner, the Esquimaux is thin; at the end, he is fat, and not to be recognized! It is true that his dinner often lasts a whole day."

"Evidently," said Altamont, "this voracity is peculiar to the inhabitants of cold countries!"

"I think so," answered the doctor; "in the arctic regions one has to eat a great deal; it is a condition not only of strength, but of existence. Hence the Hudson's Bay Company gives each man eight pounds of meat a day, or twelve pounds of fish, or two pounds of pemmican."

"That's a generous supply," said the carpenter.

"But not so much as you imagine, my friend; and an Indian crammed in that way does no better work than an Englishman with his pound of beef and his pint of beer a day."

"Then, Doctor, all is for the best."

"True, but still an Esquimaux meal may well astonish us. While wintering at Boothia Land, Sir John Ross was always surprised at the voracity of his guides; he says somewhere that two men—two, you understand—ate in one morning a whole quarter of a musk-ox; they tear the meat into long shreds, which they place in their mouths; then each one, cutting off at his lips what his mouth cannot hold, passes it over to his companion; or else the gluttons, letting the shreds hang down to the ground, swallow them gradually, as a boa-constrictor swallows an animal, and like it stretched out at full length on the ground."

"Ugh!" said Bell, "the disgusting brutes!"

"Every one eats in his own way," answered the American, philosophically.

"Fortunately!" replied the doctor.

"Well," said Altamont, "since the need of food is so great in these latitudes, I'm no longer surprised that in accounts of arctic voyages there is always so much space given to describing the meals."

"You are right," answered the doctor; "and it is a remark which I have often made myself; it is not only that plenty of food is needed, but also because it is often hard to get it. So one is always thinking of it and consequently always talking of it!"

"Still," said Altamont, "if my memory serves me right, in Norway, in the coldest countries, the peasants need no such enormous supply: a little milk, eggs, birch-bark bread, sometimes salmon, never any meat; and yet they are hardy men."

"It's a matter of organization," answered the doctor, "and one which I can't explain. Still, I fancy that the second or third generation of Norwegians, carried to Greenland, would end by feeding themselves in the Greenland way. And we too, my friends, if we were to remain in this lovely country, would get to live like the Esquimaux, not to say like gluttons."

"Dr. Clawbonny," said Bell, "it makes me hungry to talk in this way."

"It doesn't make me," answered Altamont; "it disgusts me rather, and makes me dislike seal's flesh. But I fancy we shall have an opportunity to try the experiment. If I'm not mistaken, I see some living body down there on the ice."

"It's a walrus," shouted the doctor; "forward silently!"

Indeed, the animal was within two hundred feet of the hunters; he was stretching and rolling at his ease in the pale rays of the sun. The three men separated so as to surround him and cut off his retreat; and they approached within a few fathoms' lengths of him, hiding behind the hummocks, and then fired. The walrus rolled over, still full of strength; he crushed the ice in his attempts to get away; but Altamont attacked him with his hatchet, and succeeded in cutting his dorsal fins. The walrus made a desperate resistance; new shots finished him, and he remained stretched lifeless on the ice-field stained with his blood. He was a good-sized animal, being nearly fifteen feet long from his muzzle to the end of his tail, and he would certainly furnish many barrels of oil. The doctor cut out the most savory parts of the flesh, and he left the corpse to the mercies of a few crows, which, at this season of the year, were floating through the air. The night began to fall. They thought of returning to Fort Providence; the sky had become perfectly clear, and while waiting for the moon to rise, the splendor of the stars was magnificent.

"Come, push on," said the doctor, "it's growing late; to be sure, we've had poor luck; but as long as we have enough for supper, there's no need of complaining. Only let's take the shortest way and try not to get lost; the stars will help us."

But yet in countries where the North Star shines directly above the traveller's head, it is hard to walk by it; in fact, when the north is directly in the zenith, it is hard to determine the other cardinal points; fortunately the moon and great constellations aided the doctor in determining the route. In order to shorten their way, he resolved to avoid the sinuosities of the coast, and to go directly across the land; it was more direct, but less certain; so, after walking for a few hours, the little band had completely lost its way. They thought of spending the night in an ice-house and waiting till the next day to find out where they were, even if they should have to return along the shore; but the doctor, fearing that Hatteras and Johnson might be anxious, insisted on their going on.

"Duke is showing us the way," he said, "and he can't be wrong; he has an instinct which is surer than needle or star. Let us follow him."

Duke went forward, and they all followed confidently. And they were justified in so doing. Soon a distant light appeared on the horizon; it was not to be confounded with a star in the low clouds.

"There's our light!" cried the doctor.

"Do you think so, Doctor!" asked the carpenter.

"I'm sure of it. Let us push on."

As they approached the light grew brighter, and soon they enjoyed its full brilliancy; they advanced in full illumination, and their sharply cut shadows ran out behind them over the snow. They hastened their gait, and in about half an hour they were climbing up the steps of Fort Providence.

"They advanced in full illumination, and their sharply cut shadows ran out behind them over the snow."

CHAPTER IX.

COLD AND HEAT.

Hatteras and Johnson had waited for the three hunters with some uneasiness. When they returned they were delighted to find a warm and comfortable shelter. That evening the temperature had decidedly fallen, and the thermometer outside stood at -31°. The three were very much fatigued and almost frozen, so that they could hardly drag one foot after the other; fortunately the stoves were drawing well; the doctor became cook, and roasted a few walrus cutlets. At nine o'clock they all five sat down before a nourishing supper.

"On my word," said Bell, "at the risk of passing for an Esquimaux, I will say that food is an important thing in wintering; one ought to take what one can get."

Each of them having his mouth full, it was impossible for any one to answer the carpenter at once; but the doctor made a sign that he was right. The walrus cutlets were declared excellent; or, if they made no declarations about it, they ate it all up, which is much more to the purpose. At dessert the doctor made the coffee, as was his custom; he intrusted this task to no one else; he made it at the table, in an alcohol machine, and served it boiling hot. He wanted it hot enough to scald his throat, or else he did not think it worth

- 344 -

drinking. That evening he drank it so hot that his companions could not imitate him.

"But you'll burn yourself, Doctor," said Altamont.

"O no!" was the answer.

"Is your throat lined with copper?" asked Johnson.

"No, my friends; I advise you to take counsel from me. There are some persons, and I am of the number, who drink coffee at a temperature of 131°."

"One hundred and thirty-one degrees!" cried Altamont; "but the hand can't support that heat!"

"Evidently, Altamont, since the hand can't endure more than 122° in the water; but the palate and tongue are not so tender as the hand; they can endure much more."

"You surprise me," said Altamont.

"Well, I'm going to convince you."

And the doctor, bringing the thermometer from the parlor, plunged the bulb into his cup of boiling coffee; he waited until it stood at a 131°, and then he drank it with evident joy. Bell tried to do the same thing, but he burned himself and shouted aloud.

"You are not used to it," said the doctor.

"Clawbonny," asked Altamont, "can you tell me the highest temperature the human body can support?"

"Easily," answered the doctor; "various experiments have been made and curious facts have been found out. I remember one or two, and they serve to show that one can get accustomed to anything, even to not cooking where a beefsteak would cook. So, the story goes that some girls employed at the public bakery of the city of La Rochefoucauld, in France, could remain ten minutes in the oven in a temperature of 300°, that is to say, 89° hotter than boiling water, while potatoes and meat were cooking around them."

"What girls!" said Altamont.

"Here is another indisputable example. Nine of our fellow-countrymen in 1778, Fordyce, Banks, Solander, Blagden, Home, North, Lord Seaforth, and Captain Phillips, endured a temperature of 295°, while eggs and roast beef were cooking near them."

"And they were Englishmen!" said Bell, with an accent of pride.

"Yes, Bell," answered the doctor.

"O, Americans could have done better!" said Altamont.

"They would have roasted," said the doctor, laughing.

"And why not?" answered the American.

"At any rate, they have not tried; still, I stand up for my countrymen. There's one thing I must not forget; it is incredible if one can doubt of the accuracy of the witnesses. The Duke of Ragusa and Dr. Jung, a Frenchman and an Austrian, saw a Turk dive into a bath which stood at 170°."

"But it seems to me," said Johnson, that that is not equal to other people you mentioned."

"I beg your pardon," answered the doctor; there is a great difference between entering warm air and entering warm water; warm air induces perspiration, and that protects the skin, while in such hot water there is no perspiration and the skin is burned. Hence a bath is seldom hotter than 107°. This Turk must have been an extraordinary man to have been able to endure so great heat."

"Dr. Clawbonny," asked Johnson, "what is the usual temperature of living beings?"

"It varies very much," answered the doctor; "birds are the warmest blooded, and of these the duck and hen are the most remarkable; their temperature is above 110°, while that of the owl is not more than 104°; then come the mammalia, men; the temperature of Englishmen is generally 101°."[*]

"I'm sure Mr. Altamont is going to claim something more for the Americans," said Johnson.

"Well," said Altamont, "there are some very warm; but as I've never placed a thermometer into their thorax or under their tongue, I can't be sure about it."

"The difference of temperature," resumed the doctor, "between men of different races is quite imperceptible when they are placed in the same circumstances, whatever be the nature of their bringing-up; I should add, that the temperature varies but little between men at the equator and at the pole."

"So," said Altamont, "our temperature is about the same here as in England?"

"About the same," answered the doctor; "as to the other mammalia, their temperature is a trifle higher than that of man. The horse is about the same, as well as the hare, the elephant, the porpoise, the tiger; but the cat, the squirrel, the rat, panther, sheep, ox, dog, monkey, goat, reach 103°; and the warmest of all, the pig, goes above 104°."

"That is humiliating for us," said Altamont.

"Then come amphibious animals and fish, whose temperature varies very much according to that of the water. The serpent does not go above 86°, the frog 70°, and the shark the same in a medium a degree and a half cooler; insects appear to have the temperature of the water and the air."

"That is all very well," said Hatteras, who had not yet spoken, "and I'm much obliged to the doctor for his information; but we are talking as if we had to endure torrid heats. Would it not be wiser to talk about the cold, to know to what we are exposed, and what is the lowest temperature that has ever been observed?"

"True," added Johnson.

"There's nothing easier," continued the doctor, "and I may be able to give you some information."

"I dare say," said Johnson; "you know everything."

"My friends, I only know what others have taught me, and when I've finished you'll know exactly as much. This is what I know about cold and the lowest temperatures observed in Europe. A great many noteworthy winters have been known, and it seems as if the severest has a periodic return about every forty-one years,—a period which nearly corresponds with the greater appearance of spots on the sun. I can mention the winter of 1364, when the Rhone was frozen as far as Arles; that of 1408, when the Danube was frozen its whole length, and when wolves ran over to Jutland without wetting their feet; that of 1509, during which the Mediterranean at Cette and Marseilles and the Adriatic at Venice were frozen, and the Baltic as late as April 10; that of 1608, which killed all the cattle in England; that of 1789, when the Thames was frozen—as far as Gravesend, six leagues—below London; that of 1813, of which the French retain such a terrible memory; and that of 1829, the earliest and longest winter of this century. So much for Europe."

"But what temperature has been reached above the Arctic Circle?" asked Altamont.

"Really," said the doctor, "I believe we have experienced the greatest cold that has ever been observed, since our spirit thermometer indicated one day -72°; and if I remember aright, the lowest temperatures ever observed before were only -61° at Melville Island, -65° at Port Felix, and -70° at Fort Reliance."

"Yes," said Hatteras; "we were delayed, and unfortunately too, by a very severe winter!"

"You were delayed?" exclaimed Altamont, staring at the captain.

"In our journey westward," interposed the doctor, hastily.

"So," said Altamont, continuing the conversation, "the maximum and minimum temperatures endured by men vary about two hundred degrees?"

"Yes," answered the doctor; "a thermometer exposed to the open air and sheltered from reflection has never risen above 135°, and in the greatest colds it never falls below -72°. So, my friends, you see we can take our ease."

"But still," said Johnson, "if the sun were to be extinguished suddenly, would not the earth endure greater cold?"

"The sun won't be extinguished," answered the doctor; "but even if it should be, the temperature would not fall any lower, probably, than what I have mentioned."

"That's strange."

"O, I know it used to be said that in the space outside of the atmosphere the temperature was thousands of degrees below zero! but since the experiments of the Frenchman Fourrier, this has been disproved; he has shown that if the earth were placed in a medium void of all heat, that the temperature at the pole would be much greater, and that there would be very great differences between night and day; so, my friends, it is no colder a few millions of miles from the earth than it is here."

"Tell me, Doctor," said Altamont, "is not the temperature of America lower than that of other countries of the world?"

"Without doubt; but don't be proud of it," answered the doctor with a laugh.

"And what is the reason?"

"No very satisfactory explanation has ever been given; so it occurred to Hadley[2] that a comet had come into collision with the earth and had altered the position of its axis of rotation, that is to say, of its poles; according to him, the North Pole, which used to be situated at Hudson's Bay, found itself carried farther east, and the land at the old Pole preserved a greater cold, which long centuries of the sun have not yet heated."

"And you do not admit this hypothesis?"

"Not for a moment; for what is true of the eastern coast of America is not true of the western coast, which has a higher temperature. No! we can prove that the isothermal lines differ from the terrestrial parallels, and that is all."

"Do you know, Doctor," said Johnson, "that it is pleasant to talk about cold in our present circumstances?"

"Exactly, Johnson; we can call practice to the aid of theory. These countries are a vast laboratory where curious experiments on low temperatures can be made. Only, be always careful; if any part of your body is frozen, rub it at once with snow to restore the circulation of the blood; and if you come near the fire, be careful, for you may burn your hands or feet without noticing it; then amputation would be necessary, and we should try to leave nothing of ourselves in these lands. And now I think it would be well for us to seek a few hours of sleep."

"Willingly," answered the doctor's companions.

"Who keeps watch over the stove?"

"I do," answered Bell.

"Well, my friend, take care the fire does not fall out, for it's most abominably cold this evening."

"Don't be uneasy, Doctor; it's very sharp, but see, the sky is all ablaze!"

"Yes," answered the doctor, going up to the window, "it's a magnificent aurora. What a glorious sight! I should never get tired of looking at it!"

In fact, the doctor admired all these cosmic phenomena, to which his companions paid but little attention; he had noticed, besides, that their appearance always preceded disturbances of the magnetic needle, and he was preparing some observations on the subject which he intended for Admiral Fitz-Roy's "Weather Book."

Soon, while Bell was on watch near the stove, all the rest, stretched on their beds, slept quietly.

CHAPTER X.

THE PLEASURES OF WINTER-QUARTERS.

There is a gloomy monotony about life at the Pole. Man is wholly the sport of the changes of the weather, which alternates between intense cold and severe storms with savage relentlessness. The greater part of the time it is impossible to set foot out of doors; one is imprisoned in the hut of ice. Long months pass in this way, so that men lead the life of moles.

The next day the thermometer was several degrees lower, and the air was full of clouds of snow, which absorbed all the light of day. The doctor saw himself kept within doors, and he folded his arms; there was nothing to be done, except every hour to clear away the entrance-hall and to repolish the ice-walls which the heat within made damp; but the snow-house was very finely built, and the snow added to its resistance by augmenting the thickness of its walls.

The stores were equally secure. All the objects taken from the ship had been arranged in order in these "Docks of Merchandise," as the doctor called them. Now, although these stores were at a distance of only sixty feet from the house, it was yet on some days almost impossible to get to them; hence a certain quantity of provisions had always to be kept in the kitchen for daily needs.

They had been wise in unloading the *Porpoise*. The ship was exposed to a gentle, but persistent pressure, which was gradually crushing it; it was evident that nothing could be done with its fragments; still the doctor kept hoping to be able to build a launch out of them to return to England in, but the time for building it had not yet come.

So for the most part the five men remained in complete idleness. Hatteras was pensive and always lying on the bed; Altamont was drinking or sleeping, and the doctor took good care not to rouse him from his slumbers, for he was always afraid of some distressing quarrel. These two men seldom spoke to one another.

So during meal-time the prudent Clawbonny always took care to guide the conversation and to direct it in such a way as not to offend the susceptibilities of either; but he had a great deal to do. He did his best to instruct, distract, and interest his companions; when he was not arranging his notes about the expedition, he read aloud some history, geography, or work on meteorology, which had reference to their condition; he presented things pleasantly and philosophically, deriving wholesome instruction from the slightest incidents; his inexhaustible memory never played him false; he applied his doctrines to the persons who were with him, reminding them of such or such a thing which happened under such or such circumstances; and he filled out his theories by the force of personal arguments.

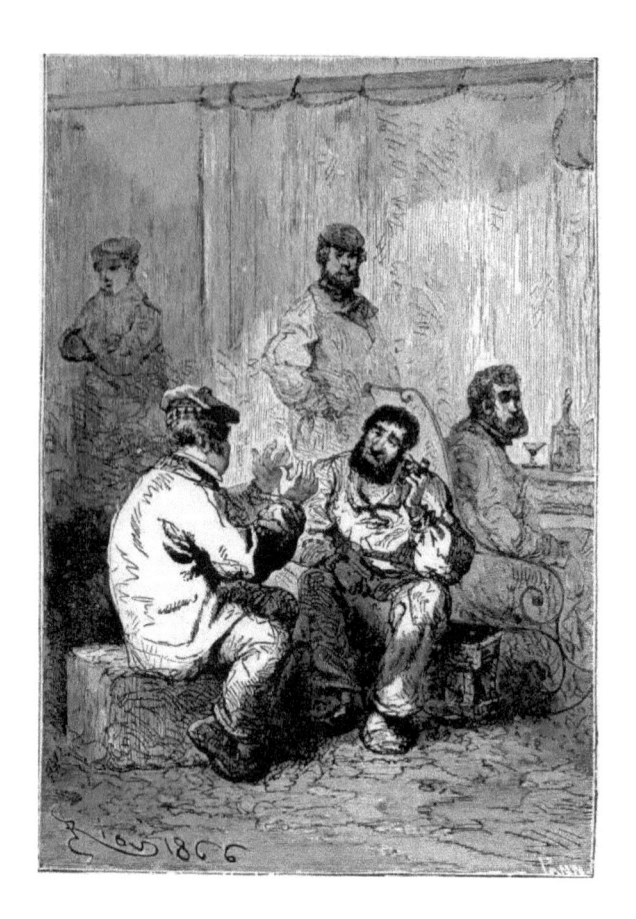

"He did his best to instruct and interest his companions."

This worthy man may be called the soul of this little world, a soul glowing with frankness and justice. His companions had perfect confidence in him; he even improved Captain Hatteras, who, besides, was very fond of him; he made his words, manners, and custom so agreeable, that the life of these five men within six degrees of the Pole seemed perfectly natural; when he was speaking, any one would have imagined he was in his office in Liverpool. And yet this situation was unlike that of castaways on the islands of the Pacific Ocean, those Robinsons whose touching history always aroused the envy of their readers. There, the natural richness offers a thousand different resources; a little imagination and effort suffice to secure material happiness; nature aids man; hunting and fishing supply all his wants; the trees grow to aid him, caverns shelter him, brooks slake his thirst, dense thickets hide him from the sun, and severe cold never comes upon him in the winter; a grain tossed into the earth brings forth a bounteous return a few months later. There, outside of society, everything is found to make man happy. And then these happy isles lie in the path of ships; the castaway can hope to be picked up, and he can wait in patience.

But here on the coast of New America how great is the difference! This comparison would continually occur to the doctor, but he never mentioned it to the others, and he struggled against the enforced idleness.

He yearned ardently for the spring, in order to resume his excursions; and yet he was anxious about it, for he foresaw difficulties between Hatteras and Altamont. If they pushed on to the Pole, there would necessarily be rivalry between the two men. Hence he had to prepare for the worst, and still, as far as he could, to try to pacify these rivals; but to reconcile an American and an Englishman, two men hostile to one another from their birth, one endowed with real insular prejudice, the other with the adventurous, irreverent spirit of his country, was no easy task. When the doctor thought of their eager rivalry, which in fact was one of nationalities, he could not help, not shrugging his shoulders, but lamenting human weakness. He would often talk to Johnson on this subject; he and the old sailor agreed in the matter; they were uncertain what view to take, and they foresaw complications in the future.

Still, the bad weather continued; they could not leave Fort Providence even for an hour. Night and day they had to remain in the snow-house. They all found it tedious, except the doctor, who found diversion for himself.

"Isn't there any way we can amuse ourselves?" said Altamont one evening. "This isn't really living, lying here like sluggish reptiles all winter."

"It's a pity," said the doctor, "that we are too few to organize any system of distractions."

"Do you mean it would be easier for us to combat idleness if there were more of us?" asked the American.

"Yes; when whole crews have wintered in boreal regions, they have found out the way to avoid idleness."

"To tell the truth," said Altamont, "I should like to know how they did; they must have been very ingenious to get any fun out of these surroundings. They didn't ask one another riddles, I suppose?"

"No," answered the doctor, "but they introduced into these lands two great means of amusement, the press and the theatre."

"What! did they have a newspaper?" asked the American.

"Did they act plays?" asked Bell.

"Yes, and with much amusement. While he was wintering at Melville Island, Captain Parry offered his crews these two entertainments, and they enjoyed them very much."

"Well," said Johnson, "I should have liked to be there; it must have been funny enough."

"Funny indeed; Lieutenant Beecher was manager of the theatre, and Captain Sabine editor of the 'Winter Chronicle, or Gazette of North Georgia.'"

"Good names," said Altamont.

"The paper appeared every Monday morning, from November 1, 1819, to March 20, 1820. It contained an account of everything that happened, the hunts, accidents, incidents, and of the weather; there were stories written for it; to be sure, it lacked the humor of Sterne, and the delightful articles of the 'Daily Telegraph'; but they got amusement from it; its readers were not over-critical, and I fancy no journalists ever enjoyed their occupation more."

"Well," said Altamont, "I should like to hear some extracts from this paper, my dear Doctor; its articles must all have been frozen solid."

"No, no," answered the doctor; "at any rate, what would have seemed simple enough to the Liverpool Philosophical Society, or the London Literary Institution, was perfectly satisfactory to the crews beneath the snow. Do you want a sample?"

"What! Do you remember—"

"No, but you had 'Parry's Voyages' on board the *Porpoise*, and I can read you his own account."

"Do!" shouted the doctor's companions.

"There's nothing easier."

The doctor got the book from the shelves, and soon found the passage.

"See here," he said, "here are some extracts from the newspaper. It is a letter addressed to the editor:—

"'It is with genuine satisfaction that your plan for the establishment of a newspaper has been received. I am convinced that under your charge it will furnish us with a great deal of amusement, and will serve to lighten materially the gloom of our hundred days of darkness.

"'The interest which I, for my part, take in it has caused me to examine the effect of your announcement upon the members of our society, and I can assure you, to use the consecrated phrase of the London press, that it has produced a profound impression upon the public.

"'The day after the appearance of your prospectus, there was on board an unusual and unprecedented demand for ink. The green cloth of our tables was suddenly covered with a deluge of quill-pens, to the great injury of one of our servants, who, in trying to remove them, got one under his nail.

"'Finally, I know that Sergeant Martin has had no less than nine pocket-knives to sharpen.

"'Our tables are groaning beneath the unaccustomed weight of inkstands, which had not seen the light for two months; and it is even whispered that the depths of the hold have been often opened to secure many reams of paper, which did not expect to issue so soon from their place of repose.

"'I shall not forget to say to you that I have some suspicions that an effort will be made to slip into your box some articles, which, lacking complete originality, and not being wholly unpublished, may not suit your plan. I can affirm that no later than last evening an author was seen bending over his desk, holding in one hand an open volume of the "Spectator," while with the other he was thawing his ink by the flame of the lamp. It is useless to recommend you to keep a lookout against such devices; we must not see reappearing in the "Winter Chronicle" what our ancestors used to read at breakfast more than a century ago.'"

"Well, well," said Altamont, when the doctor had finished reading, "there is really good humor in that, and the writer must have been a bright fellow."

"Bright is the word," answered the doctor. "Stop a moment, here is an amusing advertisement:—

"'Wanted. A middle-aged, respectable woman to help dress the ladies of the troupe of the "Theatre Royal of North Georgia." Suitable salary given, tea and beer free. Address the Committee of the theatre.—N. B. A widow preferred.'"

"They were not disgusted, at any rate," said Johnson.

"And did they get the widow?" asked Bell.

"Probably," answered the doctor, "for here is an answer addressed to the committee:—

"'Gentlemen: I am a widow, twenty-six years old, and I can produce warm testimonials as to my morals and talents. But before taking charge of the dresses of the actresses of your theatre, I am anxious to know if they intend to keep their trousers on, and whether I can have the aid of some strong sailors to lace their corsets properly. This being arranged, gentlemen, you may count upon your servant.

"'A. B.

"'P. S. Can you not substitute brandy for beer?'"

"Bravo!" shouted Altamont. "I suppose they had ladies'-maids to lace you by the capstan. Well, they were jolly fellows!"

"Like all who do what they set out to do," remarked Hatteras.

Hatteras uttered these words, and then he relapsed into his usual silence. The doctor, unwilling to dwell on that subject, hastened to resume his reading.

"See here," he said, "here is a picture of arctic sufferings; it may be varied infinitely; but a few of the observations are wise enough; for instance:—

"'To go out in the morning to take the air, and on setting foot off the ship, to take a cold bath in the cook's trough.

"'To go on a hunting-party, get near a fine reindeer, take aim, try to fire, and miss the shot on account of a damp cap.

"'To start out with a piece of fresh bread in the pocket, and when one gets hungry to find it frozen hard enough to break one's teeth.

"'To leave the table suddenly on hearing a wolf is in sight of the ship, and to come back and find one's dinner eaten by the cat.

"'To return from a walk rapt in thought, and to be awakened suddenly by the embrace of a bear.'

"You see, my friends," said the doctor, "we should not find it hard to imagine other polar troubles; but from the moment it becomes necessary to endure these miseries, it would be a pleasure to narrate them."

"Upon my word," said Altamont, "that's an amusing paper, and it's a pity we can't subscribe to it."

"Suppose we should start one," suggested Johnson.

"We five!" answered Clawbonny; "we should all be editors, and there would be no readers."

"Nor audience either, if we should act a play," said Altamont.

"Tell us, Doctor," said Johnson, "something about Captain Parry's theatre; did they act new plays there?"

"Of course; at first they made use of two volumes which were put on board of the *Hector*, and they had plays every fortnight; but soon they had acted all; then they resorted to original authors, and Parry himself wrote a suitable play for the Christmas holidays; it was very successful, and was called 'The Northwest Passage, or the End of the Voyage.'"

"A capital title," answered Altamont; "but I confess, if I had to write on that subject, I should be puzzled about the end."

"You are right," said Bell; "who can say how it will end?"

"True," answered the doctor; "but why bother about the end, since the beginning is so favorable? Let us trust in Providence, my friends; let us act our part well, and since the end depends on the Author of all things, let us have confidence in him; he will know what to do with us."

"Let us sleep on it," answered Johnson; "it is late, and since bedtime has come, let us turn in."

"You are in a great hurry, my old friend," said the doctor.

"Naturally enough, Doctor, I am so comfortable in bed! And then my dreams are pleasant. I dream of warm countries; or that, to tell the truth, half of my life is spent at the equator and half at the Pole!"

"The deuce," said Altamont, "you have a happy temperament."

"True," answered the boatswain.

"Well, it would be cruel to detain Johnson any longer. His tropical sun is waiting for him. Let us go to bed."

CHAPTER XI.

DISQUIETING TRACES.

In the night of April 26-27, the weather changed; the thermometer fell many degrees, and the inhabitants of Doctor's House perceived it from the cold which made its way beneath their coverings; Altamont, who was watching the stove, took care not to let the fire get low, and he was kept busy putting on enough coal to keep the temperature at 50°. This cold weather announced the end of the storm, and the doctor was glad of it, for now they could resume their usual occupations, their hunting, excursions, and explorations; this would put an end to the apathy of their loneliness, which in time sours even the finest characters.

The next morning the doctor rose early, and made his way over the drifts to the lighthouse. The wind was from the north; the air was clear, the snow was hard under his feet. Soon his five companions had left Doctor's House; their first care was to dig away the drifted snow, which now disguised the plateau; it would have been impossible to discover any traces of life upon it, for the tempest had buried all inequalities beneath fifteen feet of snow.

After the snow was cleared away from the house, it was necessary to restore its architectural outline. This was very easy, and after the ice was removed a few blows with the snow-knife gave it its normal thickness. After two hours' work the granite appeared, and access to the stores and the powder-house was free. But since, in these uncertain climates, such things can happen every day, a new supply of food was carried to the kitchen. They were all wearied of salt food and yearned for fresh meat, and so the hunters were charged with changing the bill of fare, and they prepared to set out.

Still the end of April did not bring with it the polar spring, which was yet six weeks off; the sun's rays were still too feeble to melt the snow or to nourish the few plants of these regions. They feared lest animals should be scarce, both birds and quadrupeds. But a hare, a few ptarmigans, even a young fox, would have been welcome to the table of Doctor's House, and the hunters resolved to shoot whatever should come within range.

The doctor, Altamont, and Bell determined to explore the country. Altamont, they felt sure from his habits, was a bold and skilful hunter, and, with all his bragging, a capital shot. So he went with the hunters, as did Duke, who was equally skilful and less prone to boasting.

The three companions ascended the east cone and set out towards the large white plains; but they had gone no farther than two or three miles before they saw numerous tracks; from that point, they ran down to the shore of Victoria Bay, and appeared to surround Fort Providence with a series of concentric circles.

After they had followed these footprints for a short time, the doctor said,—

"Well, that is clear enough."

"Too clear," said Bell; "they are bear tracks."

"Good game," continued Altamont, "and there is only one fault in it to-day."

"What's that?" asked the doctor.

"The abundance," answered the American.

"What do you mean?" asked Bell.

"I mean that there are distinct tracks of five bears; and five bears are a good many for five men."

"Are you sure of what you say?" asked the doctor.

"Judge for yourself; this mark is different from any other; the claws on this one are farther apart than those. Here is the print of a smaller bear. If you compare them together, you'll find traces of five animals."

"You are right," said Bell, after a careful examination.

"Then," said the doctor, "there is no need of useless bravado, but rather of caution; these animals are famished at the end of a severe winter, and they may be very dangerous; and since there is no doubt of their number—"

"Nor of their intentions," interrupted the American.

"Do you suppose," he asked, "that they have discovered our presence here?"

"Without a doubt, unless we've fallen on a whole band of bears; but in that case, why do their prints go about in a circle, instead of running out of sight? See, they came from the southwest and stopped here, and began to explore the country."

"You are right," said the doctor, "and it's certain they came last night."

"And the other nights too," answered Altamont; "only the snow has covered their tracks."

"No," said the doctor; "it's more likely that they waited for the end of the storm; they went to the bay to catch some seals, and then they scented us."

"True," said Altamont; "so it is easy to know whether they will return to-night."

"How so?" asked Bell.

"By rubbing out some of their tracks; and if we find new ones to-morrow, we can be sure that they are trying to get into Fort Providence."

"Well," said the doctor, "we shall at least know what to expect."

The three then set to work, and soon effaced all the tracks over a space of about six hundred feet.

"It's strange, however," said Bell, "that they could scent us at so great a distance; we didn't burn anything greasy which could attract them."

"O," answered the doctor, "they have very fine sight, and delicate sense of smell! Besides, they are very intelligent, perhaps the most intelligent of animals, and they have found out something strange here."

"Perhaps," continued Bell, "during the storm, they came up as far as the plateau."

"Then," said the American, "why should they have stopped there?"

"True, there is no answer to that," answered the doctor; "and we ought to believe that they are shortening the circle about Fort Providence."

"We shall see," answered Altamont.

"Now, let us go on," said the doctor; "but we'll keep our eyes open."

They kept careful watch, through fear lest some bear should be hidden behind the masses of ice; often they took the blocks for animals, from their shape and whiteness, but soon they discovered their mistake.

They returned at last to the shore beneath the cone, and from there their eyes swept in vain from Cape Washington to Johnson Island. They saw nothing; everything was white and motionless; not a sound was to be heard. They entered the snow-house.

Hatteras and Johnson were informed of the condition of affairs, and they resolved to keep a strict watch. Night came; nothing occurred to alarm them, or to mar its beauty. At dawn the next morning, Hatteras and his companions, fully armed, went out to examine the condition of the snow; they found the same tracks as on the previous day, only nearer. Evidently the enemy was preparing to lay siege to Fort Providence.

"They have opened their second parallel," said the doctor.

"They have made a point in advance," answered Altamont; "see those footprints coming nearer the plateau; they are those of some strong animal."

"Yes, they are gaining ground gradually," said Johnson; "it is evident that they are going to attack us."

"There's no doubt of that," said the doctor; "let us avoid showing ourselves. We are not strong enough to fight successfully."

"But where do these devilish bears come from?" asked Bell.

"From behind those pieces of ice to the east, where they are spying us; don't let us get too near them."

"And our hunt?" asked Altamont.

"Let us put it off for a few days," answered the doctor; "let us again rub out these nearest marks, and to-morrow we shall see if they are renewed. In this way we can see the manoeuvres of our enemies."

The doctor's advice was taken, and they returned to the fort; the presence of these terrible beasts forbade any excursion. Strict watch was kept over the neighborhood of Victoria Bay. The lighthouse was dismantled; it was of no real use, and might attract the attention of the animals; the lantern and the electric threads were carried to the house; then they took turns in watching the upper plateau.

Again they had to endure the monotony of loneliness, but what else was to be done? They dared not risk a contest at so fearful odds; no one's life could be risked imprudently. Perhaps the bears, if they caught sight of nothing, might be thrown off the track; or, if they were met singly, they might be attacked successfully. However, this inaction was relieved by a new interest; they had to keep watch, and no one regretted it.

April 28th passed by without any sign of the existence of the enemy. The next morning their curiosity as to the existence of new tracks was succeeded by astonishment. Not a trace was to be seen; the snow was intact.

"Good," shouted Altamont, "the bears are thrown off the track! They have no perseverance! They are tired of waiting, and have gone! Good by, and now off to the hunt!"

"Eh!" answered the doctor, "who can say? For greater safety, my friends, I beg one more day of watching; it is certain the enemy did not approach last night, at least from this side—"

"Let us make a circuit of the plateau," said Altamont, "and then we shall make sure."

"Willingly," said the doctor.

But with all their care in exploration, not the slightest trace could be found.

"Well, shall we start on our hunt?" asked Altamont, impatiently.

"Let us wait till to-morrow," urged the doctor.

"All right," answered Altamont, who had some reluctance, however, about conceding.

They returned to the fort. Each one had to watch for an hour, as on the previous evening. When Altamont's turn came, he went to relieve Bell. As soon as he was gone, Hatteras called his companions together. The doctor left his notes, and Johnson his furnaces. It might have been supposed that Hatteras was going to discuss the dangers of the situation; he did not even think of them.

"My friends," he said, "let us take advantage of the absence of this American, to talk over our affairs; some things don't concern him at all, and I don't care to have him meddling with them."

The others looked at one another, uncertain of his meaning.

"I want to speak with you," he said, "about our future plans."

"Well," answered the doctor, "let us talk now we are alone."

"In a month, or six weeks at the latest," Hatteras began, "we shall be able to make distant excursions. Had you thought of what might be done in the summer?"

"Had you, Captain?" asked Johnson.

"I? I can say that not an hour passes without my mind's recurring to my plan. I suppose no one of you has any thought of returning—"

There was no immediate answer to this insinuation.

"As for me," continued Hatteras, "if I have to go alone, I shall go to the North Pole; we are only three hundred and sixty miles from it at the outside. No men have ever been so near it, and I shall not let such a chance go by without the attempt, even if it be impossible. What are your views in the matter?"

"Your own," answered the doctor.

"And yours, Johnson?"

"The same as the doctor's," answered the boatswain.

"It is your turn to speak, Bell," said Hatteras.

"Captain," answered the carpenter, "it is true we have no family awaiting us in England, but our country is our country: don't you think of going back?"

"We shall go back easily as soon as we shall have discovered the Pole. In fact, more easily. The difficulties will not increase, for, on our way thither, we leave behind us the coldest spots on the globe. We have supplies of all sorts for a long time. There is nothing to hinder us, and we should be to blame if we did not push on to the end."

"Well," answered Bell, "we are all of your opinion, Captain."

"Good!" replied Hatteras. "I have never doubted of you. We shall succeed, my friends, and England shall have all the glory of our success."

"But there is an American with us," said Johnson.

Hatteras could not restrain a wrathful gesture at this remark.

"I know it," he said in a deep voice.

"We can't leave him here," continued the doctor.

"No, we cannot," answered Hatteras, coldly.

"And he will certainly come."

"Yes, he will come, but who will command?"

"You, Captain."

"And if you obey me, will this Yankee refuse to obey?"

"I don't think so," answered Johnson; "but if he is unwilling to obey your orders—"

"It would have to be settled between him and me."

The three Englishmen looked at Hatteras without a word. The doctor broke the silence.

"How shall we travel?" he asked.

"By keeping along the coast as much as possible," answered Hatteras.

"But if we find the sea open, as is likely?"

"Well, we shall cross it."

"How? We have no boat."

Hatteras did not answer; he was evidently embarrassed.

"Perhaps," suggested Bell, "we might build a launch out of the timbers of the *Porpoise*."

"Never!" shouted Hatteras, warmly.

"Never?" exclaimed Johnson.

The doctor shook his head; he understood the captain's unwillingness.

"Never!" the latter answered. "A launch made out of the wood of an American ship would be an American launch—"

"But, Captain—" interposed Johnson.

The doctor made a sign to the old boatswain to keep silent. A more suitable time was required for that question. The doctor, although he understood Hatteras's repugnance, did not sympathize with it, and he determined to make his friend abandon this hasty decision. Hence he spoke of something else, of the possibility of going along the coast to the north, and that unknown point, the North Pole. In a word, he avoided all dangerous subjects of conversation up to the moment when it was suddenly ended by the entrance of Altamont. He had nothing new to report. The day ended in this way, and the night was quiet. The bears had evidently disappeared.

CHAPTER XII.

THE ICE PRISON.

The next day they determined to arrange the hunt, in which Hatteras, Altamont, and the carpenter were to take part; no more tracks were to be seen; the bears had decidedly given up their plan of attack, either from fear of their unknown enemies, or because there had been no sign of living beings beneath the mass of snow. During the absence of the three hunters, the doctor was to push on to Johnson Island to examine the condition of the ice, and to make some hydrographic investigations. The cold was sharp, but they supported it well, having become accustomed to it by this time. The boatswain was to remain at Doctor's House; in a word, to guard the house.

The three hunters made their preparations; each one took a double-barrelled rifled gun, with conical balls; they carried a small quantity of pemmican, in case night should fall before their return; they also were provided with the snow-knife, which is so indispensable in these regions, and a hatchet which they wore in their belts. Thus armed and equipped they could go far; and since they were both skilled and bold, they could count on bringing back a good supply.

At eight in the morning they set out. Duke sprang about ahead of them; they ascended the hill to the east, went about the lighthouse, and disappeared in the plains to the south, which were bounded by Mount Bell. The doctor, having agreed on a danger-signal with Johnson, descended towards the shore so as to reach the ice in Victoria Bay.

The boatswain remained at Fort Providence alone, but not idle. He first set free the Greenland dogs, which were playing about the Dog Palace; they in their joy rolled about in the snow. Johnson then gave his attentions to the cares of housekeeping. He had to renew the fuel and provisions, to set the stores in order, to mend many broken utensils, to patch the coverings, to work over the shoes for the long excursions of the summer. There was no lack of things to do, but the boatswain worked with the ease of a sailor, who has generally a smattering of all trades. While thus employed he began to think of the talk of the evening before; he thought of the captain, and especially of his obstinacy, which, after all, had something very heroic and very honorable about it, in his unwillingness that any American man or boat should reach the Pole before him, or even with him.

"Still, it seems to me," he said to himself, "no easy task to cross the ocean without a boat; and if we have the open sea before us, we should need one. The strongest Englishman in the world couldn't swim three hundred miles. Patriotism has its limits. Well, we shall see. We have still time before us; Dr. Clawbonny has not yet said his last word in the matter; he is wise, and he may persuade the captain to change his mind. I'll bet that in going towards the island he'll glance at the fragments of the *Porpoise*, and will know exactly what can be made out of them."

Johnson had reached this point in his reflections, and the hunters had been gone an hour, when a loud report was heard two or three miles to windward.

"Good!" said the sailor; "they have come across something, and without going very far, for I heard them distinctly. After all, the air is so clear."

A second and then a third report was heard.

"Hulloa!" continued Johnson, "they've got into a good place."

Three other reports, in quicker succession, were heard.

"Six shots!" said Johnson; "now they've fired off everything. It was a hot time! Is it possible—"

At the thought, Johnson grew pale; he quickly left the snow-house, and in a few moments he had run up to the top of the cone. He saw a sight that made him tremble.

"The bears!" he shouted.

The three hunters, followed by Duke, were running rapidly, followed by five enormous animals; their six bullets had not disabled them; the bears were gaining on them; Hatteras, behind the others, could only keep his distance from the animals by throwing away his cap, hatchet, and even his gun. The bears stopped, according to their habit, to sniff at the different objects, and lost a little on this ground on which they would have outstripped the swiftest horse. It was thus that Hatteras, Altamont, and Bell, all out of breath, came up to Johnson, and they all slid down the slope to the snow-house. The five bears were close behind, and the captain was obliged to ward off the blow of a paw with his knife. In a moment Hatteras and his companions were locked in the house. The animals stopped on the upper plateau of the truncated cone.

"Hatteras could only keep his distance from the animals by throwing away his cap, hatchet, and even his gun."

"Well," said Hatteras, "we can now defend ourselves better, five to five!"

"Four to five!" shouted Johnson in a terrified voice.

"What?" asked Hatteras.

"The doctor!" answered Johnson, pointing to the empty room.

"Well?"

"He is on the shore of the island!"

"Poor man!" cried Bell.

"We can't abandon him in this way," said Altamont.

"Let us run!" said Hatteras.

He opened the door quickly, but he had hardly time to shut it; a bear nearly crushed his skull with his claw.

"They are there," he cried.

"All?" asked Bell.

"All!" answered Hatteras.

Altamont hastened to the windows, heaping up the bays with pieces of ice torn from the walls of the house. His companions did the same without speaking. Duke's dull snarls alone broke the silence.

But it must be said these men had only a single thought; they forgot their own danger, and only considered the doctor. Poor Clawbonny! so kind, so devoted! the soul of the little colony! for the first time he was missing; extreme peril, a terrible death, awaited him; for when his excursion was over he would return quietly to Fort Providence, and would find these ferocious animals. And there was no way of warning him.

"If I'm not mistaken, he will be on his guard; your shots must have warned him, and he must know something has happened."

"But if he were far off," answered Altamont, "and did not understand? There are eight chances out of ten that he'll come back without suspicion of danger! The bears are hiding behind the scarp of the fort, and he can't see them."

"We shall have to get rid of these dangerous beasts before his return," answered Hatteras.

"But how?" asked Bell.

To answer this question was not easy. A sortie seemed impossible. They took the precaution to barricade the entrance, but the bears could easily have overcome the obstacles if the idea had occurred to them; they knew the number and strength of their adversaries, and they could easily have reached them. The prisoners were posted in each one of the chambers of Doctor's House to watch for every attempt at entrance; when they listened, they heard the bears coming and going, growling, and tearing at the walls with their huge paws. But some action was necessary; time was pressing. Altamont resolved to make a loop-hole to shoot the assailants; in a few minutes he had made a little hole in the ice-wall; he pushed his gun through it; but it had scarcely reached the other side before it was torn from his hands with irresistible force before he could fire.

"The devil!" he cried, "we are too weak."

And he hastened to close the loop-hole. Thus matters went for an hour, without any end appearing probable. The chances of a sortie were discussed; they seemed slight, for the bears could not be fought singly. Nevertheless, Hatteras and his companions, being anxious to finish it, and, it must be said, very much confused at being thus imprisoned by the beasts, were about to try a direct attack, when the captain thought of a new means of defence.

He took the poker and plunged it into the stove; then he made an opening in the wall, but so as to keep a thin coating of ice outside. His companions watched him. When the poker was white hot, Hatteras said,—

"This bar will drive away the bears, for they won't be able to seize it, and through the loop-hole we will be able to fire at them, without their taking our guns away from us."

"A good idea!" cried Bell, going towards Altamont.

Then Hatteras, withdrawing the poker from the stove, pushed it through the wall. The snow, steaming at its touch, hissed sharply. Two bears ran to seize the bar, but they roared fearfully when four shots were fired at once.

"Hit!" shouted the American.

"Hit!" repeated Bell.

"Let us try again," said Hatteras, closing the opening for a moment.

The poker was put again into the fire; in a few minutes it was red hot.

Altamont and Bell returned to their place after loading their guns; Hatteras again pushed the poker through the loop-hole. But this time an impenetrable substance stopped it.

"Curse it!" cried the American.

"What's the matter?" asked Johnson.

"The matter! These cursed animals are heaping up the ice and snow so as to bury us alive!"

"Impossible!"

"See, the poker can't go through! Really, this is absurd!"

It was more than absurd, it was alarming. Matters looked worse. The bears, which are very intelligent beasts, employed this method of suffocating their prey. They heaped the ice in such a way as to render flight impossible.

"The bears heaped the ice in such a way as to render flight impossible."

"This is hard," said Johnson, with a very mortified air. "It's well enough to have men treat you in this way, but bears!"

After this reflection two hours passed by without any material change in their situation; a sortie became impossible; the thickened walls deadened all sound without. Altamont walked to and fro like a bold man in face of a danger greater than his courage. Hatteras thought anxiously of the doctor, and of the great danger awaiting him when he should return.

"Ah," shouted Johnson, "if Dr. Clawbonny were only here!"

"Well, what would he do?" asked Altamont.

"O, he would be able to help us!"

"How?" asked the American, with some asperity.

"If I knew," answered Johnson, "I shouldn't want him here. Still, I can think of a piece of advice he would give us at this moment."

"What is that?"

"To take some food. It can't hurt us. What do you think, Mr. Altamont?"

"Let us eat if you care to," was the answer; "although our condition is stupid, not to say disgraceful."

"I'll bet," said Johnson, "that we'll find some way of driving them off after dinner."

They made no reply, but sat down to dinner. Johnson, as a pupil of the doctor, tried to be a philosopher in the face of danger, but he succeeded ill; his jokes stuck in his throat. Besides, they began to feel uncomfortable; the air was growing bad in this hermetically sealed prison; the stove-pipe drew insufficiently, and it was easy to see that in a short time the fire would go out; the oxygen, consumed by their lungs and the fire, would be replaced by carbonic acid, which would be fatal to them, as they all knew. Hatteras was the first to detect this new danger; he was unwilling to hide it from the others.

"So, at any risk we must get out!" said Altamont.

"Yes," answered Hatteras; "but let us wait till night; we will make a hole in the snow that we may get fresh air; then one shall take his place here and fire at the bears."

"It's the only thing we can do," said the American.

Having agreed on this, they waited for the time of action; and during the following hours, Altamont did not spare imprecations against a state of things in which, as he put it, "there being men and bears concerned, the men were getting the worst of it."

CHAPTER XIII.

THE MINE.

Night came, and the lamp began to burn dimly in the close air of the room. At eight o'clock they made their final preparations. The guns were carefully loaded, and an opening was begun in the roof of the snow-house. Bell worked cleverly at this for a few minutes, when Johnson, who had left the bedroom, where he was on guard, for a few minutes, returned rapidly to his companions. He seemed disturbed.

"What is the matter?" the captain asked.

"The matter? nothing!" answered the old sailor, hesitatingly, "yet—"

"What is it?" asked Altamont.

"Hush! Don't you hear a strange sound?"

"On which side?"

"There! There is something happening to the wall of that room."

Bell stopped his work; each one listened. A distant noise could be heard, apparently in the side wall; some one was evidently making a passage-way through the ice.

"It's a tearing sound!" said Johnson.

"Without a doubt," answered Altamont.

"The bears?" asked Bell.

"Yes, the bears," said Altamont.

"They have changed their plan," continued the sailor; "they've given up trying to suffocate us."

"Or else they think they've done it," added the American, who was getting very angry.

"We shall be attacked," said Bell.

"Well," remarked Hatteras, "we shall fight against them."

"Confound it!" shouted Altamont; "I prefer that decidedly! I've had enough working in the dark! Now we shall see one another and fight!"

"Yes," answered Johnson; "but with our guns it is impossible in so small a space."

"Well, with a hatchet or a knife!"

The noise increased; the scratching of claws could be heard; the bears had attacked the wall at the angle where it joined the snow fastened to the rock."

"Evidently," said Johnson, "the animal is within six feet of us."

"You are right, Johnson," answered the American, "but we have time to prepare ourselves to receive it!"

The American took the axe in one hand, his knife in the other; resting on his right foot, his body thrown back, he stood ready to attack. Hatteras and Bell did the same. Johnson prepared his gun in case fire-arms should be necessary. The noise grew louder and louder; the ice kept cracking beneath the repeated blows. At last only a thin crust separated the adversaries; suddenly this crust tore asunder like paper through which a clown leaps, and an enormous black body appeared in the gloom of the room. Altamont raised his hand to strike it.

"An enormous black body appeared in the gloom of the room. Altamont raised his hand to strike it."

"Stop! for heaven's sake, stop!" said a well-known voice.

"The doctor, the doctor!" shouted Johnson.

It was indeed the doctor, who, carried by the impetus, rolled into the room.

"Good evening, my friends," he said, springing to his feet.

His companions remained stupefied; but joy succeeded their stupefaction; each one wished to embrace the worthy man; Hatteras, who was much moved, clasped him for a long time to his breast. The doctor answered by a warm clasp of the hand.

"What! you, Dr. Clawbonny!" said the boatswain.

"Why, Johnson, I was much more anxious about your fate than you about mine."

"But how did you know that we were attacked by bears?" asked Altamont; "our greatest fear was to see you returning quietly to Fort Providence without thought of danger."

"O, I saw everything!" answered the doctor; "your shots warned me; I happened to be near the fragments of the *Porpoise;* I climbed up a hummock; I saw five bears chasing you; ah, I feared the worst for you! But the way you slid down the hill, and the hesitation of the animals, reassured me for a time; I knew you'd had time to lock yourselves in. Then I approached gradually, climbing and creeping between cakes of ice; I arrived near the fort, and I saw the huge beasts working like beavers; they were tossing the snow about, heaping up the ice so as to bury you alive. Fortunately, they did not think of hurling the blocks down from the top of the cone, for you would have been crushed without mercy."

"But," said Bell, "you were not safe, Doctor; couldn't they leave their place and attack you?"

"They didn't think of it; the Greenland dogs which Johnson let loose would sniff around at a little distance, but they didn't think of attacking them; no, they were sure of better game."

"Thanks for the compliment," said Altamont, smiling.

"O, you needn't be vain of it! When I saw the tactics of the bears, I resolved to join you; to be prudent, I waited till night; so at twilight I slipped noiselessly towards the slope, on the side of the magazine; I had my own idea in choosing this point; I wanted to make a gallery; so I set to work; I began with my snow-knife, and a capital tool it is! For three hours I dug and dug, and here I am, hungry and tired, but here at last—"

"To share our fate?" asked Altamont.

"To save all of us; but give me a piece of biscuit and some meat; I'm half starved."

Soon the doctor was burying his white teeth in a large slice of salt beef. Although he was eating, he appeared willing to answer the questions they put to him.

"To save us?" Bell began.

"Certainly," answered the doctor, "and to rid us of the malicious pests who will end by finding our stores and devouring them."

"We must stay here," said Hatteras.

"Certainly," answered the doctor, "and yet rid ourselves of these animals."

"There is then a means?" asked Bell.

"A sure means," answered the doctor.

"I said so," cried Johnson, rubbing his hands; "with Dr. Clawbonny, we need not despair; he always has some invention handy."

"Not always handy; but after thinking for a while—"

"Doctor," interrupted Altamont, "can't the bears get through the passage-way you cut?"

"No, I took the precaution of closing it behind me; and now we can go from here to the powder-magazine without their suspecting it."

"Good! Will you tell us what means you intend to employ to rid us of these unpleasant visitors?"

"Something very simple, and which is already half done."

"How so?"

"You'll see. But I forgot I didn't come alone."

"What do you mean?" asked Johnson.

"I have a companion to introduce to you."

And with these words he pulled in from the gallery the newly killed body of a fox.

"A fox!" cried Bell.

"My morning's game," answered the doctor, modestly, "and you'll see no fox was ever wanted more than this one."

"But what is your plan, after all?" asked Altamont.

"I intend to blow the bears up with a hundred pounds of powder."

They all gazed at the doctor with amazement.

"But the powder?" they asked.

"It is in the magazine."

"And the magazine?"

"This passage-way leads to it. I had my own reason for digging this passage sixty feet long; I might have attacked the parapet nearer to the house, but I had my own idea."

"Well, where are you going to put the mine?" asked the American.

"On the slope, as far as possible from the house, the magazine, and the stores."

"But how shall you get all the bears together?"

"I'll take charge of that," answered the doctor; "but we've talked enough, now to work; we have a hundred feet to dig out to-night; it's tiresome work, but we five can do it in relays. Bell shall begin, and meanwhile we can take some rest."

"Really," said Johnson, "the more I think of it, the more I admire Dr. Clawbonny's plan."

"It's sure," answered the doctor.

"O, from the moment you opened your mouth they are dead bears, and I already feel their fur about my shoulders!"

"To work, then!"

The doctor entered the dark gallery, followed by Bell; where the doctor had gone through, his companions were sure to find no difficulty; two reached the magazine and entered among the barrels, which were all arranged in good order. The doctor gave Bell the necessary instructions; the carpenter began work on the wall towards the slope, and his companion returned to the house.

Bell worked for an hour, and dug a passage about ten feet long, through which one might crawl. Then Altamont took his place, and did about as much; the snow which was taken from the gallery was carried into the kitchen, where the doctor melted it at the fire, that it might take up less room. The captain followed the American; then came Johnson. In ten hours, that is to say, at about eight o'clock in the morning, the gallery was finished. At daybreak the doctor peeped at the bears through a loop-hole in the wall of the powder-magazine.

The patient animals had not left their place; there they were, coming and going, growling, but in general patrolling patiently; they kept going around the house, which was gradually disappearing beneath the snow. But at length they seemed to lose patience, for the doctor saw them begin to tear away the ice and snow they had heaped up.

"Good!" he said to the captain, who was standing near him.

"What are they doing?" he asked.

"They seem to be trying to destroy what they have done and to get to us! But they'll be destroyed first! At any rate, there is no time to lose."

The doctor made his way to the place where the mine was to be laid; then he enlarged the chamber all the height and breadth of the slope; a layer of ice, only a foot thick at the outside, remained; it had to be supported lest it should fall in. A stake resting on the granite soil served as a post; the fox's body was fastened to the top, and a long knotted cord ran the whole length of the gallery to the magazine. The doctor's companions followed his orders without clearly understanding his intention.

"This is the bait," he said, pointing to the fox.

At the foot of the post he placed a cask holding about a hundred pounds of powder.

"And here is the charge," he added.

"But," asked Hatteras, "sha'n't we blow ourselves up at the same time?"

"No, we are far enough off from the explosion; besides, our house is solid; and if it is hurt a little we can easily repair it."

"Well," continued Altamont; "but how are you going to set it off?"

"This way. By pulling this cord we pull over the post which holds up the ice above the powder; the fox's body will suddenly be seen on the slope, and you must confess that the starving animals will rush upon this unexpected prey."

"Certainly."

"Well, at that moment I shall explode the mine, and blow up guest and dinner."

"Well, well!" exclaimed Johnson, who was listening eagerly.

Hatteras had perfect confidence in his friend, and asked no question. He waited. But Altamont wanted it made perfectly clear.

"Doctor," he began, "how can you calculate the length of the fuse so exactly that the explosion will take place at the right moment?"

"It's very simple," answered the doctor; "I don't make any calculation."

"But you have a fuse a hundred feet long?"

"No."

"Shall you set a train of powder simply?"

"No! that might fail."

"Will some one have to volunteer and light the powder?"

"If you want any one," said Johnson, eagerly, "I'm your man."

"It's not necessary, my friend," answered the doctor, grasping the boatswain's hand; "our five lives are precious, and they will be spared, thank God!"

"Then," said the American, "I can't guess."

"Well," answered the doctor, smiling, "if we couldn't get out of this little affair, what would be the use of physics?"

"Ah!" said Johnson, brightening up, "physics!"

"Yes! Haven't we here an electric pile and wires long enough,—those, you know, which connected with the lighthouse?"

"Well?"

"Well, we shall explode the powder when we please, instantly, and without danger."

"Hurrah!" shouted Johnson.

"Hurrah!" repeated his companions, not caring whether the enemy heard them or not. Soon the electric wires were run through the gallery from the house to the chamber of the mine. One of the extremities remained at the pile, the other was plunged into the centre of the cask, the two ends being placed at but a little distance from one another. At nine of the morning all was finished, and it was time; the bears were tearing the snow away furiously. The doctor thought the proper time had come. Johnson was sent to the magazine and charged with pulling the cord fastened to the post. He took his place.

"Now," said the doctor to his companions, "load your guns in case they should not be all killed at once, and take your place near Johnson; as soon as you hear the explosion, run out."

"All right!" said the American.

"And now we have done all that men can do! We have helped ourselves; may God help us!"

Hatteras, Altamont, and Bell went to the magazine. The doctor remained alone at the pile. Soon he heard Johnson's voice crying,—

"Ready?"

"All right!" he answered.

Johnson gave a strong pull at the rope; it pulled over the stake; then he ran to the loop-hole and looked out. The surface of the slope had sunk in. The fox's body was visible upon the shattered ice. The bears, at first surprised, crowded about this new prey.

"Fire!" shouted Johnson.

The doctor at once established the electric current between the threads; a loud explosion followed; the house shook as if in an earthquake; the walls fell in. Hatteras, Altamont, and Bell hastened out of the magazine, ready to fire. But their guns were not needed; four of the five bears fell about them in fragments, while the fifth, badly burned, ran away as fast as he could.

"A loud explosion followed."

"Hurrah! hurrah! hurrah!" shouted the doctor's companions, while they crowded about him and embraced him.

CHAPTER XIV.

THE POLAR SPRING.

The prisoners were set free; they expressed their joy by the warmth of their thanks to the doctor. Johnson regretted somewhat the skins, which were burned and useless; but his regret did not sour his temper. They spent the day in repairing the house, which was somewhat injured by the explosion. They took away the blocks heaped up by the animals, and the walls were made secure. They worked briskly, encouraged by the cheery songs of the boatswain.

The next day the weather was much milder; the wind changed suddenly, and the thermometer rose to +15°. So great a difference was soon felt by both man and nature. The southerly wind brought with it the first signs of the polar spring. This comparative warmth lasted for many days; the thermometer, sheltered from the wind, even rose as high as +31°, and there were signs of a thaw. The ice began to crack; a few spirts of salt-water arose here and there, like jets in an English park; a few days later it rained hard.

A dense vapor arose from the snow; this was a good sign, and the melting of the immense masses appeared to be near at hand. The pale disk of the sun grew brighter and drew longer spirals above the horizon; the night lasted scarcely three hours. Another similar symptom was the reappearance of some ptarmigans, arctic geese, plover, and flocks of quail; the air was soon filled with the deafening cries which they remembered from the previous summer. A few hares, which they were able to shoot, appeared on the shores of the bay, as well as the arctic mice, the burrows of which were like a honeycomb. The doctor called the attention of his friends to the fact that these animals began to lose their white winter plumage, or hair, to put on their summer dress; they were evidently getting ready for summer, while their sustenance appeared in the form of moss, poppy, saxifrage, and thin grass. A new life was peering through the melting snows. But with the harmless animals returned the famished foes; foxes and wolves arrived in search of their prey; mournful howling sounded during the brief darkness of the nights.

The wolf of these countries is near of kin to the dog; like him, it barks, and often in such a way as to deceive the sharpest ears, those of the dogs themselves, for instance; it is even said that they employ this device to attract dogs, and then eat them. This has been observed on the shores of Hudson's Bay, and the doctor could confirm it at New America; Johnson took care not to let loose the dogs of the sledge, who might have been destroyed in that way. As for Duke, he had seen too many of them, and he was too wise to be caught in any such way.

During a fortnight they hunted a great deal; fresh food was abundant; they shot partridges, ptarmigans, and snow-birds, which were delicious eating. The hunters did not go far from Fort Providence. In fact, small game could almost be killed with a stick; and it gave much animation to the silent shores of Victoria Bay,—an unaccustomed sight which delighted their eyes.

The fortnight succeeding the great defeat of the bears was taken up with different occupations. The thaw advanced steadily; the thermometer rose to 32°, and torrents began to roar in the ravines, and thousands of cataracts fell down the declivities. The doctor cleared an acre of ground and sowed in it cresses, sorrel, and cochlearia, which are excellent remedies for the scurvy; the little greenish leaves were peeping above the ground when, with incredible rapidity, the cold again seized everything.

In a single night, with a violent north-wind, the thermometer fell forty degrees, to -8°. Everything was frozen; birds, quadrupeds, and seals disappeared as if by magic; the holes for the seals were closed, the crevasses disappeared, the ice became as hard as granite, and the waterfalls hung like long crystal pendants.

It was a total change to the eye; it took place in the night of May 11-12. And when Bell the next morning put his nose out of doors into this sharp frost, he nearly left it there.

"O, this polar climate!" cried the doctor, a little disappointed; "that's the way it goes! Well, I shall have to begin sowing again."

Hatteras took things less philosophically, so eager was he to renew his explorations. But he had to resign himself.

"Will this cold weather last long?" asked Johnson.

"No, my friend, no," answered Clawbonny; "it's the last touch of winter we shall have! You know it's at home here, and we can't drive it away against its will."

"It defends itself well," said Bell, rubbing his face.

"Yes, but I ought to have expected it," said the doctor; "and I should not have thrown the seed away so stupidly, especially since I might have started them near the kitchen stove."

"What!" asked Altamont, "could you have foreseen this change of weather?"

"Certainly, and without resorting to magic. I ought to have put the seed under the protection of Saints Mamert, Panera, and Servais, whose days are the 11th, 12th, and 13th of this month."

"Well, Doctor," said Altamont, "will you tell me what influence these three saints have on the weather?"

"A very great influence, to believe gardeners, who call them the three saints of ice."

"And why so, pray?"

"Because generally there is a periodic frost in the month of May, and the greatest fall of temperature takes place from the 11th to the 13th of this month. It is a fact, that is all."

"It is curious, but what is the explanation?" asked the American.

"There are two: either by the interposition of a greater number of asteroids between the earth and the sun at this season, or simply by the melting of the snow, which thereby absorbs a great quantity of heat. Both explanations are plausible; must they be received? I don't know; but if I'm uncertain of the truth of the explanation, I ought not to have been of the fact, and so lose my crop."

The doctor was right; for one reason or another the cold was very intense during the rest of the month of May; their hunting was interrupted, not so much by the severity of the weather as by the absence of game; fortunately, the supply of fresh meat was not yet quite exhausted. They found themselves accordingly condemned to new inactivity; for a fortnight, from the 11th to the 25th of May, only one incident broke the monotony of their lives; a serious illness, diphtheria, suddenly seized the carpenter; from the swollen tonsils and the false membrane in the throat, the doctor could not be ignorant of the nature of the disease; but he was in his element, and he soon drove it away, for evidently it had not counted on meeting him; his treatment was very simple, and the medicines were not hard to get; the doctor simply prescribed pieces of ice to be held in the mouth; in a few hours the swelling went down and the false membrane disappeared; twenty-four hours later Bell was up again.

When the others wondered at the doctor's prescriptions: "This is the land of these complaints," he answered; "the cure must be near the disease."

"The cure, and especially the doctor," added Johnson, in whose mind the doctor was assuming colossal proportions.

During this new leisure the latter resolved to have a serious talk with the captain; he wanted to induce Hatteras to give up his intention of going northward without carrying some sort of a boat; a piece of wood, something with which he could cross an arm of the sea, if they should meet one. The captain, who was fixed in his views, had formally vowed not to use a boat made of the fragments of the American ship. The doctor was uncertain how to broach the subject, and yet a speedy decision was important, for the month of June would be the time for distant excursions. At last, after long reflection, he took Hatteras aside one day, and with his usual air of kindness said to him,—

"Hatteras, you know I am your friend?"

"Certainly," answered the captain, warmly, "my best friend; indeed, my only one."

"If I give you a piece of advice," resumed the doctor, "advice which you don't ask for, would you consider it disinterested?"

"Yes, for I know that selfish interest has never been your guide; but what do you want to say?"

"One moment, Hatteras; I have something else to ask of you: Do you consider me a true Englishman like yourself, and eager for the glory of my country?"

Hatteras looked at the doctor with surprise.

"Yes," he answered, with his face expressing surprise at the question.

"You want to reach the North Pole," resumed the doctor; "I understand your ambition, I share it, but to reach this end we need the means."

"Well, haven't I so far sacrificed everything in order to succeed?"

"No, Hatteras, you have not sacrificed your personal prejudices, and at this moment I see that you are ready to refuse the indispensable means of reaching the Pole."

"Ah!" answered Hatteras, "you mean the launch; this man—"

"Come, Hatteras, let us argue coolly, without passion, and look at all sides of the question. The line of the coast on which we have wintered may be broken; there is no proof that it runs six degrees to the north; if the information which has brought you so far is right, we ought to find a vast extent of open sea during the summer months. Now, with the Arctic Ocean before us, free of ice and favorable for navigation, what shall we do if we lack the means of crossing it?"

Hatteras made no answer.

"Do you want to be within a few miles of the Pole without being able to reach it?"

Hatteras's head sank into his hands.

"And now," continued the doctor, "let us look at the question from a moral point of view. I can understand that an Englishman should give up his life and his fortune for the honor of his country. But because a boat made of a few planks torn from a wrecked American ship first touches the coast or crosses the unknown ocean, can that diminish the honor of the discovery? If you found on this shore the hull of an abandoned ship, should you hesitate to make use of it? Doesn't the glory of success belong to the head of the expedition? And I ask you if this launch built by four Englishmen, manned by four Englishmen, would not be English from keel to gunwale?"

Hatteras was still silent.

"No," said Clawbonny, "let us talk frankly; it's not the boat you mind, it's the man."

"Yes, Doctor, yes," answered the captain, "that American; I hate him with real English hate, that man thrown in my way by chance—"

"To save you!"

"To ruin me! He seems to defy me, to act as master, to imagine he holds my fate in his hands, and to have guessed my plans. Didn't he show his character when we were giving names to the new lands? Has he ever said what he was doing here? You can't free me of the idea which is killing me, that this man is the head of an expedition sent out by the government of the United States."

"And if he is, Hatteras, what is there to show that he is in search of the Pole? Can't America try to discover the Northwest Passage as well as England? At any rate, Altamont is perfectly ignorant of your plans; for neither Johnson nor Bell nor you nor I has said a single word about them in his presence."

"Well, I hope he'll never know them!"

"He will know them finally, of course, for we can't leave him alone here."

"Why not?" asked the captain, with some violence; "can't he remain at Fort Providence?"

"He would never give his consent, Hatteras; and then to leave him here, uncertain of finding him again, would be more than imprudent, it would be inhuman. Altamont will come with us; he must come! But since there is no need of suggesting new ideas to him, let us say nothing, and build a launch apparently for reconnoitring these new shores."

Hatteras could not make up his mind to accede to the demands of his friend, who waited for an answer which did not come.

"And if he refused to let us tear his ship to pieces!" said the captain, finally.

"In that case, you would have the right on your side; you could build the boat in spite of him, and he could do nothing about it."

"I hope he will refuse," exclaimed Hatteras.

"Before he refuses," answered the doctor, "he must be asked. I will undertake to do it."

In fact, that evening, before supper, Clawbonny turned the conversation to certain proposed expeditions in the summer months for hydrographic observations.

"I suppose, Altamont," he said, "that you will join us?"

"Certainly," was the reply; "we must know how large New America is."

Hatteras gazed earnestly at his rival while he made his answer.

"And for that," continued Altamont, "we must make the best use we can of the fragments of the *Porpoise;* let us make a strong boat which can carry us far."

"You hear, Bell," said the doctor, quickly; "to-morrow we shall set to work."

CHAPTER XV.

THE NORTHWEST PASSAGE.

The next day Bell, Altamont, and the doctor went to the *Porpoise;* they found no lack of wood; the old three-masted launch, though injured by being wrecked, could still supply abundant material for the new one. The carpenter set to work at once; they needed a seaworthy boat, which should yet be light enough to carry on a sledge. Towards the end of May the weather grew warmer; the thermometer rose above the freezing-point; the spring came in earnest this time, and the men were able to lay aside their winter clothing. Much rain fell, and soon the snow began to slide and melt away. Hatteras could not hide his joy at seeing the first signs of thaw in the ice-fields. The open sea meant liberty for him.

"The carpenter set to work at once."

Whether or not his predecessors had been wrong on this great question of an open polar sea, he hoped soon to know. All chance of success in his undertaking depended on this. One evening, after a warm day in which the ice had given unmistakable signs of breaking up, he turned the conversation to the question of an open sea. He took up the familiar arguments, and found the doctor, as ever, a warm advocate of his doctrine. Besides, his conclusions were evidently accurate.

"It is plain," he said, "that if the ocean before Victoria Bay gets clear of ice, its southern part will also be clear as far as New Cornwall and Queen's Channel. Penny and Belcher saw it in that state, and they certainly saw clearly."

"I agree with you, Hatteras," answered the doctor, "and I have no reason for doubting the word of these sailors; a vain attempt has been made to explain their discovery as an effect of mirage; but they were so certain, it was impossible that they could have made such a mistake."

"I always thought so," said Altamont; "the polar basin extends to the east as well as to the west."

"We can suppose so, at any rate," answered Hatteras.

"We ought to suppose so," continued the American, "for this open sea which Captains Penny and Belcher saw near the coast of Grinnell Land was seen by Morton, Kane's lieutenant, in the straits which are named after that bold explorer."

"We are not in Kane's sea," answered Hatteras, coldly, "and consequently we cannot verify the fact."

"It is supposable, at least," said Altamont.

"Certainly," replied the doctor, who wished to avoid useless discussion. "What Altamont thinks ought to be the truth; unless there is a peculiar disposition of the surrounding land, the same effects appear at the same latitudes. Hence I believe the sea is open in the east as well as in the west."

"At any rate, it makes very little difference to us," said Hatteras.

"I don't agree with you, Hatteras," resumed the American, who was beginning to be annoyed by the affected unconcern of the captain; "it may make considerable difference to us."

"And when, if I may ask?"

"When we think of returning."

"Returning!" cried Hatteras, "and who's thinking of that?"

"No one," answered Altamont; "but we shall stop somewhere, I suppose."

"And where?" asked Hatteras.

For the first time the question was fairly put to Altamont. The doctor would have given one of his arms to have put a stop to the discussion. Since Altamont made no answer, the captain repeated his question.

"And where?"

"Where we are going," answered the American, quietly.

"And who knows where that is?" said the peace-loving doctor.

"I say, then," Altamont went on, "that if we want to make use of the polar basin in returning, we can try to gain Kane's sea; it will lead us more directly to Baffin's Bay."

"So that is your idea?" asked the captain, ironically.

"Yes, that is my idea, as it is that if these seas ever become practicable, they will be reached by the straightest way. O, that was a great discovery of Captain Kane's!"

"Indeed!" said Hatteras, biting his lips till they bled.

"Yes," said the doctor, "that cannot be denied; every one should have the praise he deserves."

"Without considering," went on the obstinate American, "that no one had ever before gone so far to the north."

"I like to think," said Hatteras, "that now the English have got ahead of him."

"And the Americans!" said Altamont.

"Americans!" repeated Hatteras.

"What am I, then?" asked Altamont, proudly.

"You are," answered Hatteras, who could hardly control his voice,—"you are a man who presumes to accord equal glory to science and to chance! Your American captain went far to the north, but as chance alone—"

"Chance!" shouted Altamont; "do you dare to say that this great discovery is not due to Kane's energy and knowledge?"

"I say," answered Hatteras, "that Kane's name is not fit to be pronounced in a country made famous by Parry, Franklin, Ross, Belcher, and Penny in these seas which opened the Northwest Passage to MacClure—"

"MacClure!" interrupted the American; "you mention that man, and yet you complain of the work of chance? Wasn't it chance alone that favored him?"

"No," answered Hatteras, warmly,—"no! It was his courage, his perseverance in spending four winters in the ice—"

"I should think so!" retorted the American; "he got caught in the ice and couldn't get out, and he had to abandon the *Investigator* at last to go back to England."

"My friends—" said the doctor.

"Besides," Altamont went on, "let us consider the result. You speak of the Northwest Passage; well, it has yet to be discovered!"

Hatteras started at these words; no more vexatious question could have arisen between two rival nationalities. The doctor again tried to intervene.

"You are mistaken, Altamont," he said.

"No, I persist in my opinions," he said obstinately; "the Northwest Passage is yet to be found, to be sailed through, if you like that any better! MacClure never penetrated it, and to this day no ship that has sailed from Behring Strait has reached Baffin's Bay!"

That was true, speaking exactly. What answer could be made?

Nevertheless, Hatteras rose to his feet and said,—

"I shall not permit the good name of an English captain to be attacked any further in my presence."

"You will not permit it?" answered the American, who also rose to his feet; "but these are the facts, and it is beyond your power to destroy them."

"Sir!" said Hatteras, pale with anger.

"My friends," said the doctor, "don't get excited! We are discussing a scientific subject."

Clawbonny looked with horror at a scientific discussion into which the hate of an American and an Englishman could enter.

"I am going to give you the facts," began Hatteras, threateningly.

"But I'm speaking now!" retorted the American.

Johnson and Bell became very uneasy.

"Gentlemen," said the doctor, severely, "let me say a word! I insist upon it, I know the facts as well, better than you do, and I can speak of them impartially."

"Yes, yes," said Bell and Johnson, who were distressed at the turn the discussion had taken, and who formed a majority favorable to the doctor.

"Go on, Doctor," said Johnson, "these gentlemen will listen, and you cannot fail to give us some information."

"Go on, Doctor," said the American.

Hatteras resumed his place with a sign of acquiescence, and folded his arms.

"I will tell the simple truth about the facts," said the doctor, "and you must correct me if I omit or alter any detail."

"We know you, Doctor," said Bell, "and you can speak without fear of interruption."

"Here is the chart of the Polar Seas," resumed the doctor, who had brought it to the table; "it will be easy to trace MacClure's course, and you will be able to make up your minds for yourselves."

Thereupon he unrolled one of the excellent maps published by order of the Admiralty, containing the latest discoveries in arctic regions; then he went on:—

"You know, in 1848, two ships, the *Herald*, Captain Kellet, and the *Plover*, Commander Moore, were sent to Behring Strait in search of traces of Franklin; their search was vain; in 1850 they were joined by MacClure, who commanded the *Investigator*, a ship in which he had sailed, in 1849, under James Ross's orders. He was followed by Captain Collinson, his chief, who sailed in the *Enterprise;* but he arrived before him. At Behring Strait he declared he would wait no longer, and that he would go alone, on his own responsibility, and—you hear me, Altamont—that he would find either Franklin or the passage."

Altamont showed neither approbation nor the contrary.

"August 5, 1850," continued the doctor, "after a final communication with the *Plover*, MacClure sailed eastward by an almost unknown route; see how little land is marked upon the chart. August 30th he rounded Cape Bathurst; September 6th he discovered Baring Land, which he afterwards discovered to form part of Banks Land, then Prince Albert's Land. Then he resolved to enter the long straits between these two large islands, and he called it Prince of Wales Strait. You can follow his plan. He hoped to come out in Melville Sound, which we have just crossed, and with reason; but the ice at the end of the strait formed an impassable barrier. There MacClure wintered in 1850-51, and meanwhile he pushed on over the ice, to make sure that the strait connected with the sound."

"Yes," said Altamont, "but he didn't succeed."

"One moment," said the doctor. "While wintering there, MacClure's officers explored all the neighboring coasts: Creswell, Baring's Land; Haswell, Prince Albert's Land, to the south; and Wynniat, Cape Walker, to the north. In July, at the beginning of the thaw, MacClure tried a second time to carry the *Investigator* to Melville Sound; he got within twenty miles of it, twenty miles only, but the winds carried him with irresistible force to the south, before he could get through the obstacle. Then he determined to go back through Prince of Wales Strait, and go around Banks Land, to try at the west what he could not do in the east; he put about; the 18th he rounded Cape Kellet; the 19th, Cape Prince Alfred, two degrees higher; then, after a hard struggle with the icebergs, he was caught in Banks Strait, in the series of straits leading to Baffin's Bay."

"A hard struggle with the icebergs."

"But he couldn't get through them," said Altamont.

"Wait a moment, and be as patient as MacClure was. September 26th, he took his station for the winter in Mercy Bay, and stayed there till 1852. April came; MacClure had supplies for only eighteen months. Nevertheless, he was unwilling to return; he started, crossing Banks Strait by sledge, and reached Melville Island. Let us follow him. He hoped to find here Commander Austin's ships, which were sent to meet him by Baffin's Bay and Lancaster Sound; April 28th he arrived at Winter Harbor, at the place where Parry had wintered thirty-three years previously, but no trace of the ships; only he found in a cairn a paper, telling him that MacClintock, Austin's lieutenant, had been there the year before, and gone away. Any one else would have been in despair, but MacClure was not. He put in the cairn another paper, in which he announced his intention of returning to England by the Northwest Passage, which he had discovered by reaching Baffin's Bay and Lancaster Sound. If he is not heard from again, it will be because he will have been to the north or west of Melville Island; then he returned, not discouraged, to Mercy Bay for the third winter, 1852-53."

"I have never doubted his courage," said Altamont, "but his success."

"Let us follow him again," resumed the doctor. "In the month of March, being on two-thirds rations, at the end of a very severe winter, when no game was to be had, MacClure determined to send back half of his crew to England, either by Baffin's Bay, or by Mackenzie River and Hudson's Bay; the other half was to bring the *Investigator* back. He chose the weakest men, who could not stand a fourth winter; everything was ready, and their departure settled for April 15th, when on the 6th, MacClure, who was walking on the ice with his lieutenant, Creswell, saw a man running northward and gesticulating; it was Lieutenant Pim of the *Herald*, lieutenant of the same Captain Kellet whom two years before he had left at Behring Strait, as I said when I began. Kellet, having reached Winter Harbor, found the paper left there by MacClure; having heard in that way of his position in Mercy Bay, he sent Lieutenant Pim to meet the captain. He was followed by a detachment of the men of the *Herald*, among whom was a midshipman of a French ship, M. de Bray, who was a volunteer aid of Captain Kellet. You don't doubt this meeting?"

"MacClure saw a man running and gesticulating."

"Not at all," answered Altamont.

"Well, see what followed, and whether the Northwest Passage was really made. If you join Parry's discoveries to those of MacClure, you will see the northern coast of America was rounded."

"But not by a single ship," said Altamont.

"No, but by a single man. Let us go on. MacClure went to see Captain Kellet at Melville Island; in twelve days he made the one hundred and seventy miles between Winter Harbor and the island; he agreed with the commander of the *Herald* to send him his sick, and returned; many others would have thought, had they been in MacClure's place, that they had done enough, but this bold young man determined to try his fortune again. Then, and please observe this, Lieutenant Creswell, with the sick and disabled men of the

Investigator, left Mercy Bay, reached Winter Harbor, and from there, after a journey of four hundred and seventy miles on the ice, reached Beechey Island, June 2d, and a few days later, with twelve of his men, he took passage on board of the *Phoenix*."

"In which I was at the time," said Johnson, "with Captain Inglefield, and we returned to England."

"And October 7, 1853," continued the doctor, "Creswell arrived at London, after having crossed over the whole distance between Behring Strait and Cape Farewell."

"Well," said Hatteras, "to enter at one end and go out by the other, isn't that going through?"

"Yes," answered Altamont, "but by going four hundred and seventy miles over the ice."

"Well, what difference does that make?"

"The whole," answered the American. "Did MacClure's ship make the passage?"

"No," answered the doctor, "for after a fourth winter, MacClure was obliged to leave it in the ice."

"Well, in a sea-voyage it's important to have the ship reach her destination. If the Northwest Passage ever becomes practicable, it must be for ships and not for sledges. The ship must accomplish the voyage, or if not the ship, the launch."

"The launch!" shouted Hatteras, who detected the hidden meaning in the American's words.

"Altamont," said the doctor, hurriedly, "you make a puerile distinction, and we all consider you wrong."

"That is easy, gentlemen," answered the American; "you are four to one. But that won't keep me from holding my own opinion."

"Keep it," said Hatteras, "and so closely that we need hear nothing about it."

"And what right have you to speak to me in that way?" asked the American in a rage.

"My right as captain," answered Hatteras.

"Am I under your commands?" retorted Altamont.

"Without doubt, and look out for yourself, if—"

The doctor, Johnson, and Bell intervened. It was time; the two enemies were gazing at one another. The doctor was very anxious. Still, after a few gentler words, Altamont went off to bed whistling "Yankee Doodle," and, whether he slept or not, he did not speak. Hatteras went out and paced up and down for an hour, and then he turned in without saying a word.

"The doctor, Johnson, and Bell intervened. It was time; the two enemies were gazing at one another."

CHAPTER XVI.

NORTHERN ARCADIA.

On May 29th, for the first time, the sun did not set; it merely touched the horizon and then rose at once; the day was twenty-four hours long. The next day it was surrounded by a magnificent halo, a bright circle with all the colors of the prism; this apparition, which was by no means rare, always attracted the doctor's attention; he never failed to note the date and appearance of the phenomenon; the one he saw on that day was of an elliptic shape, which he had seldom seen before.

Soon the noisy flocks of birds appeared; bustards and wild geese came from Florida or Arkansas, flying northward with inconceivable rapidity and bringing the spring with them. The doctor shot a few, as well as three or four cranes and a single stork. However, the snow was melting everywhere beneath the sun; the salt-water, which overran the ice-field through the crevasses and the seal-holes, hastened the melting; the ice which was mingled with salt-water formed a soft slush. Large pools appeared on the land near the bay, and the exposed soil seemed to be a production of the arctic spring.

The doctor then resumed his planting; he had plenty of seed; besides, he was surprised to see a sort of sorrel growing naturally between the dried rocks, and he wondered at the force of nature which demanded so little in order to manifest itself. He sowed some cresses, of which the young sprouts, three weeks later, were already an inch long.

The heath began to show timidly its little pale, rosy flowers. In fact, the flora of New America is very defective; still, this rare vegetation was agreeable to their eyes; it was all the feeble rays of the sun could nourish, a trace of the Providence which had not completely forgotten these distant countries. At last it became really warm; June 15th the thermometer stood at 57°; the doctor could hardly believe his eyes; the country changed its appearance; numerous noisy cascades fell from the sunny summits of the hills; the ice loosened, and the great question of an open sea would soon be decided. The air was full of the noise of avalanches falling from the hills to the bottom of the ravines, and the cracking of the ice-field produced a deafening sound.

A trip was made to Johnson Island; it was merely an unimportant, arid, barren island; but the old boatswain was no less proud of giving his name to a few desolate rocks. He even wanted to carve it on a high peak. During this excursion, Hatteras had carefully explored these lands, even beyond Cape Washington; the melting of the snow sensibly changed the country; ravines and hillocks appeared here and there, where the snow indicated nothing but monotonous stretches. The house and magazines threatened to melt away, and they had frequently to be repaired; fortunately, a temperature of 57° is rare in these latitudes, and the mean is hardly above the freezing-point.

By the middle of June the launch was far advanced and getting into shape. While Bell and Johnson were working at it, the others had a few successful hunts. Reindeer were shot, although they are hard to approach; but Altamont put in practice a device employed by the Indians of his own country; he crept over the ground with his gun and arms outstretched like the horns of one of these shy animals, and having thus come within easy gunshot, he could not fail.

But the best game, the musk-ox, of which Parry found plenty at Melville Island, appeared not to frequent the shores of Victoria Bay. A distant hunt was determined on, as much to get these valuable animals as to reconnoitre the eastern lands. Hatteras did not propose to reach the Pole by this part of the continent, but the doctor was not sorry to get a general idea of the country. Hence they decided to start to the east of Fort Providence. Altamont intended to hunt; Duke naturally was of the party.

So, Monday, June 17th, a pleasant day, with the thermometer at 41°, and the air quiet and clear, the three hunters, each carrying a double-barrelled gun, a hatchet, a snow-knife, and followed by Duke, left Doctor's House at six o'clock in the morning. They were fitted out for a trip of two or three days, with the requisite amount of provisions. By eight o'clock Hatteras and his two companions had gone eight miles. Not a living thing had tempted a shot, and their hunt threatened to be merely a trip.

This new country exhibited vast plains running out of sight; new streams divided them everywhere, and large, unruffled pools reflected the sun. The layers of melting ice bared the ground to their feet; it belonged to the great division of sedimentary earth, and the result of the action of the water, which is so common on the surface of the globe. Still a few erratic blocks were seen of a singular nature, foreign to the soil where they were found, and whose presence it was hard to explain. Schists and different productions of limestone were found in abundance, as was also a sort of strange, transparent, colorless crystal, which has a refraction peculiar to Iceland spar.

But, although he was not hunting, the doctor had not time to geologize; he had to walk too quickly, in order to keep up with his friends. Still, he observed the land and talked as much as possible, for had he not there would have been total silence in the little band; neither Altamont nor the captain had any desire to talk to one another.

By ten o'clock the hunters had got a dozen miles to the east; the sea was hidden beneath the horizon; the doctor proposed a halt for breakfast. They swallowed it rapidly, and in half an hour they were off again. The ground was sloping gently; a few patches of snow, preserved either by their position or the slope of the rocks, gave it a woolly appearance, like waves in a high wind. The country was still barren, and looking as if no living being had ever set foot in it.

"We have no luck," said Altamont to the doctor; "to be sure, the country doesn't offer much food to animals, but the game here ought not to be over-particular, and ought to show itself."

"Don't let us despair," said the doctor; "the summer has hardly begun; and if Parry met so many animals at Melville Island, we may be as lucky here."

"Still, we are farther north," said Hatteras.

"Certainly, but that is unimportant; it is the pole of cold we ought to consider; that is to say, that icy wilderness in the middle of which we wintered with the *Forward;* now the farther north we go, the farther we are from the coldest part of the globe; we ought to find, beyond, what Parry, Ross, and others found on the other side."

"Well," said Altamont, with a regretful sigh, "so far we've been travellers rather than hunters."

"Be patient," answered the doctor; "the country is changing gradually, and I should be astonished if we don't find game enough in the ravines where vegetation has had a chance to sprout."

"It must be said," continued Altamont, "that we are going through an uninhabited and uninhabitable country."

"O, uninhabitable is a strong word!" answered the doctor; "I can't believe any land uninhabitable; man, by many sacrifices, and for generations using all the resources of science, might finally fertilize such a country."

"Do you think so?" asked Altamont.

"Without doubt! If you were to go to the celebrated countries of the world, to Thebes, Nineveh, or Babylon, in the fertile valleys of our ancestors, it would seem impossible that men should ever have lived there; the air itself has grown bad since the disappearance of human beings. It is the general law of nature which makes those countries in which we do not live unhealthy and sterile, like those out of which life has died. In fact, man himself makes his own country by his presence, his habits, his industry, and, I might add, by his breath; he gradually modifies the exhalations of the soil and the atmospheric conditions, and he makes the air he breathes wholesome. So there are uninhabited lands, I grant, but none uninhabitable."

Talking in this way, the hunters, who had become naturalists, pushed on and reached a sort of valley, fully exposed, at the bottom of which a river, nearly free of ice, was flowing; its southern exposure had brought forth a certain amount of vegetation. The earth showed a strong desire to grow fertile; with a few inches of rich soil it would have produced a good deal. The doctor called their attention to these indications.

"See," he said, "a few hardy colonists might settle in this ravine. With industry and perseverance they could do a great deal; not as much as is seen in the temperate zones, but a respectable show. If I am not mistaken, there are some four-footed animals! They know the good spots."

"They are Arctic hares," shouted Altamont, cocking his gun.

"Wait a moment," cried the doctor,—"wait a moment, you hasty fellow. They don't think of running away! See, they'll come to us!"

And, in fact, three or four young hares, springing about in the heath and young moss, ran boldly towards the three men; they were so cunning that even Altamont was softened.

Soon they were between the doctor's legs; he caressed them with his hand, saying,—

"Why shoot these little animals which come to be petted? We need not kill them."

"You are right, Doctor," answered Hatteras; "we'll let them live."

"And these ptarmigan, too, which are flying towards us!" cried Altamont; "and these long-legged water-fowl!"

A whole flock of birds passed over the hunters, not suspecting the peril from which the doctor's presence saved them. Even Duke was compelled to admire them.

They were a curious and touching sight, flying about without fear, resting on Clawbonny's shoulders, lying at his feet, offering themselves to his caresses, seeming to do their best to welcome their new guests; they called one another joyously, flying from the most distant points; the doctor seemed to be a real bird-charmer. The hunters continued their march up the moist banks of the brook, followed by the familiar band, and turning from the valley they perceived a troop of eight or ten reindeer browsing on a few lichens half buried beneath the snow; they were graceful, quiet animals, with their branching antlers, which the female carried as well as the male; their wool-like fur was already losing its winter whiteness in favor of the summer brown and gray; they seemed no more timid than the hares and birds of the country. Such were the relations of the first men to the first animals in the early ages of the world.

"They were a curious and touching sight, flying about without fear, resting on Clawbonny's shoulders," etc.

The hunters reached the middle of the band without any one flying; this time the doctor found it hard to restrain the instincts of Altamont, who could not calmly look on this game without a thirst for blood rising in his brain. Hatteras looked mildly at these gentle beasts, who rubbed their noses against the doctor's clothes; he was the friend of all the animals.

"But," said Altamont, "didn't we come here to shoot?"

"To shoot musk-ox," answered Clawbonny, "and nothing else! We should have no need of this game; we have food enough, so let us enjoy the sight of man walking thus among these animals, without alarming them."

"That proves they have never seen one before," said Hatteras.

"Evidently," answered the doctor; "and so we can be sure that these animals are not of American origin."

"And why so?" said Altamont.

"If they were born on the continent of North America, they would know what to think of men, and they would have fled at the sight of us. No; they probably came from the north, from those unknown lands where our kind has never set foot, and they have crossed the continents near the Pole. So, Altamont, you can't claim them as your fellow-countrymen."

"O," answered Altamont, "a hunter does not scrutinize so closely, and the game belongs to the land where it was shot!"

"Well, calm yourself, my Nimrod! As for me, I would rather never fire a gun in my life than alarm this timid population. See, even Duke fraternizes with the charming beasts! Come, we'll be kind when we can! Kindness is a force!"

"Well, well," answered Altamont, who sympathized but slightly with this sensitiveness; "but I should be amused to see you armed with this kindness alone among a flock of bears or wolves!"

"O, I don't pretend to charm wild beasts!" answered the doctor; "I have little faith in the enchantment of Orpheus; besides, bears and wolves wouldn't come up to us like the hares, partridges, and reindeer."

"Why not," answered Altamont, "if they have never seen men?"

"Because they are naturally ferocious, and ferocity, like maliciousness, begets suspicion; a remark which is true of man as well as of animals. A wicked man is distrustful, and fear is commonly found in those who are able to inspire it."

This little lesson in natural philosophy ended the conversation.

The whole day was passed in this Northern Arcadia, as the doctor named the valley, with the consent of his companions; and that evening, after a supper which had not cost the life of a single inhabitant of the country, the three hunters went to sleep in a cleft of a rock which was admirably adapted for a shelter.

CHAPTER XVII.

ALTAMONT'S REVENGE.

The next day the doctor and his two companions woke up after a perfectly quiet night. The cold, although not keen, increased towards daybreak, but they were well covered, and slept soundly under the watch of the peaceful animals.

The weather being pleasant, they resolved to consecrate the day to a reconnaissance of the country, and the search of musk-oxen. Altamont insisted on shooting something, and they decided that, even if these oxen should be the gentlest animals in the world, they should be shot. Besides, their flesh, although strongly flavored with musk, was pleasant eating, and they all hoped to carry back to Fort Providence a good supply of it.

During the early morning hours nothing noteworthy took place; the land grew different in the northeast; a few elevations, the beginning of a mountainous district, indicated a change. If this New America were not a continent, it was at any rate an important island; but then they did not have to trouble themselves about its geography.

Duke ran ahead, and soon came across some traces of a herd of musk-oxen; he then advanced rapidly, and soon disappeared from the eyes of the hunters. They followed his clear barking, which soon grew so hasty that they knew he had discovered the object of their search. They pushed on, and in an hour and a half they came up to two of these animals; they were large, and formidable in appearance. They appeared much surprised at Duke's attacks, but not alarmed; they were feeding off a sort of reddish moss which grew on the thin soil. The doctor recognized them at once from their moderate height, their horns, which were broad at the base, the absence of muzzle, their sheep-like forehead, and short tail; their shape has earned for them from naturalists the name of "ovibos," a compound, and which expresses the two sorts of animals whose characteristics they share. Thick, long hair and a sort of delicate brown silk formed their fur.

They ran away when they saw the two hunters, who came running up after them. It was hard to reach them for men who were out of breath after running half an hour. Hatteras and his companions stopped.

"The Devil!" said Altamont.

"That's just the word," said the doctor, as soon as he could take breath. "I'll grant they are Americans, and they can't have a very good idea of your countrymen."

"That proves we are good hunters," answered Altamont.

Still, the musk-oxen, seeing they were not pursued, stopped in a posture of surprise. It became evident that they could never be run down; they would have to be surrounded; the plateau on which they were aided this manoeuvre. The hunters, leaving Duke to harass them, descended through the neighboring ravines, so as to get around the plateau. Altamont and the doctor hid behind a rock at one end, while Hatteras, suddenly advancing from the other end, should drive the oxen towards them. In half an hour each had gained his post.

"You don't object any longer to our shooting?" asked Altamont.

"No, it's fair fighting," answered the doctor, who, in spite of gentleness, was a real sportsman.

They were talking in this way, when they saw the oxen running, and Duke at their heels; farther on Hatteras was driving them, with loud cries, towards the American and the doctor, who ran to meet this magnificent prey.

At once the oxen stopped, and, less fearful of a single enemy, they turned upon Hatteras. He awaited them calmly, aimed at the nearest, and fired; but the bullet struck the animal in the middle of his forehead, without penetrating the skull. Hatteras's second shot produced no other effect than to make the beasts furious; they ran to the disarmed hunter, and threw him down at once.

"He is lost," cried the doctor.

At the moment Clawbonny pronounced these words with an accent of despair, Altamont made a step forward to run to Hatteras's aid; then he stopped, struggling against himself and his prejudices.

"No," he cried, "that would be cowardice."

He hastened with Clawbonny to the scene of combat. His hesitation had not lasted half a second. But if the doctor saw what was taking place in the American's heart, Hatteras understood it, who would rather have died than have implored his rival's interference. Still, he had hardly time to perceive it, for Altamont appeared before him. Hatteras, lying on the ground, was trying to ward off the horns and hoofs of the two animals. But he could not long continue so unequal a struggle. He was about to be torn in pieces, when two shots were heard. Hatteras heard the bullets whistling by his head.

"Don't be frightened!" shouted Altamont, hurling his gun to one side, and rushing upon the angry animals.

One of the oxen fell, shot through the heart; the other, wild with rage, was just going to gore the captain, when Altamont faced him, and plunged into his mouth his hand, armed with a snow-knife; with the other he gave him a terrible blow with a hatchet on the head. This was done with marvellous rapidity, and a flash of lightning would have lit up the whole scene.

"Gave him a terrible blow with a hatchet on the head."

The second ox fell back dead.

"Hurrah! hurrah!" cried Clawbonny.

Hatteras was saved. He owed his life to the man whom he detested most in the world. What was going on in his mind at this time? What emotion was there which he could not master? That is one of the secrets of the heart which defy all analysis.

However that may be, Hatteras advanced to his rival without hesitation, and said to him seriously,—

"You have saved my life, Altamont."

"You saved mine," answered the American. There was a moment's silence. Then Altamont added, "We are now quits, Hatteras!"

"No, Altamont," answered the captain; "when the doctor took you from your icy tomb, I did not know who you were, and you have saved me at the risk of your own life, knowing who I was."

"You are a fellow-being," answered Altamont; "and whatever else he may be, an American is not a coward."

"No, he is not," said the doctor; "he is a man! a man like you, Hatteras!"

"And like me he shall share the glory which is awaiting us!"

"The glory of going to the North Pole?" said Altamont.

"Yes," said the captain, haughtily.

"I had guessed it!" exclaimed the American. "So you dared conceive of this bold design! You dared try to reach that inaccessible point! Ah, that is great! It is sublime!"

"But you," asked Hatteras, hurriedly, "were you not on your way to the Pole?"

Altamont seemed to hesitate about replying.

"Well?" said the doctor.

"Well, no," answered the American,—"no; tell the truth, and shame the Devil! No, I did not have this great idea, which has brought you here. I was trying simply to sail through the Northwest Passage, that is all."

"Altamont," said Hatteras, holding out his hand to the American, "share our glory, and go with us to the North Pole!"

The two men then shook hands warmly.

When they turned towards the doctor, they saw his eyes full of tears.

"Ah, my friends," he murmured, as he dried his eyes, "how can my heart hold the joy with which you fill it? My dear companions, you have sacrificed a miserable question of nationality in order to unite in your common success! You know that England and America have nothing to do with all this; that mutual sympathy ought to bind you together against the dangers of the journey! If the North Pole is discovered, what difference does it make who does it? Why stand bickering about English or American, when we can be proud of being men?"

The doctor embraced the reconciled foes; he could not restrain his joy. The two new friends felt themselves drawn closer together by the friendship this worthy man had for them both. Clawbonny spoke freely of the vanity of competition, of the madness of rivalry, and of the need of agreement between men so far from home. His words, his tears and caresses, came from the bottom of his heart.

Still, he grew calm after embracing Hatteras and Altamont for the twentieth time.

"And now," he said, "to work, to work! Since I was no use as a hunter, let me try in another capacity!"

Thereupon he started to cut up the ox, which he called the "ox of reconciliation," but he did it as skilfully as if he were a surgeon conducting a delicate autopsy. His two companions gazed at him in amusement. In a few minutes he had cut from the body a hundred pounds of flesh; he gave each one a third of it, and they again took up their march to Fort Providence. At ten o'clock in the evening, after walking in the oblique rays of the sun, they reached Doctor's House, where Johnson and Bell had a good supper awaiting them.

But before they sat down to table, the doctor said in a voice of triumph, as he pointed to his two companions,—

"Johnson, I carried away with me an Englishman and an American, did I not?"

"Yes, Dr. Clawbonny," answered the boatswain.

"Well, I've brought back two brothers."

"'Well, I've brought back two brothers.'"

The two sailors gladly shook Altamont's hand; the doctor told them what the American captain had done for the English captain, and that night the snow-house held five perfectly happy men.

CHAPTER XVIII.

THE LAST PREPARATIONS.

The next day the weather changed; there was a return of cold; the snow and rain gust raged for many days.

Bell had finished the launch; it was perfectly satisfactory for the purpose it was intended for; partly decked, and partly open, it could sail in heavy weather under mainsail and jib, while it was so light as not to be too heavy a load on the sledge for the dogs.

Then, too, a change of great importance was taking place in the state of the polar basin. The ice in the middle of the bay was beginning to give way; the tallest pieces, forever weakened by the collision of the rest, only needed a sufficiently heavy tempest to be torn away and to become icebergs. Still, Hatteras was unwilling to wait so long before starting. Since it was to be a land journey, he cared very little whether the sea was open or not. He determined to start June 25th; meanwhile all the preparations could be completed. Johnson and Bell put the sledge into perfect repair; the frame was strengthened and the runners renewed. The travellers intended to devote to their journey the few weeks of good weather which nature allows to these northern regions. Their sufferings would be less severe, the obstacles easier to overcome.

A few days before their departure, June 20th, the ice had so many free passages, that they were able to make a trial trip on board of the new launch as far as Cape Washington. The sea was not perfectly free, far from it; but its surface was not solid, and it would have been impossible to make a trip on foot over the ice-fields. This half-day's sail showed the good sailing qualities of the launch. During the return they beheld a curious incident. It was a monstrous bear chasing a seal. Fortunately the former was so busily occupied, that he did not see the launch, otherwise he would certainly have pursued it; he kept on watch near a crevasse in the ice-field, into which the seal had evidently plunged. He was awaiting his reappearance with all the patience of a hunter, or rather of a fisherman, for he was really fishing. He was silent, motionless, without any sign of life. Suddenly the surface of the water was agitated; the seal had come up to breathe. The bear crouched low upon the ice, and rounded his two paws about the crevasse. The next moment the seal appeared, with his head above water; but he had not time to withdraw it. The bear's paws, as if driven by a spring, were clashed together, strangling the animal with irresistible force and dragging it out of the water.

It was but a brief struggle; the seal struggled for a few seconds, and was then suffocated on the breast of his adversary, who, dragging him away easily, in spite of his size, and springing lightly from one piece of ice to another, reached land and disappeared with his prey.

"The seal struggled for a few seconds, and was then suffocated on the breast of his adversary."

"A pleasant journey!" shouted Johnson; "that bear has got rather too many paws!"

The launch soon reached the little anchorage Bell had made for her in the ice.

Only four days were there before the time fixed for their departure. Hatteras hurried on the last preparations; he was in a hurry to leave New America, a land which was not his, and which he had not named; he did not feel at home.

June 22d they began to carry to the sledge their camp-material, tent, and food. They carried only two hundred pounds of salt meat, three chests of preserved meat and vegetables, fifty pounds of pickles and lime-juice, five quarters of flour, packets of cresses and cochlearia from the doctor's garden; with the addition of two hundred pounds of powder, the instruments, arms, and personal baggage, the launch, Halkett-boat, and the weight of the sledge itself, the whole weighed fifteen hundred pounds,—a heavy load for four dogs, especially since, unlike the Esquimaux, who never travel more than four days in succession, they had none to replace them, and would have to work them every day. But the travellers determined to aid them when it was necessary, and they intended to proceed by easy stages; the distance from Victoria Bay to the Pole was three hundred and fifty-five miles at the outside, and going twelve miles a day they could make the journey in a month. Besides, when the land came to an end, the launch would enable them to finish the journey without fatigue for dogs or men.

The latter were well, and in excellent condition. The winter, although severe, ended favorably enough. Each one had followed the doctor's advice, and escaped from the diseases common in these severe climates. In fact, they had grown a trifle thinner, which gave a great deal of pleasure to Clawbonny; but their bodies were inured to the rigors of that life, and these men were able to face the severest attacks of cold and hunger without succumbing. And then, too, they were going to the end of their journey, to the inaccessible Pole, after which their only thought would be of returning. The sympathy which bound together the five members of the expedition would aid their success in this bold trip, and no one doubted of their success.

As a precaution, the doctor had urged his companions to prepare themselves for some time beforehand, and to "train" with much care.

"My friends," he used to say, "I don't ask you to imitate the English racers, who lose eighteen pounds after two days' training, and twenty-five after five days, but we ought to do something to get into the best possible condition for a long journey. Now the first principle of training is to get rid of the fat on both horse and jockey, and this is done by means of purging, sweating, and violent exercise. These gentlemen know they will lose so much by medicine, and they arrive at their results with incredible accuracy; such a one who before training could not run a mile without being winded, can run twenty-five easily after it. There was a certain Townsend who ran a hundred miles in twelve hours without stopping."

"A good result," answered Johnson; "and although we are not very fat, if we must get thinner yet—"

"There is no need of it, Johnson; but without exaggerating, it can't be denied that training produces good effects; it strengthens the bones, makes the muscles more elastic, improves the hearing and the sight; so let us not forget it."

In short, whether in training or not, the travellers were ready June 23d; it was Sunday, and the day was devoted to absolute rest.

The time for departure drew near, and the inhabitants of Fort Providence could not see it approach without a certain emotion. It grieved them to leave this snow-hut which had served so well to protect them; Victoria Bay, this hospitable shore where they had spent the last days of the winter. Would they find these buildings standing when they returned? Would not the rays of the sun melt away its fragile walls?

In a word, they had passed pleasant hours there. The doctor, at the evening meal, called up to his companions' memory touching reminiscences, and he did not forget to thank Heaven for its evident protection.

At last the hour of sleeping came. Each one went to bed early, so as to be up betimes. Thus passed their last night at Fort Providence.

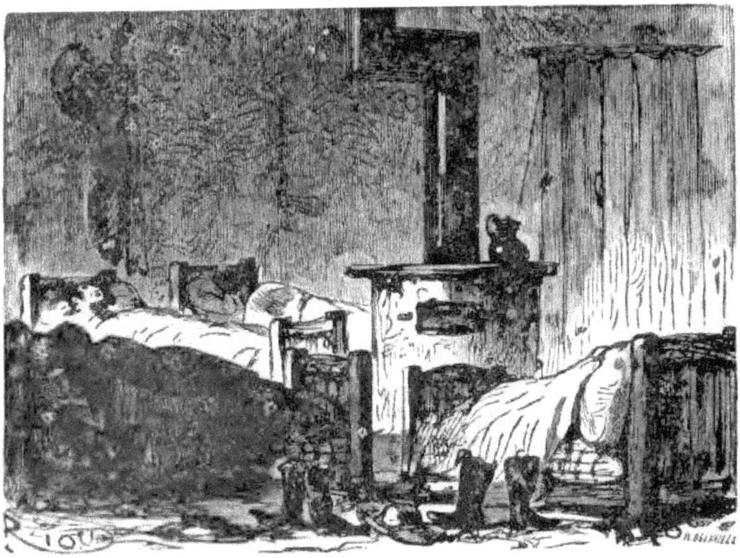

CHAPTER XIX.

THE JOURNEY NORTHWARD.

At dawn the next day Hatteras gave the signal for departure. The dogs were harnessed to the sledge; since they were well fed and had thoroughly rested, after a comfortable winter there was no reason for their not being of great service during the summer. Hence they were not averse to being put into harness.

After all, these Greenland dogs are kind beasts. Their wildness was partly gone; they had lost their likeness to the wolf, and had become more like Duke, the finished model of the canine race,—in a word, they were becoming civilized. Duke could certainly claim a share in their education; he had given them lessons and an example in good manners. In his quality of Englishman, and so punctilious in the matter of cant, he was a long time in making the acquaintance of the other dogs, who had not been introduced to him, and in fact he never used to speak to them; but after sharing the same dangers and privations, they gradually grew used to one another. Duke, who had a kind heart, made the first advances, and soon all the dogs were friends. The doctor used to pet the Greenland dogs, and Duke saw him do it without jealousy. The men were in equally good condition; if the dogs could draw well, the men could walk well.

They left at six o'clock in the morning; it was a very pleasant day. After they had followed the line of the bay and passed Cape Washington, Hatteras gave the order to turn northward; by seven the travellers lost sight of the lighthouse and of Fort Providence in the south.

"They left at six o'clock in the morning."

The journey promised well, much better than the expedition begun in the dead of winter in search of coal. Hatteras then left behind him, on board of the ship, mutiny and despair, without being certain of the object of his journey; he left a crew half dead with cold, he started with companions who were weakened by the miseries of an arctic winter; he, too, eager for the north, had to return to the south! Now, on the other hand, surrounded by vigorous, healthy friends, encouraged and aided in many ways, he was starting for the Pole, the object of his whole life! No man had ever been nearer acquiring this glory for himself and his country.

Was he thinking of all this, which was so naturally inspired by his present position? The doctor liked to think so, and could hardly doubt it when he saw him so eager. Clawbonny rejoiced in what so pleased his friend; and since the reconciliation of the two captains, the two friends, he was the happiest of men; for hatred, envy, and rivalry were passions he had never felt. What would be the issue of this voyage he did not know; but, at any rate, it began well, and that was a good deal.

The western shore of New America stretched out in a series of bays beyond Cape Washington; the travellers, to avoid this long curve, after crossing the first spurs of Mount Bell, turned northward over the upper plateaus. This was a great saving of time; Hatteras was anxious, unless prevented by seas or mountains, to make a straight line of three hundred and fifty miles to the Pole from Fort Providence.

Their journey was easy; these lofty plains were covered with deep snow, over which the sledge passed easily, and the men in their snow-shoes walked easily and rapidly.

The thermometer stood at 37°. The weather was not absolutely settled; at one moment it was clear, the next cloudy: but neither cold nor showers could have stopped the eager party. They could be followed easily by the compass; the needle was more active as they receded from the magnetic pole; it is true that it turned to the opposite direction and pointed to the south, while they were walking northward; but this did not in any way embarrass them. Besides, the doctor devised a simple method of staking out the way and thereby avoiding perpetual reference to the compass; when once they had got their bearings by some object two or three miles to the north, they walked till they reached it, when they chose another, and so on. In this way they had a straight road.

In the first two days they made twenty miles in twelve hours; the rest of the time was devoted to meals and rest. The tent was ample protection against the cold when they were sleeping. The temperature gradually rose. The snow melted away in some places, according to the shape of the ground, while in others it lay in large patches. Broad pools appeared here and there, often almost as large as lakes. They would walk in up to their waists very often; but they only laughed at it, and the doctor more than any.

"Water has no right to wet us in this country," he used to say; "it ought to appear only as a solid, or a gas; as to its being liquid, it's absurd! Ice or vapor will do, but water won't!"

They did not forget their shooting, for thereby they got fresh meat. So Altamont and Bell, without going very far away, scoured the neighboring ravines; they brought back ptarmigan, geese, and a few gray rabbits. Gradually these animals became very shy and hard to approach. Without Duke they would often have found it hard to get any game. Hatteras advised them not to go off farther than a mile, for not a day nor an hour was to be lost, and he could not count on more than three months of good weather.

Besides, each one had to be at his post by the sledge whenever a hard spot, a narrow gorge, or steep inclines lay in the path; then each one helped pull or push. More than once everything had to be taken off; and this even did not fully protect against shocks and damage, which Bell repaired as well as he could.

The third day, Wednesday, June 26th, they came across a vast lake, still frozen by reason of its being sheltered from the sun; the ice was even strong enough to bear both men and sledge. It was a solid mirror which no arctic summers had melted, as was shown by the fact that its borders were surrounded by a dry snow, of which the lower layers evidently belonged to previous years.

From this moment the land grew lower, whence the doctor concluded that it did not extend very far to the north. Besides, it was very likely that New America was merely an island, and did not extend to the Pole. The ground grew more level; in the west a few low hills could be seen in the distance, covered with a bluish mist.

So far they had experienced no hardships; they had suffered from nothing except the reflection of the sun's rays upon the snow, which could easily give them snow-blindness. At any other time they would have travelled by night to avoid this inconvenience, but then there was no night. The snow was fortunately melting away, and it was much less brilliant when it was about turning into water.

June 28th the temperature arose to 45°; this was accompanied with heavy rain, which the travellers endured stoically, even with pleasure, for it hastened the disappearance of the snow. They had to put on their deer-skin moccasins, and change the runners of the sledge. Their journey was delayed, but still they were advancing without any serious obstacles. At times the doctor would pick up rounded or flat stones like pebbles worn smooth by the waves, and then he thought he was near the Polar Sea; but yet the plain stretched on out of sight. There was no trace of man, no hut, no cairn nor Esquimaux snow-house; they were evidently the first to set foot in this new land. The Greenlanders never had gone so far, and yet this country offered plenty of game for the support of that half-starved people. Sometimes bears appeared in the distance, but they showed no signs of attacking; afar off were herds of musk-oxen and reindeer. The doctor would have liked to catch some of the latter to harness to the sledge; but they were timid, and not to be caught alive.

The 29th, Bell shot a fox, and Altamont was lucky enough to bring down a medium-sized musk-ox, after giving his companions a high idea of his bravery and skill; he was indeed a remarkable hunter, and so much admired by the doctor. The ox was cut out, and gave plenty of excellent meat. These lucky supplies were always well received; the least greedy could not restrain their joy at the sight of the meat. The doctor laughed at himself when he caught himself admiring these huge joints.

"On the 29th Bell shot a fox, and Altamont a medium-sized musk-ox."

"Let us not be afraid to eat it," he used to say; "a good dinner is a good thing in these expeditions."

"Especially," said Johnson, "when it depends on a better or worse shot."

"You are right, Johnson," replied the doctor; "one thinks less of one's food when one gets a regular supply from the kitchen."

The 30th, the country became unexpectedly rugged, as if it had been upheaved by some volcanic commotion; the cones and peaks increased indefinitely in number, and were very high. A southeast breeze began to blow with violence, and soon became a real hurricane. It rushed across the snow-covered rocks, among the ice-mountains, which, although on the firm land, took the form of hummocks and icebergs; their presence on these lofty plateaus could not be explained even by the doctor, who had an explanation for almost everything. Warm, damp weather succeeded the tempest; it was a genuine thaw; on all sides resounded the cracking of the ice amid the roar of the avalanches.

"The masses of ice took the forms of hummocks and icebergs."

"On all sides resounded the cracking of the ice amid the roar of the avalanches."

The travellers carefully avoided the base of these hills; they even took care not to talk aloud, for the sound of the voice could shake the air and cause accident. They were witnesses of frequent and terrible avalanches which they could not have foreseen. In fact, the main peculiarity of polar avalanches is their terrible swiftness; therein they differ from those of Switzerland and Norway, where they form a ball, of small size at first, and then, by adding to themselves the snow and rocks in its passage, it falls with increasing swiftness, destroys forests and villages, but taking an appreciable time in its course. Now, it is otherwise in the countries where arctic cold rages; the fall of the block of ice is unexpected and startling; its fall is almost instantaneous, and any one who saw it from beneath would be certainly crushed by it; the cannon-ball is not swifter, nor lightning quicker; it starts, falls, and crashes down in a single moment with the dreadful roar of thunder, and with dull echoes.

So the amazed spectators see wonderful changes in the appearance of the country; the mountain becomes a plain under the action of a sudden thaw; when the rain has filtered into the fissures of the great blocks and freezes in a single night, it breaks everything by its irresistible expansion, which is more powerful in forming ice than in forming vapor: the phenomenon takes place with terrible swiftness.

No catastrophe, fortunately, threatened the sledge and its drivers; the proper precautions were taken, and every danger avoided. Besides, this rugged, icy country was not of great extent, and three days later, July 3d, the travellers were on smoother ground. But their eyes were surprised by a new phenomenon, which has for a long time claimed the attention of the scientific men of the two worlds. It was this: the party followed a line of hills not more than fifty feet high, which appeared to run on several miles, and their eastern side was covered with red snow.

The surprise and even the sort of alarm which the sight of this crimson curtain gave them may be easily imagined. The doctor hastened, if not to reassure, at least to instruct, his companions; he was familiar with this red snow and the chemical analysis made of it by Wollaston, Candolle, Bäuer. He told them this red snow was not found in the arctic regions alone, but in Switzerland in the middle of the Alps; De Saussure collected a large quantity on the Breven in 1760; and since then Captains Ross, Sabine, and others had brought some back from their arctic journeys.

Altamont asked the doctor about the nature of this extraordinary substance. He was told that its color came simply from the presence of organic corpuscles. For a long time it was a question whether these corpuscles were animal or vegetable; but it was soon ascertained that they belonged to the family of microscopic mushrooms, of the genus *Uredo*, which Bäuer proposed naming *Uredo vivalis*.[*]

Then the doctor, prying into the snow with his cane, showed his companions that the scarlet layer was only nine feet deep, and he bade them calculate how many of these mushrooms there might be on a space of many miles, when scientific men estimated forty-three thousand in a square centimetre.

This coloring probably ran back to a remote period, for the mushrooms were not decomposed by either evaporation or the melting of the snow, nor was their color altered.

The phenomenon, although explained, was no less strange. Red is a rare color in nature; the reflection of the sun's rays on this crimson surface produced strange effects; it gave the surrounding objects, men and animals, a brilliant appearance, as if they were lighted by an inward flame; and when the snow was melting, streams of blood seemed to be flowing beneath the travellers' feet.

The doctor, who had not been able to examine this substance when he saw it on crimson cliffs from Baffin's Bay, here examined it at his ease, and gathered several bottlefuls of it.

This red ground, the "Field of Blood," as he called it, took three hours' walk to pass over, and then the country resumed its habitual appearance.

CHAPTER XX.

FOOTPRINTS ON THE SNOW.

July 4th a dense fog prevailed. They were only able with the greatest difficulty to keep a straight path; they had to consult the compass every moment. Fortunately there was no accident in the darkness, except that Bell lost his snow-shoes, which were broken against a projecting rock.

"Well, really," said Johnson, "I thought, after seeing the Mersey and the Thames, that I knew all about fogs, but I see I was mistaken."

"We ought," answered Bell, "to light torches as is done at London and Liverpool."

"'We ought,' answered Bell, 'to light torches, as is done at London and Liverpool.'"

"Why not?" asked the doctor; "that's a good idea; it wouldn't light up the road much, but we could see the guide, and follow him more easily."

"But what shall we do for torches?"

"By lighting tow dipped in alcohol, and fastening to the end of walking-sticks."

"Good!" said Johnson; "and we shall soon have it ready."

A quarter of an hour later the little band was walking along with torches faintly lighting up the general gloom.

But if they went straighter, they did not go quicker, and the fog lasted till July 6th; the earth being cold then, a blast of north-wind carried away all the mist as if it had been rags. Soon the doctor took an observation, and ascertained that meanwhile they had not made eight miles a day.

The 6th, they made an effort to make up for lost time, and they set out early. Altamont and Bell were ahead, choosing the way and looking out for game. Duke was with them. The weather, with its surprising fickleness, had become very clear and dry; and although the guides were two miles from the sledge, the doctor did not miss one of their movements. He was consequently very much startled to see them stop suddenly, and remain in a position of surprise; they seemed to be gazing into the distance, as if scanning the horizon. Then they bent down to the ground and seemed to be examining it closely, and they arose in evident amazement. Bell seemed to wish to push on, but Altamont held him back.

"What can they be doing?" asked the doctor of Johnson.

"I know no more than you, Doctor; I don't understand their gestures."

"They have found the track of some animals," answered Hatteras.

"That's not it," said the doctor.

"Why not?"

"Because Duke would bark."

"Still, they've seen marks of some sort."

"Let us go on," said Hatteras; "we shall soon know."

Johnson urged on the dogs, who quickened their pace.

In twenty minutes the five were together, and Hatteras, the doctor, and Johnson were as much surprised as Bell and Altamont.

There were in the snow indubitable traces of men, as fresh as if they had just been made.

"They are Esquimaux," said Hatteras.

"Yes," said the doctor, "there is no doubt of that!"

"You think so?" said Altamont.

"Without any doubt."

"Well, and this mark?" continued Altamont, pointing to another print, which was often repeated.

"That one?"

"Do you think it was made by an Esquimau?"

The doctor examined it carefully, and was stupefied. The print of a European shoe, with nails, sole, and heel, was clearly stamped in the snow. There could be no further doubt; a man, a stranger, had been there.

"Europeans here!" cried Hatteras.

"Evidently," said Johnson.

"And still," said the doctor, "it is so unlikely, that we ought to look twice before being sure."

Thereupon he looked twice, three times, at the print, and he was obliged to acknowledge its extraordinary origin.

De Foe's hero was not more amazed when he saw the footprint on the sand of his island; but if he was afraid, Hatteras was simply angry. A European so near the Pole!

They pushed on to examine the footprints; for a quarter of a mile they were continually repeated, mingled with marks of moccasins; then they turned to the west. When they had reached this point they consulted as to whether they should follow them any farther.

"No," said Hatteras. "Let us go on—"

He was interrupted by an exclamation of the doctor, who had just picked up on the snow an object even more convincing, and of the origin of which there could be no doubt. It was the object-glass of a pocket telescope.

"Now," he said, "we can't doubt that there is a stranger here—"

"Forward!" cried Hatteras.

He uttered this word so sharply that each one obeyed, and the sledge resumed its monotonous progress.

They all scanned the horizon attentively, except Hatteras, who was filled with wrath and did not care to see anything. Still, since they ran the risk of coming across a band of travellers, they had to take precautions; it was very disappointing to see any one ahead of them on the route. The doctor, although not as angry as Hatteras, was somewhat vexed, in spite of his usual philosophy. Altamont seemed equally annoyed; Johnson and Bell muttered threatening words between their teeth.

"Come," said the doctor, "let us take heart against our bad fortune."

"We must confess," said Johnson, without being heard by Altamont, "that if we find the place taken, it would disgust us with journeying to the Pole."

"And yet," answered Bell, "there is no possibility of doubting—"

"No," retorted the doctor; "I turn it all over in vain, and say it is improbable, impossible; I have to give it up. This shoe was not pressed into the snow without being at the end of a leg, and without the leg being attached to a human body. I could forgive Esquimaux, but a European!"

"The fact is," answered Johnson, "that if we are going to find all the rooms taken in the hotel of the end of the world, it would be annoying."

"Very annoying," said Altamont.

"Well, we shall see," said the doctor.

And they pushed on. The day ended without any new fact to indicate the presence of strangers in this part of New America, and they at last encamped for the evening.

A rather strong wind from the south had sprung up, and obliged them to seek a secure shelter for their tent in the bottom of a ravine. The sky was threatening; long clouds passed rapidly through the air; they passed near the ground, and so quickly that the eye could hardly follow them. At times some of the mist touched the ground, and the tent resisted with difficulty the violence of the hurricane.

The hut was pitched in a ravine for shelter.

"It's going to be a nasty night," said Johnson, after supper.

"It won't be cold, but stormy," answered the doctor; "let us take precautions, and make the tent firm with large stones."

"You are right, Doctor; if the wind should carry away the canvas, Heaven alone knows where we should find it again."

Hence they took every precaution against such a danger, and the wearied travellers lay down to sleep. But they found it impossible. The tempest was loose, and hastened northward with incomparable violence; the clouds were whirling about like steam which has just escaped from a boiler; the last avalanches, under the force of the hurricane, fell into the ravines, and their dull echoes were distinctly heard; the air seemed to be struggling with the water, and fire alone was absent from this contest of the elements.

Amid the general tumult their ears distinguished separate sounds, not the crash of heavy falling bodies, but the distinct cracking of bodies breaking; a clear snap was frequently heard, like breaking steel, amid the roar of the tempest. These last sounds were evidently avalanches torn off by the gusts, but the doctor could not explain the others. In the few moments of anxious silence, when the hurricane seemed to be taking breath in order to blow with greater violence, the travellers exchanged their suppositions.

"There is a sound of crashing," said the doctor, "as if icebergs and ice-fields were being blown against one another."

"Yes," answered Altamont; "one would say the whole crust of the globe was falling in. Say, did you hear that?"

"If we were near the sea," the doctor went on, "I should think it was ice breaking."

"In fact," said Johnson, "there is no other explanation possible."

"Can we have reached the coast?" asked Hatteras.

"It's not impossible," answered the doctor. "Hold on," he said, after a very distinct sound; "shouldn't you say that was the crashing of ice? We may be very near the ocean."

"If it is," continued Hatteras, "I should not be afraid to go across the ice-fields."

"O," said the doctor, "they must be broken by such a tempest! We shall see to-morrow. However that may be, if any men have to travel in such a night as this, I pity them."

The hurricane raged ten hours without cessation, and no one of those in the tent had a moment's sleep; the night passed in profound uneasiness. In fact, under such circumstances, every new incident, a tempest, an avalanche, might bring serious consequences. The doctor would gladly have gone out to reconnoitre, but how could he with such a wind raging?

Fortunately the hurricane grew less violent early the next day; they could leave the tent which had resisted so sturdily. The doctor, Hatteras, and Johnson went to a hill about three hundred feet high, which they ascended without difficulty. Their eyes beheld an entirely altered country, composed of bare rocks, sharp ridges entirely clear of ice. It was summer succeeding winter, which had been driven away by the tempest; the snow had been blown away by the wind before it could melt, and the barren soil reappeared.

"They climbed a hill which commanded a wide view."

But Hatteras's glances were all turned towards the north, where the horizon appeared to be hidden by dark mist.

"That may be the effect of the ocean," said the doctor.

"You are right," said Hatteras; "the sea must be there."

"That's what we call the blink of the water," said Johnson.

"Exactly," said the doctor.

"Well, let us start," said Hatteras, "and push on to this new ocean."

"That rejoices my heart," said Clawbonny to the captain.

"Certainly," was the enthusiastic answer. "Soon we shall have reached the Pole! and doesn't the prospect delight you, too, Doctor?"

"It does. I am always happy, and especially about the happiness of others!"

The three Englishmen returned to the ravine; the sledge was made ready, and they left the camp and resumed their march. Each one dreaded finding new tracks, but all the rest of the way they saw no trace of any human being. Three hours later they reached the coast.

"The sea! the sea!" they all shouted.

"And the open sea!" cried the captain.

"Three hours later they reached the coast. 'The sea! the sea!' they all shouted."

It was ten o'clock in the morning.

In fact, the hurricane had cleared up the polar basin; the shattered ice was floating away in every direction; the largest pieces, forming icebergs, had just weighed anchor and were sailing on the open sea. The wind had made a harsh attack upon the field. Fragments of ice covered the surrounding rocks. The little which was left of the ice-field seemed very soft; on the rocks were large pieces of sea-weed. The ocean stretched beyond the line of vision, with no island or new land peering above the horizon.

In the east and west were two capes gently sloping to the water; at their end the sea was breaking, and the wind was carrying a slight foam. The land of New America thus died away in the Polar Ocean, quietly and gently. It rounded into an open bay, with roadstead enclosed by the two promontories. In the middle a rock made a little natural harbor, sheltered against three points of the compass; it ran back into the land in the broad bed of a stream, through which ran down the melted snows of winter, now forming a perfect torrent.

Hatteras, after noticing the outline of the coast, resolved to make the preparations for departure that very day, to launch the boat, to put the unloaded sledge on board for future excursions. That took all day; then the tent was raised, and after a comfortable meal work began. Meanwhile the doctor took out his instruments to take an observation and determine the position of a part of the bay. Hatteras hurried on the work; he was anxious to start; he wanted to leave the land, and to be in advance in case any others should reach the sea.

At five o'clock in the evening Johnson and Bell had nothing to do but to fold their arms. The launch was rocking gently in her little harbor, with her mast set, her jib lowered, and her foresail in the brails; the provisions and most of the things on the sledge had been put on board; only the tent and a little of the camping material remained to be put on board the next day. The doctor found all these preparations complete on his return. When he saw the launch quietly sheltered from the wind, it occurred to him to give a name to the little harbor, and he proposed that of Altamont. This proposition was unanimously agreed to. So it was named Altamont Harbor.

"The launch was rocking gently in her little harbor."

According to the doctor's calculations, it lay in latitude 87° 5', and longitude 118° 35' E. of Greenwich; that is to say, less than three degrees from the Pole. The band had gone more than two hundred miles from Victoria Bay to Altamont Harbor.

CHAPTER XXI.

THE OPEN SEA.

The next morning Johnson and Bell set about carrying on board the camping material. At eight o'clock all the preparations for departure were complete. At the moment of starting the doctor's thoughts returned to the footprints they had seen. Were these men trying to gain the North? Had they any means of crossing the Polar Sea! Should they meet them again? For three days they had come across no trace of the travellers, and certainly, whoever they were, they could not have reached Altamont Harbor. That was a place which they were the first to set foot in. But the doctor, who was harassed by his thoughts, wanted to take a last view of the country, and he ascended a little hill about a hundred feet high, whence he had a distant view to the south.

When he had reached the top, he put his glass to his eyes. Great was his surprise when he found he could not see anything, either at a distance on the plains, or within a few feet of him. This seemed very odd; he made another examination, and at last he looked at the glass,—the object-glass was missing.

"The object-glass!" he cried.

The sudden revelation may be imagined; he uttered a cry so loud as to be heard by his companions, and they were much astonished at seeing him running down the hill.

"Well, what's the matter now?" asked Johnson.

The doctor was out of breath, and unable to speak. At length he managed to bring out,—

"The footprints!—the expedition!—"

"Well, what?" said Hatteras; "are they here?"

"No, no!" resumed the doctor,—"the object-glass, mine!"

And he showed his own glass.

"O, ho!" cried the American, "so you lost—"

"Yes!"

"But then the footprints—"

"Our own!" cried the doctor. "We lost our way in the fog! We went around in a circle, and came across our own footprints!"

"But the print of the shoes?" asked Hatteras.

"Bell's, you know, who walked all day in the snow after breaking his snow-shoes."

"That's true," said Bell.

Their mistake was so clear, that they all, except Hatteras, burst out laughing, and he was none the less pleased at the discovery.

"We were stupid enough," said the doctor, when they had stopped laughing. What good guesses we made! Strangers up here! Really, we ought to think before speaking. Well, since we are easy on this point, we can't do better than start."

"Forward!" said Hatteras.

A quarter of an hour later each one had taken his place on board of the launch, which sailed out of Altamont Harbor under mainsail and jib. This voyage began Wednesday, July 10th; they were then very near the Pole, exactly one hundred and seventy-five miles from it. However small the land might be at that point of the globe, the voyage would certainly be a short one. The wind was light, but fair. The thermometer stood at 50°; it was really warm.

The launch had not been injured by the journey on the sledge; it was in perfect order, and sailed easily. Johnson was at the helm; the doctor, Bell, and Altamont were lying as best they might among the load, partly on deck, partly below.

Hatteras stood forward, with his eyes turned to the mysterious point, which attracted him with an irresistible power, as the magnetic pole attracts the needle. If there should be any land, he wanted to be the first to see it. This honor really belonged to him. He noticed, besides, that the surface of the Polar Sea was covered with short waves, like those of land locked seas. This he considered a proof of the nearness of the opposite shore, and the doctor shared his opinion.

Hatteras's desire to find land at the North Pole is perfectly comprehensible. His disappointment would have been great if the uncertain sea covered the place where he wanted to find a piece of land, no matter how small! In fact, how could he give a special name to an uncertain portion of the sea? How plant the flag of his country among the waves? How take possession, in the name of her Gracious Majesty, of the liquid element?

So Hatteras, compass in hand, gazed steadily at the north. There was nothing that he could see between him and the horizon, where the line of the blue water met the blue sky. A few floating icebergs seemed to be leaving the way free for these bold sailors. The appearance of this region was singularly strange. Was this impression simply the result of the nervous excitement of the travellers? It is hard to say. Still, the doctor in his journal has described the singular appearance of the ocean; he spoke of it as Penny did, according to whom these countries present an appearance "offering the most striking contrast of a sea filled with millions of living creatures."

The sea, with its various colors, appeared strangely transparent, and endowed with a wonderful dispersive quality, as if it had been made with carburet of sulphur. This clearness let them see down into immeasurable depths; it seemed as if the sea were lit up like a large aquarium; probably some electric phenomenon at the bottom of the sea lit it up. So the launch seemed hung in a bottomless abyss.

On the surface of the water the birds were flying in large flocks, like thick clouds big with a storm. Aquatic birds of all sorts were there, from the albatross which is common to the south, to the penguin of the arctic seas, but of enormous size. Their cries were deafening. In considering them the doctor found his knowledge of natural history too scanty; many of the names escaped him, and he found himself bowing his head when their wings beat the air.

"Aquatic birds of all sorts were there."

Some of these large birds measured twenty feet from tip to tip; they covered the whole launch with their expanded wings; and there were legions of these birds, of which the names had never appeared in the London "Index Ornithologus." The doctor was dejected and stupefied at finding his science so faulty. Then, when his glance fell from the wonders of the air to the calm surface of the ocean, he saw no less astonishing productions of the animal kingdom, among others, medusæ thirty feet broad; they served as food for the other fish, and they floated like islands amid the sea-weed. What a difference from the microscopic medusæ observed in the seas of Greenland by Scoresby, and of which that explorer estimated the number at twenty-three trillions eight hundred and ninety-eight billions of millions in a space of two square miles!

Then the eye glancing down into the transparent water, the sight was equally strange, so full was it of fishes; sometimes the animals were swimming about below, and the eye saw them gradually disappearing, and fading away like spectres; then they would leave the lower layers and rise to the surface. The monsters seemed in no way alarmed at the presence of the launch; they even passed near it, rubbing their fins against it; this, which would have alarmed whalers, did not disturb these men, and yet the sea-monsters were very large.

"Then the eye glancing down into the transparent water, the sight was equally strange."

Young sea-calves played about them; the sword-fish, with its long, narrow, conical sword, with which it cleaves the ice, was chasing the more timid cetacea; numberless spouting whales were clearly to be heard. The sword-caper, with its delicate tail and large caudal fins, swam with incomprehensible quickness, feeding on smaller animals, such as the cod, as swift as itself; while the white whale, which is more inactive, swallowed peacefully the tranquil, lazy mollusks.

Farther down were Greenland anamaks, long and dark; huge sperm-whales, swimming in the midst of ambergris, in which took place thomeric battles that reddened the ocean for many miles around; the great Labrador tegusik. Sharp-backed dolphins, the whole family of seals and walruses, sea-dogs, horses and bears, lions and elephants, seemed to be feeding on the rich pastures; and the doctor admired the numberless animals, as he would have done the crustacea in the crystal basins of the zoölogical garden.

What beauty, variety, and power in nature! How strange and wonderful everything seemed in the polar regions!

The air acquired an unnatural purity; one would have said it was full of oxygen; the explorers breathed with delight this air, which filled them with fresher life; without taking account of the result, they were, so to speak, exposed to a real consuming fire, of which one can give no idea, not even a feeble one. Their emotions, their breathing and digestion, were endowed with superhuman energy; their ideas became more excited; they lived a whole day in an hour.

Through all these wonders the launch pushed on before a moderate breeze, occasionally feeling the air moved by the albatrosses' wings.

Towards evening, the coast of New America disappeared beneath the horizon. In the temperate zones, as well as at the equator, night falls; but here the sun simply described a circle parallel to the line of the horizon. The launch, bathed in its oblique rays, could not lose sight of it.

The animate beings of these regions seemed to know the approach of evening as truly as if the sun had set; birds, fish, cetacea, all disappeared. Whither? To the depths of the ocean? Who could say? But soon total silence succeeded to their cries, and the sound of their passage through the water; the sea grew calmer and calmer, and night retained its gentle peace even beneath the glowing sun.

Since leaving Altamont Harbor the launch had made one degree to the north; the next day nothing appeared on the horizon, neither projecting peaks nor those vague signs by which sailors detect their nearness to land.

The wind was good, but not strong, the sea not high; the birds and fish came as thick as the day before; the doctor, leaning over the gunwale, could see the cetacea rising slowly to the surface; a few icebergs and scattered pieces of ice alone broke the monotony of the ocean.

But the ice grew rarer, and was not enough to interfere with the boat. It is to be remembered that the launch was then ten degrees above the pole of cold; and as to the parallels of temperature, they might as well have been ten degrees to the other side. There was nothing surprising in the sea being open at this epoch, as it must have been at Disco Island in Baffin's Bay. So a sailing vessel would have plenty of sailing room in the summer months.

This observation had a great practical importance; in fact, if whalers can ever get to the polar basin, either by the seas of North America or those of the north of Asia, they are sure of getting full cargoes, for this part of the ocean seems to be the universal fishing-pond, the general reservoir of whales, seals, and all marine animals. At noon the line of the horizon was still unbroken; the doctor began to doubt of the existence of a continent in so high latitudes.

Still, as he reflected, he was compelled to believe in the existence of an arctic continent; in fact, at the creation of the world, after the cooling of the terrestrial crust, the waters formed by the condensation of the atmospheric vapor were compelled to obey the centrifugal force, to fly to the equator and leave the motionless extremities of the globe. Hence the necessary emersion of the countries near the Pole. The doctor considered this reasoning very just. And so it seemed to Hatteras.

Hence the captain still tried to pierce the mists of the horizon. His glass never left his eyes. In the color of the water, the shape of the waves, the direction of the wind, he tried to find traces of neighboring land. His head was bent forward, and even one who did not know his thoughts would have admired, so full was his attitude of energetic desire and anxious interrogation.

CHAPTER XXII.

THE APPROACH TO THE POLE.

The time flew by in this uncertainty. Nothing appeared on the sharply defined circle of the sea; nothing was to be seen save sky and sea,—not one of those floating land-plants which rejoiced the heart of Christopher Columbus as he was about to discover America. Hatteras was still gazing. At length, at about six o'clock in the evening, a shapeless vapor appeared at a little height above the level of the sea; it looked like a puff of smoke; the sky was perfectly cold, so this vapor was no cloud; it would keep appearing and disappearing, as if it were in commotion. Hatteras was the first to detect this phenomenon; he examined it with his glass for a whole hour.

Suddenly, some sure sign apparently occurred to him, for he stretched out his arms to the horizon and cried in a loud voice,—

"Land, ho!"

At these words each one sprang to his feet as if moved by electricity. A sort of smoke was clearly rising above the sea.

"I see it," cried the doctor.

"Yes! certainly!—yes!" said Johnson.

"It's a cloud," said Altamont.

"It's land!" answered Hatteras, as if perfectly convinced.

But, as often happens with objects that are indistinct in the distance, the point they had been looking at seemed to have disappeared. At length they found it again, and the doctor even fancied that he could see a swift light twenty or twenty-five miles to the north.

"It's a volcano!" he cried.

"'It's a volcano!' he cried."

"A volcano?" said Altamont.

"Without doubt."

"At this high latitude?"

"And why not?" continued the doctor; "isn't Iceland a volcanic land, so to speak, made of volcanoes?"

"Yes, Iceland," said the American, "but so near the Pole!"

"Well, didn't Commodore James Ross find in the Southern Continent two active volcanoes, Erebus and Terror by name, in longitude 170° and latitude 78°? Why then shouldn't there be volcanoes at the North Pole?"

"It may be so, after all," answered Altamont.

"Ah," cried the doctor, "I see it clearly! It is a volcano."

"Well," said Hatteras, "let us sail straight towards it."

"The wind is changing," said Johnson.

"Haul on the fore-sheet, and bring her nearer the wind."

But this manoeuvre only turned the launch away from the point they had been gazing at, and even with their closest examination they could not find it again. Still, they could not doubt that they were nearing land. They had seen, if they had not reached, the object of their voyage, and within twenty-four hours they would set foot on this unknown shore. Providence, after letting them get so near, would not drive them back at the last moment.

Still, no one manifested the joy which might have been expected under the circumstances; each one wondered in silence what this polar land might be. The animals seemed to shun it; at evening the birds, instead of seeking refuge there, flew with all speed to the south. Could not a single gull or ptarmigan find a resting-place there? Even the fish, the large cetacea, avoided that coast. Whence came this repugnance, which was shared by all the animals they saw, unless from terror?

The sailors experienced the same feeling; they gave way to the feelings inspired by the situation, and gradually each one felt his eyelids grow heavy. It was Hatteras's watch. He took the tiller; the doctor, Altamont, Johnson, and Bell fell asleep, stretched on the benches, and soon were dreaming soundly. Hatteras struggled against his sleepiness; he wished to lose not a moment; but the gentle motion of the launch rocked him, in spite of himself, into a gentle sleep.

The boat made hardly any headway; the wind did not keep her sails full. Far off in the west a few icebergs were reflecting the sun's rays, and glowing brightly in the midst of the ocean.

Hatteras began to dream. He recalled his whole life, with the incalculable speed of dreams; he went through the winter again, the scenes at Victoria Bay, Fort Providence, Doctor's House, the finding the American beneath the snow. Here remoter incidents came up before him; he dreamed of the burning of the *Forward*, of his treacherous companions who had abandoned him. What had become of them? He thought of Shandon, Wall, and the brutal Pen. Where were they now? Had they succeeded in reaching Baffin's Bay across the ice? Then he went further back, to his departure from England, to his previous voyages, his failures and misfortunes. Then he forgot his present situation, his success so near at hand, his hopes half realized. His dreams carried him from joy to agony. So it went on for two hours; then his thoughts changed; he began to think of the Pole, and he saw himself at last setting foot on this English continent, and unfolding the flag of the United Kingdom. While he was dozing in this way a huge, dark cloud was climbing across the sky, throwing a deep shadow over the sea.

It is difficult to imagine the great speed with which hurricanes arise in the arctic seas. The vapors which rise under the equator are condensed above the great glaciers of the North, and large masses of air are needed to take their place. This can explain the severity of arctic storms.

At the first shock of the wind the captain and his friends awoke from their sleep, ready to manage the launch. The waves were high and steep. The launch tossed helplessly about, now plunged into deep abysses, now oscillated on the pointed crest of a wave, inclining often at an angle of more than forty-five degrees. Hatteras took firm hold of the tiller, which was noisily sliding from one side to the other. Every now and then some strong wave would strike it and nearly throw him over. Johnson and Bell were busily occupied in bailing out the water which the launch would occasionally ship.

"The launch tossed helplessly about."

"This is a storm we hardly expected," said Altamont, holding fast to his bench.

"We ought to expect anything here," answered the doctor.

These remarks were made amid the roar of the tempest and the hissing of the waves, which the violence of the wind reduced to a fine spray. It was nearly impossible for one to hear his neighbor. It was hard to keep the boat's head to the north; the clouds hid everything a few fathoms from the boat, and they had no mark to sail by. This sudden tempest, just as they were about attaining their object, seemed full of warning; to their excited minds it came like an order to go no farther. Did Nature forbid approach to the Pole? Was this point of the globe surrounded by hurricanes and tempests which rendered access impossible? But any one who had caught sight of those men could have seen that they did not flinch before wind or wave, and that they would push on to the end. So they struggled on all day, braving death at every instant, and making no progress northward, but also losing no ground; they were wet through by the rain and waves; above the din of the storm they could hear the hoarse cries of the birds.

But at six o'clock in the evening, while the waves were rising, there came a sudden calm. The wind stopped as if by a miracle. The sea was smooth, as if it had not felt a puff of wind for twelve hours. The hurricane seemed to have respected this part of the Polar Ocean. What was the reason? It was an extraordinary phenomenon, which Captain Sabine had witnessed in his voyages in Greenland seas. The fog, without lifting, was very bright. The launch drifted along in a zone of electric light, an immense St. Elmo fire, brilliant but without heat. The mast, sail, and rigging stood out black against the phosphorescent air; the men seemed to have plunged into a bath of transparent rays, and their faces were all lit up. The sudden calm of this portion of the ocean came, without doubt, from the ascending motion of the columns of air, while the tempest, which was a cyclone, turned rapidly about this peaceful centre. But this atmosphere on fire suggested a thought to Hatteras.

"The fog, without lifting, was very bright."

"The volcano!" he cried.

"Is it possible?" asked Bell.

"No, no!" answered the doctor; "we should be smothered if the flames were to reach us."

"Perhaps it is its reflection in the fog," said Altamont.

"No. We should have to admit that we were near land, and in that case we should hear the eruption."

"But then?" asked the captain.

"It is a phenomenon," said the doctor, "which has been seldom observed hitherto. If we go on we cannot help leaving this luminous sphere and re-entering storm and darkness."

"Whatever it is, push on!" said Hatteras.

"Forward!" cried his companions, who did not wish to delay even for breathing-time in this quiet spot. The bright sail hung down the glistening mast; the oars dipped into the glowing waves, and appeared to drip with sparks. Hatteras, compass in hand, turned the boat's head to the north; gradually the mist lost its brightness and transparency; the wind could be heard roaring a short distance off; and soon the launch, lying over before a strong gust, re-entered the zone of storms. Fortunately, the hurricane had shifted a point towards the south, and the launch was able to run before the wind, straight for the Pole, running the risk of foundering, but sailing very fast; a rock, reef, or piece of ice might at any moment rise before them, and crush them to atoms. Still, no one of these men raised a single objection, nor suggested prudence. They were seized with the madness of danger. Thirst for the unknown took possession of them. They were going along, not blinded, but blindly, finding their speed only too slow for their impatience. Hatteras held the tiller firm amid the waves lashed into foam by the tempest. Still the proximity of land became evident. Strange signs filled the air. Suddenly the mist parted like a curtain torn by the wind, and for a moment, brief as a flash of lightning, a great burst of flame could be seen rising towards the sky.

"The volcano! the volcano!" was the cry which escaped from the lips of all; but the strange vision disappeared at once; the wind shifted to the southeast, took the launch on her quarter, and drove her from this unapproachable land.

"Malediction!" said Hatteras, shifting her sail; "we were not three miles from land!"

Hatteras could not resist the force of the tempest; but without yielding to it, he brought the boat about in the wind, which was blowing with fearful violence. Every now and then the launch leaned to one side, so that almost her whole keel was exposed; still she obeyed her rudder, and rose like a stumbling horse which his rider brings up by spur and reins. Hatteras, with his hair flying and his hand on the tiller, seemed to be part of the boat, like horse and man at the time of the centaurs. Suddenly a terrible sight presented itself to their eyes. Within less than ten fathoms a floe was balancing on the waves; it fell and rose like the launch, threatening in its fall to crush it to atoms. But to this danger of being plunged into the abyss was added another no less terrible; for this drifting floe was covered with white bears, crowded together and wild with terror.

"This drifting floe was covered with white bears, crowded together."

"Bears! bears!" cried Bell, in terror.

And each one gazed with terror. The floe pitched fearfully, sometimes at such an angle that the bears were all rolled together. Then their roars were almost as loud as the tempest; a formidable din arose from the floating menagerie.

If the floe had upset, the bears would have swum to the boat and clambered aboard.

For a quarter of an hour, which was as long as a century, the launch and floe drifted along in consort, twenty fathoms from one another at one moment and nearly running together the next, and at times they were so near to one another, the bears need only have dropped to have got on board. The

Greenland dogs trembled from terror; Duke remained motionless. Hatteras and his companions were silent; it did not occur to them to put the helm down and sail away, and they went straight on. A vague feeling, of astonishment rather than terror, took possession of them; they admired this spectacle which completed the struggle of the elements. Finally the floe drifted away, borne by the wind, which the launch was able to withstand, as she lay with her head to the wind, and it disappeared in the mist, its presence being known merely by the distant roaring of the bears.

At that moment the fury of the tempest redoubled; there was an endless unchaining of atmospheric waves; the boat, borne by the waves, was tossed about giddily; her sail flew away like a huge white bird; a whirlpool, a new Maelstrom, formed among the waves; the boat was carried so fast that it seemed to the men as if the rapidly revolving water were motionless. They were gradually sinking down. There was an irresistible power dragging them down and ingulfing them alive. All five arose. They looked at one another with terror. They grew dizzy. They felt an undefinable dread of the abyss! But suddenly the launch arose perpendicularly. Her prow was higher than the whirling waves; the speed with which she was moving hurled her beyond the centre of attraction, and escaping by the tangent of this circumference which was making more than a thousand turns a second, she was hurled away with the rapidity of a cannon-ball.

"Her sail flew away like a huge white bird; a whirlpool, a new Maelstrom, formed among the waves."

Altamont, the doctor, Johnson, and Bell were thrown down among the seats. When they rose, Hatteras had disappeared. It was two o'clock in the morning.

CHAPTER XXIII.

THE ENGLISH FLAG.

One cry, bursting from the lips of the other four, succeeded their first stupefaction.

"Hatteras!" cried the doctor.

"Gone!" said Johnson and Bell.

"Lost!"

They looked about, but nothing was to be seen on the storm-tossed sea. Duke barked despairingly; he tried to spring into the water, but Bell managed to hold him.

"Take a place at the helm, Altamont," said the doctor; "let us try everything to save the captain."

Johnson and Bell took their seats. Altamont took the helm, and the launch came into wind again. Johnson and Bell began to row vigorously; for an hour they remained at the scene of the accident. They sought earnestly, but in vain. The unfortunate Hatteras was lost in the storm! Lost, so near the Pole, so near the end, of which he had had but a glimpse!

The doctor called aloud, and fired the guns; Duke added his howling, but there was no answer. Then profound grief seized Clawbonny; his head sank into his hands, and his companions saw that he was weeping. In fact, at this distance from land, with a scrap of wood to hold him up, Hatteras could not reach the shore alive; and if anything did come ashore, it would be his disfigured corpse. After hunting for an hour, they decided to turn to the north, and struggle against the last furies of the tempest.

At five o'clock in the morning of July 11th the wind went down; the sea grew quieter; the sky regained its polar clearness, and within three miles of them appeared the land. This continent was but an island, or rather a volcano, peering up like a lighthouse at the North Pole. The mountain, in full eruption, was hurling forth a mass of burning stones and melting rocks. It seemed to be rising and falling beneath the successive blasts as if it were breathing; the things which were cast out reached a great height in the air; amid the jets of flame, torrents of lava were flowing down the side of the mountain; here creeping between steaming rocks, there falling in cascades amid the purple vapor: and lower down a thousand streams united in one large river, which ran boiling into the sea.

"The mountain was in full eruption."

The volcano seemed to have but a single crater, whence arose a column of fire, lighted by transverse rays; one would have said that part of the magnificence of the phenomenon was due to electricity. Above the flames floated an immense cloud of smoke, red below, black above. It rose with great majesty, and unrolled into huge layers.

The sky at a considerable height had an ashy hue; the darkness, which was so marked during the tempest, and of which the doctor could give no satisfactory explanation, evidently came from the ashes, which completely hid the sun. He remembered a similar fact that took place in 1812, at the Barbadoes, which at noon was plunged into total darkness by the mass of cinders thrown from the crater of Isle St. Vincent.

This enormous volcano, jutting up in mid-ocean, was about six thousand feet high, very nearly the altitude of Hecla. A line from the summit to the base would form with the horizon an angle of about eleven degrees. It seemed to rise from the bosom of the waves as the launch approached it. There was no trace of vegetation. There was no shore; it ran down steep to the sea.

"Shall we be able to land?" said the doctor.

"The wind is carrying us there," answered Altamont.

"But I can't see any beach on which we could set foot."

"So it seems from here," answered Johnson; "but we shall find some place for our boat; that is all we need."

"Let us go on, then!" answered Clawbonny, sadly.

The doctor had no eyes for the strange continent which was rising before him. The land of the Pole was there, but not the man who had discovered it. Five hundred feet from the rocks the sea was boiling under the action of subterraneous fires. The island was from eight to ten miles in circumference, no more; and, according to their calculation, it was very near the Pole, if indeed the axis of the world did not pass exactly through it. As they drew near they noticed a little fiord large enough to shelter their boat; they sailed towards it, filled with the fear of finding the captain's body cast ashore by the tempest.

"They noticed a little fiord."

Still, it seemed unlikely that any corpse should rest there; there was no beach, and the sea beat against the steep rocks; thick ashes, on which no human foot had ever stepped, covered the ground beyond the reach of the waves. At last the launch slipped between the breakers, and there she was perfectly sheltered against the surf. Then Duke's lamentable howling redoubled; the poor animal called for the captain with his sad wails among the rocks. His barking was vain; and the doctor caressed him, without being able to calm him, when the faithful dog, as if he wanted to replace his master, made a prodigious leap, and was the first to get ashore amid the dust and ashes which flew about him.

"Duke! Duke!" said the doctor.

Duke did not hear him, but disappeared. The men then went ashore, and made the launch fast. Altamont was preparing to climb up a large pile of rocks, when Duke's distant barking was heard; it expressed pain, not wrath.

"Listen!" said the doctor.

"Has he got on the track of some animal?" asked the boatswain.

"No," answered the doctor, quivering with emotion; "he's mourning, crying! Hatteras's body is there!"

At these words the four men started after Duke, in the midst of blinding cinders; they reached the end of the fiord, a little place ten feet broad, where the waves were gently breaking. There Duke was barking near a body wrapped up in the English flag.

"Hatteras, Hatteras!" cried the doctor, rushing to the body of his friend.

But at once he uttered an explanation which it is impossible to render. This bleeding and apparently lifeless body had just given signs of life.

"Alive, alive!" he cried.

"Yes," said a feeble voice, "living on the land of the Pole, where the tempest cast me up! Living on Queen Island!"

"Hurrah for England!" cried the five together.

"And for America!" added the doctor, holding out one hand to Hatteras and the other to Altamont. Duke, too, hurrahed in his own way, which was as good as any other.

At first these kind-hearted men were wholly given up to the pleasure of seeing their captain again; they felt the tears welling up into their eyes. The doctor examined Hatteras's condition. He was not seriously injured. The wind had carried him to the shore, where it was hard to land; the bold sailor, often beaten back, at last succeeded in clambering upon a rock above the reach of the waves. Then he lost consciousness, after wrapping himself up in his flag, and he only came to himself under Duke's caresses and barking. After receiving a few attentions, Hatteras was able to rise, and, leaning on the doctor's arm, to go to the launch.

"The Pole, the North Pole!" he repeated as he walked along.

"You are happy!" the doctor said to him.

"Yes, happy! And you, my friend, don't you feel happy at being here? This land is the land of the Pole! This sea we have crossed is the sea of the Pole! This air we breathe is the air of the Pole! O, the North Pole, the North Pole!"

As he spoke, Hatteras was the victim of a violent excitement, a sort of fever, and the doctor in vain tried to calm him. His eyes were strangely bright, and his thoughts were boiling within him. Clawbonny ascribed this condition to the terrible perils he had gone through. Hatteras evidently needed rest, and they set about seeking a place to camp. Altamont soon found a grotto in the rocks, which had fallen in such a way as to form a cavern. Johnson and Bell brought provisions there, and let loose the dogs. Towards eleven o'clock everything was prepared for a meal; the canvas of the tent served as a cloth; the breakfast, consisting of pemmican, salt meat, tea and coffee, was set and soon devoured. But first, Hatteras demanded that an observation should be made; he wanted to know its position exactly. The doctor and Altamont then took their instruments, and after taking an observation they found the precise position of the grotto to be latitude 89° 59' 15". The longitude at this height was of no importance, for all the meridians run together within a few hundred feet higher. So in reality the island was situated at the North Pole, and the ninetieth degree of latitude was only forty-five seconds from there, exactly three quarters of a mile, that is to say, towards the top of the volcano. When Hatteras knew this result, he asked that it should be stated in two documents, one to be placed in a cairn on the shore. So at once the doctor took his pen and wrote the following document, one copy of which is now in the archives of the Royal Geographical Society in London:—

"July 11, 1861, in north latitude 89° 59' 15", 'Queen Island' was discovered at the North Pole by Captain Hatteras, commanding the brig *Forward* of Liverpool, who has set his name hereto, with his companions. Whoever shall find this document is entreated to forward it to the Admiralty.

(Signed)   JOHN HATTERAS, Captain of the *Forward*.

DR. CLAWBONNY.

ALTAMONT, Captain of the *Porpoise*.

JOHNSON, Boatswain.

BELL, Carpenter."

"And now, my friends, to table!" said the doctor, gayly.

"Altamont soon found a grotto in the rocks."

CHAPTER XXIV.

POLAR COSMOGRAPHY.

Of course, to eat at table, they were obliged to sit on the ground.

"But," said Clawbonny, "who wouldn't give all the tables and dining-rooms in the world, to dine in north latitude 89° 59' 15"?"

The thoughts of each one were about their situation. They had no other idea than the North Pole. The dangers they had undergone to reach it, those to overcome before returning, were forgotten in their unprecedented success. What neither Europeans, Americans, nor Asiatics had been able to do, they had accomplished. Hence they were all ready to listen to the doctor when he told them all that his inexhaustible memory could recall about their position. It was with real enthusiasm that he first proposed their captain's health.

"They were all ready to listen to the doctor."

"To John Hatteras!" he said.

"To John Hatteras!" repeated the others.

"To the North Pole!" answered the captain, with a warmth that was unusual in this man who was usually so self-restrained, but who now was in a state of great nervous excitement. They touched glasses, and the toasts were followed by earnest hand-shakings.

"It is," said the doctor, "the most important geographical fact of our day! Who would have thought that this discovery would precede that of the centre of Africa or Australia? Really, Hatteras, you are greater than Livingstone, Burton, and Barth! All honor to you!"

"You are right, Doctor," said Altamont; "it would seem, from the difficulty of the undertaking, that the Pole would be the last place discovered. Whenever the government was absolutely determined to know the middle of Africa, it would have succeeded at the cost of so many men and so much money; but here nothing is less certain than success, and there might be obstacles really insuperable."

"Insuperable!" cried Hatteras with warmth; "there are no insuperable obstacles; there are more or less determined minds, that is all!"

"Well," said Johnson, "we are here, and it is well. But, Doctor, will you tell me, once for all, what there is so remarkable about the Pole?"

"It is this, Johnson, that it is the only motionless part of the globe, while all the rest is turning with extreme rapidity."

"But I don't see that we are more motionless here than at Liverpool."

"No more than you perceive the motion at Liverpool; and that is because in both cases you participate in the movement or the repose. But the fact is no less certain. The earth rotates in twenty-four hours, and this motion is on an axis with its extremities at the two poles. Well, we are at one of the extremities of the axis, which is necessarily motionless."

"So," said Bell, "when our countrymen are turning rapidly, we are perfectly still?"

"Very nearly, for we are not exactly at the Pole."

"You are right, Doctor," said Hatteras seriously, and shaking his head; "we are still forty-five seconds from the precise spot."

"That is not far," answered Altamont, "and we can consider ourselves motionless."

"Yes," continued the doctor, "while those living at the equator move at the rate of three hundred and ninety-six leagues an hour."

"And without getting tired!" said Bell.

"Exactly!" answered the doctor.

"But," continued Johnson, "besides this movement of rotation, doesn't the earth also move about the sun?"

"Yes, and this takes a year."

"Is it swifter than the other?"

"Infinitely so; and I ought to say that, although we are at the Pole, it takes us with it as well as all the people in the world. So our pretended immobility is a chimera: we are motionless with regard to the other points of the globe, but not so with regard to the sun."

"Good!" said Bell, with an accent of comic regret; "so I, who thought I was still, was mistaken! This illusion has to be given up! One can't have a moment's peace in this world."

"You are right, Bell," answered Johnson; "and will you tell us, Doctor, how fast this motion is?"

"It is very fast," answered the doctor; "the earth moves around the sun seventy-six times faster than a twenty-four-pound cannon-ball flies, which goes one hundred and ninety-five fathoms a second. It moves, then, seven leagues and six tenths per second; you see it is very different from the diurnal movement of the equator."

"The deuce!" said Bell; "that is incredible, Doctor! More than seven leagues a second, and that when it would have been so easy to be motionless, if God had wished it!"

"Good!" said Altamont; "do you think so, Bell? In that case no more night, nor spring, nor autumn, nor winter!"

"Without considering a still more terrible result," continued the doctor.

"What is that?" asked Johnson.

"We should all fall into the sun!"

"Fall into the sun!" repeated Bell with surprise.

"Yes. If this motion were to stop, the earth would fall into the sun in sixty-four days and a half."

"A fall of sixty-four days!" said Johnson.

"No more nor less," answered the doctor; "for it would have to fall a distance of thirty-eight millions of leagues."

"What is the weight of the earth?" asked Altamont.

"It is five thousand eight hundred and ninety-one quadrillions of tons."

"Good!" said Johnson; "those numbers have no meaning."

"For that reason, Johnson, I was going to give you two comparisons which you could remember. Don't forget that it would take seventy-five moons to make the sun, and three hundred and fifty thousand earths to make up the weight of the sun."

"That is tremendous!" said Altamont.

"Tremendous is the word," answered the doctor; "but, to return to the Pole, no lesson on cosmography on this part of the globe could be more opportune, if it doesn't weary you."

"Go on, Doctor, go on!"

"I told you," resumed the doctor, who took as much pleasure in giving as the others did in receiving instruction,—"I told you that the Pole was motionless in comparison with the rest of the globe. Well, that is not quite true!"

"What!" said Bell, "has that got to be taken back?"

"Yes, Bell, the Pole is not always exactly in the same place; formerly the North Star was farther from the celestial pole than it is now. So our Pole has a certain motion; it describes a circle in about twenty-six years. That comes from the precession of the equinoxes, of which I shall speak soon."

"But," asked Altamont, "might it not happen that some day the Pole should get farther from its place?"

"Ah, my dear Altamont," answered the doctor, "you bring up there a great question, which scientific men investigated for a long time in consequence of a singular discovery."

"What was that?"

"This is it. In 1771 the body of a rhinoceros was found on the shore of the Arctic Sea, and in 1799 that of an elephant on the coast of Siberia. How did the animals of warm countries happen to be found in these latitudes? Thereupon there was much commotion among geologists, who were not so wise as a Frenchman, M. Elie de Beaumont, has been since. He showed that these animals used to live in rather high latitudes, and that the streams and rivers simply carried their bodies to the places where they were found. But do you know the explanation which scientific men gave before this one?"

"Scientific men are capable of anything," said Altamont.

"Yes, in explanation of a fact; well, they imagined that the Pole used to be at the equator and the equator at the Pole."

"Bah!"

"It was exactly what I tell you. Now, if it had been so, since the earth is flattened more than five leagues at the pole, the seas, carried to the equator by centrifugal force, would have covered mountains twice as high as the Himalayas; all the countries near the polar circle, Sweden, Norway, Russia, Siberia, Greenland, and New Britain, would have been buried in five leagues of water, while the regions at the equator, having become the pole, would have formed plateaus fifteen leagues high!"

"What a change!" said Johnson.

"O, that made no difference to scientific men!"

"And how did they explain the alteration?" asked Altamont.

"They said it was due to the shock of collision with a comet. The comet is the *deus ex machina;* whenever one comes to a difficult question in cosmography, a comet is lugged in. It is the most obliging of the heavenly bodies, and at the least sign from a scientific man it disarranges itself to arrange everything."

"Then," said Johnson, "according to you, Doctor, this change is impossible?"

"Impossible!"

"And if it should take place?"

"If it did, the equator would be frozen in twenty-four hours!"

"Good! if it were to take place now," said Bell, "people would as likely as not say we had never gone to the Pole."

"Calm yourself, Bell. To return to the immobility of the terrestrial axis, the following is the result: if we were to spend a winter here, we should see the stars describing a circle about us. As for the sun, the day of the vernal equinox, March 23d, it would appear to us (I take no account of refraction) exactly cut in two by the horizon, and would rise gradually in longer and longer curves; but here it is remarkable that when it has once risen it sets no more; it is visible for six months. Then its disk touches the horizon again at the autumnal equinox, September 22d, and as soon as it is set, it is seen no more again all winter."

"You were speaking just now of the flattening of the earth at the poles," said Johnson; "be good enough to explain that, Doctor."

"I will. Since the earth was fluid when first created, you understand that its rotary movement would try to drive part of the mobile mass to the equator, where the centrifugal force was greater. If the earth had been motionless, it would have remained a perfect sphere; but in consequence of the phenomenon I have just described, it has an ellipsoidal form, and points at the pole are nearer the centre of the earth than points at the equator by about five leagues."

"So," said Johnson, "if our captain wanted to take us to the centre of the earth, we should have five leagues less to go?"

"Exactly, my friend."

"Well, Captain, it's so much gained! We ought to avail ourselves of it."

But Hatteras did not answer. Evidently he had lost all interest in the conversation, or perhaps he was listening without hearing.

"Well," answered the doctor, "according to certain scientific men, it would be worth while to try this expedition."

"What! really?" exclaimed Johnson.

"But let me finish," answered the doctor. "I will tell you. I must first tell you this flattening of the poles is the cause of the precession of the equinoxes; that is to say, why every year the vernal equinox comes a day sooner than it would if the earth were perfectly round. This comes from the attraction of the sun operating in a different way on the heaped-up land of the equator, which then experiences a retrograde movement. Subsequently it displaces this Pole a little, as I just said. But, independently of this effect, this flattening ought to have a more curious and more personal effect, which we should perceive if we had mathematical sensibility."

"What do you mean?" asked Bell.

"I mean that we are heavier here than at Liverpool."

"Heavier?"

"Yes; ourselves, the dogs, our guns, and instruments!"

"Is it possible?"

"Certainly, and for two reasons: the first is, that we are nearer the centre of the globe, which consequently attracts us more strongly, and this force of gravitation is nothing but weight; the second is, the rotary force, which is nothing at the pole, is very marked at the equator, and objects there have a tendency to fly from the earth: they are less heavy."

"What!" exclaimed Johnson, seriously; "have we not the same weight everywhere?"

"No, Johnson; according to Newton's law, bodies attract one another directly as their masses, and inversely to the square of their distances. Here I weigh more, because I am nearer the centre of attraction; and on another planet I should weigh more or less according to the mass of the planet."

"What!" said Bell, "in the moon—"

"In the moon my weight, which is two hundred pounds at Liverpool, would be only thirty-two pounds."

"And in the sun?"

"O, in the sun I should weigh more than five thousand pounds!"

"Heavens!" said Bell; "you'd need a derrick to move your legs."

"Probably," answered the doctor, laughing at Bell's amazement; "but here the difference is imperceptible, and by an equal effort of the muscles Bell would leap as high as on the docks at Liverpool."

"Yes, but in the sun?" urged Bell.

"My friend," answered the doctor, "the upshot of it all is that we are well off where we are, and need not want to go elsewhere."

"You said just now," resumed Altamont, "that perhaps it would be worth while to make a journey to the centre of the world; has such an undertaking ever been thought of?"

"Yes, and this is all I'm going to say about the Pole. There is no point in the world which has given rise to more chimeras and hypotheses. The ancients, in their ignorance, placed the garden of the Hesperides there. In the Middle Ages it was supposed that the earth was upheld on axles placed at the poles, on which it revolved; but when comets were seen moving freely, that idea had to be given up. Later, there was a French astronomer, Bailly, who said that the lost people mentioned by Plato, the Atlantides, lived here. Finally, it has been asserted in our own time that there was an immense opening at the poles, from which came the Northern Lights, and through which one could reach the inside of the earth; since in the hollow sphere two planets, Pluto and Proserpine, were said to move, and the air was luminous in consequence of the strong pressure it felt."

"That has been maintained?" asked Altamont.

"Yes, it has been written about seriously. Captain Symmes, a countryman of ours, proposed to Sir Humphry Davy, Humboldt, and Arago, to undertake the voyage! But they declined."

"And they did well."

"I think so. Whatever it may be, you see, my friends, that the imagination has busied itself about the Pole, and that sooner or later we must come to the reality."

"At any rate, we shall see for ourselves," said Johnson, who clung to his idea.

"Then, to-morrow we'll start," said the doctor, smiling at seeing the old sailor but half convinced; "and if there is any opening to the centre of the earth, we shall go there together."

CHAPTER XXV.

MOUNT HATTERAS.

After this solid conversation every one made himself as comfortable as possible in the cavern, and soon fell asleep. Every one, that is, except Hatteras. Why did not this strange man sleep?

Was not the object of his life attained? Had he not accomplished the bold projects which lay so near his heart? Why did not calmness succeed the agitation in his ardent mind? Would not one suppose that, when he had accomplished this end, Hatteras would fall into a sort of dejection, and that his over-stretched nerves would seek repose? After succeeding, it would seem natural that he should be seized with the feeling of sadness, which always follows satisfied desires.

But no. He was only more excited. It was not, however, the thought of returning which agitated him so. Did he wish to go farther? Was there no limit to his ambition, and did he find the world too small, because he had been around it? However this may have been, he could not sleep. And yet this first night spent at the pole of the world was pleasant and quiet. The island was absolutely uninhabited. There was not a bird in its fire-impregnated atmosphere, not an animal on the soil of cinders, not a fish in its boiling waters. Only afar off the dull murmur of the mountain, from the summit of which arose puffs of hot smoke.

When Bell, Johnson, Altamont, and the doctor awoke, Hatteras was not to be seen near them. Being anxious, they left the cave, and saw the captain standing on a rock. His eyes were fixed on the top of the volcano. He held his instruments in his hands, having evidently been calculating the exact height of the mountain. The doctor went up to him and spoke to him several times before he could rouse him from his revery. At last the captain seemed to understand him.

"They saw the captain standing on a rock."

"Forward!" said the doctor, who was examining him attentively,—"forward! let us explore our island; we are all ready for our last excursion."

"Our last," said Hatteras, with the intonation of people who are dreaming aloud; "yes, the last, indeed. But also," he continued with great animation, "the most wonderful!"

He spoke in this way, rubbing his hands over his brow as if to allay its throbbing. At that moment, Altamont, Johnson, and Bell joined him; Hatteras appeared to awaken from his revery.

"Hatteras appeared to wake from his revery."

"My friends," he said with emotion, "thanks for your courage, thanks for your perseverance, thanks for your superhuman efforts, which have allowed us to set foot on this land!"

"Captain!" said Johnson, "we have only obeyed; all the honor is due to you alone!"

"No, no!" resumed Hatteras with emotion; "to you as much as to me! to Altamont as well as to all of us! as to the doctor himself— O, let my heart well over in your hands! It can no longer restrain its joy and gratitude!"

Hatteras clasped the hands of his companions. He walked to and fro, no longer master of himself.

"We have only done our duty as Englishmen," said Bell.

"Our duty as friends," continued the doctor.

"Yes," said Hatteras, "but all have not performed this duty. Some have given way! Still, they must be pardoned, both who were treacherous, and those who were led away to it! Poor men! I forgive them. You understand me, Doctor?"

"Yes," answered the doctor, who was very uneasy at Hatteras's excitement.

"So," went on the captain, "I don't want them to lose the money they came so far to seek. No, I shall not alter my plan; they shall be rich,—if they ever see England again!"

Few could have withstood the tenderness with which Hatteras spoke these last words.

"But, Captain," said Johnson, with an effort at pleasantry, "one would say you were making your will."

"Perhaps I am," answered Hatteras, seriously.

"Still you have before you a long and glorious life," continued the old sailor.

"Who can say?" said Hatteras.

A long silence followed these words. The doctor did not dare to try to interpret the last remark. But Hatteras soon expressed his meaning, for in a hasty, hardly restrained voice, he went on:—

"My friends, listen to me. We have done a good deal so far, and yet there is a good deal to do."

His companions gazed at him in astonishment.

"Yes, we are on the land of the Pole, but we are not on the Pole itself!"

"How so?" asked Altamont.

"You don't mean it!" cried the doctor, anxiously.

"Yes!" resumed Hatteras, earnestly, "I said that an Englishman should set foot on the Pole; I said it, and an Englishman shall do it."

"What!" ejaculated the doctor.

"We are now forty-five seconds from the unknown point," Hatteras went on, with increasing animation; "where it is, I am going!"

"But that is the top of the volcano!" said the doctor.

"I'm going!"

"It's an inaccessible spot!"

"I'm going!"

"It's a fiery crater!"

"I'm going!"

The firmness with which Hatteras uttered these words cannot be given. His friends were stupefied; they gazed with horror at the volcano tipped with flame. Then the doctor began; he urged and besought Hatteras to give up his design; he said everything he could imagine, from entreaty to well-meant threats; but he obtained no concession from the nervous captain, who was possessed with a sort of madness which may be called polar madness. Only violent means could stop him, rushing to his ruin. But seeing that thereby they would produce serious results, the doctor wished to keep them for a last resource. He hoped, too, that some physical impossibility, some unsurmountable difficulty, would compel him to give up his plan.

"Since it is so," he said, "we shall follow you."

"Yes," answered the captain, "half-way up the mountain! No farther! Haven't you got to carry back to England the copy of the document which proves our discovery, in case—"

"Still—"

"It is settled," said Hatteras, in a tone of command; "and since my entreaties as a friend are not enough, I order it as captain."

The doctor was unwilling to urge him any further, and a few moments later the little band, equipped for a hard climb, and preceded by Duke, set out. The sky was perfectly clear. The thermometer stood at 52°. The air had all the brilliancy which is so marked at this high latitude. It was eight o'clock in the morning. Hatteras went ahead with his dog, the others followed close behind.

"I'm anxious," said Johnson.

"No, no, there's nothing to fear," answered the doctor; "we are here."

It was a strange island, in appearance so new and singular! The volcano did not seem old, and geologists would have ascribed a recent date to its formation.

The rocks were heaped upon one another, and only kept in place by almost miraculous balancing. The mountain, in fact, was composed of nothing but stones that had fallen from above. There was no soil, no moss, no lichen, no trace of vegetation. The carbonic acid from the crater had not yet had time to unite with the hydrogen of the water; nor the ammonia of the clouds, to form under the action of the light, organized matter. This island had arisen from successive volcanic eruptions, like many other mountains; what they have hurled forth has built them up. For instance, Etna has poured forth a volume of lava larger than itself; and the Monte Nuovo, near Naples, was formed by ashes in the short space of forty-eight hours. The heap of rocks composing Queen's Island had evidently come from the bowels of the earth. Formerly the sea covered it all; it had been formed long since by the condensation of the vapor on the cooling globe; but in proportion as the volcanoes of the Old and New World disappeared, they were replaced by new craters.

In fact, the earth can be compared to a vast spheroidal boiler. Under the influence of the central fire an immense quantity of vapor is generated, which is exposed to a pressure of thousands of atmospheres, and which would blow up the globe, were it not for the safety-valves opening on the outside.

These safety-valves are the volcanoes; when one closes, another opens; and at the poles, where, doubtless in consequence of the flattening of the earth's surface, the crust is thinner, it is not strange that a volcano should be suddenly formed by the upheaval of the bottom of the waves. The doctor noticed all this as he followed Hatteras; his foot sank into a volcanic tufa, and the deposits of ashes, volcanic stones, etc., like the syenite and granite of Iceland. But he attributed a comparatively recent origin to the island, on account of the fact that no sedimentary soil had yet formed upon it. Water, too, was lacking. If Queen's Island had existed for several years, there would have been springs upon it, as there are in the neighborhood of volcanoes. Now, not only was there no drop of water there, but the vapors which arose from the stream of lava seemed absolutely anhydrous.

This island, then, was of recent formation; and since it appeared in one day, it might disappear in another and sink beneath the ocean.

The ascent grew more difficult the higher they went; the sides of the mountain became nearly perpendicular, and they had to be very careful to avoid accident. Often columns of cinders were blown about them and threatened to choke them, or torrents of lava barred their path. On some such places these streams were hard on top, but the molten stream flowed beneath. Each one had to test it first to escape sinking into the glowing mass. From time to time the crater vomited forth huge red-hot rocks amid burning gases; some of these bodies burst in the air like shells, and the fragments were hurled far off in all directions. The innumerable dangers of this ascent may be readily perceived, as well as the foolhardiness of the attempt.

Still, Hatteras climbed with wonderful agility, and while spurning the use of his iron-tipped staff, he ascended the steepest slopes. He soon reached a circular rock, which formed a sort of plateau about ten feet broad; a glowing stream surrounded it, which was divided at the corner by a higher rock, and left only a narrow passage through which Hatteras slipped boldly. There he stopped, and his companions were able to join him. Then he seemed to estimate the distance yet remaining; horizontally there were only about six hundred feet of the crater remaining, that is to say, from the mathematical point of the Pole; but vertically they had fifteen hundred feet yet to climb. The ascent had already taken three hours; Hatteras did not seem tired; his companions were exhausted.

The top of the volcano seemed inaccessible. The doctor wished at any risk to keep Hatteras from going higher. At first he tried gentle means, but the captain's excitement amounted to delirium; on the way he had exhibited all the signs of growing madness, and whoever has known him in the different scenes of his life cannot be surprised. In proportion as Hatteras rose above the ocean his excitement increased; he lived no longer with men; he thought he was growing larger with the mountain itself.

"Hatteras," said the doctor, "this is far enough! we can't go any farther!"

"Stay where you are, then," answered the captain in a strange voice; "I shall go higher!"

"No! that's useless! you are at the Pole here!"

"No, no, higher!"

"My friend, it's I who am speaking to you, Dr. Clawbonny! Don't you know me?"

"Higher! higher!" repeated the madman.

"Well, no, we sha'n't let—"

The doctor had not finished the sentence before Hatteras, by a violent effort, sprang over the stream of lava and was out of their reach. They uttered a cry, thinking Hatteras was lost in the fiery abyss; but he had reached the other side, followed by Duke, who was unwilling to abandon him.

He disappeared behind a puff of smoke, and his voice was heard growing fainter and fainter in the distance.

"To the north!" he was shouting, "to the top of Mount Hatteras! Do you remember Mount Hatteras?"

They could not think of getting up to him; there were twenty chances to one against their being able to cross the stream he had leaped over with the skill and luck of madmen. Nor could they get around it. Altamont in vain tried to pass; he was nearly lost in trying to cross the stream of lava; his companions were obliged to hold him by force.

"Hatteras, Hatteras!" shouted the doctor.

But the captain did not answer; Duke's barking alone was heard upon the mountain.

Still, Hatteras could be seen at intervals through the column of smoke and the showers of cinders. Sometimes his arm or head would emerge from the whirlwind. Then he would disappear and be seen again higher up in the rocks. His height diminished with the fantastic swiftness of objects rising in the air. Half an hour later he seemed but a fraction of his usual size.

The air was filled with the dull noises of the volcano; the mountain was roaring like a boiler, its sides were quivering. Hatteras kept on, and Duke followed. From time to time some enormous rock would give way beneath them and go crashing down to the sea. But Hatteras did not look back. He had made use of his staff as a pole on which to fasten the English flag. His companions observed every one of his movements. His dimensions became gradually smaller, and Duke seemed no larger than a rat. One moment the wind seemed to drive down upon them a great wave of flame. The doctor uttered a cry of anguish, but Hatteras reappeared, standing and brandishing the flag.

"But Hatteras did not look back. He had made use of his staff as a pole on which to fasten the English flag."

This sight lasted for more than an hour,—an hour of struggle with the trembling rocks, with the beds of ashes into which this madman would sink up to the waist. Now he would be climbing on his knees and making use of every inequality in the mountain, and now he would hang by his hands at some sharp corner, swinging in the wind like a dry leaf.

At last he reached the top, the yawning mouth of the crater. The doctor then hoped that the wretched man, having attained his object, would perhaps return and have only those dangers before him.

He gave a last shout.

"Hatteras, Hatteras!"

The doctor's cry moved the American's heart so that he cried out,—

"I will save him!"

Then with one leap crossing the fiery torrent at the risk of falling in, he disappeared among the rocks. Clawbonny did not have time to stop him. Still, Hatteras, having reached the top, was climbing on top of a rock which overhung the abyss. The stones were raining about him. Duke was still following him. The poor beast seemed already dizzy at the sight beneath him. Hatteras was whirling about his head the flag, which was lighted with the brilliant reflection, and the red bunting could be seen above the crater. With one hand Hatteras was holding it; with the other he was pointing to the zenith, the celestial pole. Still he seemed to hesitate. He was seeking the mathematical point where all the meridians meet, and on which in his sublime obstinacy he wanted to set his foot.

Suddenly the rock gave way beneath him. He disappeared. A terrible cry from his companions rose even to the summit of the mountain. A second— a century—passed! Clawbonny considered his friend lost and buried forever in the depths of the volcano. But Altamont was there, and Duke too. The man and the dog had seized him just when he was disappearing in the abyss. Hatteras was saved, saved in spite of himself, and half an hour later the captain of the *Forward* lay unconscious in the arms of his despairing friends.

When he came to himself, the doctor gave him a questioning glance in mute agony. But his vague look, like that of a blind man, made no reply.

"Heavens!" said Johnson, "he is blind!"

"No," answered Clawbonny,—"no! My poor friends, we have saved Hatteras's body! His mind is at the top of the volcano! He has lost his reason!"

"Mad?" cried Johnson and Altamont in deep distress.

"Mad!" answered the doctor.

And he wept bitterly.

CHAPTER XXVI.

RETURN TO THE SOUTH.

Three hours after this sad conclusion to the adventures of Captain Hatteras, Clawbonny, Altamont, and the two sailors were assembled in the cavern at the foot of the volcano. Then Clawbonny was asked to give his opinion on what was to be done.

"My friends," he said, "we cannot prolong our stay at Queen's Island; the sea is open before us; our provisions are sufficient; we must set out and reach Fort Providence as soon as possible, and we can go into winter-quarters till next summer."

"That is my opinion," said Altamont; "the wind is fair, and to-morrow we shall set sail."

The day passed in great gloom. The captain's madness was a sad foreboding, and when Johnson, Bell, and Altamont thought of their return, they were afraid of their loneliness and remoteness. They felt the need of Hatteras's bold soul. Still, like energetic men they made ready for a new struggle with the elements, and with themselves, in case they should feel themselves growing faint-hearted.

The next day, Saturday, July 13th, the camping materials were put on the boat, and soon everything was ready for their departure. But before leaving this rock forever, the doctor, following Hatteras's intentions, put up a cairn at the place where the captain reached the island; this cairn was built of large rocks laid on one another, so as to form a perfectly visible landmark, if it were not destroyed by the eruption.

"The doctor put up a cairn."

On one of the lateral stones Bell carved with a chisel this simple inscription:—

JOHN HATTERAS
1861.

A copy of the document was placed inside of the cairn in an hermetically sealed tin cylinder, and the proof of this great discovery was left here on these lonely rocks.

Then the four men and the captain,—a poor body without a mind,—and his faithful Duke, sad and melancholy, got into the boat for the return voyage. It was ten o'clock in the morning. A new sail was set up with the canvas of the tent. The launch, sailing before the wind, left Queen's Island, and that evening the doctor, standing on his bench, waved a last farewell to Mount Hatteras, which was lighting up the horizon.

Their voyage was very quick; the sea, which was always open, was easy sailing, and it seemed really easier to go away from the Pole than to approach it. But Hatteras was in no state to understand what was going on about him; he lay at full length in the launch, his mouth closed, his expression dull, and his arms folded. Duke lay at his feet. It was in vain that the doctor questioned him. Hatteras did not hear him.

For forty-eight hours the breeze was fair and the sea smooth. Clawbonny and his companions rejoiced in the north-wind. July 15th, they made Altamont Harbor in the south; but since the Polar Ocean was open all along the coast, instead of crossing New America by sledge, they resolved to sail around it, and reach Victoria Bay by sea. This voyage was quicker and easier. In fact, the space which had taken them a fortnight on sledges took them hardly a week by sail; and after following the rugged outline of the coast, which was fringed with numerous fiords, and determining its shape, they reached Victoria Bay, Monday evening, July 23d.

The launch was firmly anchored to the shore, and each one ran to Fort Providence. The Doctor's House, the stores, the magazine, the fortifications, all had melted in the sun, and the supplies had been devoured by hungry beasts.

It was a sad sight.

They were nearly at the end of their supplies, and they had intended to renew them at Fort Providence. The impossibility of passing the winter there was evident. Like people accustomed to decide rapidly, they determined to reach Baffin's Bay as soon as possible.

"We have nothing else to do," said the doctor; "Baffin's Bay is not six hundred miles from here; we might sail as far as our launch would carry us, reach Jones's Sound, and from there the Danish settlements."

"Yes," answered Altamont; "let us collect all the provisions we can, and leave."

By strict search they found a few chests of pemmican here and there, and two barrels of preserved meat, which had escaped destruction. In short, they had a supply for six weeks, and powder enough. This was promptly collected. The day was devoted to calking the launch, repairing it, and the next day, July 24th, they put out to sea again.

The continent towards latitude 83° inclined towards the east. It was possible that it joined the countries known under the name of Grinnell Land, Ellesmere, and North Lincoln, which form the coast-line of Baffin's Bay.

They could then hold it for certain that Jones's Sound opened in the inner seas, like Lancaster Sound. The launch then sailed without much difficulty, easily avoiding the floating ice. The doctor, by way of precaution against possible delay, put them all on half-rations; but this did not trouble them much, and their health was unimpaired.

Besides, they were able to shoot occasionally; they killed ducks, geese, and other game, which gave them fresh and wholesome food. As for their drink, they had a full supply from the floating ice, which they met on the way, for they took care not to go far from the coast, the launch being too small for the open sea.

At this period of the year the thermometer was already, for the greater part of time, beneath the freezing-point; after a certain amount of rainy weather snow began to fall, with other signs of the end of summer; the sun sank nearer the horizon, and more and more of its disk sank beneath it every day. July 30th they saw it disappear for the first time, that is to say, they had a few minutes of night.

Still, the launch sailed well, sometimes making from sixty to seventy-five miles a day; they did not stop a moment; they knew what fatigues to endure, what obstacles to surmount; the way by land was before them, if they had to take it, and these confined seas must soon be closed; indeed, the young ice was already forming here and there. Winter suddenly succeeds summer in these latitudes; there are no intermediate seasons; no spring, no autumn. So they had to hurry. July 31st, the sky being clear at sunset, the first stars were seen in the constellations overhead. From this day on there was perpetual mist, which interfered very much with their sailing. The doctor, when he saw all the signs of winter's approach, became very uneasy; he knew the difficulties Sir John Ross had found in getting to Baffin's Bay, after leaving his ship; and indeed, having once tried to pass the ice, he was obliged to return to his ship, and go into winter-quarters for the fourth year; but he had at least a shelter against the weather, food, and fuel. If such a misfortune were to befall the survivors of the *Forward*, if they had to stop or put back, they were lost; the doctor did not express his uneasiness to his companions; but he urged them to get as far eastward as possible.

Finally, August 15th, after thirty days of rather good sailing, after struggling for forty-eight hours against the ice, which was accumulating, after having imperilled their little launch a hundred times, they saw themselves absolutely stopped, unable to go farther; the sea was all frozen, and the thermometer marked on an average +15°. Moreover, in all the north and east it was easy to detect the nearness of land, by the presence of pebbles; frozen fresh water was found more frequently. Altamont made an observation with great exactness, and found they were in latitude 77° 15', and longitude 85° 2'.

"So, then," said the doctor, "this is our exact position; we have reached North Lincoln, exactly at Cape Eden; we are entering Jones's Sound; if we had been a little luckier, we should have found the sea open to Baffin's Bay. But we need not complain. If my poor Hatteras had at first found so open a sea, he would have soon reached the Pole, his companions would not have deserted him, and he would not have lost his reason under his terrible sufferings!"

"Then," said Altamont, "we have only one course to follow; to abandon the launch, and get to the east coast of Lincoln by sledge."

"Abandon the launch and take the sledge? Well," answered the doctor; "but instead of crossing Lincoln, I propose going through Jones's Sound on the ice, and reaching North Devon."

"And why?" asked Altamont.

"Because we should get nearer to Lancaster Sound, and have more chance of meeting whalers."

"You are right, Doctor, but I am afraid the ice is not yet hard enough."

"We can try," said Clawbonny.

The launch was unloaded; Bell and Johnson put the sledge together; all its parts were in good condition. The next day the dogs were harnessed in, and they went along the coast to reach the ice-field.

Then they began again the journey which has been so often described; it was tiresome and slow; Altamont was right in doubting the strength of the ice; they could not go through Jones's Sound, and they had to follow the coast of Lincoln.

August 21st they turned to one side and reached the entrance of Glacier Sound; then they ventured upon the ice-field, and the next day they reached Cobourg Island, which they crossed in less than two days amid snow-squalls. They could advance more easily on the ice-fields, and at last, August 24th, they set foot on North Devon.

"Now," said the doctor, "we have only to cross this, and reach Cape Warender, at the entrance of Lancaster Sound."

But the weather became very cold and unpleasant; the snow-squalls became as violent as in winter; they all found themselves nearly exhausted. Their provisions were giving out, and each man had but a third of a ration, in order to allow to the dogs enough food in proportion to their work.

The nature of the ground added much to the fatigue of the journey; North Devon was far from level; they had to cross the Trauter Mountains by almost impassable ravines, struggling against all the fury of the elements. The sledge, men, and dogs had to rest, and more than once despair seized the little band, hardened as it was to the fatigues of a polar journey. But, without their noticing it, these poor men were nearly worn out, physically and morally; they could not support such incessant fatigue for eighteen months with impunity, nor such a succession of hopes and despairs. Besides, it should be borne in mind that they went forward with enthusiasm and conviction, which they lacked when returning. So they with difficulty dragged on; they walked almost from habit, with the animal energy left almost independent of their will.

It was not until August 30th that they at last left the chaos of mountains, of which one can form no idea from the mountains of lower zones, but they left it half dead. The doctor could no longer cheer up his companions, and he felt himself breaking down. The Trauter Mountains ended in a sort of rugged plain, heaped up at the time of the formation of the mountains. There they were compelled to take a few days of rest; the men could not set one foot before another; two of the dogs had died of exhaustion. They sheltered themselves behind a piece of ice, at a temperature of -2°; no one dared put up the tent. Their food had become very scanty, and, in spite of their extreme economy with their rations, they had a supply for but a week more; game became rarer, having left for a milder climate. Starvation threatened these exhausted men.

Altamont, who all along had shown great devotion and unselfishness, took advantage of the strength he had left, and resolved to procure by hunting some food for his companions. He took his gun, called Duke, and strode off for the plains to the north; the doctor, Johnson, and Bell saw him go away without much interest. For an hour they did not once hear his gun, and they saw him returning without firing a single shot; but he was running as if in great alarm.

"What is the matter?" asked the doctor.

"There! under the snow!" answered Altamont in great alarm, indicating a point in the horizon.

"What?"

"A whole band of men—"

"Alive?"

"Dead,—frozen,—and even—"

"Dead—frozen."

The American durst not finish his sentence, but his face expressed clearly his horror. The doctor, Johnson, Bell, aroused by this incident, were able to rise, and drag themselves along in Altamont's footprints to the part of the plain to which he had pointed. They soon reached a narrow space, at the bottom of a deep ravine, and there a terrible sight met their eyes.

Bodies were lying half buried beneath the snow; here an arm, there a leg, or clinched hands, and faces still preserving an expression of despair.

The doctor drew near; then he stepped back, pale and agitated, while Duke barked mournfully.

"Horror!" he said.

"Well?" asked the boatswain.

"Didn't you recognize them?" said the doctor in a strange voice.

"What do you mean?"

"Look!"

This ravine had been the scene of the last struggle between the men and the climate, despair, and hunger, for from some horrible signs it was easy to see that they had been obliged to eat human flesh. Among them the doctor had recognized Shandon, Pen, and the wretched crew of the *Forward;* their strength and food had failed them; their launch had probably been crushed by an avalanche, or carried into some ravine, and they could not take to the open sea; probably they were lost among these unknown continents. Besides, men who had left in mutiny could not long be united with the closeness which is necessary for the accomplishment of great things. A ringleader of a revolt has never more than a doubtful authority in his hands. And, without doubt, Shandon was promptly deposed.

However that may have been, the crew had evidently undergone a thousand tortures, a thousand despairs, to end with this terrible catastrophe; but the secret of their sufferings is forever buried beneath the arctic snows.

"Let us flee!" cried the doctor.

And he dragged his companions far from the scene of the disaster. Horror lent them momentary strength. They set out again.

CHAPTER XXVII.

CONCLUSION.

Why linger over the perpetual sufferings of the survivors? They themselves could never recall to their memory a clear vision of what had happened in the week after their horrible discovery of the remains of the crew. However, September 9th, by a miracle of energy, they reached Cape Horsburgh, at the end of North Devon.

They were dying of hunger; they had not eaten for forty-eight hours, and their last meal had been the flesh of their last Esquimaux dog. Bell could go no farther, and old Johnson felt ready to die. They were on the shore of Baffin's Bay, on the way to Europe. Three miles from land the waves were breaking on the edges of the ice-field. They had to await the uncertain passage of a whaler, and how many days yet?

But Heaven took pity on them, for the next day Altamont clearly saw a sail. The anguish which follows such an appearance of a sail, the tortures of disappointment, are well known. The ship seemed to approach and then to recede. Terrible are the alternations of hope and despair, and too often at the moment the castaways consider themselves saved the sail sinks beneath the horizon.

The doctor and his companions went through all these emotions; they had reached the western limit of the ice-field, and yet they saw the ship disappear, taking no note of their presence. They shouted, but in vain.

Then the doctor had a last inspiration of that busy mind which had served him in such good stead.

A floe had drifted against the ice-field.

"That floe!" he said, pointing to it.

They did not catch his meaning.

"Let us get on it!" he cried.

They saw his plan at once.

"Ah, Clawbonny, Dr. Clawbonny!" cried Johnson, kissing the doctor's hands.

Bell, with Altamont's aid, ran to the sledge; he brought one of the uprights, stood it up on the floe for a mast, making it fast with ropes; the tent was torn up for a sail. The wind was fair; the poor castaways put out to sea on this frail raft.

Two hours later, after unheard-of efforts, the last men of the *Forward* were taken aboard the Danish whaler *Hans Christian*, which was sailing to Davis Strait. The captain received kindly these spectres who had lost their semblance to human beings; when he saw their sufferings he understood their history; he gave them every attention, and managed to save their lives. Ten days later, Clawbonny, Johnson, Bell, Altamont, and Captain Hatteras landed at Korsoeur, in Zeeland, in Denmark; a steamboat carried them to Kiel; thence, *via* Altona and Hamburg, they reached London the 13th of the same month, hardly recovered from their long sufferings.

"Two hours later, after unheard-of efforts, the last men of the *Forward* were taken aboard the Danish whaler *Hans Christian*."

"A steamboat carried them to Kiel."

The first thought of the doctor was to ask permission of the Royal Geographical Society of London to lay a communication before it; he was admitted to the meeting of July 15th. The astonishment of the learned assembly, and its enthusiastic cheers after reading Hatteras's document, may be imagined.

This journey, the only one of its kind, went over all the discoveries that had been made in the regions about the Pole; it brought together the expeditions of Parry, Ross, Franklin, MacClure; it completed the chart between the one hundredth and one hundred and fifteenth meridians; and, finally, it ended with the point of the globe hitherto inaccessible, with the Pole itself.

Never had news so unexpected burst upon astonished England.

The English take great interest in geographical facts; they are proud of them, lord and cockney, from the merchant prince to the workman in the docks.

The news of this great discovery was telegraphed over the United Kingdom with great rapidity; the papers printed the name of Hatteras at the head of their columns as that of a martyr, and England glowed with pride.

The doctor and his companions were feasted everywhere; they were formally presented to her Majesty by the Lord High Chancellor.

The government confirmed the name of Queen's Island for the rock at the North Pole, of Mount Hatteras for the mountain itself, and of Altamont Harbor for the port in New America.

Altamont did not part from those whose misery and glory he had shared, and who were now his friends. He followed the doctor, Johnson, and Bell to Liverpool, where they were warmly received, after they had been thought to be long dead, and buried in the eternal ice.

But Dr. Clawbonny always gave the glory to the man who most deserved it. In his account of the journey entitled "The English at the North Pole," published the next year by the Royal Geographical Society, he made John Hatteras equal to the greatest explorers, the rival of those bold men who sacrifice everything to science.

But the sad victim of a lofty passion lived peacefully at the asylum of Starr Cottage near Liverpool, where the doctor had placed him. His madness was of a gentle kind, but he never spoke, he understood nothing, his power of speech seemed to have gone with his reason. A single feeling seemed to unite him to the outer world, his love for Duke, who was not separated from him.

This disease, this "polar madness," pursued its course quietly, presenting no particular symptom, when Dr. Clawbonny, who often visited his poor patient, was struck by his singular manner.

For some time Captain Hatteras, followed by his faithful dog, that used to gaze at him sadly, would walk for hours every day; but he always walked in one way, in the direction of a certain path. When he had reached the end, he would return, walking backwards. If any one stopped him, he would point his finger at a portion of the sky. If any one tried to make him turn round, he grew angry, and Duke would show his anger and bark furiously.

The doctor observed carefully this odd mania; he understood the motive of this strange obstinacy; he guessed the reason of this walk always in the same direction, and, so to speak, under the influence of a magnetic force.

Captain John Hatteras was always walking towards the north.

FINIS.